Achieving Excellence

Mastering Mindset for Peak Performance in Sport and Life

Achieving Excellence

Mastering Mindset for Peak Performance
in Sport and Life

Colleen M. Hacker, PhD

With Mallory E. Mann, PhD

HUMAN
KINETICS

Library of Congress Cataloging-in-Publication Data

Names: Hacker, Colleen, author. | Mann, Mallory E., 1984- author.
Title: Achieving excellence : mastering mindset for peak performance in
  sport and life / Colleen M. Hacker, PhD, Mallory E. Mann.
Description: First Edition. | Champaign, IL : Human Kinetics, [2023] |
  Includes bibliographical references and index.
Identifiers: LCCN 2021056734 (print) | LCCN 2021056735 (ebook) | ISBN
  9781718207707 (Paperback : alk. paper) | ISBN 9781718207714 (ePub) |
  ISBN 9781718207721 (PDF)
Subjects: LCSH: Sports--Psychological aspects. | Performance. | BISAC:
  SPORTS & RECREATION / Sports Psychology | PSYCHOLOGY / Applied
  Psychology
Classification: LCC GV706.4 .H29 2023 (print) | LCC GV706.4 (ebook) | DDC
  796.01/9--dc23/eng/20220201
LC record available at https://lccn.loc.gov/2021056734
LC ebook record available at https://lccn.loc.gov/2021056735

ISBN: 978-1-7182-0770-7 (print)

Copyright © 2023 by Colleen Hacker and Mallory Mann

Acquisitions Editor: Diana Vincer; **Developmental Editor:** Anne Hall; **Managing Editor:** Kevin Matz; **Copyeditor:** Annette Pierce; **Proofreader:** Leigh Keylock; **Indexer:** Ferreira Indexing; **Permissions Manager:** Dalene Reeder; **Senior Graphic Designer:** Nancy Rasmus; **Cover Designer:** Keri Evans; **Cover Design Specialist:** Susan Rothermel Allen; **Photograph (cover):** ULISES RUIZ / Getty Images; **Photographs (interior):** © Human Kinetics, unless otherwise noted; **Photo Asset Manager:** Laura Fitch; **Photo Production Manager:** Jason Allen; **Senior Art Manager:** Kelly Hendren; **Illustrations:** © Human Kinetics; **Printer:** Versa Press

Human Kinetics books are available at special discounts for bulk purchase. Special editions or book excerpts can also be created to specification. For details, contact the Special Sales Manager at Human Kinetics.

Printed in the United States of America   10 9 8 7 6 5 4 3 2 1

The paper in this book is certified under a sustainable forestry program.

Human Kinetics
1607 N. Market Street
Champaign, IL 61820
USA

United States and International
Website: **US.HumanKinetics.com**
Email: info@hkusa.com
Phone: 1-800-747-4457

Canada
Website: **Canada.HumanKinetics.com**
Email: info@hkcanada.com

E8324

Tell us what you think!
Human Kinetics would love to hear what we can do to improve the customer experience.
Use this QR code to take our brief survey.

To Dr. Terry Orlick, world-renowned expert in the field of sport psychology and author of *In Pursuit of Excellence*. We are indebted and grateful for his enduring contributions in sport psychology and to his commitment to teaching people how to perform to potential and to enjoy the process. We hope our book lives up to his legacy.

CONTENTS

Accessing the HK*Propel* Online Content   ix   •
Preface   xi   •   Acknowledgments   xiii

CHAPTER 1	**Getting to the Starting Line**	1
CHAPTER 2	**Believing You Can**	7
CHAPTER 3	**Chatter Matters**	27
CHAPTER 4	**Being in the Moment**	45
CHAPTER 5	**Harnessing Imagination**	65
CHAPTER 6	**Energy Management**	87
CHAPTER 7	**Control of Calm**	105
CHAPTER 8	**Revving the Engine**	125
CHAPTER 9	**The Three Cs of Performance Success**	143
CHAPTER 10	**Creating an Action Plan**	161

CHAPTER 11   **Focusing on the Right Things at the Right Time**   181

CHAPTER 12   **Preperformance Routines**   199

CHAPTER 13   **Prioritizing Self-Reflection**   215

CHAPTER 14   **Growing Through Adversity**   235

CHAPTER 15   **Bouncing Back**   253

CHAPTER 16   **Highlighting We Before Me**   273

CHAPTER 17   **Inclusive Excellence**   289

CHAPTER 18   **Career and Life Transitions**   307

EPILOGUE   **Learning More**   321

Appendix 323 • Bibliography 325 •
Index 343 • About the Authors 353

ACCESSING THE HK*PROPEL* ONLINE CONTENT

Achieving Excellence: Mastering Mindset for Peak Performance in Sport and Life comes with online content that is available to you for free upon purchase of a new print book or an ebook.

The HK*Propel* online content offers PDF's of the Chalk Talk elements and the Performer-Centered Implementation Worksheets. We are certain you will enjoy this unique online component.

Follow these steps to access the HK*Propel* online content. If you need help at any point in the process, you can contact us via email at HKPropelCustSer@hkusa.com.

If it's your first time using HK*Propel*:

1. Visit HKPropel.HumanKinetics.com.
2. Click the "New user? Register here" link on the opening screen.
3. Follow the onscreen prompts to create your HK*Propel* account.
4. Enter the access code exactly as shown below, including hyphens. You will not need to re-enter this access code on subsequent visits.
5. After your first visit, simply log in to HKPropel.HumanKinetics.com to access your digital product.

If you already have an HK*Propel* account:

1. Visit HKPropel.HumanKinetics.com and log in with your username (email address) and password.
2. Once you are logged in, navigate to Account in the top right corner.
3. Under "Add Access Code" enter the access code exactly as shown below, including hyphens.
4. Once your code is redeemed, navigate to your Library on the Dashboard to access your digital content.

Access code: HACKER1E-H8DN-HK3P-HNC6

Once you have signed in to HK*Propel* and redeemed the access code, navigate to your Library to access your digital content. Your license to this digital product will expire 7 years after the date you redeem the access code. You can check the expiration dates of all your HK*Propel* products at any time in My Account.

For technical support, contact us via email at HKPropelCustSer@ hkusa.com. **Helpful tip:** You may reset your password from the login screen at any time if you forget it.

PREFACE

The mental skills that are critical for performance excellence are known and well documented. This book offers a variety of training strategies to help people hone their mental game. Although we are unwavering and unapologetic about centering the text on athletes in sport, we also provide an application of the same principles to a range of performance domains in which the reader might engage over the course of a lifetime. We view that as a strength of this book. Rather than putting the onus on the reader to apply the psychological skills presented in the text to other achievement domains, we tried to weave in diverse examples from other areas to facilitate integration across performance arenas. We recognize that each domain carries its own personal and situational variables that absolutely must be considered. The fact that you may know about military science, for example, does not mean those strategies will work similarly in sport, and the fact that you know sport science does not mean that every skill in athletics can be applied to the corporate world. Yet we also believe there are enduring and foundational principles that transcend any one particular achievement area. We made concerted efforts in this text to identify those themes and provide application examples across domains when appropriate.

We wanted to move this book beyond mere anecdotes. As such, we grounded information in each chapter in the published literature, in scholarship, and in science. We used citations and references so that you can understand the evidence that supports each skill and strategy we present. It is important for you to know that these skills are evidence based and effective, but we also went to great lengths to present the information in an applicable, user-friendly format that requires active investment with the material on your part. You will get the most from this book if you integrate these strategies into your life, into your career, and into your chosen area of performance. It is not enough to simply know what to do; rather, it is essential to *do* what you know. And so, it is not just knowing and reading about sport psychology terms and strategies found in this book that will unlock your potential and increase your best-performance capabilities. Rather, our goal is to motivate you to action and to provide simple but effective worksheets for you to use to actively apply each concept or strategy to your own career. You do not get extra points for knowing about imagery and how it works. You only benefit when you implement imagery in a systematic, consistent, and scientifically validated way. Performance is not measured on multiple-choice exams where credit is given for knowing the right answer. With this fact in mind, in each chapter, we have tried to explain the science of what each technique is and how each mental skill works. Then, we provide an invitation for you to invest, to personalize, and to make it your own. We hope you will.

What follows in each chapter will become a familiar organizational pattern centered on athlete stories and testimonials (see the In Their Own Words sections), quotes, and applied activities to help you personalize the content and develop self-awareness. You will see Chalk Talk sections, performer worksheets, and Put It Into Practice sidebars throughout the book. Chalk Talks include short, pithy summary phrases that highlight key concepts from the chapter and are designed for easy retention and use. Put It Into Practice sidebars offer specific techniques and strategies for applying those concepts in meaningful ways. Implementation worksheets offer opportunities to analyze and apply chapter concepts to individual career and performance arenas. Think of these worksheets as gentle nudges for you to take the next step and integrate targeted information into your own life. You will find these opportunities for personalization and application throughout the book, and just as each performer is unique, so too is each chapter. Instead of taking a cookie-cutter organizational approach, we have allowed the content to drive the application elements within each chapter. Careful consideration was also given to the order in which the chapters are presented. They can be read in order, and there is a certain cohesiveness and flow to reading the book in this manner. However, we also recognize that each reader might be in a different moment in their journey as a performer—some in the middle of their careers, some considering transition to different performance arenas, and others just beginning their achievement pursuit. Some are at the top of their game, others are struggling to find their footing, and still others are trying to hold on.

In each moment of your life, you will need different skills, and so you will be open to new strategies and performance demands as your career unfolds. We wanted to honor those realities as we wrote, so each chapter can also be read as a stand-alone topic. They all matter; each psychological skill is scientifically supported to enhance performance. But one may be most useful to you in this exact moment of your career, and a different strategy might resonate more later. Either is appropriate. Take what you can from the text and implement it now. Then as your journey continues, revisit, reapply, reassess, reimagine, and recommit to different tools and techniques offered in other chapters. That is mental skills training at its best. As author Eleanor Brownn writes, "The amazing thing about a long journey is that you can miss exits, run Stop signs, head the wrong way down a one-way street, get lost, misplace your keys, find them, make a U-turn, and still, somehow, miraculously reach your proper destination."

Own your process and your unique individual pursuit of performance excellence. We hope this book serves as a useful guide that you can revisit along the way.

ACKNOWLEDGMENTS

Writing this book has been a labor of love for both of us. It has provided an opportunity to revisit the scholarly literature in our field and to do so with a commitment to the scholarship of application. We steadfastly considered how our writing might resonate, apply, and be valuable to people from all walks of life and to individuals, teams, and groups across multiple performance domains. We celebrate with each reader who benefits from this text and successfully works to apply the lessons. Hopefully the strategies and evidence-based guidance are personally relevant for each reader's path in pursuit of excellence throughout their lives. Further, we hope that readers enjoy and benefit from reading this book and share in a transformative process that is similar to what we experienced writing it.

Collaborating on this book—as mentor and mentee, as colleagues, and as friends—was a personal and professional privilege—one that we cherished. We want to thank Human Kinetics, the leading publishing company in the field of kinesiology, for offering us this opportunity. And we wish to extend special acknowledgment to Diana Vincer, our acquisitions editor, and to Anne Hall, who served as the developmental editor for this book. Diana, your gentle and respectful nudges coupled with your understanding of the toll that balancing manuscript deadlines with our other professional responsibilities as faculty members, consultants, and scholars were sincerely appreciated. To Anne, we thank you for your competent eye for detail and for guiding us through the editing process.

It is always a daunting challenge to acknowledge and highlight the significant collective and individual impact of those who have demonstratively contributed to one's life and to one's career. I often share with people my view that none of us achieves anything in life without standing on the shoulders, sacrifice, and investment of those who came before us. My life is an example of that fact. I would first like to thank my parents for providing a foundation of hard work and a commitment to give one's best in every endeavor. For many decades, there has been no greater influence than Sharon Taylor, my former intercollegiate coach, faculty member, and now dear friend. Sharon instilled in all of us under her charge the expectation to compete with integrity, excellence, and grit and to know and honor those who "paddled the canoe" before we got in. To this day, speaking with Sharon is like reading a history book; it is informative, educational, and aspirational. Two individuals in my graduate education, Dr. Donna Mae Miller and Dr. Jean Williams, provided enduring and powerful lessons on the importance of scholarship, evidence-based practices, and professional (and life) expectations and responsibilities. They each serve as exemplars in that regard to this day. I would also like to thank the hundreds of student-athletes I was privileged to coach during my 17-year intercollegiate coaching tenure at the University of Arizona and at Pacific Lutheran University. We did something special *together*. Finally, I want to share a special note of gratitude for all the Olympic and professional athletes and teams with whom I have been privileged to work. Whether working in the NFL, MLB, MLS, NWSL, PGA, and many others or being part of the staff for the women's national soccer team for 12 years and the U.S. women's national hockey team for 8 years in both World Championships and the Olympic Games, I am grateful beyond measure. In particular, the years I spent with Coach Tony DiCicco and the U.S. women's national soccer team are some of my most cherished. Thank you to those who invested in me and in my career. Deep gratitude is extended to every athlete and team who trusted and honored our work together.

Finally, I'd like to thank my family for the gift of unconditional love, understanding, and support. There are no greater gifts.

My heart is grateful and full.

—Colleen Hacker

To all of my mentors—your strength, your grace, your commitment to excellence, and your dedication to improving your respective portions of the world have served as a guiding light at critical junctures in my life. Thank you for your example and your leadership. I want to specifically acknowledge Dr. McConnell. Your decision to invest in me as an 18-year-old undergraduate student changed the direction of my life. I am forever grateful for our conversations during frequent "walk and talk" sessions across and around campus. You helped me learn to trust and believe in myself and served as an example of the power that comes from doing so. Thank you for serving as one of the most profound and enduring guides in my life.

To my coauthor and cherished mentor—to write this book with you will forever be one of the great joys of my life. Thank you for inviting me to this project. Both personally and professionally, I am who I am in large part because of your influence. You challenge me, correct me, and cheer me on (often in the same conversation). Perhaps it is that you choose to offer all three that I most respect and have learned to trust. You have helped me find my voice and continue to encourage me to forge my own path in life. Living up to your belief in and vision for me will continue to be a driving force in my life.

Finally, I want to thank my dad. It was first through our conversations and your challenges on the front porch and on drives to the gas station that I learned how to process moments of success and failure in life. I am thankful for a determined father who raised a similarly persistent young girl who has evolved into a woman buoyed by the knowledge that she is capable of pursuing her goals in a world that might, at times, suggest otherwise.

—Mallory Mann

CHAPTER 1

Getting to the Starting Line

Usain Bolt's world record 100-meter sprint (9.58 seconds) in 2009 and largest margin of improvement (.16 seconds) since electronic timing began, Serena Williams' two-hour and 18-minute come-from-behind victory in the third set (6-2, 2-6, 7-5) of the 2012 U.S. Open final, Secretariat and jockey Ron Turcotte winning the Belmont Stakes by 31 lengths in 1973, and Michael Phelps' breaking the Olympic record with eight gold medals in swimming in the 2008 Beijing Olympic Games—these experiences represent some of the greatest sport performances of all time. Peak performance is "an episode of superior functioning" (Privette 1983, p 1361), a moment when it all seems to come together. And yet, peak performances also occur in the midst of incomprehensible challenges. Think about Michael Jordan scoring 38 points and clinching an NBA finals victory while sick with food poisoning or an intestinal virus, Mario Lemieux scoring and assisting in his debut return to the ice two months after being diagnosed with Hodgkin's disease, or Gertrude Ederle swimming across the English Channel, the first woman to do so and faster than her male predecessors. She swam through six-foot waves and with a swollen tongue that made it hard to speak and was covered in jellyfish stings. Peak performance does not just happen by chance or through hope. People can train in ways that help them close their performance gap and play at a high level more consistently. What we

> My game is my mental toughness. Not only to be able to win but to be able to come back when I'm down. Both on the court and after tough losses just to continue to come back and continue to fight, it's something that takes a lot of tenacity.
>
> Serena Williams, American professional tennis player with 23 Grand Slam singles titles, the most by any player in the Open Era, and the second most of all time

> The ideal attitude is to be physically loose and mentally tight.
>
> Arthur Ashe, American professional tennis player, winner of three Grand Slam singles titles, first Black player selected to the United States Davis Cup team, and the first Black man to win the singles title at Wimbledon, the U.S. Open, and the Australian Open

Andrea Jemolo / Electa / Mondadori Portfolio via Getty Images

hope to convey in this book is that pursuing, achieving, and sustaining excellence is a lifelong pursuit and one that requires sustained effort and systematic training over time.

Four Pillars of Peak Performance

To perform at your best in any domain, you need to address each of the four pillars that exist in every performance domain: technical, tactical, physiological, and psychological. Technical aspects of performance could include positional knowledge, technique, anticipatory and perceptual skills, and biomechanics among others. In sport, it could refer to the hand positioning on a field hockey stick, which foot to drop defensively in lacrosse, or how high to propel your upper body out of the water when swimming the breaststroke. Other examples might include how a news anchor practices to improve how they read a teleprompter, how a parent delivers corrective feedback to their child, or a musician's finger placement on a piano to ensure appropriate keys can be hit on time. Performers train tactically when they learn when to take a big lead versus when to hug the base as a baserunner, when the executive team decides who to retain and which employees to move to a different project, or when a coach decides which play to run in the last few moments of a competition. Any strategic decisions about a presentation, race strategy, game plan, or event planning requires tactical training beforehand to reduce errors and increase the likelihood of success. The physical pillar refers to the training people engage in to improve their speed, power, flexibility, fitness, and nutrition. Sleep should also be added to the physical pillar because it is increasingly recognized for its powerful influence on performance as well. Most performers have well-established routines and plans for how they will train in each of these three areas. The fourth pillar refers to the mental or psychological skills required for peak performance. For example, players train their focus so they can pay attention to the right thing at the right time, or they train productive self-talk or practice imagery so that when their team gets an unfavorable call, they are able to control their emotions and stay present in the game. This fourth pillar is often neglected, but U.S. women's national soccer team player Carli Lloyd discussed its significance leading into the 2020 Tokyo Olympic Games:

> It is what makes this team really special: the mentality . . . . I've been a part of eight world championships, won four. I can tell you that we've won four because of the mentality . . . . We can spend hours upon hours doing tactical work, technical work, but if we don't have the mentality that's been built for so long, since the start of this team, we're not going to win. (Das 2021)

Think of each of these pillars as one leg on a chair. The most balanced version of a chair is when all four legs are in contact with the ground equally and simultaneously. Certainly, you could find a way to balance and remain upright on two or even three of the legs, but to do so would require an extraordinary amount of additional energy, concentration, and effort. So, too, is it possible for quality performance to occur when intentional training has occurred only within the first three pillars; however, it is more likely that consistently high performance requires that all four pillars be addressed.

You would never tell your children that they do not need to nourish their bodies before school. You know that a lack of high-quality nutrients will negatively affect their cognitive abilities in class. Similarly, you would not willingly avoid running for a month and then attempt to run a marathon, because you know your performance would suffer from a lack of physical training and you could sustain an injury. Surgeons continue practicing their sutures in simulated experiences to refine their technical and tactical approaches before surgeries. And golfer Collin Morikawa described the importance of training his mental game.

> You would be surprised just how many bogeys are made from a flawed thought process. Try taking an honest look at your rounds and ask yourself, "Were my mistakes the result of poor execution or bad decisions?" You can live with bad swings because that happens in golf, but you're in total control of decision-making, and it's such an easy thing to improve. (Rapaport 2021)

If you are not scientifically, systematically, and consistently training in all four pillars, you are leaving part of your own potential unrealized. Every performance domain has four pillars, and, if you are part of a group, then you have the plus one, which is *team*. No one ascended to their current position alone; we all rely on team members to move us forward. Sometimes, those teammates are role models or colleagues or coaches or bosses. Throughout this book, we will challenge you to not only read about mental skills training but also to implement what you are learning. This book is designed to evoke your behavioral investment. It is not enough to know that you need to integrate mental skills training to improve your performance. To achieve and sustain performance excellence over time, you must do the work.

Mental Skills Training

Olympic athletes have consistently over the last four decades identified mental preparation as a key factor in their success (Gould and Maynard 2009; Krane, Williams, and Graupensperger 2021; Orlick and Partington 1988). While there is no single set of psychological characteristics that a performer must possess in order to succeed in their work, people do need to be confident, be in control, develop and evolve over time, adapt to changing circumstances, and be able to bounce back from errors or failure quickly. Elite athletes report frequent use of imagery practice, attentional focusing, activation-control techniques, and productive self-talk (Hayslip et al. 2010). When asked about his mental routines, four-time NBA champion LeBron James replied:

> **What does it mean to be mentally fit? It means presence. No matter what I'm doing, my attention is locked. It means awareness. I can see my surroundings with clarity and I can calculate my options. It means calm and composure in those big moments when the pressure is on. It means resilience. I face a setback and I show up fresh the next game, the next quarter, the next possession.**

When playing on the 2000 Canadian men's national basketball team, Steve Nash said that through the team's commitment to sport psychology, he learned "When people get nervous, they tend to hold their breath. In order to focus, we'd remind each other to breathe normally and to take deep breaths when we were feeling a lot of pressure" (Nash 2010). Elite athletes know that mental skills training works. It is one of the most consistent differentiating factors between successful and less successful athletes.

In the next 18 chapters, we will outline the psychological skills that are necessary for performance excellence, and we will offer strategies for training and improving in each area. Although each chapter is designed to be distinct and capable of being read separately, repetitive themes will appear across multiple sections of the text. This repetition is by design and is similar to training to learn a physical skill. When you train in the tactical, technical, and physiological pillars, completing repetitions of the same skills over and over is viewed as expected, important, and necessary. Basketball players shoot free throws each and every day, even after they have learned and mastered their shooting technique. In much the same way, repeatedly reading about and practicing essential components in your psychological game is critical to successful mental skills training. This focus on the basics and commitment to repetition was an intentional decision made throughout the writing process. Two such skills that will be discussed often are *self-awareness* and *self-regulation*. They are the foundation of any effective psychological skills training program. We will set them up in this introductory chapter and draw your attention back to them throughout the text.

Self-Awareness

Self-awareness, to know oneself and one's needs in any given moment, is essential. For a performer to notice the difference between current and preferred mental and emotional states is the first step to being able to control one's own internal environment. Take, for example, an athlete who is preparing for the most significant competitive situation of their lives or a lawyer who is getting ready to try the biggest case of their legal career. If proper mental training and preparation have not occurred leading up to that event, then performers might be unaware of what they need in the pressure-packed moments when accessing their preferred performance zone is required. In that moment, as they stand when the judge enters the courtroom or listen to the national anthem before the competition, it is already too late. Each person needs to know which mental skills they need at any given moment and be able to successfully implement those skills across a range of competitive situations. Developing self-awareness of the routines and behaviors needed to bring about a preferred performance state under any condition creates a sense of control and allows a performer to assume responsibility over their personal execution (Ravizza, Fifer, and Bean 2021). As you learn about the mental skills presented in this book, you will be challenged to critically reflect about yourself as a competitor and about your own performance in order to become aware of your preferences and needs as an elite competitor.

Self-Regulation

Once you have become aware of your own needs, habits, and tendencies and start to develop the ability to recognize when you are not in your preferred performance state, learning to gain control over yourself and of your performance is the next key in mental skills training. Always remember that when the time comes to perform, the time to prepare is over.

Self-regulation refers to the ability to control one's thoughts, emotions, and behaviors. What good is recognizing when you are not in your preferred state or when you are directing your focus inappropriately if you do not follow that knowledge with the ability to redirect and correct yourself? In the earlier examples, as the lawyer rises when the judge enters and feels their heart race, that is the moment when activation control is needed to calm themselves and prepare for opening arguments. In the moment that the national anthem plays and the athlete starts to think about how much this moment means to their family and career, in that instant, the player needs to initiate their practiced and individual plan to redirect their focus to the competitive details that matter in the present. It is a performer's commitment to becoming self-aware and developing their ability to self-regulate that will determine how well they implement these skills into their daily life.

In the age of instant information and access, most people are aware of the same data, and they know the same facts and material. And regardless of their performance domain (surgeons compared to other surgeons, business leaders competing with and against other business leaders, or athletes compared to athletes), most people have the same capabilities. So time and time again, the literature shows that the psychological component is the great separator. This book addresses that reality. The skills and strategies as well as the application elements that follow are supported in the literature; they work. We wrote this book as an open invitation to you to invest in your performance and to implement these strategies in your daily life.

CHAPTER 2

Believing You Can

Developing belief in yourself might be the greatest predictor of success. In fact, one of the most consistent findings in the sport psychology literature is that confidence is a difference maker; it separates good athletes from great ones. When interviewing Olympic athletes and other elite athletes, researchers over the past three decades have found that cultivating high levels of confidence

> **Belief in oneself generates momentum . . . [confidence] far outweighs any kernel of self-doubt that may creep in.**
>
> Aimee Mullins, U.S. Paralympian, world record holder (100 meters, 200 meters, long jump)

is one of the mental links to excellence (e.g., Anderson, Hanrahan, and Mallett 2014; Orlick and Partington 1988). Believing in yourself also has a protective quality because it can buffer against the negative effects of losing or the pressure of high expectations placed on you or your team. The reason confidence is one of the first mental strategies discussed in this book is because it is part of the foundation for developing and maintaining mental toughness (Connaughton, Hanton, and Jones 2010). To develop "an unshakeable belief in your ability to achieve your competitive goals," you first have to believe you are capable (Jones, Hanton, and Connaughton 2002, 171). Throughout this chapter, you will learn about confidence: how to create it, how to regain it, and how to sustain it. You will read examples from high-performing athletes that will help you hone your self-confidence. You will also have opportunities to personalize the material and develop a plan to build or rebuild self-confidence *before* you need the plan.

The Most Important Races Ever Run

Two races, separated by 65 years, provide powerful examples of the impact of self-belief on performance. In these stories, the athletes faced what had been considered impossible. Each stared down an impenetrable barrier that runners before them had feared and faltered in front of; yet, this time, they *knew* it would be different.

In 1954, Roger Bannister stepped to the start line. For years, runners had come close to breaking the four-minute barrier. Times of 4:03, 4:02, and 4:01 had been run, but no one had broken four minutes. Experts believed the weather conditions had to be perfect, the race needed to be on a specific track, and that an audience present would lift some lucky runner to their best performance. Bannister was different. He trained alone without coaches and maintained a full schedule as a medical student. On race day, he ran on a cold, wet track at a small meet in England. And *he did it*. In 1954, Bannister ran one mile in 3:58. He broke through the "impossible" and showed the world what was possible.

Over six decades later, Eliud Kipchoge, a Kenyan marathoner, faced a barrier of his own. No runner had completed a marathon in less than two hours. Again, the conditions were less than ideal: fog, rain, and 90 percent humidity for most of the run. Kipchoge had been here before. He had come close in 2018 when he ran a world record 2:01:39 and in 2017 when he ran the distance in 2:00:25. The conditions were imperfect, and researchers suggested there was only a 5 percent chance that the two-hour barrier could be broken before 2024. Recognizing the psychological significance of the finish line, Kipchoge often remarked that running a sub-two-hour marathon would help other humans break barriers they thought impossible. Then, in 2019, in Vienna, Austria, Eliud Kipchoge held a sub-4:34-per-mile pace for 26.2 miles (42.2 km) to finish the marathon in 1:59:40. *He did it*. Kipchoge became the first marathoner to break the two-hour barrier. Because he accomplished this feat at a stage-managed event, the next significant advance will happen when a runner finishes a marathon sanctioned by the IAAF (International Governing Body of Athletics).

And, if history has taught us anything, it is that Kipchoge's feat will expand the belief system that previously unimagined marathon times are indeed possible. Soon after Bannister's feat, three runners broke the four-minute barrier in a single race, and 37 runners broke four minutes in the next year. To date, 1,400 athletes have run a sub-four-minute mile. What changed? Did they get stronger, faster, or smarter? Were they better fueled? Even if true, it is unlikely these changes would account for such a dramatic shift in mile times within the same calendar year. The most significant change was their belief. Once they witnessed runners breaking time barriers, they felt confident they could as well. As Kipchoge noted after his historic marathon in 2019, "No human is limited. . . . Physical ability determines the limits of what we are capable of, but the mind determines how close we get to that limit" (Butterworth 2019).

Two-Lane Road: Confidence and Performance

As the previous examples indicate, confidence can affect performance, and performance (executing well or playing poorly) can also affect confidence. The relationship between confidence and performance is a two-lane road.

Self-confidence is the belief that you can successfully perform (Weinberg and Gould 2018; Williams and Hacker 2020). Confident athletes are focused on their plans and strategies, feel positive about their upcoming performances, and seek challenges and also competitors who are equally skilled or better. They want to compete against the best so they can test their skills. Nadia Comaneci, a Romanian gymnast who scored the first perfect 10, explained it this way in her 2009 book, *Letters to a Young Gymnast*: "I don't run away from a challenge because I am afraid. Instead, I run toward it because the only way to escape fear is to trample it beneath your feet." It is not that confident athletes do not experience fear; rather, it is their belief in themselves that compels them to move forward anyway. These athletes give supreme effort and play to win. Confident performers believe—regardless of their circumstances—they will persevere, they will outlast, and they will make it through to the other side victorious. This is a sentiment echoed by American actor Will Smith:

> The only thing that I see that is distinctly different about me is I'm not afraid to die on a treadmill. I will not be outworked, period. You might have more talent than me, you might be smarter than me. . . . You got it on me in nine categories. But if we get on the treadmill together, there [are] two options: You're getting off first, or I'm going to die. It's really that simple.

Smith's confidence stems from his effort and his dogged determination. The more he outworks and outlasts his competitors, the more confident he is in his future success. This relationship between confidence and performance is *bidirectional* and *reciprocal*. Your thoughts and feelings are often unstable because your performance and behavior fluctuate. When people perform poorly, self-confidence typically drops, making them more likely to dwell on their poor play and worry about what their teammates or opponents think, and they are less likely to persevere. Decreased self-belief eventually changes sport behaviors, making it more likely someone might avoid challenging situations. When they find themselves in these critical performance moments, their heightened negative emotions, shaken confidence, and focus on possible failure will lead to behaviors that typically bring about more mistakes and errors.

In essence, they are engaging in a *self-fulfilling prophecy*, which occurs when a performer expects an undesirable outcome and then behaves in ways that bring that outcome to bear. This phenomenon occurs in all aspects of life: sport, business, music, medicine, health, exercise, and nutrition. A person who wants to diet but believes they will "cheat" on their plan is much more likely to do so than someone who believes they will learn strategies to build a productive food relationship. A graduate student who fears public speaking and thinks that they will forget their speech when they step behind the podium is negatively affected by those thoughts and feelings so much so that the very expectation of failure is likely to lead them to make mistakes during the presentation. This circular pattern between thoughts, behavior, and performance creates a cycle that is future oriented and prescriptive. Dwelling on a negative outcome is more likely to bring on that result, which leads the student to expect the same response during the next presentation. This belief leads to increased negative emotions under similar conditions, and the same result does, in fact, become more likely.

So how do you break the unproductive cycles you have created for yourself? How do you avoid these *negative* self-fulfilling prophecies? First, understand that positive self-fulfilling prophecies can also be learned and trained. You can develop the ability to expect successful performances and engage in thoughts and feelings that make that desired result more likely. To develop confidence, you must commit to fostering an optimistic approach to your craft, to search for the opportunities, and to believe in your impending success. As Arsene Wenger, who served as the manager of Arsenal Football Club from 1996 to 2018, says, "If you do not believe you can do it, then you have no chance at all."

The Confidence Road Is Always Under Construction

Your self-beliefs can be long lasting and grow over time. For example, you might feel confident that you will commit to an exercise program, cope well with distractions during board meetings, stick the landing in gymnastics, improve your vocal range through practice, or perform well on an exam. In other words, you might be a confident person who believes you will succeed across multiple performance arenas, or you might experience confidence that is unstable and dynamic (Vealey and Chase 2008). Because of this fact, confidence is transient and changing. State-like confidence, a belief that fluctuates based on the situation or circumstance, is unstable and dynamic. It is this type of confidence that seems to cause athletes and performers the most angst.

Often, performers feel they have to be confident in order to play well. Yes, confidence affects performance, but you do not have to have your best confidence to perform at a high level. That knowledge should take some pressure off. Throughout a career, you will feel moments of self-confidence, and you will have drops in confidence. There will be times when you will need to regain your confidence and occasions when the goal is to maintain your self-belief. Know that the confidence road is *always* under construction. It is a task that is never done, a problem that is never solved, a challenge that never goes away. *The need to normalize that fact is critical.* It is not a matter of whether you will experience changes in your confidence levels. You will. What matters is that you become aware of your confidence and the related impact those fluctuations can have on performance. Take a look at the confidence V in figure 2.1*a* and compare it with the U in figure 2.1*b*.

Because confidence is transient, every performer has lulls in their self-belief. It is a universal experience. The difference between figure 2.1*a* and 2.1*b* is that the performer in figure 2.1*b* likely feels low levels of confidence for longer periods between spells of high self-belief. Realistically, you should expect drops in your belief system from time to time. It is normal to have self-doubt. It stems from a biological, evolutionary need to focus on your deficiencies and hold on to negative events. When you put your hand on a hot stove as a child, it is useful to retain that memory to avoid replicating the error and risk burning yourself again. From an evolutionary perspective, the decision to retain that adverse memory is both helpful and important. So the propensity to remember negative events has served us well and kept us safe for genera-

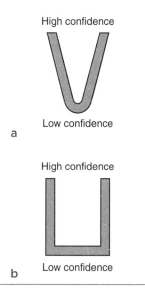

FIGURE 2.1 *(a)* Confidence V and *(b)* confidence U.

tions, but that same mechanism is a burden for us from a performance standpoint. People tend to remember in greater detail and replay with increased frequency their failures and shortcomings. We have to recognize that tendency and remember that, as a result, developing and sustaining confidence is an ongoing task throughout life. The good news is that we can take greater control of that process.

Rather than fearing a lack of confidence or feeling frustrated when you feel a drop in confidence, pay attention to your perceptions of self-belief. As you look at figure 2.1 *a* and *b*, consider: *When do periods of heightened confidence occur for me? What brings me out of those periods of confidence? When I lose confidence [and you will], what causes me to lose it? How low does my confidence drop? How long does it take me to regain my confidence?* For each person, there are both personal factors (e.g., goal orientation, optimism, motivation, anxiety) and situational factors (e.g., playing a preferred position, performing in a comfortable environment, coach's behaviors) that affect self-confidence. For example, a baseball player who is focused on the outcome (winning or outperforming others) might experience a drop in confidence that remains low for longer if they are in a hitting slump and lose their starting position in the middle of a contract season (e.g., they need to play well to earn a better contract next season or avoid being traded). In this situation, with those personal factors, the player's confidence might look like a U. It is the interaction between the individual and the situation that influences self-belief. Read through the In Their Own Words sidebar on page 12 for an example of how situational and personal factors can affect performance.

IN THEIR OWN WORDS **A Tale of the Trade in the National Basketball Association**

Being traded is a difficult reality for National Basketball Association (NBA) players. They often report feeling isolated, worrying about their families, and experiencing a lack of confidence with their new teams. Typically, this is an experience that role players share. When Jimmy Butler entered the NBA, he was a highly regarded player—the type of player a franchise would build around, not the person you would expect to be traded. Yet, since he was drafted in 2011, he has already played for four NBA teams.

Regardless, his confidence and performance rarely faltered. He has already made three All-NBA Teams and five All-Defensive Teams and, in 2020, was the best player on the Miami Heat, who made it to the coveted NBA finals.

Although Butler has not always been accepted by teammates or within team cultures that do not prioritize winning, he continuously performs at a high level and averaged 20 points per game, almost 7 rebounds, and over 6 assists per game during the 2020 season. With a smile on his face and his shoulders back, Butler remains confident and performance has improved now that he is playing with the Miami Heat (Friedell 2020).

Jimmy Butler has had every reason to pout or complain or give less than his best effort. He has been shipped around the league every year or two since entering in 2011. His story demonstrates that there will always be situational factors that could affect your confidence (e.g., new team, new coaching staff, new position, new living situation, new arena). You will always face situations in which you are comfortable and others that stretch or push you. What will you do to be confident in any situation? You cannot always control the environment or culture, but you can direct your focus and implement a plan to enhance self-confidence. Because the confidence road is always under construction, you need a go-to plan—something you do well, something you can control. Focus on those elements.

These factors are not the same for everyone, and they change over the course of a person's life and career. The first step in the confidence construction process is to become aware of when you feel confident, the factors that promote confidence, elements that cause self-doubt, and how you are able to regain your confidence after you lose it. *Self-awareness* is at the heart of every chapter in this book. You can perform well with doubts *if* you know what is causing those doubts and how to correct them.

An important acknowledgement about our propensity to focus on deficiencies or errors is that this habit negatively affects our self-belief. *Confidence follows focus*. When working with performers who have confidence issues, we have to backward chain. There is power in knowing that it is first and foremost a focus issue. We must become aware of that reality.

When you lack confidence, you are likely thinking about your shortcomings. As self-doubt develops, performers often feel anxious, distracted, and unsure. It is inconceivable, impossible even, to lack confidence and be focused on your strengths and accomplishments. What can be jarring to highly successful performers is that all of the behaviors during practice that helped them excel—the drive for perfection, constant repetition, error correction, and refinement orientation—can actually be a detriment to their confidence during performance. They might feel that focusing on reducing errors and analyzing their mistakes is their "superpower" because that is how they honed their craft—through hard work and practice. Being hard on themselves and focusing on deficiencies during practice has served them well. However, the behaviors that help people improve and get better in practice are different from the behaviors that are best suited to games, matches, and competitions. There are times to trust the training, to focus on strengths, and to believe in their ability to succeed, and it is not helpful from a confidence or performance perspective to do this during competition. In competition, as opposed to practice, they need to focus on their strengths, their unique capabilities. Concentrating on their assets will positively affect confidence, which will, in turn, enhance performance.

If you can extend moments of confidence, and if you can bring yourself out of low confidence sooner, then you will have made an improvement. There will always be dips in self-belief. The point is to decrease how often and for how long you experience those decrements in self-belief. You want your periods of confidence to look like figure 2.2. Notice how the distance between the drops in confidence increases so that the performer is experiencing higher levels of confidence for longer periods of time. Then, look at the Vs specifically—they represent a decrease or drop in confidence—and pay attention to how their width decreases. The performer is regaining confidence quicker over time as they learn strategies to build and develop their self-belief.

Once you have developed an awareness of your confidence, then you can begin to develop a *self-regulation* plan. That is the goal: to be able to sustain high levels of confidence for as long as possible, to recognize when your belief is suffering, and to effectively implement strategies to regain it as quickly as possible. The best performers know they must train their minds the same way they discipline their bodies; they must work on their confidence day after day and year after year. Before discussing how you might create confidence training plans, read through the Chalk Talk checklist on page 14, which highlights a few of the key techniques for building your self-belief we have covered.

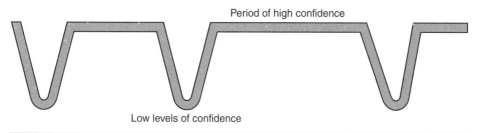

FIGURE 2.2 Quicker confidence recoveries and longer high-confidence periods.

Chalk Talk

Quick Hits for Building Confidence

☐ Focus on your strengths.
☐ Search for opportunities and reasons to perform well.
☐ Identify challenges to your self-confidence and create plans to counter them.
☐ Recognize that confidence is an ongoing, lifelong task.
☐ Expect a successful outcome.

The remainder of this chapter highlights several sources of confidence and strategies for you to integrate into your practice to improve, recover, and sustain your self-belief.

Strategies for Strengthening the Belief

Arthur Ashe, the first African American tennis player to win the U.S. Open and Wimbledon singles titles and the first man of color to be ranked number one in the world, acknowledged that "An important key to self-confidence is preparation." It is a prerequisite for building confidence. Scholars review the literature and comb over their notes to prepare for presentations, young guitarists strum the chords over and over before recitals, and pilots pore over their flight patterns and landing plans before takeoff. In each of these examples, performers' confidence in their abilities is bolstered by their commitment to preparation. For athletes, it is their physical conditioning and training that serve as the foundation upon which their confidence is built. Many sport performers rate physical preparation as one of their top sources of belief because it provides them with the confidence to believe they will win points late in matches, outreach their opponent at the line, or have a final kick in the last 50 meters that separates them from the pack. Two-time gold medalist and two-time FIFA Women's World Cup champion Mia Hamm summed it up like this: "I've worked too hard and too long to let anything stand in the way of my goals." Winner of 23 Grand Slam tennis titles, the most by any player in the Open Era, Serena Williams' mantra is "Overpower. Overtake. Overcome." Do you think their confidence stems from their physical conditioning? Elite and internationally competitive performers

Clive Brunskill/Getty Images

consistently point to their training as an entrance ticket. It gets them in the room. It is not the sole differentiator, but without it a solid belief system could not exist.

The other essential elements of preparation are mental skills training and developing a confidence plan. What will you do when it is time to perform and you are not feeling confident? How will you respond after you make a mistake and you lose your belief? What strategies will you employ when you perform in your first major arena or in front of a large crowd or away from your hometown for the first time? Regardless of your answers to these questions, if you are waiting until you are in these positions to decide on the solution, then you are already too late. You need a go-to plan so you know what to do *before* you need to do it. Planning and practicing your identified strategies improve confidence.

Repeating your plans under various conditions so that you know how to shorten your routines if you get a flat tire, for example, on the way to your performance or so you are ready to stretch your preperformance regimen if the competition is delayed can strengthen your self-belief. It gives your mind somewhere to go in moments when you might otherwise be distracted or taken out of the present moment. You know that you have the ability to be successful no matter the circumstances. Once your foundation is set and you are ready to build your belief, it is time to identify the sources of self-efficacy, which is simply a task-specific type of confidence. It refers to your belief that you can perform a particular task successfully (Bandura 1977). Initially, we think of specific tasks such as putting a golf ball, hitting a baseball, or swimming breaststroke, but self-efficacy can also refer to your perception that you will overcome challenges such as completing your workout even after a 12-hour workday or executing a takedown maneuver in the final round of a fight. To feel confident as a performer, you must have high levels of self-efficacy. A basketball player, for instance, would not feel confident in their offensive abilities if they did not have high self-efficacy in their ability to dribble, pass, and shoot the basketball. Self-efficacy, then, is important to consider and is the path to take when addressing confidence issues. Enhancing belief in your ability to perform a specific task would likely lead to an increase in your overall self-belief in that particular performance domain. Further, you need to become aware of the four sources of self-efficacy (verbal persuasion, vicarious experiences, past performance accomplishments, physiological states) and how these particular sources offer strategies for influencing efficacious beliefs (Bandura 1997).

Verbal Persuasion

When you commit an error (and you will), imagine your teammate patting you on the back and telling you to go for it again or your coach encouraging you to continue working hard. These examples might prevent drops in self-belief that could otherwise accompany an error. Occasionally, you might experience a lowered or negative mood before a performance and so you begin listening to music or a self-recorded audio file that includes words or short phrases that can elevate your mood and help you feel more confident. Each of these examples highlights the effect verbal persuasion can have on self-efficacy and demonstrates how this source of self-efficacy includes any credible, trustworthy, and expert feedback regarding your performance. It can come from you as the performer, from a trusted teammate, from your coach or boss or leader, from music, or from some other respected person in your life. The purpose of these words and phrases is to persuade or convince you to maintain your effort, elevate your mood, remind you of your capabilities, or, in some other way, attempt to enhance your confidence.

Talking to yourself is typically described as self-talk in sport psychology. Specific strategies for targeting your self-talk are provided in chapter 3. In this chapter, the focus is on explaining the purpose and effect of such words and phrases on your confidence specifically. Verbal persuasion might sound like "Stay focused," "I've been here before; they can't stop me," or "I'm ready for this moment." These phrases should be stated in the present tense and should come from someone who matters most to you. First-person language (an "I" statement) is powerful when implementing verbal persuasion; however, some athletes have had success recording a parent or guardian or teammate reading a script they created that contains second-person language. The most important elements of successful verbal persuasion are that the words are *believable* and *credible*. They

PUT IT INTO PRACTICE

Coaches and sport leaders cannot control athletes' feelings of confidence; however, they oversee the environment in which athletes perform. The following suggestions are supported by the literature and will allow coaches to provide a culture that encourages athletes to develop self-confidence. These suggestions are separated into several categories to promote quick, effective implementation.

Creating an Effective Team Climate

- Recognize and reward effort (more than outcome).
- Focus on individual improvement and comparing athletes with their previous performances.
- Reduce uncertainty (e.g., share practice plans, disseminate travel itineraries in advance).

Responding to Errors

- Recognize athletes' effort and reinforce *any* attempts to "go for it."
- Involve athletes in the correction of the technical or tactical error.
- Focus on the solution rather than the problem or error.

Training Athletes Physically

- Balance challenging drills and competitive situations with opportunities for success.
- Put athletes and teams in pressure situations to test their strategies and positively reinforce them when they are successful.
- Maximize opportunities to practice and perform; minimize waiting time.

Considering the Individual

- Learn each athlete's strategies for sustaining and regaining confidence.
- Identify, with the athlete, moments in which their confidence is under siege.
- Remember that confidence levels constantly fluctuate and will change over the course of a season for each performer.

should be meaningful to you as the performer and should ideally come from you or a trusted, respected source.

One person or group of people whose words and behaviors can have a significant impact on athletes' self-efficacy is their coach or coaching staff. For many sport performers, the leader of their team or their personal trainer becomes one of the most significant influencers in their life during their competitive years. As such, it seems particularly important to offer strategies for coaches and other sport leaders to address athletes' self-efficacy and confidence (see the Put It Into Practice sidebar on page 17).

Vicarious Experience

Observing others is another way to improve confidence. Vicarious experiences can be particularly powerful and useful when an athlete or performer is injured or unable to participate in practice or preparation. This source of confidence is also helpful when someone is attempting a challenging skill or a task that involves high risk or includes a situation that the person has yet to experience. Rock climbers might watch videos of Alex Honnold, known for his free solo ascents, in hopes of ascertaining possible strategies or approaches. In the same way, a novice teacher would intern or work with an experienced teacher and, after a period of observing, would begin teaching short portions of lessons before taking over their own class. Most of the time, the model should be someone who is an expert and skilled in the task. However, if a beginner or novice performer is struggling to execute a specific task, then it is appropriate for them to observe someone who might commit similar errors while performing. It may seem counterintuitive, but doing so can help the athlete or performer recognize the mistake and identify strategies for correcting it without negatively affecting their confidence. Vicarious experiences and modeling offer a way for athletes and nonsport performers to build their confidence before they attempt the feat themselves or when they cannot complete the skill or task for some reason. See the Chalk Talk checklist on page 19 for critical strategies for increasing the effectiveness of the model or demonstrator.

People could also imagine themselves performing the selected task successfully or correcting their error to improve confidence through vicarious experiences. Specific strategies for conducting successful imagery sessions will be addressed later in this text.

Past Performance Accomplishments or Mastery Experiences

Enhancing confidence by reflecting on previous successes and accomplishments is the most dependable source of self-efficacy. These reflections are based on actual mastery experiences of the athletes and performers them-

Chalk Talk

Quick Hits for Improving Model Effectiveness

Observers should do the following:

- ☐ Pay attention to the demonstration.
- ☐ Look for the key or critical points.
- ☐ Practice the skill or task after observation.
- ☐ Be motivated and excited to perform the task and understand the importance of completing it.

Demonstrators should do the following:

- ☐ Be enthusiastic about the task.
- ☐ Provide two to four demonstrations from various angles and distances.
- ☐ Give verbal cues that direct the athlete's attention to critical or key elements of the task.
- ☐ Offer reinforcement to the athlete or performer when they attempt to re-create the movement (if it is a live demonstration).

selves. For example, an athlete could create their own video recording of multiple performances of executing the same task successfully. Then, that person would watch the video to re-create the experience and build their confidence. The images should be examples of mastery or successful execution and should include the appropriate emotion associated with such a performance to be effective. Overall, the videos should last only a few minutes to ensure athletes maintain interest and attentional focus (Selk 2009). Athletes could also re-create these experiences through imagery. For example, a field hockey player who had not performed her individual task or assignment during a corner play could imagine herself setting up before the official blowing the whistle and then take the play to completion, seeing herself performing correctly. These images would help to build the player's confidence before the next practice or competitive event. Because imagery will be the focus of a later chapter, further specificity will not be offered here.

Coaches, consultants, teachers, and other leaders could facilitate performers' mastery experiences by providing opportunities for successful

MichaelSvoboda/iStockphoto

practice. For example, youth sport athletes could play on smaller fields or decrease the distances between scoring apparatuses. Changes to equipment such as lowering basketball hoops or shortening a tennis racket handle would also offer increased chances at accomplishing their goals. Other performers could have their attempts charted and successes recorded. These decisions by sport and nonsport leaders could help performers draw from more frequent and robust past performance achievements, thereby increasing a person's confidence.

Emotional and Physiological States

Activation levels influence performance through athletes' interpretations of their activation or physiological and emotional states. For example, if an athlete notices sweaty palms or a shaky voice and interprets that as fear of failure or signs of physical pain, then they will likely experience a decrease in their confidence and a related increase in anxiety levels or worry, resulting in poor play. On the other hand, if they perceive their sweaty palms as an indication of their commitment, excitement, and desire to succeed, then it is more likely that the athlete will feel confident, prepared, and ready to play well. *Interpretation matters.* Learning how to think productively about the signals the body is providing is important in developing confidence. When considering emotions specifically, positive states such as happiness, excitement, and tranquility are more likely to improve efficacy judgments than are emotions like fear or anxiety (Martin 2002).

Now that you understand the sources of self-efficacy, consider completing the homework to help you personalize the content of this chapter. The worksheet on pages 24-25 provides an opportunity for you to become more aware of your own confidence needs and to begin the process of self-regulation. Each chapter and every mental skill is structured around your personal commitment to developing self-awareness and self-regulation.

Conclusion

While mental skills coaches and consultants often discuss performers' thoughts and feelings, a focus of this book will be to explain how those same thoughts and feelings can and should be measured through observable behaviors. How do athletes or performers look when they are feeling confident versus when they are experiencing a drop in their self-belief? For an outside back in soccer, for example, who is the best in the world at her position, playing confidently means that she would not only perform well defensively but that she would also get forward on the attack. When she is playing well, feeling good, and going into the match with a confident mindset, she should get forward on attack more often. And, as a consultant or leader, I would expect to hear that she feels differently about performances when she is doubting herself. In soccer, a player lacking confidence is often less likely to go forward and move into an attacking position, preferring instead to play it safe and stay back on defense.

However, focusing primarily on thoughts and feelings can be misleading and inaccurate. Your opponents don't care how you feel; what matters in performance is what you do. Your coach does not care what you are thinking about or considering; your coach cares about your actions and your behaviors. It is important, then, to operationally define thoughts and feelings—to name them and identify them through behaviors. And, when you put your thoughts in behavioral terms, the direct effect might be less dramatic but more impactful than you initially thought. When thinking about a previous performance, you may feel that the experience was awful and horrific and that you could not do anything right. If you are playing while also feeling less confident, it often feels like you are behaving and performing differently than you would if you had high levels of confidence when, in fact, the difference may seem great only to you.

Every athlete needs to establish a baseline, so you may have to watch film or observe a practice or training session and measure the targeted behavior. In this case, the behavior is a defender getting forward. The world-class outside back, then, might suggest she got forward often when she was feeling good, when it was a great game, and when the video represents how she wants to play the position. Yet, when you watch the film or count the number of times she actually got forward during the match, it is two or three times per half, a measured baseline of getting forward six times per competition. This is a perfect example of confidence making us overestimate our behaviors and actual impact. When we objectively count and measure the behavioral outcome of the feelings of confidence, it is often less than what we thought or felt during competition. So, in this scenario, pushing forward as an outside back six times per game is a baseline indication of self-defined confidence.

Now, imagine what would happen after a game in which the athlete felt less confident. How would she answer the same questions if she felt afraid to get forward? Would she use language like "I never got forward; I was scared to get beat, so I didn't get forward like I normally would"? Here, her language indicates her thoughts and feelings may or may not match actual behavior. If she is not careful, those thoughts could take her away from her desired goal. Instead, we measure the actual behavioral outcomes associated with a lack of confidence. In this case, maybe the athlete got forward one or two times during each half. When she was supremely confident, she got forward three or four times. The behavioral difference is workable and certainly not as negative as the feelings indicate.

As an athlete, when you can see the film and count the behavioral outcomes that you associate with demonstrations of confidence (or a lack of it), you can deal with the discrepancy between your thoughts, feelings, and behaviors. Often, what athletes think is terrible is not as bad as they assume, and when they see it was not as bad as they thought or felt, they can move on from that performance without their confidence taking a hit. The key is to operationally define the thought or feeling. What does it yield from a behavioral or performance perspective? Then measure the behavior. Focus on behavior, not just thinking and feelings. In short, measure confidence by the behaviors and competitive actions displayed.

The other element that is important when focusing on behaviors and outcomes is how to correct the thought or feeling as quickly as possible to avoid further disruptions to performance. So when you lack confidence, and self-doubt creeps in at some point, you have to make behavioral adjustments. Go to your 80 percent game. Make decisions that have a likely completion or success rate of 80 percent. For example, a soccer player should choose the sure pass, the pass with an 80 percent likelihood for success, rather than trying to thread the needle between defenders. In other examples, a person should state the sentence in the simplest terms rather than using jargon during a business presentation, and students might choose to skip a tough question on an exam and find one that they can answer correctly and then go back to the tough one. If you have to perform a riskier move or task when you are already doubting yourself, then deciding to complete that task is not in your best interest. Self-doubt lowers the chance of success of that skill—perhaps to as low as 20 percent—so if the ball is intercepted or you lose your place in the sentence or you miss the exam question, then you might begin saying things like "I can't pass" or "I never do well on exams." Those things are not true. You just made a poor decision. Go to your 80 percent game instead, and let the next person play the ball. Then you can say "Man, I'm connecting my passes." *Change the probabilities*.

When you do not believe in yourself and when you are doubting your capabilities, make 80 percent probability decisions. After you make enough successful decisions and experience enough successful behavioral outcomes, confidence will begin to increase. As suggested in the preface, do the work through your actions, not just psychologically or emotionally. You must commit to changing your behaviors. If you are willing and ready to behave differently, then the strategies presented in the rest of this book can make a significant impact on your life.

The chapters that follow highlight cognitive strategies that can target confidence. The following mental skills, in particular, could be used: imagery, self-talk, goal setting, cognitive restructuring, mindfulness, focus, and concentration. These topics will be expanded on later in the book. Confidence remains one of the greatest differentiators among highly successful and less successful performers and serves as the foundation for what follows. While each of these strategies can be used to target a variety of performance issues, they can also directly enhance confidence once the performer is educated, engages in consistent practice over time, and begins implementing the mental skills during performances and competitive situations. As you read the chapters that follow, think about the various ways each of the strategies discussed could be integrated into your daily practice in life and in sport.

Sources of Confidence

Use this worksheet after reading about or teaching performers how to strengthen their beliefs. In particular, the sections in this chapter dedicated to the four sources of self-efficacy (verbal persuasion, vicarious modeling, mastery experiences, emotions and physiological states) should be considered before completing this worksheet. The purpose of this homework is to individualize the information in this chapter and to provide an opportunity to create a go-to plan before you need it. Filling in the table will help you become more self-aware and better able to self-regulate so that you can reap the benefits of enhanced confidence.

Directions

Each of the columns is dedicated to a source of self-efficacy: verbal persuasion, vicarious modeling, mastery experiences, emotions and physiological states. For each of the columns, fill in the boxes with your responses to the prompts. You should limit yourself to three phrases in each column.

Prompts

- *Verbal persuasion:* Write three examples of credible, trustworthy phrases that would enhance your confidence. Indicate who you would seek for this type of feedback or information (e.g., yourself, coach, teammate, music, quote from a respected elite performer in your sport).
- *Vicarious experiences (modeling or observing):* Identify and describe three examples of people and situations that offer the ideal models. These people could be parents or guardians, teammates, coaches, or other performers who compete in your position or whom you admire and respect. They must be meaningful and accurate for you.
- *Past performance accomplishments or mastery experiences:* Record three past performance accomplishments that you are most proud of in your life in that particular achievement domain. Be as specific as possible by including the date, location, opponent, and so on.
- *Physiological states:* Write three emotions that you feel when you are confident. And write a word or short phrase that you would use to bring about each physiological state.

All responses should be as detailed and specific as possible. Please review the example provided before beginning your worksheet.

Verbal persuasion	Vicarious experiences (modeling, observing)	Past performance accomplishments or mastery experiences	Physiological states
Example: *I am the floor general. I direct the show (tell myself).*	Example: *Sue Bird during game one of the 2020 WNBA Finals against the Las Vegas Aces*	Example: *Playing point guard during the FIBA World Cup on October 1, 2020, in Sydney, Australia*	Example: *I am strong. I am calm and steady.*

From C. Hacker and M. Mann, *Achieving Excellence: Mastering Mindset for Peak Performance in Sport and Life* (Champaign, IL: Human Kinetics, 2023).

CHAPTER 3

Chatter Matters

In the 2019 World Cup, the U.S. women's national soccer team faced Spain, with the winner advancing to the quarterfinals. In the seventh minute of the match, Team USA scored and went up 1-0. However, in less than a minute, the match had swung the other way after a costly error. U.S. goalkeeper Alyssa Naeher tried to clear the ball after a shot on goal from

> **If you want to break through, your mind should be able to control your body.**
>
> Eliud Kipchoge, Kenyan distance runner, first marathoner to break the two-hour barrier (1:59:40)

Spain (Goff 2019). With a soft pace, she played the ball short out of the penalty area to a teammate who did not clear it in time. A Spanish player sprinted to intercept the pass and put it in the back of the net: 1-1. In that moment one lapse in judgment changed everything.

What do you think happened next? Did the player hang her head? Did she hustle to grab the ball and get it to midfield for the restart? Did she yell at her teammate for not clearing the ball under pressure? The answer to those questions is key. The answers affect her behavior and that of her teammates and, perhaps, even the final score. After a poorly played ball that resulted in a match-tying goal in a sport where goal scoring happens infrequently, the U.S. goalkeeper could have responded in various ways. There were plenty of reasons: her teammate had more than enough time to clear it, it was routine to play the ball to that player from the box, or her coach had directed her to do so, among others. Excuses and reasons are always available. You can always find an excuse. Just know that when you do, there are consequences.

Had the player put her head down and focused on the error, she likely would have negatively affected her own performance and that of her teammates. In this instance, the goalkeeper regained composure by reminding herself that she was part of the best team in the world and that they had more than 80 minutes left to score a single goal. She was confident in her teammates and directed herself to "play her role" (Goff 2019). *Self-talk* is a cognitive strategy in which cues are used to activate appropriate and preferred responses. In a moment when she had erred, the keeper implemented productive self-talk to direct her behaviors and, ultimately, her in-match response appropriately. Then, late in the match, one of her teammates converted a penalty kick, which put the United States into the next round as they defeated Spain 2-1. Choices have consequences. This player made the decision to direct her self-talk to productive and positive statements, and her behavior followed. In fact, many analysts used that match as an indicator that this goalkeeper was ready for the international stage.

Competitions are made of more than one moment. The purpose of this story is not only to highlight the significance of one event but also to emphasize the importance of carefully choosing your thoughts and responses. Whether playing in a World Cup, preparing for your first surgery as a resident, giving a presentation in front of clients, or talking to a nervous youth sport athlete before a league-deciding hockey game, you are performing. And your performances, your behaviors, are affected by your thoughts. This chapter outlines the elements of effective self-talk and offers strategies for becoming aware of your inner dialogue and learning to self-regulate.

Significance of Self-Talk

One of the reasons self-talk is so critical in sport and exercise psychology is because people think in words, and those words have important implications for performance. Self-talk, then, is infinitely more than simply talking to oneself. Language, whether silent or spoken, reveals a person's psychological state in that moment. Their words are the behavioral manifestation of underlying factors that have a direct impact on performance and emotions in and out of sport settings. It communicates expectations; it indicates self-belief; it demonstrates self-confidence; it expresses persistence (or lack of it); it signals discrepancies between how someone is performing and how they think they should be performing. To understand the significance of self-talk, you need to look at the effect it is having on expectations, effort, confidence, and performance. Is it working for you? Is it encouraging you to keep going or to seek out more challenging situations? Does it help you listen to and implement criticism? This is the powerful effect of self-talk on behaviors, and behaviors change performance, and performances change careers, and careers change the world. If you look at the result and follow the steps back to the source, you can see how powerful that mental skill is. Self-talk, a silent or spoken thought, provides a window into an athlete's soul.

As with all the mental skills and strategies described in this text, training self-talk requires awareness and practice. When systematically trained over time and effectively integrated with physical practice, it has been proven to enhance performance (see reviews by Hatzigeorgiadis et al. 2011; Tod, Hardy, and Oliver 2011). Self-talk has been proven effective across a variety of tasks and when used by participants who possess a range of capabilities (Hatzigeorgiadis et al. 2014). In other words, all performers, in every domain, executing any motor skill can benefit from actively choosing productive, purposeful thoughts. Whether someone is a corporate executive presenting material at a business meeting, a golfer trying to sink a five-foot (1.5 m) putt on the 18th hole for the championship, a surgeon repairing an anterior cruciate ligament, a kindergartener writing their name for the first time, a student completing a final exam, or a coach leading during a timeout or a drill, there is benefit in training self-talk. And for novel tasks that require precision and accuracy, like shooting an arrow or playing the violin, implementing effective self-talk is particularly important (Hatzigeorgiadis et al. 2014).

As a leader or consultant, you must listen for, observe, and be aware of the self-talk patterns of your employees, coaches, students, or athletes. Do they hang their head after an error or hit their thigh after a mistake, for example? Tuning into these moments and understanding how much additional baggage those words reveal can have a significant impact on the experiences in sport and exercise that follow. Watch their eyes light up when they see their favorite opponent after the schedule is posted. You do not need to hear the actual words that are being said to understand how their inner dialogue is influencing their emotions and behavior. Performers' self-talk can affect their confidence, effort, persistence, and motivation, and it can affect their ability to manage their emotions, control their activation, and direct and sustain attentional focus (Hatzigeorgiadis et al. 2011; Tod, Hardy, and Oliver 2011). Observing an athlete take a deep breath when they see the game against Norway on the schedule, for example, is a clue, an indication of their beliefs and expectations of success against a top-level opponent. This brief encounter signals the need for a self-talk intervention. The efficacy of such interventions was shown in a study with scuba divers (Van Raalte et al. 2018). Imagine diving 165 feet (50 m) under water only to have your mask fill with fog or water from a leak.

This equipment issue in diving is a common occurrence, but novice divers who suddenly lose the ability to see their immediate surroundings often panic and develop inadvertent, distracting thoughts, like "Oh no, it's happening again. I can't see anything." Self-talk interventions taught divers to prioritize clear thinking directed to the task at hand, and as a result, they were able to clear their masks quickly and efficiently in a high-risk context when seconds mattered. Learning to create effective thoughts and direct self-talk appropriately is important for anyone looking to improve their performance.

The Relationship Between Self-Talk and Performance

Self-talk and behavior operate through a reciprocal, bidirectional relationship. Self-talk reflects beliefs, confidence, energy, and expectations and is influenced by a performer's beliefs, confidence, and expectations. An athlete thinking about and focusing on how tired they are during practice is likely to feel even more exhausted as their thoughts lead them to slouch their shoulders and grab their shorts. In this way, internal thought patterns affect behavior, but performance can also affect self-talk. In preparation for her first trial case, a novice lawyer practiced her opening remarks repeatedly during a mock trial she organized with her colleagues. Standing in front of the jury months later to deliver her opening remarks on day one of the trial, she presses her shoulders back, levels her chin, takes a deep breath, and thinks "I am ready. Just like the mock trial. I've got this" as she confidently approaches the jury box.

Events like this, despite the potential personal significance, are neutral. All students do not fear oral presentations in front of their peers just as all athletes do not feel cool, calm, and confident before a competitive match. It is not the event itself that causes specific or predetermined thoughts or feelings. Rather, as these examples demonstrate, a person's thoughts and feelings can influence their behavior and performance in either a positive or negative direction. Similarly, a person's performance can influence how they think. These examples highlight the reciprocal, bidirectional relationship between thoughts and behaviors as shown in figure 3.1.

FIGURE 3.1 Bidirectional relationship between thoughts and behaviors.

To better understand this relationship, you need to know the physiology of the connection. While the focus of this text is on developing mental skills, sometimes specifically explaining how these strategies work helps performers better understand the skill itself. It is an indisputable fact that when you think (or tell yourself) that you are energized and excited to perform, certain neurochemicals are released (e.g., anandamide and epinephrine) that make you actually feel joyful and excited. Internal thoughts and words spoken aloud have both a physiological and emotional impact. Emotions, behaviors, and, ultimately, performances then are a byproduct of your interpretation of those physiological changes. Knowing about this relationship is important as you recognize elements within your control. Is it possible for you to perform without errors? No. To play and to compete is to err. The power comes when you recognize that you have complete control over the thoughts that follow an error.

And your choice will determine the actions you take next. The next time you prepare for a performance, remember that your thoughts affect your physiology, and your interpretation of those physical changes will affect your performance. So choose wisely.

Types and Timing of Self-Talk

Although some athletes might suggest they do not talk to themselves and that they don't think at all when they are competing at their highest level, the truth is that performers are constantly analyzing, processing, and thinking about their behaviors. In fact, new evidence from brain imaging studies suggests that, on average, human beings generate approximately 6,200 unique thoughts per day (Tseng and Poppenk 2020). What these athletes are asserting when they claim not to think is that they have automated their performances to the point that their thoughts are not conscious. They *are* thinking, but those actions and thoughts are so well rehearsed that they are not aware of them nor are they interrupted by their self-talk. It is important to note that we are not suggesting that we want performers to think more or to engage in more frequent self-talk patterns. What we hope to demonstrate is that, whether you want to be or not, you *are* engaging in thought before, during, and after each performance. The choice, then, is not *if* you should engage in self-talk, but instead the decision lies in *how* you will train your inner dialogue. How will you create and implement productive and purposeful self-talk?

Selecting productive and purposeful thoughts does not mean having only positive self-talk, just as unproductive and dysfunctional thoughts are not necessarily negative. Productive and purposeful means you have carefully and intentionally chosen thoughts that will bring you closer to what you desire. They are more likely to bring the results you are hoping to achieve. See the sidebar on page 32 about Tom Brady's negative, purposeful, and productive self-talk.

Whether the thought is negative or positive is less important than its effect. What do you want to have happen? Select your self-talk as it relates to outcome and purpose. If the thought does not increase your ability to bounce back from an error or enhance your ability to perform well, then it needs to be adjusted. The outcome of the thought should always be part of the consideration. If it is not bringing you what you want (more confidence, more resilience, more energy, for example), if it is not working productively *for* you, then change it. Select a different thought. Many athletes leave their dialogue to chance, to situation, or to habit. You can always find a reason for poor performance. Do you want to find a reason or find a way? "Find a way" people make it work no matter what conditions they are in. These people are dogged. They are determined. And their thoughts reflect their approach.

To direct your thoughts effectively and to engage in productive, purposeful self-talk, you need to know how the different types of self-talk

IN THEIR OWN WORDS **Tom Brady**

Six-time Super Bowl champion, four-time Super Bowl MVP, and three-time league MVP Tom Brady said, "If you want to perform at the highest level, you have to prepare at the highest level mentally" during one of the documentaries of his life. He went on to describe how, at the age of 43, as the oldest player in the National Football League (NFL), he viewed his mental game the same as the technical and tactical skills such as throwing, avoiding sacks, and reading the defense. In fact, he noted, "I still work on running and jumping, but, you know, it's a very minimal part of what I do." Instead, he focused most of his time and energy on training mental skills (Rivera 2021).

In a 2014 article in NFL News, Brady described how he uses self-talk to prepare himself to excel during each game and every season. He tells himself "Tom, you're not very good," "What are you doing? That was a bad play. You have to work harder at this" during games. When asked why he, as one of the best quarterbacks in the league, makes these statements, he responded, "I think that's a lot of motivation for me to always feel like I have to prove it to myself first" and "get on the right emotional level" (Kremer 2014).

A high-achieving quarterback, Tom Brady provides an example of using negative self-talk productively and purposefully. In so doing, it is effective for him. Often, athletes and mental skills coaches think that performers must use positive language, but it is how they interpret that language and how meaningful it is that matters most. Whether positive or negative, athletes and nonsport performers should think in ways that are intentional and purposeful.

affect skill execution. More than 47 studies examining the effect of *motivational* and *instructional* self-talk collectively demonstrated that both are equally effective in enhancing performance (Tod, Hardy, and Oliver 2011). Performing any skill, whether shooting in lacrosse, tackling a ball carrier in American football, tying surgical sutures, completing a flip turn in the pool, playing the piano, or running a marathon, can benefit from both types of self-talk. It is knowing *when*, *why*, and *how* to implement each type of self-talk that is essential for success.

Instructional Self-Talk

Instructional self-talk refers to cues that can be used to direct learners' attention, correct errors, or change bad habits. It is often used early in the learning process when trying out a new skill to help performers focus on the most essential elements of the task. When field hockey players are trying to redirect the ball, a coach might say "drop step" to cue athletes to reposition their bodies for a quick change of direction. An acronym in basketball is BEEF (balance, eyes, elbow, follow-through), which can highlight a few aspects of the jump shot at a time. The key is to keep these instructional statements brief and use them sparingly. When someone is learning a skill for the first time, they are already contending with a significant amount of information and inner dialogue. Adding more language can cause some performers to overthink.

Performers might notice that their movements have developed a hitch or that they need to slow down. These are signs of contending with too many thoughts while simultaneously performing a skill. Particularly in conditions when anxiety is already high, using short, simple phrases that bring an immediate change in behavior might be the best form of self-talk. It is important for each performer to experiment with phrases that are productive for them. Then they should practice and refine to ensure the identified thoughts and words yield the intended effect. *Experiment. Practice. Refine.*

For every athlete or performer, self-talk, or their thinking, is an ongoing area of consideration or concern. There are no exceptions. This can be especially true when an athlete commits an error. The key is in learning to choose their thoughts with purpose and to be in control. Often after a mistake, athletes and performers think about the error repeatedly, even creating images of the error to repeatedly replay in their mind. Rather than allowing their thoughts to occur at random and defaulting to the negative event, they should be purposeful and intentional. Using instructional self-talk to change a bad habit or addressing an error means developing self-statements that focus on the correction, not the original mistake. Thinking about the mistake can make the appropriate actions even more difficult to execute, particularly in high-anxiety conditions (Woodman, Barlow, and Gorgulu 2015). In other words, telling themselves what to avoid (e.g., don't play it too wide, don't turn it over, don't get out hustled today) often makes what they want to prevent more likely to happen. Cues like "bend knees, stay low" can be more useful and help a defender adjust their stance quicker than "don't stand up" or "don't lock your knees." With the latter, the immediate image is of a person standing tall and still, which requires the performer to create that image, recognize the error, and correct the error before they execute the skill differently. If a performer wants to feel confident and prepared, then their internal dialogue must include verbal and nonverbal cues that convince the mind of these thoughts and feelings. Similarly, saying "I'm not good at speaking in public" or "I always play poorly in preseason" often leads to performances that confirm the original self-statements. Instead, athletes and performers need to actively construct short, productive, action-oriented self-talk focused on desirable performance or behaviors.

As skills are mastered, instructional cues become even shorter and may be needed less frequently as these self-talk statements become internalized and the movements become automatic. Skilled performers might also want to shift from thinking about the technical or mechanical elements of the task (e.g., bend knees, extend elbow, reach) to focusing on the outcome of the task. Hitters might think "level through the zone" rather than thinking about how to move their body to ensure a level swing, or swimmers might say "explode" or "spring" to propel themselves off the wall for the last leg of the race. Focusing on what they want to accomplish can cue their bodies quickly once the movement patterns have been automated and they know how to execute the skill.

Motivational Self-Talk

In contrast to instructional self-talk, *motivational self-talk* is useful when you need to psych yourself up or bring about more energy and effort. It is about creating the desired emotion and affect those performers want. When feeling lethargic or underactivated, performers can say "Everything you've got on the next rep" to themselves to create the ideal activated state. Right before presenting material to the chief executive officer and the board, a new employee who was up the night before with a sick pet or child might go the restroom, look themselves in the mirror, and say "I've got this. I can do anything for 30 minutes." In general, performers tend to select motivational self-talk over instructional self-talk, but both are necessary and important. It is about knowing when, why, and how to implement each. When motivational self-statements are paired with rapid breathing, an athlete's mood is likely to improve, which can elevate

Per Breiehagen/Stone RF/Getty Images

performance. It is important for every performer to develop a few go-to phrases they can use when they are tired at a morning training session, nervous just before an evaluative or competitive event, or want to maintain effort amid challenging circumstances. Short, simple statements like "strong," "calm," "drive," "explode," and others can help performers cultivate their ideal emotional state when it counts.

Before you head out for your next run, swim, or cycling session, identify a phrase for those moments when you are ascending a hill or disrupted by someone swimming too close to the lane line next to you. Think of a word or statement that you will integrate into practice that will help you feel the way you want to feel in those moments—confident, steady, determined. Then, try it out.

Remember, the words must be meaningful to you and cue your desired effect or feeling.

With both types of self-talk, you should construct your thoughts in the present moment. Be concerned with what is happening right now. Telling yourself "I am confident" rather than "I was confident" or "I will be confident" will have a stronger impact. It is also important to remember the timing of your self-talk. As a performer, there are certain moments that you can take in information and other times when talking to yourself would pull you out of the moment. For skills that you initiate—bowling a ball, swinging a golf club, throwing a ball, delivering a speech—use self-talk before the action begins. In this way, you are priming yourself for success. For skills that require you to respond to someone or something else—receiving a puck in ice hockey, catching a softball, digging up a spike in volleyball—you need to wait until there is a pause in action to engage in self-talk. These breaks offer opportunities to focus on self-talk so that a change can be made or affirmation of the previous performance emphasized. You can incorporate self-talk while executing this latter group of skills if the phrases are short and focused on building confidence or directing attention (Williams and Hacker 2020).

The goal is to teach athletes to regulate themselves, for them to manage their own thoughts, emotions, and behaviors. As such, coaches and leaders should encourage performers to determine their own cues and to identify their own plans for using self-talk during competitive and evaluative moments (Hardy, Hall, and Hardy 2006; Latinjak, Torregrosa, and Renom 2010). Allowing performers to participate in determining how to integrate self-talk into their daily performances can increase participants' interest in it, commitment to using it, and belief in its effectiveness.

However, assigning self-talk cues to performers might be warranted if the athlete, for example, is not old enough or experienced enough to know the appropriate cues. When those moments arise, Van Raalte and colleagues (2016) suggest that coaches and leaders should assign self-talk that is in line with performers' gut feelings or impressions. In other words, the client or performer must believe these words and cues in order to experience their benefit. Teaching an athlete to say "I've got the next one" after committing an error might negatively affect their performance if they do not believe they actually do have the next one. This example underscores, again, the need for athlete belief and buy-in during self-talk training. The positive effects of self-talk on performance are limited if the athlete does not believe what they are saying to themselves.

Buy-in is fundamental to any change in mindset. As a performer, you are interested in cause and effect. You know what went wrong and now you want to know how to fix it. Think of the effect of your thoughts or your beliefs on performance. If you walked into practice thinking about the lack of sleep you experienced the night before, how would that thought affect you? Would it help you have more energy? Are you more focused on your training goal? Or would it make you feel even more tired? Think of the effect of that self-talk focus. Every thought has a related behavioral response. It affects you. What is important to remember is that your thoughts are under your control. Use that control to your advantage. When you have a night of restless sleep and walk into training the next day, think "I am ready for the day. I have played well tired. I am focused and ready now." Take a deep breath and remind yourself you have plenty of energy for today's practice. These thoughts are productive and purposeful. See the Chalk Talk checklist on page 37 for strategies to create and select effective thoughts on demand. When it matters most, choose thoughts that bring about what you want. Thoughts are like actions; they have consequences.

Affirmations for Successful Performance

Affirmations represent a special case or category of self-talk. They are succinct, positively framed words or phrases that are often future oriented or stated as if the performer has already attained what they desire. They are extremely helpful for any athlete, but especially for those who struggle with dysfunctional or unproductive thought patterns. As mentioned previously, human beings are patterned people. Creating and repeating affirmations intentionally is one way to develop self-enhancing cognitive and behavioral patterns. The more these thoughts are accepted and internalized, the less time and space the brain has to consider unproductive self-talk.

There are many examples of affirmations across a variety of performance sectors. Perhaps one of the first athletes to come to mind regarding affirmations is acclaimed boxer and social justice icon Muhammad Ali. Ali is known for affirmations like "I am the greatest." While they may have seemed shocking to some, Ali recognized the significance of his statements and stated, "I said that [I was the greatest] even before I knew I was." He knew that it was the repetition of affirmation that led

Chalk Talk

Quick Hits for Effective Self-Talk

Self-talk statements should be as follows:

- ☐ Short and concise
- ☐ Self-generated
- ☐ Action oriented
- ☐ Focused in the now (present tense)
- ☐ Productive
- ☐ Purposeful
- ☐ Instructional when learning a new skill, correcting an error, or directing attention
- ☐ Motivational when controlling effort or affecting mood or energy
- ☐ Personally meaningful
- ☐ Focused on elements under the performer's control

to belief. It is important to point out that for Ali, these statements were stretching him, but they were not out of his reach. He believed he could be the greatest boxer in the world. Similarly, your affirmations must be believable to you. You do not need to have accomplished them yet, but you should believe they are possible. Effective affirmations are *accurate*, *vivid*, and *internalized*.

To create your own affirmations, try building them from previous successful performances. Think about how you felt while competing and write down that list of words or phrases. Or you could start by writing a list of your strengths as a performer. Then, think of the feelings you want to consistently have that would help bring your game to its highest level—either re-creating that successful performance or strengthening your assets. Construct action-oriented, present-tense "I" statements. For example, you might write "I am ready for this moment," "I am at my best when my plate is full," "I am steady under pressure," or "I am the come-back queen (or king)." Each of these statements is focused on what you want to happen. It may not be true yet that you perform well when an opponent is winning, but repeating the affirmation of being a comeback player helps you create a sense of expectation that the next time that situation arises, success will be imminent. Place the affirmative statement in a place you see frequently (e.g., on shoes, notecards, equipment, clothes, recorded on your phone). The point is to intentionally notice and practice the affirmation multiple times each day until it becomes automatic. You want to see it or hear it every single day. Consistent rehearsal over time will bring about change. Once you have mastered that statement and it has become a part of your daily routine, you can create another statement to train your focus on the positive and then thoughtfully and intentionally create your expectations for future success.

The Importance of Controlling Self-Talk

As a point of distinction, self-talk is more than talking to oneself; it is controlled, intentional, and on time. Purposeful and controlled self-talk is achieved once you can create and re-create productive thoughts in a variety of environments. Never forget that effectively directing your inner dialogue requires consistent training over time. The first step to developing purposeful self-talk is to become *aware* of the ways in which you are talking with yourself before, during, and after performances. You must become aware of when you use self-talk, the content of that self-talk, and when you may need to but currently are not making helpful self-talk choices. Do you only talk to yourself before a performance when you are nervous? What words do you use to recover from an error? Answering these questions can help you better understand your self-talk and how it affects your thoughts, feelings, and behaviors. Perhaps most importantly, along with identifying the conditions in which you use self-talk, you should recognize which parts of your inner dialogue are useful and help you perform or recover from errors and which elements of your self-talk are dysfunctional and unhelpful.

One way to increase awareness of their inner dialogue is for performers to put coins or paper clips in one pocket of their pants and switch the object to the other pocket each time they make a negative or unproductive comment to themselves. Doing so can help them become more aware of what and when they are predicting future failures or focusing on unhelpful thoughts. Another strategy for building awareness is to have performers reflect on recent excellent and poor performances, identifying the thoughts they had before and during those moments. As Latinjak and colleagues (2014) noted, the idea is to recognize typical thoughts associated with positive performance outcomes. Becoming more aware of the types of self-talk that are useful and the conditions under which they occur can help performers more consistently and purposefully re-create those statements. Learning to control self-talk can positively affect behaviors and performances as well as expectations for future success.

Becoming aware of your thoughts is an important step; unfortunately, simply knowing that negative or harmful thoughts exist does not prevent them from happening. In fact, dwelling on how negative your self-talk is can be debilitating. The next step, then, is to consider techniques for effectively controlling and adjusting self-talk as needed. In this chapter, we focus on thought stoppage followed by cognitive restructuring to help direct your self-talk. However, this is simply one strategy of many. Some performers benefit from thought acceptance (a component of acceptance and commitment therapy), for example, which will be discussed in chapter 4.

Thought Stoppage

Thought stoppage is used to eliminate unwanted or harmful thoughts that often distract people from their performance and take them out of the present moment. To interrupt or stop an unproductive thought, performers should use a trigger or cue such as "stop" or clapping their hands one time. The cue can be verbal or nonverbal as long as it is meaningful and is natural for the athlete to integrate into their behavior. It should not require an additional thought process to remember this routine; instead, the best forms of cues to stop unwanted thoughts are those that the athlete or performer already engages in. The difference is that they are now engaging in this technique with purpose. Although this skill seems simple, it will only work if athletes are aware of their less-than-desirable thoughts and are motivated to change them *and* practice the thought-stopping technique consistently.

As with the other mental skills in this book, thought stoppage should be practiced away from the competitive or evaluative environment initially to prevent solidifying bad habits. One way to practice is to imagine being in a situation in which you usually have unproductive, self-defeating thoughts. As you create that image in your mind, use your trigger word or action to stop the thought and continue with your performance. Saying the cue out loud or actually practicing the action trigger will help you become more aware of its effect and will allow your coaches or consultants to monitor and intervene if necessary. The imagery practice should continue until the image you create is of you experiencing the situation without dysfunctional self-talk. Only practice thought stoppage during physical preparation or the actual performance itself *after* having mastered the imagined scenario.

Shift to Productive Thoughts

In trying to get rid of unwanted thoughts, some athletes and performers become even more focused on the very thoughts they are trying to eliminate (Woodman, Barlow, and Gorgulu 2015). This second strategy, then, involves teaching performers to shift from unproductive thoughts to appropriate, affirming, productive language. Remember, it is not the unproductive thought that is unusual or debilitating. All performers experience self-defeating thoughts from time to time. Take National Basketball Association (NBA) superstar Kevin Durant for example. He recalled an incident early in his career when he was fouled at the end of a game. He remembers that as he walked to the free throw line, "All I could think of was what if I missed. I knew those feelings, and I knew I would drown in them" (MacMullan 2019). The moment he released the shot, he knew his free throw had no chance of going in.

These moments happen. The key is what happens *after* that thought occurs. Snowboarder Lindsey Jacobellis has talked about how, after several mishaps at the Olympic Games, she had to finally recognize and acknowledge her dysfunctional self-talk instead of pretending like she was the only athlete who didn't have self-defeating thoughts (KSN 2018). The greatest performers learn how to face their unproductive talk, and over time they develop the ability to correct or transform their unhelpful thoughts quickly and efficiently. Instead of repeating the unproductive statement over and over again, these athletes train themselves to replace those thoughts with facilitative, self-enhancing statements. With awareness and self-regulation, like these athletes, you can learn this same mental skill.

To practice, performers can create a self-talk log and note unhelpful statements, when they make them, and under what conditions they occur. Then they can identify self-affirming statements to substitute in the same situation. This process is outlined in the sidebar on page 41. As stated earlier, the productive thoughts and self-statements identified should always bring the performer back to the present moment and, in so doing, decrease unproductive self-talk (Hatzigeorgiadis, Zourbanos, and Theodorakis 2007).

Cognitive Restructuring

Often underlying unproductive self-talk is irrational thinking. There are many types of irrational thoughts such as demanding perfection from oneself, catastrophizing (expecting a disastrous mistake), believing self-worth depends on accomplishments, and blaming oneself as the cause of a failure, among others. A basketball player thinking about letting her team down if she misses the game-tying free throw in overtime just as she steps to the line, a violinist struggling before each performance because he feels like he is not good enough to be on stage, a sprinter feeling like he will not run well in the meet because he performed poorly the last time he ran with strong winds, or a corporate executive feeling incapable of leading her C-suite colleagues because she has been told she is too shy her entire life—these are all examples of irrational thinking. And it is these debilitating cognitions—not the weather or lack of ability or opponents' perceptions—that affect behavior. When people are focused on their irrational thoughts, they have fewer resources to devote to their

PUT IT INTO PRACTICE

Creating Self-Talk Logs

One challenge coaches, consultants, and other professionals working in performance domains face is trying to convince clients that their thoughts matter. Some performers think they do not engage in self-talk, and a few athletes might claim that thinking causes their performance to deteriorate. Here, the challenge is a lack of awareness of their self-talk and how their thoughts influence their performance.

In these instances, encourage performers to create self-talk logs. These logs help people identify, for themselves, the language they use and its impact on their behaviors. In other words, creating these logs offers opportunities to bring about self-awareness, which is a prerequisite for behavior change.

One strategy for creating a self-talk log is to have performers think about their most recent best performance, and then write down the elements that qualified it as a high-quality performance. Next, ask them to write down how it felt, what it looked like, and how it sounded. Allow them to write the statements they were making to themselves. Once they have completed that task, have them repeat the process for their worst performance. Ask them to identify differences between how it looked, felt, or sounded when they performed well and when they performed poorly.

Once they have recognized some of those variations, ask them to write down one to three examples of words, thoughts, or statements they might use to bring about the affective, attentional, or confidence-related experience during a good performance.

These self-talk logs can be used to target other issues as well (e.g., becoming aware of thoughts that help them maintain focus instead of distracting them or recognizing self-talk that occurs after an error when they recover quickly compared to self-talk when they take longer to bounce back). These tasks and logs promote self-recognition, which is an ongoing process.

performance. As a result, these maladaptive beliefs must be identified and modified to prevent the resulting negative impact on self-confidence and skill execution.

One strategy to transform these self-defeating thoughts is to use cognitive restructuring (Turner and Barker 2014). The goal is to identify, dispute, and replace irrational thoughts with facilitative, flexible, adaptive beliefs (Williams and Hacker 2020). The process of replacing unproductive thoughts with performance-enhancing thoughts is called cognitive restructuring. To do this, performers need to identify an event and the dysfunctional self-talk they typically engage in before, during, and after those moments. Once the dysfunctional and unhelpful thought has been identified, performers describe the consequences of that self-talk.

Scott Taetsch/Getty Images

Thoughts such as "I did it again; I'm killing my team" or "Ugh, I can't get anything right today" are common examples, so the athlete explains how those thoughts made them feel or behave (e.g., *what happened next?*) and they answer whether or not that thought was true or logical. Is it logical that they cannot get anything right or is it true that they are the sole person to dictate the success of their team? Once the thoughts are established as untrue or illogical, the performer is able to establish a new, effective, rational belief associated with the event. The worksheet on page 44 outlines one way to work through these questions and identify new, facilitative, and flexible thoughts that are more likely to lead to a quicker recovery from errors and other associated performance benefits.

A critical element of successfully restructuring thoughts is for athletes and nonsport performers to repeat the substituted, productive thought until they believe it. Again, this process takes time and repetition. Just as someone's physical skills and fitness progress through practice and targeted repetitions, so, too, does their self-talk. Spending time focusing on positive experiences and productive self-talk is critical for enhanced self-confidence and, ultimately, enhanced performance.

Conclusion

The most successful athletes learn how to think in ways that allow them to correct unproductive thoughts and cultivate the emotions and effect they want on demand. They do not rely on random utterances or default thinking patterns. In this chapter, you learned strategies for controlling self-talk. As you will learn throughout this text, it is not a question of whether or not these skills or strategies work—they do! The impact on performance will occur *if* you are willing to consistently practice and eventually integrate self-talk with physical training.

Systematic training occurs consistently and over time. It is this type of training that is crucial for appropriate, accurate, and timely use of this cognitive strategy (Hatzigeorgiadis et al. 2011). Plans and programs to improve self-talk should always provide opportunities for you to learn about self-talk and its effects, develop your own self-determined cues, and identify moments when they would be useful to implement. You should integrate self-talk strategies during training and then into competitive and evaluative moments, and consistently reevaluate your strategies to ensure the effectiveness of their applications.

Prolonged, systematic training is what leads to changes in thoughts and behaviors. Rather than leaving your thoughts to chance, begin making a choice about your self-talk in the same way you make a choice about the type of pitch to throw. Although random thoughts and utterances occur during performance, if you want to improve, then you must know what to say or think and when to think or say it. You must also learn how to shift unproductive thoughts to productive thoughts. Finally, you must train self-talk strategies through repeated simulations until they are mastered. The reward is that you will be able to select productive and purposeful thoughts on demand and when it matters most. Remember, your thoughts are within your control, *and* they have consequences. *Choose* wisely.

Performer-Centered Implementation Worksheet

Thought Stoppage and Replacement With Productive Thoughts

The purpose of this worksheet is to help you identify and replace dysfunctional thoughts with facilitative and helpful self-talk.

Directions

Identify one to three events in which you commonly experience unproductive self-talk. Be specific. Then, use columns three and four to identify a productive, helpful, accurate replacement thought that will bring about a preferred behavior or response.

Competitive event or moment	Typical response	Preferred response	Facilitative, flexible, adaptive thought (to bring about preferred response)
Example: *Make a poor pass to a teammate that results in a turnover.*	Example: *Clap my hands together and put my head down. "Ugh, again. Get it together. You're awful today."*	Example: *Mentally correct and sprint back defensively.*	Example: *"Head up."* *"Stay aggressive."* *"Make the easy play first."*

From C. Hacker and M. Mann, *Achieving Excellence: Mastering Mindset for Peak Performance in Sport and Life* (Champaign, IL: Human Kinetics, 2023).

CHAPTER 4

Being in the Moment

When writing this book, we discussed which cognitive strategies to include. Dr. Hacker, a mental skills coach in six Olympic Games, recounted one of her favorite stories that illustrates the importance of cognitive strategies in achieving performance success. It happened during the 1996 Olympic Games, which was the first time the U.S. women's soccer team fully integrated a mental skills coach into its staff. In the lead-up to the games, she presented mental skills to the team, and several times athletes said, "You know, Doc, I've been doing this my entire life. I just didn't have a name for it." They thought she might be offended, but she simply reminded them that *that* is why they were an Olympic champion; that is why they were a World Cup champion.

The value of this book is that it points out to athletes and performers that they don't have to leave their success to chance. They don't have to stumble onto the benefits of mental skills training in general and of mindfulness in this case. Whether or not an athlete engages in individualized mindfulness practice should not be left to chance. In the last decade, through numerous continuing education programs, countless books, and personal experience, mindfulness is now part of the suite of psychological strategies that Dr. Hacker presents to every client and team. That is how powerful mindfulness is both as a performance tool and as a life enhancement practice. That is how valuable and applicable it is to both life and sport.

The greatest athletes (and other high-achieving individuals) across decades and generations have used mindfulness practice and a mindfulness orientation to performance, and for many, they do so without knowing there are specific evidence-based tenets. The point of this text

> I really think of mindfulness as being a form of brain hygiene.
>
> Dan Siegel, M.D., clinical professor of psychiatry at the UCLA School of Medicine, executive director of the Mindsight Institute

> I meditate every day. I do a lot of things that center around the mental training . . . so that I can rise to the challenge of whatever comes at me and really stay present on just doing my best in the moment.
>
> Kate Courtney, professional mountain bike racer (2019 World Cup cross-country overall champion)

is to avoid leaving this effective cognitive tool to chance. As with all the cognitive strategies presented, the evidence is clear: Mindfulness works. The question remains, Will you train it? And will you practice mindfulness? Developing this personal and psychological orientation to both sport and life will help enhance your performance across all competitive levels and performance domains as well as increase life satisfaction. The hope is that, after reading this chapter, you will thoughtfully and intentionally implement a mindfulness practice every day and that, ultimately, you will become more aware in each waking moment.

The purpose of this chapter is to describe the historical roots of mindfulness, explain its usefulness in sport and exercise settings, describe its unique contributions to performance enhancement, and identify the applications of mindfulness beyond sport. As with all the chapters, the focus is on offering evidence-based strategies for immediate implementation of mindfulness in both performance domains and activities of daily living. Toward that end, there will be opportunities to practice and suggestions for integrating mindfulness throughout this chapter.

The Roots of Mindfulness

Some of you might think mindfulness is too passive or too soft. (We will address that perception in the next section.) Others of you, particularly performers growing up in the late 20th and early 21st century who have heard and read about experts and athletes discussing their mindful practice (see sidebar on page 48), tend to believe that mindfulness has always been part of sport, business, and life.

It is important to acknowledge the often overlooked historical context of mindfulness. Versions and iterations of this cognitive strategy and framework have existed for over 2,500 years as a key element of Buddhist teachings and philosophies (Epstein 1995). According to Buddhist teachings, mindfulness is intended to help end suffering and painful thoughts and feelings. Being mindful, or intentionally aware of the present moment, can disrupt patterns of reacting, thus "offering possibilities of relief" (Mannion 2020). As Dr. Hacker says, "Things are not good because they are old; they are old because they are good," and this adage is certainly true of mindfulness. Mindfulness practice has stood the test of time and has been "newly discovered" by recurring generations.

Mindfulness garnered attention in medicine and psychology in North America more than 100 years ago (Mannion 2020). Although there was scattered interest in the West throughout the early 1900s, it was not used consistently or systematically until the 1970s and 1980s, when Jon Kabat-Zinn's mindfulness meditation interventions were used for stress management and other medical conditions (e.g., cancer treatment, pain management). Kabat-Zinn (1982) defined mindfulness as a deliberate nonjudgmental awareness of present-moment thoughts, feelings, body sensations, and the environment. Figure 4.1 provides a way to understand the importance of a present-moment focus.

Performers learn to be curious and accepting of a situation—to allow the situation to be what it is rather than trying to change it, avoid it, or judge it. Medical professional and winner of four national ultrarunning titles, Dr. Megan Roche noted, "Whether in running or business, there are moments that feel like the most immense failures, but that's where the good stuff happens" (Roche and Roche 2020). It is this type of approach to unpleasant and undesirable competitive moments (e.g., poor performances, bad calls, arguments with a teammate, admonishments from a coach) that mindful engagement can bring about.

Kabat-Zinn fits mindfulness to a need that almost everyone has or will face: medical issues. And as a result of his work with Oprah Winfrey, the concept took off in the United States. Kabat-Zinn made mindfulness practical, accessible, and meaningful. Specifically, during the 1970s, at the University of Massachusetts Medical School, Kabat-Zinn created the mindfulness-based stress reduction (MBSR) program to assist people in coping with stress, anxiety, pain, and depression, among other ailments (Kabat-Zinn 2013). The MBSR program combines meditation, mindfulness, self-awareness training, and yoga to examine thoughts, feelings, and behavioral patterns. To date, this eight-week program that encourages both informal and formal daily mindfulness practice is the most scientifically tested and established mindfulness training program in the world.

Still, the field of sport psychology lagged in its implementation of this proven technique. In fact, we did not study mindfulness as part of our initial graduate training. And Dr. Hacker did not use a mindfulness-based approach to sport or for her clients in the first 20 years of her career. It was not part of the most commonly accepted mental skills interventions

FIGURE 4.1 These three figures represent the three points in time. The far left shows a person whose body is present in the current moment but their mind is thinking about or focused on the past or some past event. The figure on the right represents a person whose body is present in the current moment but their mind is thinking about or focused on the future or some future event. The middle figure represents a person whose body is in the present moment and their mind is fully focused on the present as well.

IN THEIR OWN WORDS **Mindful Performers**

In 2013, Arianna Huffington, founder of the Huffington Post, said, "Our world has become unmanageable," opening the door for many corporate executives to publicly acknowledge their use of mindfulness to combat the stressors and constant message bombardment (Nirell 2014). For example, Jeff Weiner, executive chairman of LinkedIn, has highlighted his mindful communication as he learned to slow down and truly listen to the struggles his management team and employees shared with him. Rather than turn taking, where one person is quiet and waits their turn to say what they have been planning during the other person's talking time, mindful communication means Weiner is committed to fully engaging in the conversation and actively listening to the speaker. Bill Ford, executive chairman of Ford Motor Co., detailed "how the practice of mindfulness kept me going during the darkest days" when he almost declared bankruptcy (Schwartz 2013).

Sport is much the same. Goalkeeper Erin McLeod, one of Canada's most capped players and Olympic bronze medalist, recently reported she is enjoying soccer now more than at any other time in her career. She has touted the positive effects of mindfulness, stating, "I've learned our brains are incredibly powerful," and described how staying in the present moment helped her become more consistent and less nervous during matches. She went on to say, "As high performers, we have this concept of perfection . . . we put the pressure of the world on our shoulders, and there should be more enjoyment taken from what we do. Mindfulness is so ingenious in that respect because it's all about being in the present moment, and as athletes that's invaluable" (FIFA 2020). And baseball fans would be hard pressed to identify a mental strategy that is garnering more attention and public praise than mindfulness among its players and managers. In the medical community, even the top doctor in the United States in 2015, Surgeon General Vivek Murthy, reports practicing mindful meditation daily (Jain 2015).

or frameworks in the 1980s or early 1990s. It was often critiqued for seeming too passive or mystical and less applicable to high-pressure and highly stressful performance domains than other more traditional approaches to mental skills training.

Mindfulness-Based Approach to Mental Skills Training

Most of the cognitive strategies offered in this text follow the cognitive behavioral therapy (CBT) approach to mental skills training. CBT strategies, often considered as the most common and traditional mental skills training, appeal to elite athletes and corporate executives because these people are high achievers and accustomed to being in control of their competitive lives. They also want to control their thoughts and behaviors in achievement domains whether in elite sport performance or in life. For example, CBT skills such as thought stoppage, which was introduced in the previous chapter, require performers to alter or enhance their thoughts to improve their performance, and goal setting or action planning teaches performers to identify preferred outcomes and regulate their behaviors in ways that move them closer to achieving their goals. To do so, people must first judge their thoughts, feelings, or behaviors as either undesirable and unproductive or as desirable and helpful, then either edit, alter, stop, or enhance them. Athletes, businesspeople, surgeons, lawyers, and educators, among other performers then become intentional, aware, and active agents of change. Through CBT techniques, performers develop awareness of and an ability to control their thoughts, feelings, and behaviors.

Mindfulness represents a very different orientation or approach to peak performance, whereby performers learn to stay connected to the present moment. Standout college basketball player Aaron Gordon noted, "Peak performance lives in the present moment and presence can be trained." His quote gets at the core of mindfulness in sport. Athletes become aware of their thoughts and feelings without having to *do* anything or change anything. They simply notice and allow the thought to exist and stay focused on the *now*. Rather than judging or evaluating thoughts for accuracy and usefulness, the tenets of mindfulness—which stem from acceptance and commitment therapy (Zettle and Hayes 1986)—suggest that thoughts and feelings are neither helpful nor unhelpful (McCracken and Vowles 2014) and are in fact neutral.

The goal of cognitive strategies associated with acceptance and commitment therapy is to produce a psychologically flexible person who can stay in the present moment with an open, nonjudgmental stance as they experience a range of thoughts and feelings. Professional basketball player Andre Iguodala acknowledged, "The struggle for me is thinking too much . . . my mind tends to wander a lot. [Mindfulness] has given me the confidence to know it's okay to wander" (Thrive Global 2016). Rather than fighting or trying to limit his wandering mind, taking a mindful approach helped Iguodala continue to play and perform without forcing or controlling his thoughts. Look through the scenarios in the sidebar on pages 50-51 to better understand the difference between a *mindful approach* to applied sport psychology and *traditional* mental skills training.

Both approaches are useful for anyone who wants to enhance their performance and increase life satisfaction. Traditional psychological skills training works for many performers, but in some instances, trying to eliminate or replace a thought can create even more emphasis on that

PUT IT INTO PRACTICE

Differentiating Mindful and Traditional Approaches to Mental Skills Training

All performers need to understand the different approaches to mental skills training in order to know when and how to implement various cognitive or behavioral strategies. The following hypothetical scenario will help you better understand the differences between taking a mindful approach to sport psychology and engaging in traditional mental skills training techniques such as self-talk. Read through the scenario and examine how a performer using each approach would handle that situation.

Scenario

In a packed high school gym it is match point for the high school conference championship, and the serving team, playing on their rival's home court, is bombarded with loud chants against them. A player catches the volleyball from a line judge. She hears the crowd roaring as they wave their handmade posters in the air and sees the hopeful faces of teammates and the readied body position of the opponents in a serve-receive position. Coach is signaling the area of the court to serve to. The player walks to the service line. A successful serve and ace would win the match. In that moment, the athlete starts thinking about how her last service attempt caused the middle hitter to duck as it landed in

Jonathan Daniel /Allsport/Getty Images

the center of the net. *Just get it over the net. Don't mess up. Everyone is counting on you.* The athlete's mind races as thoughts dart from the significance of the moment to self-doubt from the last failed serve to the worried look on coach's face. The referee makes eye contact and blows the whistle to initiate the serve.

Mental Skills Interventions

A Mindful Approach

- A mindful athlete would focus on the current breath and become aware of her thoughts, all without judging them.
- "Where am I now?" and "What is required of me now?" might be two questions the server would ask herself to facilitate a "right now" focus.
- The server would, then, take a deep abdominal breath and either focus on the breath or bring her attention to an element of the moment such as the weight of the volleyball in her nondominant hand or the feeling of her fingers on the seams of the volleyball.

A Traditional Approach (Using Self-Talk or Thought Stoppage)

- An athlete skilled in self-talk would attempt to quickly shift from unproductive, unwanted thoughts to productive and helpful thoughts as she stepped to the service line.
- She might think "stop" to disrupt the unproductive thoughts such as "Don't mess up" and "Everyone is counting on you."
- Then, she would replace those thoughts with productive thoughts like "Serve the six" (a location on the opponent's side of the court) or "Contact high and snap." These replacement thoughts would focus the athlete's attention on the critical elements of the skill or the desired, controllable next step.

thought or feeling and further disrupt performance (Gardner and Moore 2004). Consider a time when you were getting ready to perform and a memory of a previous poor performance creeped in. The more you tried to prevent or stop a thought or feeling from occurring, the more you might have experienced that exact thought. Wegner and Erber (1992) refer to this common experience as *ironic processing* (i.e., in trying to avoid or control unwanted cognitions, you might be more likely to bring them about). In these moments, developing mindfulness would present an alternative approach whereby the performer would simply accept the thought rather than try to control it or judge it and might, therefore, be able to perform better.

It is necessary to understand two concepts when learning about mindfulness: *cognitive defusion* and *nonjudgmental awareness*. What does nonjudgment mean? It means that, regardless of what the reality of the situation is, the performer evaluates it as neither positive, great, or desirable nor do they view it as negative, bad, or undesirable. That place between positive and negative, that neutral zone, is nonjudgment. The performer is aware of what the thought is or what is happening in the situation, but they are not judging it. Like a car that is turned on and not yet advancing forward or moving in reverse, it is in neutral. *Nonjudgmental awareness* means the performer does not have to label every thought or attach an emotion to it. There is no hierarchy of good or bad thoughts. It is simply noticing and accepting what is. That does not mean that the performer has given up or given in. Rather, they can stay focused in the *now*, regardless of the circumstance.

Cognitive defusion occurs when you can separate yourself from your thoughts. You are more than your thoughts. Thoughts occur and they change in relation to your circumstances, but you do not have to give your physiology over to them. Not only are you nonjudgmentally aware of the present moment and your thoughts, but you are also able to recognize that the thought is not *you*. The present moment is about what you are thinking now, what you are focused on now, and what you are doing now. Of course, if you commit an error, you will have thoughts and feelings about that moment. But giving thoughts more power or more of your energy, physiology, or judgmental language does not bring you closer to connecting with this moment, which is the only place action can occur. Instead, you must begin to ask "What is required of me now?" If a rugby player misses a tackle, they might think "Ugh, I should have gotten there sooner, sprinted to catch up." The requirement, what is needed, is to keep playing and to catch up with the opponent. A mindful athlete will become aware of their thought and return to the present moment as soon as possible.

In a nonsport example, imagine that you are a trial lawyer and have just completed your entire case—all of the witnesses have testified, and all of the evidence has been presented. Then comes the moment when it is your job to stand up and make the closing arguments. You are tasked with highlighting the strengths of the evidence and weaving the facts together into a story that compels the jury to reach the desired verdict. As you stand up from your chair, your mind races with thoughts like "Did I put in all the evidence I needed? Did I establish everything I needed to establish? Did the jury understand the evidence? Can I tie this together?"

In the internal chaos of that moment, the value of mindfulness is that it can give you confidence in your ability to be in the *now* even when your mind is filled with self-doubt, and you are feeling worried or apprehensive. As the litigator, in this case, you can become *nonjudgmentally aware* of your thoughts and engage in *cognitive defusion* so you stay in the present moment in order to deliver your remarks. Here, that might mean that, as the lawyer, you become aware of your thoughts and you take a deep breath, you feel the edges of your pen and hear the sound it makes when you set it on your yellow legal pad. Then, you look up to meet the gaze of the jury. You are aware of where you are standing, how your suit feels. You notice the care and concern in the jury's eyes as you take one more deep breath and then exhale fully and slowly. You are in the present moment and aware of each word of your closing statement.

Mindfulness provides a great check system so that you know whether you were truly focused in the moment. The value of mindfulness is that, as you leave the court room, you can be aware of the sights, sounds, and feelings of that moment.

Becoming mindful is developing a skill that permeates your life. The truth is that people spend very little of their waking hours in the present tense and the present moment. *Mindfulness is the answer to that reality*. Other mental skills in this text are taught to be implemented at a certain moment or time in your life, whereas mindfulness helps you become more aware of each waking moment. At its best, mindfulness is practiced throughout the day and not simply implemented in performance or high-stress situations. Because people are so infrequently in the present, mindfulness helps you accomplish what Dr. Hacker encourages clients to do: "Be where your feet are." Be here. Be present. Be in the now. The goal to live a more mindful life allows you to truly be with your kids when you are picking them up from school, be with your pets when you are walking them around the neighborhood, and be in your car when you are changing lanes on the interstate. *Be where your feet are*.

Mindful athletes have demonstrated increased awareness, improved focus, enhanced coping skills, reduced negative perfectionism, reduced anger and hostility, and decreased stress, among other benefits (Gross et al. 2018; Kaiseler et al. 2017). And many elite sport performers, such as tennis legend Billie Jean King, have recognized the need for a mindful approach to their game. King has said, "Each point I play is in the now. The last point means nothing, the next point means nothing." And 11-time NBA championship coach Phil Jackson implemented "One breath, One mind, One team," to teach mindfulness to both the Chicago Bulls and Los Angeles Lakers. A shortened version of this same mantra is "One breath, One mind." People have been engaged in mindfulness practice across performance domains and in both professional and personal settings.

Even if you prefer traditional mental skills training strategies (e.g., imagery, self-talk), mindfulness can and should be added to your repertoire because mindfulness highlights the heart of effective mental skills training: self-awareness. To be a mindful performer, you must develop awareness of the present moment, your thoughts, your feelings, and your behaviors. As we outlined in the preface and first chapter of this book, to become more aware of yourself—your thoughts, feelings, and behaviors—is the first step in implementing any of the cognitive strategies in this book. Think of it like this: If you want to engage in imagery of a previous best performance so that you can try to replicate that experience, then you must first become aware of that exact moment (i.e., what it looked like, sounded like, smelled like, tasted like, and felt like). Mindfulness training can support these traditional cognitive strategy approaches to performance. Look at table 4.1 for a short summary of differences among these two approaches to peak performance.

TABLE 4.1 Differences Between Traditional and Mindfulness-Based Training Strategies

Category of difference	Traditional mental skills training strategies	Mindfulness-based approaches
Focus of the performer	Past or future oriented: Thought stoppage and imagery can be either past or future oriented, and skills like goal setting are future oriented and based on past performances.	Right now focus: There is no other requirement than to become aware of the present; the entire purpose is to be present in the moment in a nonjudgmental way.
Time to implement the strategy	Strategy is implemented in appropriate, as-needed situations in response to a performance issue or to enhance an element of performance.	Strategy is implemented multiple times throughout the day, training session, and competition; the goal is to become mindfully aware and present in all phases of life, such as mindful conversations, mindful eating, mindful exercising.
Role of the performer	Person is an active agent of change, in control of their experiences.	Person focuses on awareness rather than control, change, or enhancement.

As mentioned at the start of this chapter, mindfulness-based approaches differ from traditional sport psychology perspectives that stem from CBT. Be clear about the approach you are taking to performance: Recognize it and own it. A mindful orientation to peak performance can serve as your go-to strategy if it matches your way of being in the world, or it can help you develop the necessary self-awareness before implementation of other mental skills such as goal setting. The ways in which you benefit from mindfulness training are, in part, yours to determine, but it should be part of your overall suite of mental skills and strategies.

The Practice of Mindfulness

Reading about mindfulness does not create a performance advantage; understanding the language of mindfulness does not enhance performance; watching videos on mental skills does not yield improvement. As with all mental skills, our reminder to leaders who want to introduce mental skills training into the corporate world, to mental performance coaches who want to share this book with their clients, and to clients who are going to use this book in their own lives regardless of the level or sport is that you must do more than read and know about or understand each cognitive strategy. Every mental skills framework and strategy outlined in this book is included for a reason. The research and evidence support its efficacy. But it is not the knowledge of each strategy or technique that improves performance, it is the consistent implementation of mindfulness practice that enhances performance.

It is incredibly challenging to stay in the present tense in a nonjudgmental way. To experience thoughts without judging them, assigning value to them, or associating emotions with events is difficult. And while remaining neutral in stressful situations is incredibly difficult, ironically, it is the act of trying to control your thoughts that takes you out of the present moment. That's when you shift into either the past or the future mode, neither of which you can control, nor can you affect either a past or a future event. Being in a competitive or performative moment without

Greg Epperson/Fotolia

trying to actively change or edit your thoughts is exactly the self-aware-ness that mindfulness highlights.

The next time you are doubting yourself, try to stay in the moment—feel your cleats on your feet or listen for the sound of the dirt moving as you dig in and take your stance in the box or feel the handle of the hockey stick resting in your glove. Again, remind yourself of Dr. Hack-er's advice, "Be where your feet are." Mindful athletes resist the urge to label every thought or associate it with a feeling. You don't ignore it, you don't deny it, you don't reject it, and you don't stop it. You simply become aware of each thought and allow it to exist, staying connected to what is required of you right now, in this moment. Mindfulness helps you bring 100 percent of your awareness to the present moment. When you give all of your awareness to the present tense, no other subset of your attention exists. You simply are not able to have all of your awareness in the pres-ent moment if you are holding on to thoughts about the past or future. You cannot be in the past, thinking about your errors or mistakes, and you cannot be in the future, worrying about what might go wrong if 100 percent of your awareness is in the now.

Another error people make when they practice mindfulness is holding the belief that it needs to be implemented during a specific time or seg-ment of the day. Remember, training and competition represent only one element of your daily experiences. Try to eliminate thinking that "Now it's exercise time, next I'll head into the office, and then at the end of the day I'll meditate." Rather than segmenting and designating mindfulness practice as a stand-alone, separate-from-life activity, work to integrate mindfulness throughout all of your waking hours and activities. When you are more mindful, you are more aware and in the present. The goal is not to check mindfulness practice off a to-do list. Mindfulness is not a thing to do, but rather a way to be in the world and in life. Look for ways to integrate mindfulness practice throughout your day. Certainly, scheduling mindfulness practice works better for some performers. Bernie Holliday, the mental skills coach with the Pittsburgh Pirates for many years, explained it like this:

> I think there's a value in scheduling it once or twice in your day, to develop a little stillness program where you spend 10 or 15 minutes, and you just shut down sensory input and focus on breathing and on being in that moment with you and your breath. I think once in the morning, once in the afternoon—I think there's also value to looking at your schedule. . . . You might have a busy period from 3:00 to 4:30 in the afternoon, so maybe try to put a [mindfulness practice] session in there at 2:15 or one at 4:45. (Bac-cellieri 2020)

To be in the present, you must practice becoming aware of what each moment looks like, sounds like, and feels like. Like Holliday outlined, that does not mean you have to spend 30 or 45 minutes sitting in stillness and meditating. The beautiful thing about mindfulness is that you can start today. You can do it right now. In fact, you can become more mindful as you are reading the words on this page.

Converting the Skeptic

We have a challenge for you as you begin to practice mindfulness. Keep it simple. Although technology (PET scans and fMRI, for example) has shown how mindfulness works, you do not need expensive equipment, significant time, or specialized training. Start small. Look at the following sidebar for strategies to try.

Concomitant benefits of mindfulness include accountability and awareness. You might get away with lying to other people and claim complete focus in the moment, but you cannot lie to yourself. When you practice

PUT IT INTO PRACTICE

The Start Small Challenge

Try to complete 15 seconds of present-tense focus just being aware of your breathing and not having any other thoughts. The goal is slow and complete abdominal breaths. Try inhaling on a count of 4 and exhaling on a count of 6. Be aware only of your breathing. If you put one hand over your chest (palm resting gently) and the other hand over your abdomen (palm resting gently), this is one way to check yourself and ensure that you are belly breathing. You should feel the gentle pressure against the hand on your abdomen as your belly expands as you inhale and feel the belly return to rest as you exhale. You could even imagine a small string pulling your belly out as it expands and gently receding as you exhale. Inhale on a 4 count, exhale on a 6 count. With practice, you will soon discover your own preferred ratio of inhalation and exhalation. The key is to expand your belly fully and ensure that the exhalation is a bit longer than the inhalation.

Can you focus on just your breathing for 15 seconds? You may soon discover that it sounds easier to do than it is. Our active minds love to wander. Truly focused, present-tense awareness is rarer than most folks imagine. For a certain percentage of the population, the answer is no. So you start small. Try to engage in 15 seconds of focused, present-tense breathing for 15 seconds every day, five days this week.

If you accomplish it, then great. Try to add 5 seconds of mindfulness practice each day the following week or try to add two sessions of 15 seconds on at least two of the five days. If you are mindful for 15 seconds for three consecutive days without your mind wandering or thinking about either the past or future, then add 5 seconds to the next day's practice. If, however, you do not reach your goal, then simply reduce the length of practice or start the five-day cycle again until you are successful. Start where you are. Remember, you cannot give all your attention to your breath and be thinking about whether or not you are doing mindfulness correctly. If you are aware of your breath, then you are being mindful.

mindfulness, you know with absolute certainty whether you allowed other thoughts in while you were attending to your breathing. You will always know. When you are being honest with yourself and you focus on your breath for 15 seconds, that gives you confidence moving forward that you absolutely can be in the *now* in a nonjudgmental way. Do *now* well.

The way you start practicing mindfulness is to bring all your focus and attention to your breathing. You can only give all your attention to your breathing if you are *right now* focused. During this challenge, it is common for many people to worry about or judge whether they are doing *it* correctly. Virtually every person wonders whether they are doing mindfulness right. Right or wrong evaluations are judgments. Judgment. Judgment. Judgment. Set a timer and start breathing. If you become distracted or have a different thought before the timer goes off, simply become aware that you went 10 seconds instead of 15 seconds. There is no need to judge that fact or criticize yourself or feel unsuccessful. It simply is. You are not good because you made it 15 seconds or bad because you only completed 10 seconds.

When those evaluative or emotional thoughts occur, or when judgment creeps in, simply notice that fact. You are aware of the thoughts, but they do not require anything of you. Simply bring your awareness back to your breathing and start again being in the present moment. If you start thinking "When is this going to end?" or "Am I doing this right?" remind yourself to "Do now well." The *now* moment is when the basketball is in your hands and you become aware of how your fingers feel on the ball, aware of your breathing, aware of your knee bend. Do what is required of you to shoot a free throw in this moment—not the last time you stepped to the line or the future consequences of making or missing the shot. Stay present. Stay in the moment.

Keep It Simple

As a businessperson, athlete, or coach, until you have personally experienced mindfulness practice, it is all too tempting to think that mindfulness is for others or is too "out there" or too New Age or Eastern philosophy. Certainly, as we outlined earlier in this chapter, mindfulness may have its roots in Eastern philosophy, but it is also true that mindfulness can help improve the quality of your present life experiences as well as the quality of your own performances whether in sport or in your professional life. Simply stated, mindfulness can be used across performance domains and can serve as a stand-alone performance enhancement practice or as an adjunct to other cognitive behavioral strategies already used.

If you are a leader wanting to help performers recognize the importance of mindfulness, it's important to be clear, keep practice simple, and use language familiar to the person. In business, use the behavioral strategies and principles with which people are already familiar, and in sport, use examples related to the competitive demands and to common situations athletes face. Then begin to integrate and overlay a mindful-ness orientation. For example, if you are coaching a tennis player, you might explain nonjudgmental, present-tense focus by talking to them about how the ball sounds when they bounce it on the court or how the racket feels in their hand before the serve. You might ask the athlete what helps them serve well? If they prefer not to think about serving, then they do not have to organize their thoughts sequentially based on the order of the physical skill components. The key is to meet athletes where they are. Have performers examine their best performance aware-ness. They should know what works for them when they are executing at their best. So for the tennis example, the athlete should bring their awareness to the present moment, which is the serve. As they continue practicing mindfulness, they will be better able to recognize when they are not in the present and when their thoughts are wandering to the past or the future. In those moments, coaches, educators, and other leaders across performance domains might ask "Is your previous attempt part of this one?" No one says yes to that question. Or you might ask "Was the off-target shot in the first period a factor for this shot in the third period?" They might respond that the missed shot is really bothering them now and is affecting their current shot. Then you can follow up with "And how is that working for you?" It's hard enough to shoot well and on target in any game let alone trying to shoot two pucks at once—the puck from the first period and the puck from the third period. Regardless of their answer, the point is made. Best performances occur in the *now*, and holding on to past or future thoughts or negatively judging themselves makes playing their best that much more difficult.

Be Where Your Feet Are.

If you are the athlete from our tennis example who is about to serve, your nonjudgmental awareness is not that you are losing 40-15 or that you must win this set or that it is an elimination match or that you have not been serving well lately. Rather, nonjudgmental present-tense focus is on the strings of your racket or the familiarity of the ball in your hand. Simply be aware of the ball in your hand or the strings of your racket. Then when it's time to serve, you are aware of the release of the toss and the reach of your arm as you contact the ball. There is only *this* serve in *this* moment and at *this* time. That is what being fully present is and what a mindful approach to performance requires. It is neither hoping for a good serve nor remembering a bad serve. It is simply this serve, in this moment.

You Are Here Right Now. Do Now Well.

A second critique of mindfulness from some elite performers comes from what may initially seem a departure from the very characteristics that have made them successful to begin with. Elite performers are accustomed to being in control. They control their technique practice. They control their tactical development. They control their physical preparation. In fact, it is common for elite performers to be engaged agents in their own lives and constantly active in shaping and changing their world. Nonjudgmental awareness initially may seem rather passive, comparatively speaking, and they may feel as though they are merely watching their lives and careers unfold. For this group of people, mindfulness can feel like it is the antithesis of all that made them successful in business, in sport, and in life in the first place. Nothing could be further from the truth, however. Mindful athletes are active agents in their lives, in training, and in performance; they are simply focused on right now rather than on the future or past. A similar issue often occurs when trying to convince elite athletes to devote more time to rest and recovery. To many athletes, rest seems passive, inactive, and a willful waste of time. However, expert Canadian sport psychology consultant Dr. Orlick (2016) has discussed the importance of considering rest as a form of work. This subtle shift in language, awareness, and understanding of the critical value of rest and recovery in peak performance can help elite athletes view rest as an active, intentional, and purposeful element of their training program. Often, with the proper sport science education, athletes begin to embrace the critical role of rest, recovery, and sleep in achieving excellence.

Performers often experience a similar shift in their beliefs about mindfulness. Although this cognitive strategy does not encourage people to control their thoughts or actively alter their feelings or emotions, it does not make it a passive or inactive approach. Instead, there is both a cognitive and behavioral element to mindfulness just as there is with self-talk and other traditional mental skills. The difference is in the effort exerted. Without trying, there is a behavioral component to mindfulness (breathing), and there is a cognitive element (present-tense, nonjudgmental focus, and awareness). Competitive or professional situations simply become neutral events. The situation is simply that: the current situation. It does not require appraisal or judgment. It requires a present focus on what is required now. Through mindfulness practice, performers become aware of when they are thinking about the past or future and when they are bringing evaluation or judgment to the situation.

As we have discussed throughout this chapter, to be mindful is to be focused in the now, the present moment. At its core, mindfulness is the opposite of multitasking. People spend much of their lives developing the ability to perform multiple tasks at the same (or similar) time. To take a different approach—to become more mindful—they must first become aware of how often they are multitasking throughout the day. They must notice when their mind is full of thoughts, to-do lists, and planning for the next action while completing the current task rather than being mindful.

In sport, this awareness helps you recognize that you are thinking about the last ball as you stand close to the line ready to serve again. Consider completing the exercise on page 62 every day during the next week so that you can become more aware of when you are not being mindful.

As you become more aware of the amount of time spent multitasking and the combination of tasks you perform simultaneously, you also become aware of when and how to insert mindfulness into your daily practice. This awareness becomes your cue during moments of chaos to take a mindfulness breath. You do not stop the thought or try and control the thought. You simply notice the thought and gently bring your attention back to this moment, right now, and keep your mind and your feet in the same moment and at the same time. The fundamentals of best performance regardless of the sport or achievement domain—self-awareness and self-regulation—do not change. Regulation, in this sense, occurs through the mindful breath.

Conclusion

Mindfulness is a cognitive strategy and an approach to both mental skills training and to life. As such, it is useful across all performance and achievement domains, but that is only one aspect of the totality of our lives to which mindfulness could be applied. Because we are constantly evolving and changing as human beings, we want as many tools in the toolbox as we can access. What is good for us at age 18 might be unhelpful for us as a 28-year-old. What is helpful for us as athletes might need to be adjusted when we become educators or doctors or businesspeople.

Remember, the goal of mindfulness is to become more mindfully aware of the present moment without judgment. Doing so enhances who we are, our satisfaction and enjoyment, and our full immersion into all aspects of life. Our hope is that by understanding the challenge and the importance of being in the present and yet realizing how often our thoughts, self-talk, worry, and personal evaluation are part of most of our current awareness, the importance of mindfulness is seen as valuable and transformative. Instead of focusing on what we have or have not done in the past or what we need or hope to do in the future, athletes and other high achievers will more readily adopt a mindfulness practice frequently and consistently throughout all of life's endeavors. Mindfulness is a more robust way to fully experience the most important moment in our lives: *this* moment.

Performer-Centered Implementation Worksheet

	Describe examples of multitasking (e.g., eating while watching television, engaging on social media while playing with your children)	Record the number of times you were multitasking each day
Monday		
Tuesday		
Wednesday		
Thursday		
Friday		
Saturday		
Sunday		

From C. Hacker and M. Mann, *Achieving Excellence: Mastering Mindset for Peak Performance in Sport and Life* (Champaign, IL: Human Kinetics, 2023).

Two Sets of Five

If you find that you are ruminating—that you have a busy brain—or that you just cannot seem to shake your worry or nervousness, use this simple mindfulness practice. Try one or both techniques if you are feeling stuck in the past or thinking about the future. You can implement each mindfulness practice at home or in a performance situation or while transitioning from one task to another. Each can be done indoors or outdoors. Both exercises begin with mindful breathing, like what we describe in the four-square breathing exercise in chapter 7. With practice, you can become mindful with just one breath.

Directions

Exercise 1: Five-Step Mindfulness Walk

As you notice that your thoughts are pulling you out of the present moment, bring your awareness to five things you see. Do not judge these items or describe any memories or stories associated with them. Simply become aware of them. Next, bring your attention to four things you hear followed by three things that you feel, two things you smell, and one thing you taste. When you have finished this task, you have created a multisensory, mindful, present-tense focus connection (sight, sound, touch, smell, taste) with the present moment. As part of this exercise, complete the following worksheet.

	Examples associated with each step
5. Sight	
4. Sound	
3. Touch	
2. Smell	
1. Taste	

> continued

Two Sets of Five > *continued*

Exercise 2: Five-Finger Breathing

Start by placing your nondominant hand palm down on a flat surface (e.g., on your thigh, table, desk, or floor). Take a few mindful breaths from your abdomen (inhale 4 counts, exhale 6 counts), and then take the pointer finger of your dominant hand and touch the midrange of your nondominant hand outside of your pinky finger. Make sure that as you continue to engage in abdominal breathing, you are locked on to the tactical and visual sensation associated with your pointer finger and its movement.

Now, starting on the outside of your pinky finger (nondominant hand) at the midrange point of your hand, begin moving your pointer finger (dominant hand) along the outside of your pinky finger. Inhale as you slide your pointer finger to the apex, or top, of the nondominant pinky finger; exhale as your pointer finger traces the inside of the pinky finger. Then inhale as you reach the fleshy base between your fourth and fifth finger, and continue inhaling until you reach the apex of your fourth finger. Now exhale as your pointer finger of your dominant hand traces the inside of that fourth finger. Continue this process—inhaling as you trace the outside of a finger on your nondominant hand and exhaling as you trace the inside of the same finger—with your middle finger, pointer finger, and thumb. The exercise is complete when you have traced each finger of your nondominant hand and finish by your wrist on the thumb side of that hand.

The key is to never hold your breath and never run out of breath as you match your inhalations and exhalations with the tracing of each finger on your hand. Because your fingers are different lengths, this requires you to engage in focused breathing. That type of breathing is present tense and multisensory (visual and tactile/kinesthetic) and is incredibly engaging. One practice set occurs when all five fingers are traced with focused breathing on the inhalation and exhalation. Tracing only three or four fingers, for example, is not a complete set. Continue this five-finger breathing practice for as many sets as necessary to help you center yourself and get back into present-focus awareness.

From C. Hacker and M. Mann, *Achieving Excellence: Mastering Mindset for Peak Performance in Sport and Life* (Champaign, IL: Human Kinetics, 2023).

CHAPTER 5

Harnessing Imagination

It does not take much time or effort to find elite athletes, coaches, and other leaders in business and in sport talking about the benefits of imagery. Since the 1980s, Olympic athletes have been touting this mental skill as a critical factor

> The soul never thinks without a picture.
>
> Aristotle, Ancient Greek philosopher

in their quest for excellence. In a survey at the United States Olympic and Paralympic Training Center, 97 percent of athletes believed imagery helped their performance, and 94 percent of their coaches used imagery during their training sessions (Murphy, Jowdy, and Durtschi 1990). Since the 1980s, 99 percent of Canadian Olympians have reported using imagery (Orlick and Partington 1988). To have that level of adoption across sports, across genders, and across disciplines is impressive. It provides compelling evidence for the integration of this mental skill within any training program. Findings from hundreds of studies over the last three decades support athletes' anecdotal experiences and demonstrate the efficacy of implementing imagery sessions to enhance performance (Cumming and Ramsey 2009). This chapter includes scientifically validated strategies for creating effective images and tips for implementing consistent and systematic imagery training.

See It to Be It

Imagery involves creating or re-creating a situation or experience in your mind. You could create an image of yourself responding the way you want to when your name is called by the announcer before the first competitive match of the season or you are introduced for your first presentation as a keynote speaker. You might also use imagery to re-create the best performance from your career or vividly imagine a time when you demonstrated mental toughness. Read the In Their Own Words sidebar on page 66 as elite soccer performers praise the importance of incorporating imagery into their physical training regimens. Pay attention to how they describe their imagery training, the variables they considered, and their attention to detail.

IN THEIR OWN WORDS **Three Soccer Legends Discuss Imagery Training**

Carli Lloyd is a two-time Olympic gold medalist, two-time World Cup champion, and two-time FIFA player of the year. During the 2015 World Cup, in a match against Japan, she scored three goals in the first 16 minutes of play. When asked how she was able to perform this feat, Lloyd explained,

> **I dreamed of and visualized playing in a World Cup final and visualized scoring four goals. Sounds pretty funny but that's what it is all about. At the end of the day you can be physically strong, have all the tools but if your mental state isn't good enough you can't bring yourself to bigger and better things. For me I am just constantly visualizing . . . (Guardado 2019)**

Brazilian legend, Ronaldinho, is the only footballer in history to win all nine major trophies. Over the course of his career, he scored 313 goals and played in 816 matches. Ronaldinho explained,

> **When I train, one thing I concentrate on is creating a mental picture of how best to deliver that ball to a teammate, preferably leaving him alone in front of the rival goalkeeper. So, what I do, always before a game, always, every night and every day, is try and think up things, imagine plays which no one else will have thought of, and to do so always bearing in mind the particular strengths of each teammate to whom I am passing the ball. When I construct those plays in my mind, I take into account whether one teammate likes to receive the ball at his feet or ahead of him, if he's good with his head and how he prefers to head the ball, if he's stronger on his right or his left foot. That's my job. That is what I do. I imagine the game. (Carlin 2006)**

Tony DiCicco coached the United States women's national soccer team to an Olympic gold medal in 1996 and a FIFA World Cup Championship in 1999. In what many have called a defining moment in sport for girls and women, DiCicco's team won the World Cup in front of a record-setting crowd of 90,185 in Pasadena, California. Tony said,

> **I had them visualize performing their unique abilities on the soccer field over and over again. . . . 'If you're a great header, visualize yourself winning headers. If you're a great defender, visualize yourself stripping the ball from an attacking player. If you're a great passer of the ball, visualize yourself playing balls in.' . . . I made a special point of saying, 'Visualize the special skills that separate you from the rest.'**

Notice how Lloyd, Ronaldinho, and DiCicco all worked to image unique strengths and capabilities. As you read their quotes, did you pick up on the details they included? One way to increase the effectiveness of the image is to ensure that it involves all of the available senses relevant to performing the actual task (visual, kinesthetic, auditory, tactile, gustatory, and olfactory elements). Including tactile senses might help you imagine your grip on a golf club just before teeing off on a par-5 hole or imagine the seams on a baseball or softball as you prepare to pitch. Rather than simply creating the picture of the environment, using multiple senses helps to create a vivid, realistic image that shows you executing a task at your highest level or capability. Taste (gustatory) elements, for example, might not always be significant or available in your performance; however, American football players might taste their mouthguard after sprinting 80 yards (73 m) on a kickoff return. Integrate this sensory data intentionally and authentically so that the image feels, sounds, looks like, and resembles the competitive moment.

Imagery is a learned skill that, when trained effectively, can be almost as useful as physical practice. In fact, evidence indicates that combining physical practice with mental rehearsal can improve performance above and beyond that which occurs merely through physical training alone (Frank et al. 2014). As Dr. Bob Rotella, a sport psychology consultant known for his work with professional golfers, said, "There is no such thing as muscle memory."

Your muscles do not store memories of movement patterns or performances, so we must create vivid, multisensory images to deepen the performance memories. Regardless of how skilled you become as a surgeon performing life-saving maneuvers or as a cross-country skier ascending a mountain, it is not your brain and not your muscles that are responsible for remembering how to execute the skills you need to perform when you need to perform them. Memories are consolidated and retained in your central nervous system, and imagery strengthens that mental blueprint of appropriate skill execution or accurate and productive emotional responses to competitive demands.

It's All in the Name

When high achievers discuss their imagery sessions, they often use the term *visualization* rather than *imagery*. Words matter. There are several reasons why performers and professionals working with athletes and nonsport performers should consistently use the term *imagery*.

First, we now know that for imagery to be effective, it must contain all the essential environmental, sensory, and emotional components. Essentially, environmental components refer to the details of the situation and the environment. Examples include the location, time of day, people present, and as many details of the external environment as possible. Emotional components refer to the feelings you have as you are performing. It is best to imagine the exact emotional elements you experience when performing. Examples might include excitement, high energy, calmness, focus, or butterflies in your stomach. There is strong science outlining the elements of effective imagery. It is not the Wild West where anything goes; rather, every opinion should be supported by the evidence or scientifically validated. We must follow the science, and the science is clear: All imagery practice is *not* the same. So if you are going to invest in mental skills training, then you want to invest in getting it right. That means using all your senses to create meaningful imagined experiences. It includes visual sensory data, but it is not limited to what you "see." In fact, it might be the sounds or the feel of the movement that matter more in creating a realistic, powerful mental blueprint of the performance. Effective images are best and most impactful when they are multisensory. And when you use the word *imagery*, it signals broader, more inclusive imagination rather than just visual images.

Another reason to stop using the term *visualization* is because imagery should include the physiological and emotional correlates that are important when you are executing that skill. In other words, images should be emotionally congruent. For example, when imaging a surgery, medical professionals should include sensory information that promotes poise and calmness just as a golfer might need to include words and phrases that replicate a quiet mind. On the other hand, physiological elements like explosive power and high energy might be used by a tennis player imagining their serve or hitting a crosscourt winner. Simply visualizing a serve or a putt or any other motor skill is not enough. It does not bring that image close enough to the actual, lived experience. As a result, the effectiveness of that type of imagery is decreased. While the emotional and physiological needs will differ based on the performer, the sport or performance domain, and the type of skill being performed, the importance of addressing those elements remains. There is not one single emotion to incorporate for every person or every performance, but emotion *is* necessary for successful imagery training. All free throw shots in basketball are not the same. If you want to prepare yourself to sink the game-winning free throw with no time left on the clock in an international tournament, then you better include the sensory elements that will be present in real life (e.g., crowd noise, coaches organizing players, opponents trying to throw you off, and the bright scoreboard showing no time left and a tied game). Further, you should imagine yourself controlling your emotions amid all the noise and other distractions so that you are loose, confident, and able to move through your full range of motion as you sink the winning shot. Effective imagery carries with it imaginal correlates that are both emotional and physiological. As such, it is important to use the term *imagery* to describe this broader, more inclusive process.

Uses of Imagery

As noted, imagery has been proven effective for all performers across a variety of sports and competitive levels. Experienced performers and those who become skilled at imagery are likely to create more vivid and controllable images, so they tend to get even greater results than people who are new to their sport or to practicing imagery. However, with time and training, everyone can learn to cultivate impactful imagery experiences.

Imagery training can enhance performers' motivation and confidence as well as control emotional responses and make accurate, on-time decisions (Westlund-Stewart and Hall 2016). There are two primary reasons why performers tend to use imagery: to enhance their cognitive performance abilities or to address motivational elements associated with their performance. When imagery is used to target and improve cognitive skills, the image is typically focused on learning, practicing, or correcting technical aspects of motor skills (e.g., getting the puck on net from the point) or implementing a performance strategy to solve a problem or win a competitive event. Arguably one of the top basketball players of all time and six-time NBA champion Michael Jordan was known for wanting to prevent overanalyzing while he played, saying, "I find that after I play, my mind is clearer, and I can come up with a better solution. . . . It relaxes me and allows me to solve problems." Imaging the cognitive aspects of a motor skill can also be effective immediately before a performance so that the imaginal experience "primes" the correct movement execution (Cumming and Williams 2012).

The second use for imagery is for competitors to develop images targeting the motivational aspects of a performance. For example, an Olympian might image themselves walking into the stadium with their country's delegation or see themselves winning their competition and then later hearing their anthem and feeling the weight of the gold medal on their neck. Imagery could also be used to help performers psych themselves up by imaging themselves warming up before competition and hearing the crowd and feeling high-fives from teammates. Or they could use it to calm down before an event by imagining themselves taking a deep breath and feeling their muscles relax just before they get into the blocks for a 100-meter sprint. Imagery that focuses on the motivational elements can also be useful when coping with pain or injury because athletes must control their emotions before a medical examination. If they use imagery consistently and systematically and construct the image correctly, their performance will benefit. However, some athletes and nonsport performers may still feel skeptical about the positive impact of imagery. The Put It Into Practice sidebar on page 70 outlines considerations for the most ardent cynics.

When to Use Imagery

We want performers to use imagery before, during, and after physical training and competitive performances. Coaches should encourage athletes to mentally rehearse running their route or executing their role in a play during a water break or between drills. Athletes who struggle to sleep the night before games might use imagery to relax and rehearse at night. The point is that imagery can and should be used in daily life and across a variety of performance domains. It can be even more powerful when performers find themselves in conditions that do not allow them to physically train. For example, an injured athlete might imagine fully healing, or they might image themselves returning to play at an even higher level after they have increased the range of motion or strength at the affected joint. Working professionals might use imagery when they have a presentation but are feeling fatigued from their work schedule or

PUT IT INTO PRACTICE

Considerations for the Skeptic

If you feel like imagery is not working for you, then ask yourself these three questions:

1. Am I using it consistently?
2. Am I using it systematically through all aspects of my performance and training?
3. Am I following all required imagery elements?

If you are saying "yes" to all these questions, then it *is* working.

You must be consistent in your daily imagery practice. Create images in short clips rather than for long periods. Image on your way to work, as you walk into the locker room, while you stretch—any moment you have available is an opportunity for imagery practice. Finally, as the performer, you must use all the requisite components (vividness, controllability, emotional affect). You cannot bake and only use a portion of the ingredients. If you do not use flour, then you do not get cake. Using another analogy, if you have a car but do not keep it either charged or filled with gas, then it will not run. The same is true for imagery. For it to be effective and for you to maximize the positive effects of mental rehearsal, you must include all the essential elements.

This protocol is not a matter of opinion. How you practice imagery or what you include is not a matter of preference. You must follow the science and the evidence. It is clear and consistent. It is compelling. It is robust. Imagery works. Period.

family events. As they prepare for the meeting, they might spend a few minutes imagining themselves walking into the boardroom, standing in front of other employees or colleagues, and feeling energetic and excited. Using imagery in this way is more likely to bring about the desired affect for quality performance. Imagery is even more important when athletes and performers cannot gain the necessary physical reps because creating effective images allows them to practice and habituate behaviors without breaking rules or increasing injury risks.

Create Functionally Equivalent Images

In the last two decades, neuroimaging studies have proven that functionally equivalent images activate the same areas in the brain that initiate the actual movement. For example, a high jumper could imagine herself performing in a meet, and her brain would contract her muscles as if she were physically leaping over the bar (Suinn 1980; Roure et al. 1999). Specifically, techniques such as transcranial magnetic stimulation (TMS), functional magnetic resonance imaging (fMRI), positron emission tomography (PET) scan, and electroencephalography (EEG) have shown that imagery can yield activity in the supplementary motor area (SMA), cerebellum, and premotor cortex, which are the areas of the brain responsible for selecting remembered movements so performers can execute actions (Mizuguchi, Kanosue, and Nakata 2012). In essence, when a ground ball was hit, these brain areas would help the shortstop remember how to put their glove on the dirt and initiate the requisite movement to catch the ball. Neuroimaging has demonstrated that these brain areas light up during both actual performance and vividly imagined performance and that motor learning can accrue from imagery practice (Skottnik and Linden 2019).

Although a detailed explanation of neuroimaging techniques is outside the scope of this text, look at figure 5.1*a*, which shows an fMRI of the brain of a person executing a skill. Figure 5.1*b* shows that the activated areas of the brain of a person imaging their performance matches those activated during actual execution of the skill.

There is no question that science and technology have evolved and improved our understanding of how imagery works and enhanced our ability to show performers evidence of what is happening in their mind and body during imagery training. It is important that performers construct functionally equivalent images to enhance their performance. There are two approaches: using the PETTLEP (physical, environment, task, timing, learning, emotion, perspective) model (Holmes and Collins 2001) or emphasizing the vividness, controllability, and affect or emotion of the image. Both models represent a departure from the traditional and outdated way of looking at imagery as a practice that should be done with shoes off in a dark room with eyes closed. The current use of imagery has performers wearing the gear, holding the equipment, smelling the potent chlorine of the pool, or holding the lacrosse stick. Performers can use

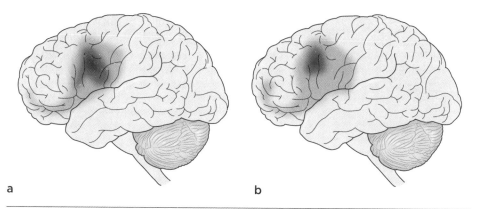

a   b

FIGURE 5.1 *(a)* Functional MRI of a person performing a skill and *(b)* fMRI of a person who is using imagery to re-create the performance.

either approach, but they must use *all* of the essential elements in either imagery model to reap the benefits. Table 5.1 shows the elements of the PETTLEP model, which is the most researched, supported, and robust.

A few of the PETTLEP elements require additional explanation. When selecting which perspective to take—internal or external—the research is clear that the internal perspective is best. An internal perspective means you are imagining your performance from your own eyes, inside your body. You might see yourself defending as if you were actually playing defense. External imagery allows you to see yourself as if you were watching game film of yourself. As a practitioner, both internal and external imagery can be used for different reasons and at different times, however. If you want to correct errors or alter emotional responses to difficult situations, then implementing extrinsic imagery might be effective; see yourself

TABLE 5.1 Elements of the PETTLEP Model

Model element	Explanation of each element	Sport examples (during imagery . . .)
Physical	As close to the physical experience as possible	Hold sport equipment, wear the uniform, grasp barbell
Environment	As similar to the performance environment as possible	Sit in the locker room, stand on pool deck, step into batter's box
Task	As similar to the actual competitive task, skill level, attentional focus as possible	Look at opponent's midsection as a defender, hear the sound of the club hitting the golf ball cleanly off the tee
Timing	As close to real-time speed and length of performance as possible	Create images that last as long as the actual performance (mostly)
Learning	As similar to actual thoughts and feelings (content) and skill level as possible	Image changes with skill development: peek to see teammate is open and prepared to catch the frisbee
Emotion	As realistic to actual competitive emotions as possible	Hear the opposing crowd before a free throw, see the lane line and feel the cold water as you dunk goggles before swim meet, feel your heart beat faster and muscles tighten as you walk to the service line in volleyball
Perspective	Internal or external based on purpose and preference	See your performance through your own eyes (internal) or like watching yourself on a selfie camera (external)

losing control and then correcting that image. On the other hand, it can be easier to feel the movement when using an internal perspective. Williams and Cumming (2012) found that internal imagery benefits tasks like hitting a pitched softball or returning a serve in tennis that require or depend on perception.

Alternately, external imagery might be useful for tasks that emphasize exact posture or form (e.g., as in figure skating or diving). It is also important to recognize that some people's default imagery style is external. In those situations, practitioners should bring as much vividness, controllability, and affect using an external perspective as they can. Rather than forcing the client to adopt their nonpreferred imagery style, integrate as many PETTLEP elements as possible into an external imagery perspective. Both have value.

In terms of the timing (i.e., temporal components) of imagery, PETTLEP research suggests that imagery should be conducted in real time. Penalty kick imagery should take as long as it takes for the person to get from the midfield line to the successful conclusion of the kick. Elite athletes image with incredible temporal consistency, completing the imagery session within one second of the actual performance. There are, however, moments when slow or fast motion might be useful. For example, if an athlete is learning a new skill or correcting a technical aspect of the skill, then slow motion is effective because it allows them to tease out particular performance elements and analyze them. Fast-motion imagery can energize athletes and enhance their focus and is useful when using a quick-hit strengthening image or a skill revisit, especially with well-learned tasks. In fact, all types of imagery timing can enhance performance if they match the purpose of the imagery session (O and Munroe-Chandler 2008), but the primary imagery style should be in real time.

The second approach to imagery is to emphasize the controllability, vividness, and emotionally equivalent elements of mental rehearsal. In terms of affect (anger, anxiety, pain, excitement), athletes' experiences should prioritize the feelings they desire in competition. Athletes should imagine themselves feeling energized and motivated when the 5 a.m. wake-up call for training comes, or a politician should create an imaginal experience that includes the positive and confident emotions experienced when walking onto a debate stage. They might feel their muscles tighten and image themselves taking a long, slow breath to quiet their mind and release any lingering muscular tension. Athletes and performers need to train themselves to include this type of information in their imagery notes and scripts so they can create images that are emotionally reflective of and physiologically congruent with the actual performance.

Vividness refers to the number of senses being used when engaging in imagery. Probably the biggest error that athletes make is creating images that are not multisensory. Vision and kinesthesis have the most significant role in ensuring the image reflects the actual, lived scenario. Kinesthesis refers to the awareness of the position of every critical body part in the execution of skills such as the legs, arms, head, torso, feet, and arm positions. It also encompasses the perception of movement, speed, and pressure of those body parts. However, all relevant senses should be included because involving more senses increases the impact of the image. In some sports, the sounds are familiar and necessary for re-creating the experience, for example. Any basketball player knows the sound of a shot going through the net, and every golfer knows the sound of a perfectly struck golf ball. Auditory vividness should take up as much of the image as it plays in the authentic, live example. The same is true for the olfactory elements like the smell of freshly cut grass, which is incredibly evocative for field sport athletes. It signals game day for many outdoor sport athletes because the fields are not cut every day, so that smell may be a critical olfactory element for game day imagery but may not be as important in practice imagery. The gustatory element—the taste of sweat on your lips during training, for example—should be part of the imagery. When focusing on imagery vividness, try to split up 100 percent of an image and think through how much of each sense should be represented. Imagining the performance of one skill might be 40 percent vision, 50 percent kinesthetic, and only 10 percent auditory, gustatory, and olfactory combined, while a different imagery session of a separate skill or scenario might have different sensory percentages.

People who have more control over their image—the ability to imagine exactly what they intend and to manipulate aspects of the images they desire—will benefit more from imagery (Vealey and Forlenza 2020). You ought to know what sets you apart, what makes you unique in your competitive world. You ought to be searching for every opportunity to exert your strength onto the current performance, and imagery facilitates that process. You should be able to exert control across multiple settings and situations. For example, imagine being a soccer forward and your signature strength is playing with your back to pressure and being defensively impactful. You ought to be able to imagine yourself pressuring in the defensive third, in the middle of the field, out at the 18-yard box, as well as receiving a ball under pressure with your back to the goal. Can you control who your opponent is or the weather? Can you control where you are on the sheet of ice or on the track? Can you control at what point in the surgery you are applying suction or when you initiate your pitch during a business sales call? Being able to control all elements of the external environment is critical in imagery training.

The purpose of these imagery approaches is to help performers do more than simply "watch" their performance, skill, or execution. Knowing the essential elements of each protocol helps performers load images with

emotion and kinesthetic components and imagine the behavioral, psychological, and physiological responses desired. These approaches teach athletes to swim on pace, hear the start signal for the race, feel the stick in their hands, see themselves squaring up for the shot, and feel their muscles ready to explode. Using meaningful verbal cues and symbolic images can also improve athletes' abilities to create multisensory images. For example, sprinters and swimmers might imagine themselves coiled like a snake on the blocks ready to start the race, and gymnasts might imagine a steel pole running through their body to steady themselves on the rings between maneuvers. These techniques and approaches should lead to functionally equivalent images that will maximize the positive effect of imagery.

Although most elite athletes understand the benefit of imagery, learning to control their images and implement an intentional and systematic imagery program often requires training, a process that is outlined on pages 76-77 in the In Their Own Words sidebar.

A Master Class on Imagery and Systematic and Systemic Buy-In

What follows is a conversation between the authors of this text focused on sharing Dr. Hacker's consulting experiences and outlining some of the strategies she used to gain performer buy-in.

Q: *Can you tell me how you have implemented imagery when you have worked with clients?*

A: In the 2014 Olympic Games in Sochi, Russia, we used more of a broad brush stroke approach to mental training. We taught the U.S. women's ice hockey team several mental skills, and we became fairly proficient at those mental skills. After the silver medal finish in Sochi, the general manager and coaching staff made a concerted effort to look at which mental skills we thought would yield the greatest results. Which skills would move our performance to a higher level and our outcome from silver to gold? It is significant to me that imagery was identified as *that* mental skill. We committed to imagery training in all aspects of our individual and collective performance and as an entire program. I view that imagery focus as one of the reasons we moved the dial from a silver to a gold medal performance in 2018.

Q: *And how did you decide that imagery would be the mental skill you targeted over that four-year cycle?*

A: We wanted to play a different way as a team, we wanted to feel a different way when we were playing on the ice, and we wanted to reinvent ourselves as individual contributors to the team. One way we could accomplish those hierarchical goals without putting ourselves at greater risk physically was to use imagery. We could collectively imagine our patterns of play and vividly control each person's role and who each athlete is playing off as well as who they are receiving the puck from. The rhythmic, full-team style of playing that we wanted to employ really lent itself to vivid, controllable imagery practice.

Q: *Earlier you indicated imagery was used in all aspects of training. What did that look like?*

A: We focused the greatest amount of our mental skills training time—in practice, after practice, before practice, in team meetings—on imagery. We spent more time implementing imagery than all of the other mental skills combined. We changed *where* we imaged, *how* we imaged, and the *frequency* of our imagery. We used imagery after we received photos of the Olympic Village, of the rinks, and of the trip from the Olympic Village to the practice and competition rinks. We used imagery to simulate training. We used imagery to highlight signature strengths, roles, and go-to plans. We used imagery in absolutely every aspect of preparation and individual performance. There was complete individual buy-in from every athlete whether they were a first-time Olympian or three-time Olympian. We had complete buy-in from the team, the captains, and the coaching staff. That kind of buy-in, that kind of systemic and systematic adoption of a mental skill and having that mental skill woven into every practice and performance elevated our individual and collective performances.

Q: *How did you achieve that level of systemic buy-in with the national team? How might other practitioners get performers to buy in to a similar degree?*

A: One way you can enhance buy-in is to use examples of highly accomplished athletes being explicit about their use of imagery. Mindful athletes are probably going to use the word visualization, but we are talking about the same mental skill. The second way is to involve athletes in the decision-making. We asked athletes where they saw us getting even greater benefits from mental skills training. Imagery allowed us to develop and to replicate practice above and beyond what they could do physically. There is no athlete who is going to do this consistent type of training if the coaches are not invested. The key stakeholders must see the value and know the benefits as well. I think a third powerful strategy for buy-in is achieving positive results. When athletes see that they can cope more quickly and in a preferred manner because they have been using imagery, then they are motivated to try it in another area. If they have had ineffective emotional responses to, for example, not starting, playing on the fourth line rather than the second line, being asked to play on a new line, or being injured, then they use imagery to create effective responses to those situations. When they see how it translates to improved performance or improved team contributions or both, then it becomes cyclically used and reinforcing. Athletes then want to learn how to use imagery in other areas. Success begets success. Improvement begets increased motivation; increased motivation leads to looking at more ways to implement and adopt a technique or strategy. It really is a built-in, motivational reinforcement loop. It is fun to see.

Tools for Implementation

This chapter has offered both evidence-based anecdotes and scholarly evidence proving the efficacy of incorporating imagery into your training regimen. As you begin (or continue) the process of honing your imagery skills, start simple. See yourself performing well, then move on to work through more challenging situations. Begin by imaging in places where you have positive memories and that are mostly successful and easily controllable. Then incorporate imagery into practice conditions with increasingly stressful demands. Give yourself an opportunity to build the skill in practice before testing it in competitive moments. You would not complete your first mile run two days before a half marathon. In the same way, you should not begin imagery sessions in the most competitive performance arenas.

Imagery seems to be one of the few skills where less is more. It is not a skill that has to be practiced for long periods. Rather, shorter imagery training sessions throughout the day at different times (e.g., when you are lacing up skates, waiting in line for your turn, or getting water between drills) is advantageous. And if you lose concentration during imagery training, break those imagery sessions into even shorter time blocks. It is also true that imagery training, even when done in clips, should be intentional, consistently used, and systematic. There is no evidence that random imagery or spontaneously seeing a previous performance enhances performance (Anuar, Cumming, and Williams 2016). Regular practice over time is critical to effective implementation and to maximum results. You would not expect bulging muscles after lifting weights one day per week for two weeks; similarly, effective imagery requires consistent and purposeful integration with physical training (Ramsey, Cumming, and Edwards 2008).

Imagery scripts can be used with video or turned into audio recordings for performers to listen to across situations. Athletes and nonsport performers can re-create their own personal highlight films. Kristine Lilly, U.S. women's soccer two-time gold medalist and two-time World Cup champion, said, "The [imagery] videos give me that little extra confidence, remind me about who I am and what I can give. I'm inspired watching my teammates' tapes. And I'm reminded of what they do well, so I'll never second-guess them" (personal communication). Lilly's comments support the strength-based imagery mentioned earlier in this chapter.

Weinberg and Gould (2019) highlight the five Ws for effective imagery scripts (who, where, when, why, and what). Performers and professionals making the scripts must know *who* the script is for (age, sport, competitive level), *where* the skill or performance occurs (elements of the training or competition environment), *when* (before, during, after competition or practice), *why* the image is needed (goal or purpose of imagery), and *what* elements are essential to the performance (content of the image). If adding audio scripts to video highlights, the film should be arranged into three to five outstanding, randomly ordered performance moments with crisp transitions (no inadvertent visual images) that performers watch for one to two minutes at least once a day (Gabriele, Hall, and Lee 1989; Selk 2009). These videos with imagery scripts can be used for both individual and team performance enhancement and can also positively affect confidence and other mental skills.

To begin or continue your imagery training, complete the worksheets on pages 80-85 at the end of this chapter. As we mention throughout this text, mental skills are just like physical skills; likewise, they benefit from progressions and specific techniques. Similarly, these worksheets will help you develop increasingly vivid, controllable, and emotionally accurate images as you move from simple and easy to complex and difficult, and you should start cultivating images of familiar, well-known situations before imagining unusual and infrequent scenarios.

Conclusion

The first step to improving imagery skills is to become aware of the performance areas that could benefit from increased repetitions. Once you have identified the strengths you want to highlight, your imagery script will write itself. Remember, imagery is a skill that can be learned, but it takes time and purposeful and systematic training. If you are consistent with your imagery practice and follow the evidence-based protocol, your performance will benefit.

Imagining a Location or Piece of Equipment

Directions

Create a vivid image of a piece of equipment or being in a specific performance location. See the example below of a swimmer creating a vivid (including vision, kinesthetic, auditory, olfactory, gustatory, and tactile senses) scenario while standing on deck next to the pool. The goal is to imagine the location or piece of equipment from different angles and distances and to highlight the most relevant senses in that location or with that piece of equipment. In the swimming example, an athlete could imagine the string of flags hanging 15 feet above the pool surface. Next, use two examples from a sport environment and then do so twice in any other performance arena (e.g., music, business, school).

Sport imagery practice

Focus on creating images in your sport domain

Equipment or location	Visual	Kinesthetic	Auditory	Olfactory, gustatory, tactile	Preferred emotional response
Example: *Standing on the pool deck barefoot in team travel gear, with swim cap on and holding goggles after practice with no one else around*	Example: *Calm and steady water, championship banners on the opposite side of the pool, windows to coach's office, water on pool deck, lane lines, string of flags holding still above the pool at 25-meter and 50-meter marks, lane lines bobbing up and down in the water*	Example: *Cold water under my feet; grout lines of the pool deck under my feet; shoulders, back, and posture is long and tall; body feels loose and relaxed in travel gear; feel light like I will glide on top of the water*	Example: *Rest of team in the locker room talking about practice, two managers putting the kickboards in the bin and rolling the marker board across the deck*	Example: *Rubber band of my goggles between the fingers of my right hand; tightness of the cap on my head, tucking strands of hair under my cap*	Example: *Calm, confident, smiling*

Sport imagery practice

Focus on creating images in your sport domain

Equipment or location	Visual	Kinesthetic	Auditory	Olfactory, gustatory, tactile	Preferred emotional response

Performance psychology imagery

Create examples in any nonsport performance domain (e.g., school, music, medicine, business)

From C. Hacker and M. Mann, *Achieving Excellence: Mastering Mindset for Peak Performance in Sport and Life* (Champaign, IL: Human Kinetics, 2023).

Imagining a Frequent or Anticipated Skill

Directions

Make a list of at least three of the most frequently used or necessary skills in your competitive environment. Create a vivid, controllable image, with accurate emotional responses for each skill. Remember, you want to imagine yourself successfully performing the skill in each requisite situation. For example, a basketball player would associate different sensory descriptions with a jump shot from the corner than from the top of the key. Doing so helps you develop controllable images. This worksheet includes a nonsport and sport performance domain so that you can practice imagery in different areas of your life.

Sport imagery practice

Focus on creating images in your sport domain

Frequent or anticipated skill	Visual	Kinesthetic	Auditory	Olfactory, gustatory, tactile	Preferred emotional response
Example: The last 10 strokes into the wall at the end of a 200-meter freestyle race	Example: One last look at coach signaling last breath, bottom of the pool, black line in the center of the lane at the bottom of the pool, wall under water during the last 3 strokes	Example: Muscles fatigued, lungs filled with air as I take my last breath with 9 strokes left, arms pulling through the water, elbow high above my head as I reach the top of my stroke, thumb enters the water first, lungs burning, cupping the water, legs are strong, powerful kick propelling my body forward, gliding on top of the water, reaching to the wall	Example: Fans cheering, coach yelling "finish, finish, head down, reach," my count of final strokes into the wall (7-6-5-4-3 . . .), teammates clapping and chanting my name, announcer calling the end of the race	Example: Forcing my head back into the water, easy pull through the water with my hands, water sliding effortlessly around my head as I glide on top, goggles pulled tight against my face, tasting the water on my lips after my last breath, touching the wall with my middle finger	Example: Powerful, fatigued, determined, spent emotionally, happy, proud

Sport imagery practice

Focus on creating images in your sport domain

Frequent or anticipated skill	Visual	Kinesthetic	Auditory	Olfactory, gustatory, tactile	Preferred emotional response

Performance psychology imagery

Create examples in any nonsport performance domain (e.g., school, music, medicine, business)

Performer-Centered Implementation Worksheet

Imagining a Signature Strength

Directions

As a performer, you should highlight and practice your signature strength. Similar to the two previous worksheets, the format and the formula remain the same. Some sports might require an offensive, transition, and defensive strength, while other performance domains require competitors to exert their strength in multiple spots on the field or in the classroom, for example. You could also imagine your signature strength in response to various challenges (e.g., mistake routines, calls against your team or you). Controlling images of where to exert a signature strength and under what conditions will help you habituate your signature strength so that you know when, where, and how to employ it at any point throughout the competition or performance.

Sport imagery practice

Focus on creating images in your sport domain

Signature strength	Visual	Kinesthetic	Auditory	Olfactory, gustatory, tactile	Preferred emotional response
Example: *Staying underwater when pushing off the block to get more distance at the start of a race*	Example: *Flags above the pool, spot on the black line that runs under the pool to enter the water, more distant spot underwater to try to reach before surfacing for air, coach signaling last-minute strategy reminders*	Example: *Coiled like a spring, right foot ahead of the left, fingers tightly gripping the edge of the block, shoulders locked and ready to send me forward, legs feel strong and tight, quad muscles engaged, body feels light and quick and sleek*	Example: *Squeaky sound of goggles as I wipe last drops of water off before placing them on my eyes, coach yelling, fans cheering, teammates calling my name, opponents' names and schools being announced as they step onto the blocks, announcer saying "take your marks," high-pitched brief beep to start the race*	Example: *Dunk goggles in water and place them on top of cap, ridges on top of the block under my feet, edge of the block as I grab it with my fingers, coldness of the water as I dunk my goggles and place them over my eyes, smell of chlorine wafting through the air*	Example: *Excited, energized, prepared, focused, locked on and locked in*

Sport imagery practice

Focus on creating images in your sport domain

Signature strength	Visual	Kinesthetic	Auditory	Olfactory, gustatory, tactile	Preferred emotional response

Performance psychology imagery

Create examples in any nonsport performance domain (e.g., school, music, medicine, business)

CHAPTER 6

Energy Management

We feel stress and pressure to perform well every day, whether at home, at work, or in sport. Often, as Coach Iapoce's quote highlights, the difference between rising to meet those challenging demands or not lies within us. We often hear athletes and other high-level performers talk about playing or performing their best when their best is needed. We listen and try to learn about their strategies for peak performance by locking into the language they use and the insights they provide and then try to emulate those strategies in our own sphere of performance. We soon learn that translating those insights into successful action, however, is more difficult than expected. The greats have a knack for making things seem and look easy. In our own lives, we may wake up on the first day of starting a new career, walk into a major exam at school, or arrive at a significant competitive moment, and, in truth, we hope that things will turn out well. We hope that we will feel energized, confident, well-rested, and ready to perform. Although few people admit it, our thoughts and emotions are often left to hopeful chance. How we feel before a critical performance becomes a matter of luck and hope rather than resulting from a practiced and clear design.

> There are really good players in the minor leagues, but the separator is who can handle their emotions better under duress, under extreme stress. . . . I think that's why some guys get into the big leagues faster. It's not that they're so much more talented than everyone. They just think better. They understand anxiety, and they're able to calm themselves down sooner.
>
> Anthony Iapoce, hitting coach for the Chicago Cubs baseball team

In this chapter, we aim to change that line of thinking. Like the rest of this book, this chapter emphasizes specific activation-control skills you can learn so you can put yourself in the best position to perform well and to repeat those moments under pressure. As Mildred "Babe" Didrikson Zaharias—founder of the Ladies Professional Golf Association; Olympic gold medalist; and a record holder in track and field, golf, and basketball—stated when asked whether her performance was based in luck, "Luck? Sure. But only after long practice and only with the ability to think under pressure." This chapter outlines how you can manage anxiety and control your activation levels. Because there is no one-size-fits-all approach, we offer well-researched guidelines for developing awareness of your emotions during your best performance, and we teach you how to access the range of appropriate emotions useful for your performance and how to correct your path when you are more excited or nervous or more emotionally flat than you would prefer to be before or during performance. Instead of attempting to replicate the emotional state that helps another performer succeed, this chapter will help you identify how to access the zone of activation that works best for you and how to compete even when you are outside of that performance zone. As Babe Didrikson noted, performing well in a variety of conditions is not about luck. Luck comes *after* you have become aware of what helps you perform well and have developed the skills necessary to control or mitigate the negative effects of inappropriate activation when moments in life are less than ideal.

Managing Stress and Anxiety

The first skill you must develop is the ability to handle stress and manage anxiety and activation in response to competitive challenges and stressors. The list of challenging, pressure-filled situations in both sport and life are endless: competing against a top opponent, trying to earn an athletic scholarship, attempting to make a team, having an administrator or boss evaluate your performance, playing for a national or world title in front of your home crowd, delivering a presentation in front of a class or business group, and performing during a contract year as a professional athlete or coach are just a few examples. Each of these moments is considered a stressor. Each is an event that involves specific high-stakes tasks and places demands on you as the performer. How you handle that pressure influences how you perform, how you feel about your performance, and how satisfied you are with the results. To "own the moment" and perform well in high-pressure situations, you need to recognize and understand the following:

1. The relationship between stress, anxiety, and activation
2. The importance of perception as a controllable factor
3. That each performer has their own unique preferred activation range

Then you can begin to focus on developing the skills necessary to either activate or deactivate yourself and to be able to do so on demand when it matters most (the latter of which will be discussed in more detail in chapter 7).

Stress, Anxiety, and Activation

Stress, anxiety, and activation are all factors that interrelate and can affect performance. The key is to understand how these variables affect performance so that you can begin exerting control in ways that can moderate or control activation, cope with stress, and mitigate the negative effects of anxiety. *Stress* is the perceived imbalance between a competitive demand (e.g., public speaking, batting in the bottom of the ninth inning, headlining a Broadway musical) and a performer's capability (McGrath 1970). Famed spiritual advisor Eckhart Tolle (2010) noted, "Stress is caused by being 'here' but wanting to be 'there,' or being in the present but wanting to be in the future." Both are true. People tend to experience stress when they are unsure of whether they can meet the challenge they are facing. And stressful thoughts and feelings are much more likely to occur when people begin thinking too far in advance, when, as mentioned in chapter 4, performers are not where their feet are. Two common sources of stress are (1) the importance of an event or situation, or the value placed on an event, and (2) event or situation uncertainty (Weinberg and Gould 2019). The following sidebar describes what leaders

PUT IT INTO PRACTICE

Suggestions for Leaders

Business leaders and coaches can help their employees and athletes handle competitive demands by limiting self-induced stress. The more important an event feels and the more uncertain a performer feels, the more stress and anxiety they are likely to experience. To help, leaders should do the following:

- Tell performers about the plan for the upcoming practice or meeting (research does not support the belief that people will loaf or be less productive if they know details of the upcoming events).

- Learn which performers are trait anxious (that is, they generally view competitive situations as threatening) because they will likely need increased support to cope and perform well in the face of stressful challenges.

- Be aware of uncertainties that a new team member or coworker might be experiencing in their daily life (e.g., relocation, new school for their children, playing status) because those uncertainties can negatively affect performance.

- Ensure people are aware of policies and procedures that might affect them, such as how the company handles sick leave or the injury rehabilitation process in sport.

- Consistently assess and evaluate the importance of an event to specific members of the team or group and make necessary adjustments.

- When addressing performers before a significant event, avoid using language that might increase the perceived importance for someone who might already be worried or anxious about the outcome (e.g., this is a must-win situation, we must do well today).

can do to mitigate the negative effect these sources of stress can have on employees, coworkers, and athletes.

Expect that any person in a stressful, competitive situation will feel physically *activated*, meaning they might experience any of the following: increased heart rate, respiration, and sweating; cold, clammy hands; dry mouth; flushed face or upper body; jittery legs. This physical activation is neither good nor bad. Rather, people's arousal and activation levels can vary along a continuum throughout the day from a deep sleep at night to a frenzied feeling before competition (Gould, Greenleaf, and Krane 2002). In fact, to perform well, each person needs to feel some level of activation (although the preferred amount of activation varies as we will discuss later in this chapter). The literature indicates that ideal or preferred levels of activation change based on the individual, the sport (e.g., rugby requires higher activation levels than archery), and the position played (e.g., a lineman in American football might require higher activation levels than a place kicker). Some physical manifestations of heightened activation might be quite pronounced. Mikaela Shiffrin, the most decorated female alpine skier in history, for example, is famous for throwing up before races. Many athletes would panic if they vomited before an event or performance. It would cause them to question their confidence or their preparation or their training; it would give them an excuse for not performing well. For Shiffrin, throwing up signals "It's race day." The signs and symptoms of activation in and of themselves are neutral. They are simply events or experiences. What matters most is how people interpret their activation symptoms and responses.

Stress is generally regarded as a perceived imbalance between the demands placed on the individual and their perceived capacity to respond successfully. *Anxiety*, on the other hand, is a negative emotional state marked by nerves, worry, and apprehension that stem from changes in physical arousal levels (Cheng, Hardy, and Markland 2009; Weinberg and Gould 2019). In other words, if Mikaela Shiffrin perceived throwing up or running to the restroom before a race as a sign that she was worried or unprepared or that she was not going to ski well, then she would likely experience increased anxiety (and, consequently, be at increased risk for performing poorly). When people experience anxiety before a performance, called *competitive anxiety*, they typically have both thought disturbances and negative interpretations of the physical activation responses they are experiencing. It is the negative thinking and worrying that have the most deleterious effect on performance. When a person is called on as a demonstrator in front of their peers for example, worrying what will happen if they are incorrect makes it more likely that the student-performer will struggle to answer the question appropriately and to their capability. Why? Because anxiety—both anxious thoughts and negative interpretations of the body's activation—can negatively affect performance.

Athletes might report that they do not feel well, they feel like throwing up, or that their muscles feel tight. Once they know what to look for, it is easy to see the negative effects of anxiety on performance. The unhelpful effects of anxiety and activation occur when baseball and softball players, for example, flinch or tense up when fielding a hard-hit ground ball. Rather than simply putting their glove on the dirt as they have thousands of times in practice, they shrug their shoulders, and their glove is pulled just off the dirt, allowing the ball to get past them. Performers experiencing high competitive anxiety might also fatigue faster, or their motions might develop hitches or seem stiff and robotic rather than smooth and effortless.

In addition to behavioral changes, too much activation and increased anxiety can affect performers' attention, concentration, and vision as well (Vine and Wilson 2010). Think about a sprinter who is taking a handoff from a teammate during a 4 × 400-meter relay. As the teammate running the third leg rounds the curve of the track, the anchor runner notices the crowd rising to their feet and clapping as they cheer for a comeback from the team in the neighboring lane. The anchor runner starts to feel their heart beat faster, and their mouth becomes dry. Their muscles tighten as they hope their teammate hangs on to the lead coming down the stretch. They start to zone in on their teammate and do not notice that they need to make positional adjustments because another team has just taken the lead. As a result, they get to their position late and the handoff is disrupted, causing them to drop the baton. This example demonstrates how increased anxiety and activation, if not within the performer's control, can cause people to concentrate on the wrong cues (e.g., crowd noise, internal self-talk) rather than focusing on what they need to do to take a successful handoff, in this case, or to perform well, more generally. High activation and in-the-moment anxiety can also lead to tunnel vision, a narrowing of the athlete's visual field, so that they do not see or even notice important elements they would normally pick up on in practice. Performers might also feel like they cannot stop looking at one element of the competitive environment (the baton, for example), and their attention becomes rigid and fixed, and they struggle to scan the entire playing or performing area for additional relevant cues (the speed of their teammate's approach or the lane switch by their opponents, for example).

As we have mentioned, performance can break down when a performer hasn't learned how to control their activation. And often, athletes and other performers realize too late that they have not mastered the ability to control their optimal activation levels, usually during a competition or performance or immediately afterward, when it is far too late to either learn or implement the requisite self-regulation strategies. People do not get credit in sport or in life for knowing what to do, they only benefit when they both know and *do* it—take the necessary actions when needed and on demand. Athletes often fail to realize the significant role that activation control, once developed, can play in all aspects of their performance and generally in other life pursuits. For example, athletes might have a plan in place that dials them in to their preevent routine or pregame warm-up. In fact, pregame and preperformance moments are when we see the most attention given to activation control. But competitors also need activation control *during* the event and *after* the performance. After an event, many performers are stuck in rumination and replaying what they should have done and what they could have done differently or better. Although postevent analysis is valuable for many reasons, knowing what you *should have* done after the fact does not help with the most recent performance. Generally, postevent evaluations are negative and unhelpful. Those assessments must be turned into action and into identification of needed capabilities going forward. Merely identifying what went wrong is not helpful unless that awareness is also accompanied by a commitment to take action in practice.

Often, athletes think only about errors and the disappointment of a loss or poor performance. They hang on to tension, to worry, to doubt, and to fear that it might happen again, and each of those emotions exerts a somatic (physical) toll on the performer. Instead, athletes need to engage in activation control after the event ends either to prevent a downward spiral or to quickly regain control of their physical selves. A competitive advantage can be gained by learning to control activation after an event. In many sports, such as softball and baseball, where athletes play doubleheaders, being able to return to an ideal activation level between games is essential. Another example is in soccer. Athletes need to return to their preferred activation level when they have back-to-back matches on Saturday and Sunday. They need to recover from Saturday's match before Sunday begins. Psychological and physiological recovery activation control is absolutely essential from a competitive standpoint because so often teams perform well in one but not both events. Consistency in performance is a hallmark of competitive excellence.

Being able to control energy and activation is not only important for team sport athletes, but it's also a vital skill set for individual athletes and performers. Take distance runners, for example. Often, during a race or training run, energy management is required to set and maintain the desired pace from the outset. Going out too fast in a race can have disastrous results later.

During the first few minutes of a run at a pace that is too fast, the runner might feel like they are running out of oxygen or are not properly trained. But if they get into their proper pace and rhythm early and comfortably, not only do they experience the psychological benefits of confidence and comfort, but they experience physiological benefits as well. Most runners have had that moment where they question themselves and take the first few minutes or first mile (1,600 m) of a run at a pace that is too fast as a sign that they are not ready, that they are "gassed," or that they cannot keep pace with the field. As a result, they give themselves an excuse for a lower physical output, and say things like "It's not my day today" or "I am not as good as these other runners." They are in conservation or preservation mode for the rest of the race (or, if it is a team sport, until halftime, a time-out, or the end of the period). However, if they know how to control their activation and can quickly recognize that they are expending too much energy early, then they can quickly adjust their pace or calm the frenetic energy and realize that they can control their activation and calm the initial and temporary feeling of worry or exhaustion. Runners might remind themselves that if they are smart in the next 45 seconds and run at their practiced pace, then they can return to their best performance levels more quickly.

This skill of activation control is also important in sports like the biathlon, where a central feature of the sport itself is going from high aerobic output and gross motor movements (skiing) to immediately calming oneself and firing a rifle with controlled, fine motor movements under lower activation levels. The same is true for basketball players shooting free throws. The game itself is quick and powerful and largely aerobic, but the transition to free throw shooting requires a calmer, more controlled activation level. Very often, to compete well requires someone to move from gross to fine motor skills and from a high energy output to a low, slow, and calm energy output in a snap of the fingers. Similar activation changes and transitions happen in lacrosse and soccer. For example, in soccer, when a person is fouled in the penalty box and goes to the spot for a penalty kick, they must slow their breathing and calm themselves immediately to cope with the added pressure and stress. Read the sidebar on pages 94-95 to learn how members of the United States women's national soccer team (USWNT) learned how to practice and prepare for these required changes in activation to propel themselves into the World Cup and Olympic Games.

The rest of this chapter is dedicated to helping you learn how to activate yourself appropriately and consistently to your best and preferred activation level (either up or down) and to manage your own anxiety. We want you to learn what works for *you*, and then learn how to access that level of activation *consistently* and *on demand*.

Perception Matters

Often, we watch and hear people talk about competitive moments as being *stressful*, while others mention how exciting the *clutch* moment felt. Both can be true, and neither must occur, meaning the stressor is only a moment, an event, an experience, an interaction. It does not yield a predetermined response. Instead, the effect of stress and the initiation of an activated emotional state or anxiety that results from an objective

IN THEIR OWN WORDS

In the 1990s and 2000s, the USWNT was the number one ranked team in the world. They had been World Cup champions and had won Olympic gold numerous times. Suffice it to say, the team and coaching staff were getting things right more often than not. When asked to share a story about one of her proudest moments as a member of the USWNT coaching staff, Dr. Hacker offered the following:

In soccer, set pieces are traditionally practiced in similar ways to free throw shooting in basketball. During practice, you spend about 15 minutes on set pieces just like in basketball practice you might shoot 10, 20, 30 free throws in a row. But that is not how those skills are performed during matches and games. How many times in a basketball career do you get to shoot 10 free throws in a row? Zero. The same is true in soccer. A team does not have the opportunity to run multiple set pieces in a row. Yet, basketball and soccer teams around the world practice those skills under a set of psychological and physiological activation parameters that do not match what will be required during competition. As we know from the motor learning literature on open skills (performed in dynamic environments—for example, catching an object, defending a shot on a goal) versus closed skills (performed in a predictable environment that does not change to affect performance—for example, bowling, running, swimming), athletes experience fewer benefits from repetitive, closed practice of set pieces because the demands of practice are almost entirely different from the demands experienced during games.

Now remember, the USWNT was the number one team in the world during this time. So the players did not see much need to change how they practiced, you know "Why fix it if it ain't broken?" But I knew we could close our performance gap and improve our set piece conversion rate if we changed how we practiced. I felt that if we could improve in this one area of the game, we could close the gap between our current performance level and our team and individual potential. It took a year and a half to convince all the coaches, one and a half years of discussing the research and explaining the rationale, but we started practicing our set pieces differently. Our success rate for set pieces before this change was under 20 percent. In essence, we converted 2 out of every 10 opportunities.

We started practicing set pieces under the same or similar activation and psychological demands that we needed players to execute in match conditions. For example, we challenged players during practice to go from full scrimmage mode straight into a set piece in the middle of practice and at random times throughout practice rather than practicing set pieces in a block of practices at the end of training. The coach would blow a whistle randomly and say "Free, free, free," and everyone would sprint to their respective positions both offensively and defensively for a corner kick. Rather than setting aside time to practice corners separately from other segments of the game, we integrated them into scrimmages and competitive moments in practice. That change forced athletes to scramble, to transition from an intense moment of sprinting and defending or looking to score, to suddenly needing to stand still, become calm, and execute the set piece. We changed the practice demands to better mirror the match demands and simulate the transition from high psychological and physiological activation to moments that required lower activation levels.

Within six months of following this new practice protocol, we moved from a 20 percent success rate to higher than 70 percent. In one World Cup, the USWNT scored 73 percent of their goals from set pieces: 73 percent! Just think what that success rate means in typically low-scoring soccer matches. I am proud of that change in practice conditions and in the success rate of our team. I credit our coaching staff for believing in the science and for trusting that recommendation. It is truly one of my proudest moments as a mental skills coach.

This example highlights the effects of activation control. It can be a hard sell for people when they have only coached or played one way, under one set of conditions, but training under the requisite psychological demands and physiological activation levels required in competition is essential to success. Whether you are a top surgeon or the lowest-ranked conference team in a preseason poll, you can become more efficient and effective by learning activation control and being able to enter your preferred activation level on time, when it counts. The value of this protocol is that it facilitates the development of appropriate activation control strategies on demand and in both competition and practice.

---

situation depends entirely on how a person perceives that moment. For example, when a person is called on to perform a skill in front of their teammates or answer a question in front of their classmates, it is assumed that the individual will feel nervous or anxious. And while some people might experience nerves, those emotions are not inevitable and certainly not directly caused by the event.

Emotional responses stem from people's perceptions of their abilities to cope with and meet the challenge they are facing. As a result, someone who is asked to perform in front of others might experience increased worries (*cognitive state anxiety*) and increased activation (*somatic state anxiety*). A different individual in the same set of circumstances, when called on, might feel like they are prepared to respond correctly and are excited to demonstrate their knowledge or skill expertise. It is key to understand that a person's perception of the event and their increased physical activation do not necessarily mean they will perform well or perform poorly; it simply means that they are preparing to do something that is meaningful and important to them. Everything that happens after that moment is a result of each person's own interpretation. They have control.

Identify Your Preferred State

As we mention throughout this book, one of the most important skills you can learn that will improve performance consistency is self-awareness. Our goal is to help you recognize that you have a preferred best-performance

ferrantraite/E+/Getty Images

state, and you must be self-aware when you are moving outside of that preferred range or state. When you start feeling stressed, when you are not in your preferred state, you tend to rush, and that speeding up of performance is a common competitive problem. You must take control and be able to appropriately intervene when things are not going well.

In the late 1990s, Yuri Hanin, a Russian sport psychology researcher, found that top athletes have a zone of optimal state anxiety (often distinct for various competitive situations) in which they perform at their best (Weinberg and Gould 2019). To explain this idea, Hanin constructed what is now known as the *individualized zones of optimal functioning* (IZOF) model, one of the most widely applied models used to explain sport performance (Ruiz, Raglin, and Hanin 2017). What Hanin (1997) suggested was that every performer has an individualized range of emotions, including feelings of nervousness or anxiety, within which their best performances occur. Some members of a world-renowned orchestra might need to feel calm and relaxed before performing at the revered Carnegie Hall in New York City. Other members of the same musical ensemble might need to experience entirely different emotions. The IZOF model suggests that even performers who need to experience a sense of relaxed calm may still perform well in moments when they are slightly more anxious than they prefer to be. Performers do not *have* to be at the center of their best emotional state to perform well; rather, they might be on the upper end of their performance zone or just barely entering it. According to Hanin, it is important for coaches, leaders, and sport psychology professionals to help performers recognize and consistently access their unique optimal zone of state anxiety and emotions so that they can perform at a high level. Some athletes and nonsport performers struggle to identify their IZOF. Use the information in the following sidebar to better understand your own IZOF or help performers access theirs.

The purpose of the task described in the sidebar is to help performers intentionally develop or become more aware of their personal performance roadmap. They learn what behaviors, feelings, and emotions they experience when they are competing at a high level. The goal then becomes learning how to repeat those actions, thoughts, activation levels, and experiences. Always remember that there is a cognitive bias to remember what went wrong in a past performance rather than what went well. Unfortunately, in good performances, performers often think "It just happened" or "I was lucky." Too often people succumb to a magical kind of thinking about performance rather than recognizing that controlling anxiety and activation is a skill and is under their control.

For example, you might tend to believe that if you slept well the night before an event or ate a particular food the day you performed well, then

PUT IT INTO PRACTICE

Creating Your Own IZOF

To help performers identify when they perform well and to better understand the amounts and types of emotions and anxiety necessary for them to play well, try the following exercise:

1. Ask competitors to think of a time when they experienced their preferred or best performance. "When did you perform the way you wanted to perform?"

   List demographic data such as year, day, opponent (when appropriate), and name of the event. Doing so helps the performer to reenter that specific competitive moment and to recall a specific event rather than generally review performances.

2. Examine the behavioral manifestations of that match, game, or performance. Ask "When you played your best, what were the characteristics of that experience? What did you see, hear, say to yourself, and feel?

   List behaviors associated with preevent routines. For example, what did you do on your walk to the performance arena, during the night before, when you woke up on the day of the competition or performance, during meals, and throughout the warm-up? The performer should list what they did from the moment they started preparing for the event (the night before, the morning of, two hours before) through to the end of the performance.

3. Repeat steps 1 and 2 for a performance or a competition in which they did not perform their best.

it was that happenstance experience that caused the performance to go well. Instead, the sidebar exercise makes it clear that, if you play well when you sleep for at least six hours and you tend to perform worse when you are sleep deprived, then you learn that you need to improve your sleep habits and commit to prioritizing rest and recovery. Rather than saying "Oh, I didn't sleep well, so I doubt that I'll run fast today," it is more facilitative to think that while you might have preferred to sleep longer or better, you do not have to have a perfect night's sleep to be able to run fast. Further, it is also valuable to learn that sleep is important, and therefore you need to prioritize choices and behaviors that will facilitate better sleep so you can go to sleep more quickly or return to sleep more consistently when it is disrupted during the night. The goal is to identify a roadmap to create the behaviors and skills necessary to cultivate the likelihood for best performances to occur. Remember, it is the zone that matters. Do not feel like you must mirror other athletes who may have a different set of best-performance preferences and parameters.

Playing Outside Your Preferred Zone

We are advocates of Hanin's IZOF, and research supports its efficacy among performers. It is great if you can identify and consistently access your ideal range of emotions and nerves that propel you to a good performance. In fact, this chapter is designed to help you recognize and access that zone more often. However, it is also important to realize that you do not *have* to be at your best to have an impactful, positive, and productive performance. Professional athletes discuss this principle in the sidebar on page 99.

We note that people develop performance preferences within a range rather than as an exact point and acknowledge that no universal performance requirements yield a best performance. There is no singular way every athlete prefers to feel before a performance just as all lawyers do not prepare for trial in the same manner, and teachers do not prepare a lesson the same way. From our perspective, Hanin (1997) was accurate in this sense. Individual performers might prefer to feel a certain set of emotions or amounts of anxiety to play well. However, perspective also helps explain the fact that performers do not have to be perfectly situated in their IZOF to perform well.

Often, athletes have been taught, in a well-meaning but unhelpful way, that they need to experience their highest levels of confidence, have the best night's sleep, or feel optimally focused to play their best. That type of all-or-none thinking is neither accurate nor helpful. The truth is, most of the time, athletes are not feeling optimal confidence, they often feel nervous or anxious, and they are often fatigued during a difficult training cycle. In these moments, as famed sport psychology expert Dr. Ken Ravizza often said, performers must "bring 100% of their 80% game" (Hays 2017).

Shortly after her successful performance, Olympic gold medal cross-country skier Jessie Diggins acknowledged the following:

> **So while the 10 km individual skate race that I narrowly won on Friday was undoubtedly one of my better races, I think it's important to acknowledge that you don't have to feel perfect the morning before the race or even at the start line to pull off a great performance. Even if your body doesn't feel on fire, being able to refocus on the positive, narrow down your window to what you CAN do, what you need to do technically and with your pacing to achieve a good race, is important. (Diggins 2021)**

Similarly, English professional footballer and center back Peter Clarke noted, "We have this thing in our mind of I gotta feel perfect, calm and confident and THEN I'll perform well. Mate, if that's the case you're going to perform well a very, very small portion of the time."

Key generalizations about energy management and performance are critical to understanding best performance. However, it is also true that great performances have occurred all around the edges, so to speak, of the ideal target as well. As outlined earlier, people possess performance preferences—desired activation levels, intensity, and types of emotions—but that does not mean there are rigid, performance requirements. The reality is that people perform well even when not feeling their best. In fact, that happens often.

Similarly, we argue that it is as important to know *your* preferred zone as it is to learn how to play well when you are not able to access it. When a cricketer, for example, has a sore hamstring or did not sleep well, they must still play and, hopefully, play well. They do not have the luxury of listing all the reasons they might not play their best, nor is it advisable. Rather than create excuses for why you are not feeling or thinking your best, you need to recognize that even though you are not in your preferred zone, you can still devote 100 percent of your current capabilities to today's performance. Learning to perform at 100 percent of your 80 percent game is both a skill and a competitive mindset. It also represents a significant shift in perspective for most people.

What you need to implement in these less-than-ideal moments or situations, is a go-to plan. A go-to plan is simply a behavior or series of behaviors over which you have complete control. You may not be able to score like you usually do, but you can still play tough defense and be a positive support for teammates. For example, in lacrosse, if you are not able to make the give-and-go runs you typically make, it is critical to know what your go-to plan is and execute it immediately. You can double-team your opponents on defense, for example, make better off-ball runs to open the field, or serve as a vocal leader for teammates either on the field or from the bench. In other words, there are many go-to options available that will allow you to productively and significantly affect your performance or your team's. The key is that you must be in total control of your go-to plan. For example, you can control your reaction to errors. You can control your effort. You can control how you respond to coaching criticism or teammate mistakes. The truth is that every performer has experienced a moment, a game, a half, or a period when, from their perspective, nothing went the way they planned. It is essential to spend time developing a go-to plan for what you will do and how you will respond when you are having a less-than-ideal performance. We suggest that developing a "good

Julian Finney/Getty Images

enough" plan is another valuable tool and offers a perspective that can aid rather than hurt performance.

For example, in many sports and for many athletes across competitive levels, getting quality sleep the night before competition and a nap on the day of the event are viewed as critical for performance success. In the 21st century, it seems everyone knows the importance of sleep, that there may in fact be a greater performance benefit from taking a half-hour nap or sleeping an hour longer than what is gained from another half hour practicing or lifting weights for 30 more minutes. In other words, the data is showing just how valuable naps and sleep are to performance. Dr. Terry Orlick discussed the importance of rest and recovery in his 2016 book, *In Pursuit of Excellence,* as he implored performers to commit to rest and recovery in the same ways they commit to practice. Value it. Prioritize it. Commit to it. Sleep has become a prized possession for many athletes and nonsport performers alike. But what happens on days when you cannot get a nap in or you cannot seem to fall asleep? Often, individuals start feeling frustrated and upset because they know that sleep is important, so they start fighting themselves and looking at the clock, thinking "Now

I only have 15 minutes to nap," or they start watching each minute pass on the clock and getting more anxious and agitated with each passing moment. These negative thoughts create a recurring cycle of anxiety, frustration, and concern that takes the performer further and further from what they want: rest. Instead, performers must learn to manage that moment. In this case, it is better to direct their focus to breathing and to taking a long slow, belly breath and then exhale fully with each breath, keeping a this-breath focus. They could also conduct a body scan from toes to head, looking for signs of tension or tightness. When found, they can relax that muscle group and focus on breathing.

Whether it is writing a book on mental skills training or preparing for an important performance event, Dr. Hacker often shares the adage that "Perfection is the enemy of progress." Often in our quest to be perfect, we fail to notice, respect, and appreciate that starting, even starting small, is better than doing nothing or waiting until conditions are perfect to start. It is often best to start small or to start imperfectly than it is to not to start at all. Recognize the gains and the improvements made however imperfectly. Be better today than yesterday. Focus on what you can accomplish rather than engage in all-or-none thinking. This is not a small point of distinction. Let's unpack that idea a little bit more as it relates to activation control. We talk often about ideal and preferred, but we also need to acknowledge and respect *good enough* sometimes. Pursuing excellence is motivating. Pursuing perfection is often demoralizing. In sport and other performance domains, we often avoid good enough. We are trained to believe that those words are blasphemous and reflect a lack of commitment, motivation, or competitiveness. Perhaps if we start with an example other than sport, the principle will make more sense. Think about a time when you had only a few minutes to clean your house or take care of your lawn. You originally hoped to spend two hours on a Saturday doing yardwork and housecleaning, but you needed to finish an office project, spend time with the family, and pick up a few groceries. And so, a *good enough* and appropriate adjustment had to be made. It would not be helpful to say "Well, I cannot clean or work on the yard for as long as I wanted, so why bother to do anything?"

Sadly, that is a decision many people make. Instead, it is more productive to say "If I can't dust the entire house or pull every weed in the lawn, I will weed the front lawn and dust the living room only." It may not be perfect. It may not be preferred. It may not be ideal, but it is a start and considering all that you must accomplish in limited time, for today it is good enough. How would it be better to conclude that because you cannot dust everything or pull all the weeds, that it is pointless to do anything at all? Instead, it would be wise to devote the time you can and recognize that you started; you made a few things better and therefore, have less to do the next chance you get. Of course, we are not suggesting that your ultimate goal in either sport or life is to aspire to *good enough* standards but rather to recognize that there are times when the good enough plan can become the preferred strategy (when compared to the *do nothing* plan).

Let's apply this principle to the previous sleep example. There are amounts of sleep between a 15-minute nap and a 30-minute nap. Why not adjust the focus to getting 15 minutes of peaceful rest and recovery instead of striving for 15 more minutes that will result in agitation and stress? Similarly, there are hours between "I did not sleep at all last night" and "I slept for nine hours." You must learn to love the nuance of good enough. You might not have achieved your ideal and preferred sleep or rest time, but you did commit to fully engaging in the benefits of recovery for the time you did have. To embrace the nuance between ideal, preferred, and good enough (on occasion) and prevent the quest for perfection from disrupting your commitment to excellence, learn to control what you can, do your best with the options available, and make the most of the opportunities available. The point is you have control over how you respond to each setback. So, in this case, you might say "While I'm not happy with only a 15-minute nap, I can engage in systematic and targeted progressive relaxation." In this response, although your brain does not enter rapid eye movement sleep, you can still use the time you have to scan your body for areas of tension, focus on that area, control your breathing, and achieve a restorative somatic relaxation response even in the absence of sleep. It is good for your body because you are searching for areas of tension and letting them go, so it provides that immediate physical benefit *and* it is practice for focusing on what you can control. That nap time was good enough. You may not have gotten the sleep you wanted, but you were able to calm your mind, practice breath control, and reduce tension in your body—all of which allow you to recover more quickly. That fact alone should be reassuring.

The calm, breathing-focused, tension-releasing go-to plan is certainly superior to one that leaves you feeling agitated, annoyed, worried, and disappointed in yourself. For so many of us, perfection becomes the enemy of excellence. You might think "If I cannot get my full workout in, then why work out at all?" Instead, you could say "I only have 15 minutes, so at least I can get two rounds of high-intensity training cycles in and still have a minute to spare!" In those moments, it is best to immediately enact your go-to plan, thus ensuring some benefits rather than none.

What we are saying is that there are moments and there are times when your go-to plan becomes a good enough plan. Implementing it still helps you enter your range of excellence, even though it is not perfect. Do not make a bad situation worse by striving for perfection when it is not possible in a particular moment. The scenarios you are likely to face that require either a go-to plan or a good enough plan are numerous and could include the team bus arriving late to the match, leaving only 15 minutes to warm up, or the speaker before you covering some of your material, thus necessitating you having to eliminate or change your remarks, or you just finished a 12-hour round as a nurse and you get called back for a consult on a challenging case. Make these less-than-perfect and less-than-preferred situations better by focusing on what you can control in the moment (e.g., breathing, self-talk) and commit to desirable activation control techniques.

Identifying Activation Strategies

We close this chapter by offering a few specific activation strategies, which are useful when performers feel sluggish and fatigued. In those moments, performers might seem distracted, and both their focus and movements are usually slower. Some athletes report feeling heavy or like they have no bounce in their step. When they need to perform with high output to succeed and are feeling too calm, too fatigued, or disengaged, then activation-inducing techniques are useful. See the following Chalk Talk sidebar.

Breath control is key for either energizing or relaxing yourself. When using the breath to produce energy, use short breaths. With each exhalation, push air out quickly and with power or force. Doing so activates the nervous system and helps you feel more energized and alert (Weinberg and Gould 2019). Using *positive self-statements* and images such as "Be quick. Plant and go" or "Push, and attack like a lion" can also help prepare your body to increase activation. Similar techniques can be used for calming or lowering one's activation levels. In this case, focus on long,

Chalk Talk

Quick Hits for Activation Strategies

The following could be included in your activation strategy:

☐ Control your breath: Use short breaths and during exhalation force air out quickly.

☐ Use positive, powerful self-statements and images to activate your body.

☐ Play loud or upbeat music.

☐ Engage in intentional, energizing behaviors (clap your hands, jump up and down).

full exhalations. Slow your breathing rate. Listen to calming music. Use language that provides both assurance and clarity about your ability and capabilities. For example, before his races, track and field gold medalist Carl Lewis said his thoughts were "really simple. . . . I would tell myself: Get out of the blocks, run your race, stay relaxed. If you run your race, you'll win . . . channel your energy. Focus." In this case, he discussed how he attempted to relax himself before the race began. *Music* (listening to it or imagining it) can also be useful because it has been shown to reduce perceived exertion and enhance mood and activation (Karageorghis et al. 2012). The number of beats per minute of a song has been a useful way to think through whether a song or playlist might elicit an energizing or relaxing effect. If none of the techniques just listed are helpful in the moment, you can *act* as if you are already activated or relaxed. Here, we are not suggesting you fake it, but rather these *activation behaviors* are intentional actions that require your body to mirror and reflect the desired activation level. For example, a public speaker might activate by pacing in the green room, ice hockey goalies might hit their shoulder pads and knee pads before the puck drop, a pitcher might step off the mound and jump up and down before the start of extra innings to reenergize themselves. Conversely, a pole vaulter might lie down and relax between attempts, or field hockey players might go for a short, easy jog before the start of a competition to calm themselves. Each of these intentional behaviors helps people recapture the energy they need for their best performance.

Conclusion

This chapter has laid the foundation for why you need to develop the ability to control your anxiety and activation levels before, during, and after competitions or performances. As you have learned, it is important to train in ways that replicate the psychological and physiological conditions and demands that you will face during matches, games, and other performative events. Much of this chapter has been dedicated to introducing you to the importance of energy management, and there are two components to that ability. First, you must develop that skill to activate yourself on cue and on demand within a moment's notice. And second, you need to develop the ability to deactivate or relax yourself on demand. The next chapter will offer several relaxation techniques and outline when and how to implement each. We encourage you to integrate the strategies in chapter 6 and chapter 7 into your training so that you can control your activation and anxiety levels on demand and when it matters most.

Control of Calm

In the previous chapter, we discussed energy management, offered strategies for coping with stress effectively, and identified techniques to increase activation on demand. The purpose of that chapter was to emphasize that you can learn to control your activation levels. While you might not be able to prevent a stressor, you can learn to frame the event in ways that are useful, and you can develop the mental skills and tools that can help you perform well under less-than-ideal (and common) circumstances. In this chapter, we describe various interventions to calm yourself before competition, during competition, and after a competitive event ends so you can quickly prepare for the next training session or performance.

> Master our breath, master our mind.
>
> American Sniper.

> [Relaxation] can be as simple as sitting by yourself and drawing your attention to your breath. Pay attention to how your breath feels on the inside of your nostrils as it goes in and out. Don't make it any more complicated than that.
>
> Rich Roll, ultra-endurance athlete

As we mentioned in chapter 6, there are general guidelines for relaxation training, but it is your responsibility to identify moments in your own preparation and performance cycle to implement this work. We can teach you *how* to reduce your physiological activation and anxiety symptoms but only you know *when* doing so would be beneficial. For you, it might be before a performance, whereas someone else might struggle to relax more between two closely paired competitive events, while another person might have trouble relaxing after a significant event. And people might have different moments during the same performance in which they need to be able to slow their heart rate and relax their muscles. Relaxation—recognizing and releasing unwanted muscle tension—can yield faster injury recovery, promote sleep, reduce insomnia, and facilitate recovery from fatigue among other performance benefits (Baldock et al. 2021).

Approaches to Reducing Activation

This chapter provides a variety of relaxation scripts that you can implement in your training immediately. Many examples of relaxation techniques are available on the Internet; however, they are not all equally effective or supported in the literature. Therefore, this chapter provides as many interventions as possible that are well-researched and supported by evidence.

Relaxation techniques or interventions are typically classified into two approaches: muscle-to-mind strategies and mind-to-muscle techniques. The strategies that you use to control your calm should target and match the dominant anxiety symptoms that you experience before, during, and after performances (Davidson and Schwartz 1977) with the intervention that you employ. After reading chapter 6, you should have an idea of whether you are more affected by cognitive anxiety (e.g., negative, unproductive thoughts about performance, typically classified as a "busy brain") or somatic anxiety (e.g., butterflies in stomach, sweaty palms, rapid heart rate). *Mind-to-muscle* techniques might be most helpful when you are experiencing high levels of cognitive anxiety, whereas *muscle-to-mind* techniques are useful for moments when you are feeling overactivated physically (Baldock et al. 2021). The truth is, however, that often performers experience anxiety problems that affect both their physical, or somatic, activation as well as their thoughts (e.g., "I can't make this play" or "I hope I don't mess up this presentation"). When that is the case, the most effective interventions target and help reduce both cognitive and somatic symptoms. The key is that the approach should match the intended outcome. For example, there is evidence that athletes and other performers might use muscle-to-mind techniques when they are coping with competitive anxiety and mind-to-muscle strategies during their daily lived experiences (Kudlackova, Eccles, and Dieffenbach 2013).

Along with the two dominant approaches to relaxation techniques, there are two additional skills one must also develop, namely, the ability to completely or totally relax and the ability to initiate momentary relaxation. The ability to completely relax helps athletes and performers get to sleep or return to sleep faster or to completely reset between more closely connected performances. Momentary relaxation can be done quickly, on the spot, and in performance and offers brief feelings of relaxation that might be useful before performing a specific skill like a corner kick in soccer, free throw in basketball, or just before walking on stage to give a keynote presentation. Both of these skills are necessary for achieving high levels of performance. Complete or total relaxation can help a performer recover quickly after one performance and get the most out of their rest time before the next performance and might also facilitate deep sleep in the nights leading up to competition. On the other hand, momentary relaxation is useful in lowering activation just before important evaluative moments in a given performance domain or in important situations within a specific competition. Developing this second skill can help a performer reduce muscle tension and cognitive worries and doubt, both crucial for good performance.

Francois Nel/Getty Images

The point of this text is to demonstrate the efficacy for using a variety of mental skills in numerous ways to help you achieve your desired performance outcomes. Other mental skills and strategies are presented throughout this text that could help either to increase activation or decrease activation. In this chapter, we focus on relaxation techniques and how they can be used to reduce activation levels and enhance feelings of calm. Each of the two approaches to relaxation (muscle-to-mind and mind-to-muscle) will be outlined, and interventions within each group will be offered.

Muscle-to-Mind Relaxation Techniques

Muscle-to-mind relaxation techniques target the physical signs and symptoms associated with somatic anxiety. In other words, these strategies will help a performer slow their breathing or relax and release the tension in their muscles that might result from experiencing a stressful situation. The idea behind these interventions is that if a performer can relax their body, then their cognitive worry or apprehension will decrease as well. This connection is based on the common tendency of athletes equating heightened levels of physical activation as cause for worry, anxiety, or apprehension. Each of the techniques in this section might help a performer experience either momentary or complete and total relaxation. To become aware of when and for what purpose each intervention might be most useful is an important feature of this chapter.

The two major types of relaxation strategies outlined in this section are breathing exercises and progressive relaxation.

We encourage you to learn about each technique, practice each, and then decide which to train first. Once you have become skilled in one strategy or technique, revisit this chapter and move to the next.

Breathing Exercises

Learning to breathe properly can either activate or calm and relax your body. You can use the following two breathing exercises to slow your heart rate and calm yourself. Rather than engaging in short, shallow, rapid chest breathing, as people commonly do during high-pressure or stressful situations, using these techniques will help you learn to decrease physical activation by taking full, slow diaphragmatic breaths, known as abdominal or belly breathing. The first step in any breathing exercise, and most relaxation techniques in general, is to become aware of what it feels like to engage in diaphragmatic breathing.

To attempt this type of breath control right now, put one hand over your chest and the other hand over your navel. Now take a full inhalation through your nose. You want to feel your abdomen expanding and filling with air before you notice your chest moving. You should notice the air moving up from your abdomen and up through your chest, and then as you bring the air through your lungs, you will notice your shoulder blades widen. All of this movement happens continuously as you inhale. The key is to notice the location of the breath and become more aware of how it begins around your navel and then moves up toward the chest and shoulder. As you exhale, the reverse occurs. You experience your shoulder blades lowering and chest letting air out first, and then you notice the air being forced out of your abdominal area as your belly retracts.

Take three or four diaphragmatic breaths before reading further. Now that you have engaged in diaphragmatic breathing, try the breathing exercises described in the sidebar on page 109.

Learning to control your breath is one of the quickest and most effective strategies for controlling anxiety and activation. And yet, breathing exercises are often overlooked. Breathing in (inhaling) increases muscle tension, while breathing out (exhaling) releases that tension, so learning to control when and how you take a breath can be useful (Weinberg and Gould 2019). Discus throwers, for example, who learn to exhale as they release the disc might increase the distance of their throw and doing so requires consistent practice. Baldock and colleagues (2021) recommend that athletes and performers engage in 30 to 40 deep breaths each day or engage in one breathing exercise every day (or both) to continue with this training. The key is to make focused breathing a habit. Connecting this form of breathing with everyday tasks is one way to integrate breath control into your lived experiences and to ensure that you become aware of and release tension as needed and under your own control.

PUT IT INTO PRACTICE

Four-Square Breathing

In this exercise, you will create a square while you engage in slow, full diaphragmatic breathing.

- As you inhale, slowly count to 4 (count evenly throughout the inhalation process).
- Hold your breath for four seconds.
- Slowly exhale as you count to 4 (count evenly throughout the exhalation process).
- Once all of the air is smoothly forced out, count to 4 again.
- Imagine drawing one line of the square for each inhalation or exhalation.
- Repeat the process until the square is complete.
- At the end of this process, you are likely to experience enhanced relaxation and a slower breathing rate.

This exercise can be used before training and evaluative situations.

One-to-Five Breathing

- Count to 5 as you inhale while taking a slow, full diaphragmatic breath (1, 2, 3, 4, 5).
- "See" the number with each inhalation.
- During each exhalation, think "I am calm and relaxed."
- On the second breath, repeat that process starting with the 2 (2, 2, 3, 4, 5). Repeat for 3 through 5 (3, 2, 3, 4, 5; 4, 2, 3, 4, 5, and so on).
- The entire exercise should take one to two minutes and should result in enhanced relaxation.

This exercise can be used before training and evaluative situations.

Abbreviated Five-to-One Breathing

- Count backward from 5 as you inhale while taking a slow, full diaphragmatic breath (5, 4, 3, 2, 1).
- Focus on expanding the belly as you inhale slowly, evenly, and fully.
- During each exhalation, think "Calm and relaxed."
- On the second breath, repeat process, starting with 4 (4, 3, 2, 1 as you inhale). Repeat for 3 through 5 (3, 2, 1; 2, 1).
- The entire exercise should take less than 90 seconds and should result in enhanced relaxation.

This exercise can also be used before training and evaluative situations depending on athlete preference.

Progressive Relaxation

Jacobson (1938) constructed the progressive relaxation technique that forms the foundation for many strategies in this chapter. There are multiple forms of progressive relaxation, and they all involve systematically tensing and relaxing muscle groups throughout the body until a sense of total physical relaxation is achieved. Jacobson believed that it was impossible to be both tense and relaxed at the same time and, as a result, if people could become aware of when their body was tense and what a lack of tension felt like, then they could re-create those experiences as needed and under their own control.

In active progressive relaxation (PR), sometimes called progressive muscle relaxation (PMR), every muscle group has a contraction, or tension, phase, in which the muscle is contracted and held for approximately five seconds, and a relaxed phase, in which tension is released. The relaxation phase for each muscle group should last for 20 to 30 seconds before you move to the next muscle group. During the relaxation phase, direct your attention to what the muscle feels like when there is no tension. Try active progressive relaxation by reviewing the script in the following sidebar.

PUT IT INTO PRACTICE

Active Progressive Relaxation

Find a comfortable position and either sit or lie down. Close your eyes if you choose. Be sure your body feels comfortable and supported before starting this training. Remove all jewelry, and loosen or remove outer clothing that restricts you (e.g., jacket, shoes). If you are prone to back problems, it may be best to elevate your knees and rest them on a chair, backpack, or stack of pillows. Bending and resting the knees in an elevated position will help to flatten the spine on the floor and relieve pressure on the back.

- Begin by taking a deep breath and noticing the feeling of air filling your lungs. Pause.
- Release the breath slowly and let the tension leave your body.
- Take another deep breath in and hold. Pause.
- Again, slowly breathe out to release the air.
- Continue taking slow, deep breaths from your belly as you continue this relaxation training.

For the next several minutes, you will tense and then relax each muscle group or body part. As you work your way through the body, be aware of discomfort while tensing a particular muscle group. If you notice discomfort or signs of injury, relax the muscles, take a couple of deep, diaphragmatic breaths, and then move to the next muscle group.

- Continue to take long, slow complete inhalations and then slowly exhale all of the air out of your lungs.
- Breathe in. Pause. Breathe out.
- Guide your attention to the muscles in your arms, hands, and fingers.

Hands

- Make a fist and clench your fingers together. Feel all of the muscles in your arms squeezing together. (Hold this tension for 5 to 7 seconds.)
- Relax. Allow your hands to open and lie on your lap or by your side, with palms open and facing up. Pause for 15-20 seconds.
- Clench your fingers and hands into a fist one more time. Hold that tension for 5 to 7 seconds.
- Relax and pause for 20 to 30 seconds. Notice how relaxed your hands feel.

Next bring your attention to your upper arms and biceps.

Upper Arms and Biceps

- Bend your elbows and clench your fists. Hold the tension in your biceps muscles. Feel them firing and tightening for 5 to 7 seconds.
- Relax and allow your arms to gently fall and rest on your lap or by your side. Pause for 15 to 20 seconds.
- Tense your biceps again and hold for 5 to 7 seconds.
- Relax and pause for 20 to 30 seconds.

Continue taking long, slow complete breaths as you bring your awareness to your shoulders and the muscles in your upper back.

Shoulders and Upper Back

- Slowly raise your arms straight out in front of you. Notice the muscles in your arms begin to tense as you lift them.
- Make a fist and clench your fingers together. Feel all of the muscles in your upper arms, shoulders, and back squeeze together. Hold for 5 to 7 seconds.
- Relax for 15 to 20 seconds.
- Again, stretch your arms out in front of you and hold that tension for 5 to 7 seconds.
- Relax and allow your arms to gently fall by your sides. Pause for 20 to 30 seconds.

Notice how relaxed and loose the muscles in your upper arms, forearms, and hands are. Your palms and fingers are relaxed.

All of the tension is released in this area. Let it all go.

As you continue to breathe, feel more of your body letting go.

Slowly, bring your focus and attention toward your neck and up to your face—your forehead, eyes, and jaw.

> continued

Active Progressive Relaxation > *continued*

Forehead

- Become aware of the tension in your forehead and scalp.
- Wrinkle your forehead by raising your eyebrows and hold for 5 to 7 seconds.
- Relax and pause for 15 to 20 seconds.
- Raise your eyebrows again. Hold that tension for 5 to 7 seconds.
- Relax and notice the sense of calm and relaxation in your forehead. Pause for 20 to 30 seconds.

Eyes

- Bring your awareness to the muscles around your eyes and cheeks.
- Lower your eyebrows and squint your eyes. Notice the tension in your forehead and your eyes. Hold for 5 to 7 seconds.
- Relax and pause for 15 to 20 seconds.
- Again, squint your eyes and furrow your brow. Hold for 5 to 7 seconds.
- Relax and feel the tension around your eyes and cheeks release. Pause for 20 to 30 seconds.

Jaw

- Now bring your awareness to your jaw and begin to clench your teeth. Feel the tension in your jaw and cheeks. Hold for 5 to 7 seconds.
- Relax and pause for 15 to 20 seconds.
- Now, clench your jaw and clench your teeth together one more time. Hold for 5 to 7 seconds.
- Relax and pause for 20 to 30 seconds. Feel that sense of relaxation in your jaw and cheeks.

Tongue

- Bring your tongue up to the roof of your mouth like you're going to say the letter N.
- Press your tongue into the roof of your mouth as hard as you can and hold for 5 to 7 seconds.
- Relax and pause for 15 to 20 seconds.
- Press your tongue into the roof of your mouth one more time and hold for 5 to 7 seconds.
- Relax and pause for 20 to 30 seconds. Allow your tongue to relax gently in the bottom of your mouth.

Mouth

- Bring your attention to your mouth and lips.
- Press your lips together as tight as they can go. Hold for 5 to 7 seconds.
- Relax and pause for 15 to 20 seconds.

- Press your lips together and feel the tension around your mouth and face. Hold for 5 to 7 seconds.
- Relax and pause for 20 to 30 seconds.
- Let your mouth and facial muscles relax completely, with your lips slightly parted.

Neck

- Now bring your awareness to your neck—the muscles in the back of your neck in particular.
- Press your head back into an imaginary wall and hold for 5 to 7 seconds.
- Relax and pause for 15 to 20 seconds.
- Again, press your head backward and tighten your neck muscles. Hold for 5 to 7 seconds.
- Relax and pause for 20 to 30 seconds.

Shoulders

- Bring your attention to your shoulder muscles and the muscles in your neck.
- As you slowly draw in a full belly breath, pull your shoulders up toward your ears and squeeze these muscles firmly for 5 to 7 seconds.
- Relax and pause for 15 to 20 seconds.
- Pull your shoulders up toward your ears again. Hold that tension in your shoulders for 5 to 7 seconds.
- Relax and pause for 20 to 30 seconds. Allow your contracted muscles to become loose and limp.

Chest

- Feel yourself becoming more and more deeply relaxed.
- Now focus on your chest.
- To tighten your chest and shoulder muscles, press or push the palms of your hands together. Hold for 5 to 7 seconds.
- Relax and pause for 15 to 20 seconds.
- Press your palms together again. Feel the squeeze and tightness in your chest. Hold for 5 to 7 seconds.
- Relax and pause for 20 to 30 seconds. Concentrate on the relaxation in your chest.

Abdomen

- Now bring your awareness to your abdomen.
- Draw in a complete, deep breath and then tighten the abdominal muscles.
- Imagine you are trying to touch your belly button to your spine. Hold for 5 to 7 seconds.

> continued

Active Progressive Relaxation > *continued*

- Relax and pause for 15 to 20 seconds.
- Tighten your abdominal muscles again, pulling your belly button to your spine. Hold for 5 to 7 seconds.
- Relax and pause for 20 to 30 seconds.

Back

- Bring your awareness to the muscles in your lower back.
- Arch your back slightly and tighten these muscles. Hold for 5 to 7 seconds.
- Relax and pause for 15 to 20 seconds.
- Arch your back slightly and tighten these muscles again. Hold for 5 to 7 seconds.
- Relax and pause for 20 to 30 seconds.

Now tense and tighten all of the muscles in your upper body. Squeeze all of your muscles. Feel the tension in your face and shoulders and back and arms and hands. Hold for 5 to 7 seconds.

Now relax. Release all of the tension in your upper body. Enjoy this feeling of relaxation in your upper body as you continue complete, slow belly breathing.

Pause for 15 to 20 seconds.

Now, bring your attention to your lower body—your gluteal muscles, thighs and hamstrings, calves, and feet.

Gluteal Area

- Bring your attention to your gluteal muscles.
- Tighten your glutes and hold for 5 to 7 seconds.
- Relax and pause for 15 to 20 seconds.
- Again, tighten your glutes and hold for 5 to 7 seconds.
- Relax and pause for 20 to 30 seconds.

Thighs

- Bring your awareness to your legs. Extend your legs in front of you, raising them about six inches (15 cm) off the ground.
- Tense your thigh muscles and hold for 5 to 7 seconds.
- Relax and pause for 15 to 20 seconds.
- Again, raise your legs and tighten your thigh muscles. Hold for 5 to 7 seconds.
- Relax and pause for 20 to 30 seconds. Enjoy the feeling of relaxation in your legs.

Calves and Feet

- Bring your attention to your feet, and point your toes away from your body. Tense your feet and hold that tension for 5 to 7 seconds.
- Relax and pause for 15 to 20 seconds.

- Again, point your toes and hold that tension in your calves and feet for 5 to 7 seconds.
- Relax and pause for 20 to 30 seconds.
- Now curl your toes as tightly as you can and hold for 5 to 7 seconds.
- Relax and allow your toes to rest apart from one another in your shoes (or socks).
- Relax and pause for 15 to 20 seconds.
- Again, curl your toes tightly and hold for 5 to 7 seconds.
- Release and feel the sense of relaxation in your feet and toes.
- Relax and pause for 20 to 30 seconds.

Now concentrate on each section of the body in order. Focus your attention on that part for 10 to 20 seconds and allow it to relax even more than it is right now.

Begin with the face.

Relax the neck.

Relax the shoulders.

Relax the arms and hands.

Relax the torso.

Relax the hips.

And, finally, relax the legs and feet.

Allow yourself to drift away into a deep state of calm relaxation.

Continue to rest and enjoy this state of total relaxation for a few more moments.

Now as you begin to count backward from 5, start bringing yourself back to a state of alertness. Keep your eyes closed until each breath brings you closer to alertness. Begin to feel your body becoming more aware and calm.

5. Become aware of the blood moving through your body. Feel its energy. You might even feel a tingling in the tips of your fingers and toes. That is perfectly fine. Allow all of these feelings. Pause for 5 to 10 seconds.

4. Feel the blood flow through your organs, your heart, your liver. Feel its warmth and energy. Pause for 5 to 10 seconds.

3. Notice the oxygen that the blood takes to each of your muscles. Feel its light airiness and the energy it brings to your entire body. This might cause a twitch here or there. That is perfectly fine. Enjoy that relaxed yet alert feeling. Pause for 5 to 10 seconds.

2. Feel the blood moving through your brain. It makes you feel alert, excited, and full of energy. Pause for 5 to 10 seconds.

1. Slowly open your eyes as you feel completely refreshed from the relaxation session you just experienced. Pause for 5 to 10 seconds.

Progressive relaxation typically proceeds from either head to toes or from toes to head. The difference between passive and active progressive relaxation (PR) is that during active PR, muscles are tensed first and then relaxed; whereas, in passive PR, a person thinks about the muscle groups, focuses their attention on that particular muscle group, and then releases muscular tension in that area without physically tensing the body part.

The first few sessions of progressive relaxation might take 30 minutes or even longer to complete, but the time demands decrease as you become more skilled (Weinberg and Gould 2019). Once you become both comfortable and proficient at PMR, you can begin combining some of the muscle groups to reduce the amount of time required. For example, rather than tensing or tightening the wrists and hands separately, you can learn to tense and tighten all of the muscles in your arms or your entire upper body at once and then relax those muscles all together. To achieve this combined muscle group capability, relaxation training sessions should ideally occur daily and over several months. Again, the goal of either of the progressive relaxation techniques, active PR or passive PR, is to increase awareness of the tension–relaxation cycle and, over time, for you to develop the skills to relax your muscles and reduce muscular tension on demand and with complete control.

Although active and passive progressive relaxation might take longer initially, over time momentary, progressive muscle relaxation can be completed in less than 30 seconds, right before a motor skill is performed. For example, a triple jumper, before beginning their sprint, could engage in momentary relaxation. This form or type of PMR occurs during performance (e.g., while running a 5K race, just before stepping to the plate as a hitter) (Baldock et al. 2021). Momentary relaxation typically includes a quick body scan from head to toe, during which a performer stops at any muscle group experiencing tension. After becoming aware of the tension, the performer releases that tension and continues the scan of their body. This quick body scan could ideally be finished within a few seconds; however, it can take more than a year of consistent and deliberate practice to develop the ability to release muscle tension that quickly and efficiently and on demand.

Mind-to-Muscle Relaxation Techniques

Unlike the previous set of relaxation interventions, mind-to-muscle techniques target thoughts. Performers learn to control their thoughts in order to relax their physical bodies. Rather than simply adjusting their breath or muscle tension, performers focus on an image or repeat a cue word to stimulate physical relaxation. Mind-to-muscle techniques are particularly useful for performers who experience cognitive anxiety and for performers who in competitive moments are dominated by worry or apprehension and thoughts like "What if I miss?" or "I can't do this." The goal is to quiet the mind so that the body can relax. This approach includes a variety of techniques. We highlight two in this chapter: autogenic training and imagery training.

Autogenic Training

The focus of autogenic training, which was created by Schultz and Luthe (1969), is to produce sensations of warmth and heaviness to elicit a relaxation response. There are six stages of autogenic training: (1) heaviness, (2) warmth, (3) regulation of heart rate, (4) regulation of breathing, (5) abdominal warmth, and (6) cooling of the forehead (Weinberg and Gould 2019). During autogenic training, the participant repeats statements such as "My left leg is heavy," followed by statements like "My left leg is warm." These repetitive statements occur when awareness is brought to various muscle groups throughout the body. Typically, it takes several months of daily 30-minute practice sessions to be able to bring about feelings of warmth and relaxation. Instructions for autogenic training are presented in the following sidebar.

PUT IT INTO PRACTICE

Autogenic Training Script

Autogenic training uses imagery and expressive phrases to cue the body to experience feelings of quietness, heaviness, and warmth. A relaxed state can be produced by reading or listening to a series of suggestive statements such as those that follow.

Begin this autogenic training session by taking several full and complete breaths. Make sure that the exhalation is longer than the inhalation. With each breath cycle (one inhalation plus one exhalation equals one cycle), notice the increase in calmness and relaxation. We recommend taking four to five complete breath cycles prior to beginning autogenic training practice. After completing the breathing warm-up, repeat each phrase three times.

- I feel quiet.
- I am beginning to feel relaxed.
- My feet feel heavy and relaxed.
- My ankles, knees, and hips feel heavy and relaxed.
- My chest and abdominal area feel relaxed and quiet.
- My hands, arms, and shoulders feel heavy and relaxed.
- My neck, jaw, and forehead feel relaxed, smooth, and calm.
- My whole body feels quiet, heavy, comfortable, and relaxed.

Pause to feel the quietness, heaviness, and warmth for one minute. Then continue on with the phrases:

> continued

Autogenic Training > *continued*

- I am completely relaxed.
- My arms and hands are heavy and warm.
- I feel quiet and centered.
- My entire body is relaxed.
- My hands are warm.
- Warmth is flowing into my hands . . . they are warm . . . warm . . . warm.
- I notice the warmth flowing down my arms into my hands.
- My hands are warm, heavy, and relaxed.

Pause to feel the quietness, heaviness, and warmth for one minute. Then continue on with the phrases:

- My whole body feels quiet, warm, and relaxed.
- My mind is quiet.
- My mind and body feel serene and still.
- My thoughts are turned inward. I am at ease.
- I imagine and experience myself relaxed, comfortable, and still.
- My mind is calm and quiet.
- I feel a sense of quietness, calm, and warmth.

Feel the quietness, heaviness, and warmth for one minute.

Consistent practice is necessary to achieve proficiency in autogenic training. Over time, you may find that you only need to repeat each sentence once or twice to achieve a calm, pleasant, and relaxed state.
Adapted from Dr. J.H. Schultz (1969).

Imagery Training

Once you have become skilled in autogenic training, you might try imagery relaxation to produce feelings of calmness and complete relaxation. You learned about imagery and its many uses earlier in this text. You can use the imagery relaxation script in the sidebar on pages 119-121 to create a sense of calm by imaging yourself in a preferred place of comfort and relaxation. The exercise highlights the comfort that might come from imaging yourself floating on a cloud, but any type of imagery that is calming or relaxing (a warm beach day, a serene path in the woods) could be used as part of this technique. Select images that will bring your preferred sense of relaxation.

PUT IT INTO PRACTICE

Imagery Relaxation Script

Find a relaxed position—lying down is best—and get comfortable.

First, relax your body. Start at the top of your head, and allow a feeling of relaxation to begin. Feel the relaxation grow with each breath you take.

Inhale. Relax your scalp and head. Exhale. Let the tension release even more.

Breathe in relaxation . . . exhale all the tension.

Take another breath, drawing in relaxation all the way down to your feet. From the top of your scalp to the bottom of your feet, breathe in relaxation. And breathe out tension and tightness in your body.

Now you are feeling deeply relaxed. Deeply relaxed and calm.

Begin to create a picture in your mind. Imagine that you are floating on a soft, fluffy white cloud.

Feel the surface beneath you becoming softer . . . more cloudlike. Feel the cloud rising out of the surface you are on, surrounding you in its protective support. Soon you are floating on just the cloud.

Let it rise a little farther, taking you with it. See the walls and ceiling around you disappearing as you float into the sunny sky . . . drifting on the cloud.

Feel the cloud beneath you. It is soft but supportive. Feel your body relax into the cloud. Experience the cloud supporting your whole body.

Notice each place where your body is touching the cloud. Feel how soft and comfortable the cloud is. It is almost like floating in the air.

Notice how the cloud feels. It might be a little bit cool and moist like fog. Your body relaxes and sinks into the cloud. It is a wonderful feeling.

The sky above you is bright blue, sunny, and inviting. You are warmed by the sun's rays shining down peacefully.

Notice the other clouds in the sky, floating gently. They might be above you or floating lazily right beside you.

Start to create an image in your mind of where you are. You might be floating just barely above the ground. You can choose to float wherever you like. If you enjoy being high up, you can let your cloud rise into the sky. It is very safe . . . calming . . . and relaxing.

You are relaxed.

You are floating on your supportive, light, cool cloud and are fully supported as you allow your body to sink farther into the cloud. You're surrounded by its protective embrace.

See the sights around you as you float on your cloud. Imagine the green grass below, gently blowing in the wind. Notice the smell of fresh-cut grass as the green fades as you rise into the sky. From above, the grass

> *continued*

Imagery Relaxation Script > *continued*

looks like a soft carpet. Pay attention to the wind creating gentle waves in the grass as if it were water.

Feel the light, crisp air as you float through the atmosphere. Notice the leaves on the trees whispering in the gentle breeze.

As you gaze below, notice the housetops, country roads, and rolling hills. Notice in the distance how the hills appear almost yellow . . . slightly hazy as the sun shines on the roads below.

Listen to the quiet breeze as the wind gently pushes your cloud along. Hear the birds communicating back and forth with one another. Their chirping is relaxing and peaceful.

Continue floating on a cloud, enjoying the sights and sounds around you. The air smells clean and fresh.

Continue floating on a cloud, drifting, rising even higher if you wish.

The ground below you appears like a patchwork quilt: green grass, golden fields, blue patches of water . . . rivers and lakes and oceans. Bring your cloud down, closer to the ocean and listen to the sounds of the water as the waves move effortlessly—in and out—along the coastline.

Just as the water moves gently, so is your cloud moving you through the air.

Notice the shadow your cloud makes and how it drifts silently across the ground below.

Relax in this beautiful scene, floating on a cloud.

As you lie on your cloud, look up at the sky above you. The clouds that were high above you are much closer now. Notice a few of the clouds around you gently passing by. Some of them are so close you can touch them.

As you reach your arm out, you can feel the light, soft fluffiness of the cloud next to yours. It is cool to the touch, and your hand gently passes right through the gas and moisture of that neighboring cloud. As you bring your arm back to your side, you notice it is slightly wet and cooler than before. You are aware of the mist on your hand.

You can look down on the clouds you just passed and see the white, fluffy peaks and valleys of these clouds below. It looks like perfect snow. Looking around below you, it is as if you were above a land of snow.

You can even rise higher still and pass right through the clouds above. Feel the mist on your cheeks as you rise through the clouds. Around you it is a glorious white, like fog. The sun shines through just enough that the white all around you glows vibrantly. Up here on your cloud, it is quiet and peaceful. There is no rush. Only calm and peace.

Lie back on your cloud, floating and relaxing on your cloud.

Feel the cloud beneath you and the warmth from the sun above you. You glide through the air effortlessly, feeling fully supported.

Take your cloud wherever you wish . . . higher, lower . . . Drift wherever you want to go.

Enjoy the sights and sounds and smells around you, flying wherever you wish.

(pause)

Continue floating. Imagine wherever you would like to go. Your cloud can take you there.

You can travel anywhere you wish. You can look down on forests, the countryside, the ocean, mountains, even your own home. Float wherever you like.

(pause)

Enjoy the sights and sounds and smells around you . . . floating on a cloud.

You are so relaxed . . . at peace.

(pause)

Now it is time to return to your day. Let your cloud take you there. Feel your cloud flying through the sky back to where you need to go.

Let your cloud lower you back toward the ground.

Feel the cloud meld with the chair or floor, the surface you are on. Feel the cloud slowly disappear as the real surface becomes more solid beneath you.

Gradually come back to the present. Begin to notice your surroundings. Hear the sounds around you. Become more and more aware and alert.

Wiggle your fingers and toes, feeling your body reawaken. Shrug your shoulders. Move your arms and legs. Turn your head.

When you are ready, open your eyes and look around. See your surroundings. You can now return to your day feeling refreshed and alert.

A Note on Implementation

It can be tempting to believe that you do not need to learn how to relax on command, that because your preferred performance state includes some level of activation, you do not need to know how to calm yourself. Although it might seem obvious that performing a surgical procedure, playing violin, or landing a jump on the balance beam are motor skills in which relaxation is needed, it might be less apparent why a hockey player sprinting on ice, a football player tackling an opponent, or a cricket player bowling might want to relax or calm their activation. Previously, we mentioned that preferred activation zones might differ based on the competitive moment, positions, individual performers, and other factors. In addition to each of these factors, which all offer a rationale for learning to create a sense of calm, performers who can create a complete sense of relaxation might also become more sensitive to their somatic (or physical) experiences and aware of when they are rising, thus being able to intervene more quickly and appropriately.

To develop and improve the implementation of activation reduction skills, performers must practice them consistently and over time. Rather than coaches shouting "calm down" to their athletes right before a major competitive moment or a performer attempting to reduce their activation only in moments when they need to be calm, relaxation techniques should be taught and learned in a series of steps or phases (see the following Chalk Talk sidebar). Each phase or step should be assessed and evaluated by the performer and in consultation with the sport psychology practitioner with whom the performer is working. The purpose of these check-ins or evaluations is to ensure proper use and to address issues that emerge as the performer moves closer to integrating the technique into their daily, lived experiences and then into more stressful and evaluative situations.

The goal of each step in the Chalk Talk sidebar is to add or increase pressure or stress during the relaxation training session progression. For example, in the first step, the performer encounters almost no stress or pressure. They would be sitting or lying in a dark room with relatively little, if any, noise. As they practice the particular relaxation technique and feel comfortable being able to control their activation levels in that setting, they move to the next step or phase of training. Once a performer can implement the relaxation technique in a quiet, dark room, a practitioner might start adding noise or distractions while the performer attempts to control their activation through the same technique in the same room. Eventually the performer practices in a lighted room, then,

Chalk Talk

Quick Hits for Implementing Relaxation Techniques

Phases of implementing relaxation techniques:

- ☐ Practice the technique seated (or lying down) in a comfortable position in a quiet, stress-free environment.
- ☐ Use the relaxation technique in a nonsporting, stressful environment.
- ☐ Implement the technique in a practice or training session.
- ☐ Integrate the relaxation technique into competition or performance.

Elsa/Getty Images

perhaps, in a real-world, nonsport setting. Then practice might progress in that same nonsport setting but with additional disruptions. Once a performer can consistently replicate feelings of relaxation and calm in one phase, they can move to the next. The theme is consistent success before advancement. Systematically adding pressure or stress in a new phase, after performers have consistently replicated feelings of relaxation in the previous phase, ensures they are able to cope with pressure during competition and relax or reduce their activation levels appropriately in each of those moments (Driskell, Sclafani, and Driskell 2014; Stoker et al. 2016). If problems occur when adding new pressures or demands, the athlete can simply go back to a previous level of control and success and then revisit the added pressure situation and progression.

There are guidelines for how long this process might take, and the timing is related to your skill and the specific technique you are practicing. For example, you might be able to successfully integrate breath control into your performance domain more quickly than you can master autogenic training. Rather than seeking a general time frame for mastery, recognize and respect that, just like physical skills, practicing relaxation techniques requires consistent training over time and in formal and systematic ways. You cannot occasionally practice these techniques and expect to be able to relax muscles or calm your mind on demand, especially when it matters most. To be able to accomplish that goal, you must move through these steps and honestly assess your progress consistently to ensure accurate and appropriate implementation. It might take six months to a year to be able to relax on demand, but, when trained consistently and once you are skilled in this technique, you will experience significant personal and performance benefits. In fact, in a review of 64 studies on this topic, 81 percent found stress was reduced, cognitive appraisals of stressors were modified, and performers engaged in effective coping behaviors (Rumbolt, Fletcher, and Daniels 2012). Many factors influence performance and developing multiple mental skills and strategies is necessary for achievement, but this evidence suggests that learning to control physical activation through relaxation techniques is an important element to add to your game.

Conclusion

Our hope throughout this text is that you come to recognize and appreciate that practicing and developing your mental game is an important way to separate yourself from other performers. The most elite, high-achieving performers train every element of their performance across all four pillars of sport. When compared with college- or university-level athletes and recreational competitors, for example, professional athletes used activation reduction techniques more often and more consistently each week (Kudlackova, Eccles, and Dieffenbach 2013). Mental skills training is professional work. As long as you are living and breathing and performing in various arenas of your life, you will need a strong mental game. This chapter outlined several strategies to practice relaxation techniques and train yourself to be able to calm down on cue. While you do not have control over every situation or competitive moment you might find yourself in, you do have complete control over your ability to activate and deactivate yourself so that you can perform well across challenging circumstances.

Remember, how you view stressful situations matters. It is important to interpret your resulting activation and anxiety levels as facilitative and helpful for your performance (Thomas, Hanton, and Maynard 2007). To both appropriately interpret and control your activation, you need to be skilled at both activating and relaxing yourself. We believe if you systematically practice the strategies presented in chapter 6 and this chapter, you will be able to access your preferred performance zone more consistently and perform well even when you are outside of your preferred zone. As always, keep training your mental skills!

CHAPTER 8

Revving the Engine

The quote from track and field legend Jackie Joyner-Kersee highlights the idea of intrinsic motivation, which means to strive inwardly to be competent and master the task at hand (Weinberg and Gould 2019). And it is certainly true that many performers tout the positive effects of developing an internal drive for success, knowledge, and enjoyment. We, too, argue that it is unlikely that people would be able to sustain the high levels of commitment required over years, even decades, in pursuit of their goals if they were not motivated to do so. The task then is to figure out what you are motivated to pursue, why you are motivated in that area, and how (or in what ways) you are motivated. It is perhaps equally important to also understand the factors and processes that interfere with sustained and internal motivation. This chapter explains strategies that will help you develop intrinsic motivation (or help others to cultivate it for themselves) and how, in so doing, you will be prepared to endure, overcome, invest, and persevere in pursuit of your goals and dreams.

> The rewards are going to come, but my happiness is just loving the sport and having fun performing.
>
> Jackie Joyner-Kersee, U.S. heptathlete and long jumper, three-time Olympic gold medalist (heptathlon 1988 and 1992, long jump 1988), gold medalist in 1998 Goodwill Games (heptathlon)

It Starts Within

Whether you run marathons, play a musical instrument, swim on a recreational team, or represent your country on a world stage; whether you are a high-level corporate executive, a librarian, a gastroenterologist, a sixth-grade history teacher, a politician, or a news anchor—all of your pursuits in life are driven by your motivation. Motivation determines whether you seek out or are attracted to a situation, and it affects how much effort you put forth in that situation. For example, some people are drawn to swimming and they make comments suggesting they were not made for land sports, while other people suggest they always loved piano and could never imagine participating in sport. Based on your own personality and capabilities, social and geographic upbringing, as well as the requirements of the task, you likely gravitated to the competitive and performance-related pursuits in which you now engage. And, chances are, you are more motivated to work hard and complete tasks related to your professional interests than you are to invest in other domains where you might be less skilled or less motivated.

Characteristics of High Achievers

According to the sport psychology literature, everyone has two underlying motives that influence their behavior: the need to achieve success and the need to avoid failure (Atkinson and Raynor 1974; Gill 2000). People who are high achievers are motivated to achieve success; they want to compete and have their abilities evaluated, and they worry much less about the possibility of failing. These people tend to prefer tasks and competitive situations that are challenging, moments in which they will only succeed if they perform at a high level. In the National Basketball Association (NBA), Kobe Bryant often talked about wanting to play against Michael Jordan because he knew he would be tested and, win or lose, he would get better. The U.S. women's national ice hockey team wanted to play Team Canada in the gold medal games at Worlds or at the Olympic Games. Why? Because high achievers want to be tested; they want to compete against people and teams that might outperform them. They seek out these challenges because they know that is how they will improve. High achievers also tend to perform at their best when they are being evaluated, when the game is on the line, when the patient is counting on their expertise, or when their boss is observing their performance.

Overall, high achievers are motivated by success, they feel proud of their accomplishments, and they seek out and are motivated by challenges. They perform well when it counts, they are more likely to stick with it and persist in the face of adversity, and they will attribute their performance outcomes to useful and appropriate factors (e.g., attribute success to their competitive strategy). Canadian rower Silken Laumann is the definition of a high achiever. Read a portion of her story in the sidebar on pages 127-128 to gain a better sense of how these characteristics drive thoughts, behaviors, and actions.

Among other aspirations and objectives, people are driven by their desire to feel competent and skilled at a task (Deci and Ryan 1985; 2000; Harter 1978), a point we will return to in the next chapter. For the purpose of this chapter, however, what matters is that, like the experience of Silken Laumann, no one's journey is linear, and no one is born with inherent or insatiable intrinsic motivation. Becoming intrinsically motivated to go for their dreams, cultivating the internal drive to stick with their pursuits, even when other people might give up, is how high achievers separate themselves from low achievers. The good news is that, like the other psychological skills in this book, intrinsic motivation can be learned and developed.

IN THEIR OWN WORDS **The Triumph of the Human Spirit: Silken Laumann**

After winning the single sculls at the World Championship in 1991, Canada's Silken Laumann was favored to win Olympic gold in rowing the following year. After the race, Laumann said, "I think what made that win special was how strong my competitors were and how the headwind did not favor a rower of my size. Usually in a headwind the bigger rower has the advantage. . . . It felt so great to be that good and for a brief moment in time, I really recognized I was at the top of my game."

But, in May, just 10 weeks before the Olympic Games, Laumann was injured in a brutal rowing accident that left her right leg shattered. She was told by doctors she may never walk, let alone row, again. Silken was undeterred. After the first few surgeries, she required a cane to walk. Nevertheless, she persisted. "The power of a dream is that it frees up your imagination to think about the best possible scenario in your life," she said. Twenty-seven days, five operations, and countless hours of grueling rehabilitation later, Laumann was back in her shell, ready to continue her quest for an Olympic medal. On August 2, 1992, she made Canadian sport history and captured the hearts of a nation when she won a bronze medal for herself and her country in the Barcelona Olympic Games. After her race, the *Montreal Gazette* ran a story with this quote: "In ten weeks [Silken Laumann] made the greatest comeback in Canadian sports history, becoming a symbol of hope to all." And Laumann has been quoted as saying, "Success in life comes to those . . . with a vision so strong that obstacles, failures, and loss only act as teachings."

From broken bones to Olympic glory, her story is one of courage, motivation, and the will to persevere. Laumann won three Olympic medals during her career. After writing a few books, including a memoir, Laumann continues to share her belief: "At the end of the day, it's not the medals you remember.

> *continued*

What you remember is the process—what you learn about yourself by challenging yourself, the experiences you share with other people, the honesty, the training demands—those are the things nobody can take away from you."
Based on Laumann (2021).

Silken Laumann is clearly a high achiever, and her story exemplifies the role of intrinsic motivation in helping someone overcome obstacles and, in the face of tremendous odds, continue to struggle and toil in pursuit of their goals until they finally succeed.

"Want to" Versus "Have to"

Often, people believe that developing intrinsic motivation means that the journey or pursuit is always fun or that they will always be happy. The ubiquitous saying "If you do what you love, you'll never work a day in your life" comes to mind. Of course, we believe that it is more likely someone will have fun and enjoy their experience if they develop an internal drive to pursue their chosen performance domain, but the truth is that work and training are neither easy nor fun *all* of the time. There are sacrifices. There are difficulties. It isn't always enjoyable or easy. The reason it is so important to develop intrinsic motivation, then, is that doing so can enhance someone's willingness to sacrifice for a greater purpose and their eagerness to do what it takes to succeed.

Yes, passion matters. Finding a physical activity or type of work or sport that is personally meaningful and important enough to invest in regularly is one aspect of intrinsic motivation. Sidney Crosby, one of the best Canadian professional hockey players and captain of the Pittsburgh Penguins, stated, "I've always had a passion for hockey. You can't just be putting in time, you have to enjoy what you do." But, that passion must also match with your perceived purpose in order to be helpful in driving behavior, especially when your enjoyment is tested, and your pursuit becomes more difficult.

Tying purpose with passion allows you to endure those hard times, to continue focusing on your priorities when it would be easier to take a break. Rather than *having to* get extra reps in after practice or *having to* add weight to the next lifting set or *having to* attend an additional film session with the coach, a performer can begin to *want to* complete those tasks and believe they are meaningful and important to a larger goal. That process is more likely to occur by connecting those choices with their larger purpose or overarching goal to improve in, for example, one of the four pillars of sport performance (i.e., technical, tactical, psychological, physiological). When discussing the work she has done to advance opportunities for girls and women in sport, four-time Olympic medalist and world champion in ice hockey Angela Ruggiero remarked, "That's the awesome part. Little girls now have a chance to look up and see women playing soccer, basketball, and now hockey and know they can win a gold medal, too." And Canadian Tessa Virtue, who along with her ice dance partner, is the most decorated figure skater in Olympic history, noted, "The idea of constantly pursuing something with purpose helps me to stay focused." Both of these athletes' statements edify the idea that connecting purpose and passion adds nobility to the quest.

Rewards Are Tricky

Your intrinsic motivation might be influenced by tangible rewards (e.g., certificate, trophy, scholarship, job offer) as well as how feedback is delivered (e.g., CEO praises you for execution of a task, coach high-fives you after a good play) along with other reinforcers (e.g., earning a day off after performing well, increased playing time). Initially, you might think that rewards, in particular, would be a great way to build or develop intrinsic motivation. For example, a child might not enjoy a particular task like washing the dishes or folding laundry or mowing the lawn, so parents attempt to "sweeten the pot" by offering added allowance money upon completion or providing performance incentives beyond the satisfaction of mastering the skill. These common practices are well meant and familiar. They are often phrased as a form of quid pro quo: "Do this and I'll give you that." These types of rewards are helpful in the short term in that they are motivating; they help drive effort as you take on a new challenge or less-than-thrilling task. And while initially beneficial, over time, tying extrinsic rewards to what should ideally be an intrinsically motivated action can have deleterious, long-term, even lifelong, negative effects on intrinsic motivation.

Take the classic series of studies from Lepper, Greene, and Nisbett (1973) and Lepper and Greene (1975), for example. They studied nursery school children and identified that, at this age, drawing with a felt pen was an intrinsically motivating, fun task. However, when they later paired the task of drawing with felt pens with an external reward (e.g., a good player certificate), within one week, the children began drawing for shorter periods of time unless there was a reward involved. Even preschool-aged children's enjoyment of a task can be negatively affected by rewards. In other words, young children make the connection that coloring is only worthwhile if there is a reward involved. If there is no reward, then they lose interest in the activity. This study underscores the notion that extrinsic rewards can actually decrease intrinsic motivation because they can negatively influence why someone is pursuing or participating in a task. Now, apply this knowledge to sport. Think about how college athletic scholarships or professional contracts might influence behavior and disrupt intrinsic motivation. And, indeed, both positive and negative effects from these rewards on intrinsic motivation have been proven (e.g., Deci and Ryan 1985).

That is not to say that rewards are "bad" or even that they should be eliminated. However, it is important to know *what* rewards to use, *when* to use them, *how to* implement the reward *structure*, and *why* the rewards are being offered (both for yourself and for others). It is a particularly salient issue for sport performers because at all levels of sport—from youth to elite international competition—external rewards dominate the landscape. Two elements dictate how rewards affect motivation (Deci and Ryan 1985):

1. If people perceive a reward as controlling their behavior, then their motivation to perform that skill or behavior will decrease.

2. If people perceive a reward as recognition of their competence and skill, then they will likely feel more motivated to continue engaging in that behavior.

On one hand, promising to reward athletes by eliminating a lifting session early in the morning if they train hard or focus or engage in a specific behavior can be perceived as controlling. When these controlling rewards are given, it is likely that intrinsic motivation will decrease, meaning that athletes, similar to the nursery school children described earlier, will be less likely to engage in desired behaviors unless they are rewarded. On the other hand, rewarding a middle manager with the opportunity to influence company policies or allowing a junior political staffer to introduce a high-profile political candidate can enhance someone's feeling of autonomy or control. That staffer or middle manager is more likely to believe that their behavior and their competent performance led to their reward. As a result, intrinsic motivation increases.

Withholding positive feedback or praise consistently over time and offering primarily negative or critical feedback can be viewed as both controlling and as an indication that the performer is not skilled. Whether an athlete is overly critical of themselves or experiences consistently negative feedback from important people in their lives, over time they are likely to internalize the message of incompetence, and the effect is the same: a decrease in motivation. If, however, the reward is contingent on achievement and recognizes the performer's effort and skill development or personal improvement, then the reward will reinforce motivated behavior. For example, when a Gritty Player of Practice award that is given each week of training during the season (recognizing competence) is paired with a discussion of the significance of the award and the specific actions the athlete took to win the award (reinforcing autonomy and control), then athletes will likely feel motivated to engage in gritty behaviors. There is no question that rewards can be tricky to implement effectively. Carefully considering how you reward yourself and others (why and on what behaviors) is massively important to ensuring the result leads to enhanced, intrinsic motivation and elevated performance.

Self-Reinforcement Strategies

Effectively implementing rewards and self-reinforcement is underappreciated and underused. When a person rewards themselves, they should connect the reward with the effort or accomplishment and to their greater purpose. For example, a shot-putter could choose to stay 20 minutes after practice to tweak their technique in order to generate more force and afterward could identify and reinforce one element of improvement. Thinking "I got 1 percent better today" serves to reinforce that self-selected behavior because it connects their decision to train longer (autonomy) with increased competence. A professional who records how many days during a two-week period they image themselves successfully executing the presentation they will deliver later that month and can connect that behavior with fewer errors in the speech or increased efficiency is reinforcing their own behavior. Actively recognizing the connection between waking up early to image their performance to actual delivery improvements of the presentation is an effective use of rewards. These types of reinforcement can be written, they can be verbal, or they can even be social. Socially sharing with someone important in their life that they completed a task can be reinforcing and motivating.

Train yourself to recognize your motivated behaviors and reinforce them. When you vacuum or dust a room in your house, recognize yourself for that. When you complete the first three items on your list for the day, announce it out loud. When you spend time outside of work finishing a project, pay attention to that moment of accomplishment and appreciate your action. Making the choice to reward yourself with great frequency throughout the day can pay meaningful dividends. Doing so can have a powerful influence on emotions *and* performance. It produces feelings of satisfaction, pride, and appreciation.

That does not mean that you need to reward yourself for accomplishing an easy task. You should not. Further, avoid being the person who finishes a task and then after the fact writes it down just so that they can cross it off. When nurses complete their daily rounds, they would not reinforce themselves for doing what is expected, just as parents or guardians should not reinforce a fifth grader for tying their own shoe. Praising mediocre performance or completion of a simple task is a poor choice of reinforcement because it has no effect on intrinsic motivation. At best, you learn to ignore it and continue performing your job. At worst, you lose credibility with others because of low standards for reinforcement, and the praise itself loses impact. However, when you take initiative and complete a task that others might avoid, or you complete a task at a high level, then it is reward worthy. Recognize what you bring to an achievement domain that others might not or would not be able to replicate. See the sidebar on page 132 for ideas.

> ## PUT IT INTO PRACTICE
> ### Self-Reinforcement Talking Points for Athletes
>
> After a successful performance, you might think or verbalize self-reinforcing comments such as the following:
>
> - I just hit a great cross-court shot!
> - I just outran my opponents, and they couldn't keep up with me.
> - I just took their best hit and kept going. I'm tough!
> - No one watches film like I do. I'll be ready for anything they throw at me.
> - (*After setting up the field for practice*) I can't wait to see the smile on coach's face when they don't have to set up today.
> - (*After making a pass that hits your teammate perfectly, with laces lined up and leading them to their next play*) Boom! They didn't even have to break stride. I love that I can make that play.
> - I can see the play before anyone else. I know what's coming.

Most performers just want to get done with practice, complete their fitness routine, submit the paper, pass the exam. They got done, but they did not get better. When you take actions to improve, notice it. As soon as possible, tie your action with your reinforcement and internalize that feeling of satisfaction, pride, accomplishment. Recognize and reward yourself for doing what others are either unwilling or incapable of doing.

When you exert agency to complete the task well and right, own it. Self-reinforcement strategies serve as a source of agency and feed into your knowledge of your unique competencies. Everyone needs to own what makes them a distinct member of the team or organization, so reinforcing your motivated behaviors, over time, is one way to recognize your unique skills and what Seligman calls your "signature strengths" (Peterson and Seligman 2004). Now that you know the impact of rewards on your motivation, intentionally and appropriately use them in your own performance and in life.

The Power of Anticipatory Self-Reinforcement

Once you have learned about the importance of rewarding yourself, you can start to experience the benefits of *anticipatory self-reinforcement*—feeling the satisfaction and pride in accomplishment *before* you even begin the task. Perhaps you do not love to run or you are not looking forward to running today because it is cold and raining. As you start lacing up your shoes, you think about how much you love how it feels to finish the run. You do not feel like making your bed today, but you smile knowing how satisfying it feels to walk in your bedroom after a long day at work to a room that is tidy and clean. Anticipatory reinforcement is powerful because it can compel you to perform a task or engage in a behavior that you might not do otherwise. In some ways, you are reinforcing a behavior that has not yet occurred. Rather than connecting a behavior with an external reward that controls your behavior (e.g., go for a run so you can eat ice cream tonight), you are intentionally coupling self-directed behavior (going for a run) with internal motivation (the joy you will feel) through anticipatory reinforcement (before you take your first steps out of your house). Leaders (e.g., bosses, medical school deans, teachers, band directors, coaches) also play an important role in encouraging performers to connect a dreaded or challenging task with how they will feel when it is completed to a high standard. See the following sidebar for strategies. In essence, the focus shifts from whether or not you want to do something to thinking about how good it is going to feel.

As has been the case throughout this book, we want the focus to be on rewarding, encouraging, reinforcing, and training yourself in ways that promote excellence. We want your sights set on mastery, on getting 1 percent better each and every day. Reinforce yourself and those around you for taking on and completing hard, challenging, and demanding tasks. And connect those efforts—in moments when you do not want to finish the task well and right—to your purpose, to your *why*. If you are a trial lawyer, how good will it feel and how valuable will it be to your

PUT IT INTO PRACTICE

Ideas for Connecting Behaviors With Appropriate Anticipatory Reinforcement

Encourage athletes and performers to "Think how good it will feel when X is complete." According to Dr. Hacker, this phrase can direct performers' focus away from the fatigue or dread they might feel before engaging in the behavior and direct their focus toward the positive feelings that will result. It also eliminates the focus on the decision-making process. It assumes that they *will do* this behavior and can anticipate a feeling of accomplishment and pride once completed. The following are sample responses:

- When a student is struggling with motivation to study, a teacher or a faculty advisor might say "Think how good it is going to feel to walk into the exam room feeling prepared and ready as opposed to hoping that a specific question is not on the exam."

- When an athlete is struggling to pay attention during a film session, a coach might say "Think how good it's going to feel to match up with this opponent knowing you have mentally and tactically prepared for their dominant moves and strategies. You're going to have their number. What an advantage!"

competence to practice your closing arguments three more times? Or as a science student or medical worker, focus on the feeling of accomplishment you experience when you choose to stay in the lab on Friday and Saturday nights to practice even after you passed the lab because your goal was not just to get done but to get better. Choose to do something hard each day and each week that will bring you closer to your goal, your vision for yourself. Then, pay attention to the fact that you did it. As legendary basketball coach John Wooden said, "If a task is once begun, never leave it 'till it's done. Be the labor great or small, do it well or not at all." Reinforce your efforts to master hard, monotonous, tedious tasks. Your purpose is not to graduate and become an anesthesiologist, a college athlete, or a student at a top university; if you are reading this book, your goal is to master your skills and become the best version of yourself in your respective performance domain. Pay attention to when you are training your fitness on your own, when you are in the stacks of books in the library on your own, and when you are choosing to do what other people are avoiding. It is the mastering of small, mundane tasks that can produce oversized results. It is the aggregation of marginal gains over time that will bring about true excellence. Recognize and congratulate your self-motivated behaviors.

Peathegee Inc/Tetra images RF/Getty Images.

Creating Successful Habits

Once you learn how to reward and engage in self-reinforcement strategies for taking action toward your goals and your greater purpose, the magic is in creating a habit of these efforts. Why engage in behaviors or pursuits that are challenging, that involve struggling and persevering without a guarantee of success? Take proofreading and rewriting the information in these chapters, for example. As the coauthors of this text, we could have finished and sent the manuscript to the editors without reviewing each chapter multiple times both individually and together, but for us, the answer was not in what had to be done, it was about ensuring that the message was as tight and polished as possible. We spent time writing and rewriting and talking about adjustments because we wanted to ensure that each chapter was based in the scholarly literature and was easy to digest and implement. Therefore, the power is in shifting the focus from achieving minimum competencies to taking responsibility for choices that will increase maximum capabilities and move people toward excellence. For many, this shift requires a new set of behaviors.

What the research shows is that to consistently do hard tasks well, you need to engage in the habit loop or habit cycle (Carden and Wood 2018; Wood and Neal 2007). A habit loop involves three separate elements to help you engage in a new behavior or routine. First, you identify the new behavior or routine. For example, you want to be physically active in the evening each night after work. Identify a specific behavior you want to start or establish. Then create a routine ahead of time. In this instance, you decide to lay your shoes and training gear on the table by your front door the night before so that as soon as you walk in from your workday you will set down your briefcase, pick up your training gear, and immediately go change. You have eliminated making the decision on the spot, when your motivation may have waned, and created an effective behavioral cue that makes it easier to say "yes" to the new behavior. The third step is to create a list of rewards that you could use after you have engaged in this new behavior and select one or two that you think will help you pay attention to how satisfying it feels to engage in and to complete this new behavioral choice. To develop a habit, you must pair those three components: a cue for the behavior, a behavioral routine, and a reward (see figure 8.1). Over time—when you are cued and then pair the cue with

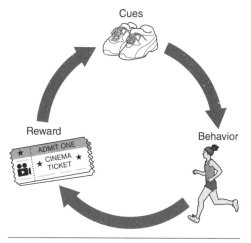

FIGURE 8.1 Habit loop.

a routine and then reward the accomplishment—those three separate processes begin to link together and become a single unit. Cue, routine, reward. Cue, routine, reward. Eventually, the extrinsic reward you might have started with becomes less important (e.g., If I work out, I get a latte in the morning). Soon, the reward is successfully and consistently completing the habit cycle, which becomes its own self-reinforcing strategy. The goal becomes to pair your choice and decision to establish a new behavior with salient cues and rewards so that ultimately, you feel proud about your actions and recognize the value in establishing this new routine for a greater purpose.

According to Wood and Neal (2007) and Carden and Wood (2018), these are the five most common cues:

1. A time of day (e.g., Each night at 6, I will work out.)
2. A particular place (e.g., When I am at the park, I will do 10 step-ups on park benches. When I am in the library, I will study my class notes.)
3. A particular emotion (e.g., When I am frustrated, I will clean my home office. When I am bored, I will go for a walk.)
4. Other people or another person (e.g., When I see my neighbor, I know we are going for a walk. When I see my professor, I know we will work on the literature review.)
5. A preceding or preestablished behavior (e.g., When teaching a child to brush their teeth in the morning, pair that with washing their hands because they are already engaged in that behavior.)

It is always best if you have more than one cue. For example, if you meet your coach or training partner at a specific time each day, then you are even more likely to engage in the new behavior because you have two cues: person and time of day.

Habit formation is one way to pursue excellence and avoid mediocrity. You start with a behavior you want to or need to perform. You make the choice to complete the task, and you create a habit cycle. It may or may not be intrinsically motivating to start, but you purposely tie your cue, routine, and reward together. Over time, that behavior and that routine become intrinsically satisfying and meaningful in your life. You can no longer retreat to your previous behavior because now, after forming the new habit, you are motivated and inspired to excel at it. Imagining it any other way is not enjoyable. You like this new you, this new way of doing things, this new standard. Of course, occasionally, a habit loop is disrupted before it has enough time to solidify, and then you might have to start the process again. But, if you stick with it, the behavior, completing the task, will become enjoyable for its own sake. And when that transformation happens, it feels like magic. You will not resort to previous or lower standards, and you will feel undeterred in your steadfast commitment to a greater purpose and vision. Like all of the skills and strategies presented in this book, it is important to intentionally plan a habit loop so that you can implement it in your daily and performance life effectively. See the worksheet on this page.

The Role of Attributions

Many people are unaware of attributions and how critical they are to past performance assessments, current performance, and future motivation. A simple definition is that *attributions* are the reasons people generate for their outcomes in performance (Weinberg and Gould 2019). So even if you have never heard of an *attribution*, you have most certainly attributed your performance successes and failures. We all do and we do so all of

---

Performer-Centered Implementation Worksheet

Developing Habits to Accomplish Hard Tasks

The purpose of this worksheet is to help you construct a habit loop that will, over time, lead you to feel more intrinsically motivated to complete a self-identified new behavior or higher-standard task.

Directions

1. Identify one new behavior that you are not engaged in consistently but is important to you. You may or may not feel intrinsically motivated to engage in this behavior, but it is one that you know is important for you to master as you continue to pursue your purpose with passion.

2. Create a list of 10 rewards that you find valuable and meaningful. Remember, avoid rewarding yourself with food or punishing yourself with physical activity. Examples of rewards are buying a new book, going on a hike with a friend, exploring a new region around where you live.

3. Establish one or more cues that will trigger that behavioral routine (time of day, place, emotion, other people, already established routine).

4. After you have completed the previous steps, identify three of the most significant challenges or barriers that might act as impediments that prevent you from engaging in this new behavior. And, even more importantly, identify a strategy to overcome each obstacle you identified.

When you are finished, put a visual, written reminder of your responses in key places throughout your house or office or training facility to remind you of your self-selected habit loop and your strategies for ensuring your success.

From C. Hacker and M. Mann, *Achieving Excellence: Mastering Mindset for Peak Performance in Sport and Life* (Champaign, IL: Human Kinetics, 2023).

---

the time, either consciously or unconsciously. Athletes try to figure out why they did not start during a particular competition, why they made or missed a shot on goal, or why they played better than usual in a particular contest. Orthopedic surgeons try to find meaning in why one ACL repair might have gone smoothly while another surgery was more difficult than anticipated. Businesspeople might ask themselves "Why did my direct report resist my request for territory reconfiguration?" Teachers attempt to decipher why some students understood the lesson while others seemed confused or uninspired. The point is that we all attempt to explain why an outcome or a performance unfolded as it did, good or bad. Every person in every achievement domain is searching for reasons that explain the outcome.

The problem with attributions, however, is that if left unexamined, they may or may not fit the facts of the situation or productively serve a performer in moving forward. An athlete might think the coach did not start them because the coach does not like them or prefers a different player, but the coach might have chosen a different player to start because that player presented a more favorable matchup in that particular game. That inaccurate attribution can have disastrous consequences for a performer. Whether the performer is right or wrong, whether the attribution given is accurate or inaccurate, complete or incomplete, it will undoubtedly affect feelings, behaviors, attitudes, and performance moving forward. Here is a nonsport example:

Imagine standing on a street corner in the rain as you prepare to cross the street. All of a sudden, a car speeds through a dip in the road as it hugs the curb. Water splashes all over you. You have a few attributional options: (1) You could believe that the driver saw you, made a decision to move closer to the curb, and sped up intentionally to ensure you were soaked; (2) you could believe that the driver just learned really bad news about a family member in the hospital and needed to speed up to get there quickly, and you were simply collateral damage; (3) you could believe that the driver was distracted by texting or changing music channels and was completely oblivious to your presence; or (4) you could believe that the driver didn't see you at all and didn't know you were splashed because they were focused on the road ahead given the inclement weather conditions.

These are not the only options, of course, but they are a few of the reasons available as you attribute the reasons for the splash. And depending on which option you identified, your response to being splashed is likely to be very different moving forward. Each attributional decision you make will undoubtedly affect the next several minutes or more of your life by affecting your mood, your thoughts, and your behavior. Inaccurate or inappropriate attributions require a tremendous amount of energy to cope and to recover. Being splashed by a car is just an innocuous example. The difference in the emotion, the cognition, and the behavioral responses in that one simple example underscores why attributions are important. You act on the basis of your beliefs. In one set of circumstances you might choose to stand back farther from the curb, while in another you might be tempted to yell at the driver, and in another still, you might hope that there's not something really serious going on with the driver.

Now, imagine attributions in response to all of the emotionally charged events and situations that occur in sport (or another achievement domain). Those situations become personal very quickly. They have great meaning to you because you have devoted your life to the performance. If attributions are important in simple, innocuous examples, then imagine how critically and pervasively impactful they become in your chosen achievement domain. Whether you know how to appropriately attribute your performance or you understand attributional impact, your selected reasons for successes and failures influence your emotions, assessments, and behaviors moving forward. Training and retraining correct and facilitative attributions are key factors in determining future motivations and actions. Facilitative attributions are useful because of their power to assist performers to cope, persist, and form positive expectations for future success.

Attributional Training

After any success or failure, you want to feel a sense of control. You want to believe that what you did, the behaviors you engaged in, helped you perform well or that you can make changes in order to bring about a different, more positive result next time. We have already suggested that attributions have significant effects on your effort and motivation. They affect your future effort, belief in your capabilities, motivation to persist in the face of difficulties, and your emotions. Training your attributions then, ensuring that you do not give power to anyone or anything else, matters. For example, when people succeed, and this is true for performers who identify as girls and women in particular, it is important to attribute those successes to accurate and stable factors, namely to internal factors *that are less likely to change* and that *you can affect or control*. Examples include your effort, your skills, your knowledge, and your race plan or competitive strategy. Own your successes rather than giving credit to other people or attributing your success to luck.

One strategy to ensure performers are constructing appropriate and productive attributions is to question the possible reasons they give for their performance. They should select reasons that are under their control and that they have the capability to change or to continue. For example, if a highly skilled athlete is trying out for the next level of competition but is eliminated from the program, then it is both appropriate and likely that the athlete will search for reasons for their deselection. Ideally, that athlete would attribute the rejection to factors that are *changeable* and *within their control*. For example, perhaps they need to exert more effort during training camps so they can improve their fitness and endurance, or they may need to work more on one specific aspect of their game that could elevate their performance. Or an aspiring medical student who was not admitted on their first application to a prestigious medical school might search for reasons to explain that rejection. If they attribute their rejection to the idea that only rich kids or people with well-connected families get into that program and they do not come from that type of family, then there is no reason for them to engage in new behaviors or to resubmit their application. Family background may be one set of reasons for not getting into medical school, but that attribution is both unhelpful and unproductive because it will likely result in the student not applying the following year, losing confidence, and not engaging in behaviors that might result in acceptance in the future. Their effort, confidence, and motivation are negatively affected. It is equally likely, however, that the applicant pool was large, extremely well-trained, diverse, and competitive. Like the athlete who was rejected from a higher-level league or team, the student would be better served to think about what capabilities they have to improve and develop so that, in the next evaluation of applications, their name moves to the top of the list. They might take additional courses, retake an entrance examination, or earn hours interning at a local clinic or hospital to demonstrate their desire to work in the field. The point is, by attributing a rejection to variables that they can both control and improve on, they can begin to act to change the direction of their career. In short, they have something positive, helpful, and impactful to *do* that can potentially change their options.

These examples illustrate the importance of questioning your current attributions and expanding your attributional framework. *Why else might this result have occurred? What are all of the possible reasons?* Look for evidence to support the attributional conclusion you draw. Think back to the elite athlete who did not make it into the next-tier program. Rather than assuming the coaches dislike them or that selections are too political, they would do better to think about additional possibilities for progress and change. Look for and hold on to reasons or explanations that are more facilitative, helpful, and under your control. It is those attributions that will sustain you as you experience failures, setbacks, and disappointments on your way to your purpose. Even in the worst-case scenario, when the most unhelpful reasons were actually accurate (e.g., the system was political, you did not have enough money, or your family was not well connected), adopting productive and facilitative attributions help you focus on what you can control. Rather than feeling discouraged or demoralized, you might look for new ways to achieve your dream or explore new opportunities for personal or performance development.

This more productive strategy leads to a second effective way to ensure accurate and facilitative attributions: *Ensure that your attribution is creating an entry point for action.* Scan for possibilities that offer you an alternative path forward or that highlight a behavior that might develop or enhance your capabilities. If the reason you scored poorly on an exam is because you forgot to review the additional articles the teacher assigned, then you must read more carefully in the future so you will be able to pass the next exam. Or, if your reason for failing is that you need to start studying sooner, then that is an action item for change before the next exam. If the attribution is within your control, then it can be enhanced or extended. These types of attributions give you something you can control and that you can change. They give you a way to stand up after you fail or get knocked down, and they offer a possibility for using the failure or rejection to grow and become a better version of yourself. In that vein, failure can serve as fertilizer moving forward and can contribute to enhanced motivation and drive.

Cultivating a Habit of Appropriate Attributions

Attributions are a type of habit. The cue is the success or the failure, rejection, or loss. Not being hired in the new position, not being accepted to graduate school, or not getting a date; conversely, passing a competency exam or being named most valuable player of the team or league are all examples that serve as the stimulus or cue of a potential attributional habit. What and whom do you blame for your failure or credit for your success?

From a habit perspective, you want to prevent yourself from blaming or crediting other people. You should recognize the role that helpful others played in your success and be appreciative of those efforts, but the credit belongs to you. You are the person in the arena. If you either blame others or give others undue credit for your performance outcomes, then an unproductive habit results because in either instance you are cheating yourself. You are preventing yourself from feeling the pride that comes with owning your achievement, or you are shortcutting the benefit of learning how to correct an error or to improve as a performer so that your own development and improvement lessens the likelihood of future failure. You may have a default, unconscious attributional style that has occurred over time and been reinforced by a well-meaning support system. The key is to actively examine each of your attributions and determine whether or not they are serving you well moving forward.

When you have a successful or poor outcome in an achievement setting, that is your cue. What is the routine? Scan for causes in line with the more productive attributions outlined earlier. For example, if you lose a game that was important to you, search for reasons that you have control over and can change going forward and that are not related to innate talent or stagnant ability. Believing you lost because you did not spend enough time in training or watching film to learn your opponent's tendencies creates a clear path for improvement. Before your next performance, change those behaviors (train more or watch more game film) so that you are likely to experience a different outcome. Once you have the routine established and you have it paired with a cue or stimulus, you need to connect the reward. Recognize how much better it feels to regain control of your performance and to know that you have clear and helpful steps that will lead you to success. It is likely that by engaging in this helpful and facilitative habit loop over time, you will be able to stay motivated even in the face of failures, difficulties, and setbacks.

Chalk Talk

Quick Hits for Cultivating Intrinsic Motivation

- ☐ Implement self-reinforcement strategies.
- ☐ Attribute successes and failures appropriately.
- ☐ Retrain incorrect attributions.
- ☐ Connect your passion with your larger purpose to get through difficult or unknown challenges.
- ☐ Implement the habit loop trio—cue, routine, reward—and be consistent and intentional about combining all three.
- ☐ Examine the reasons you give for success and failures. Engage in reattributional training to correct unhelpful and unproductive reasons for outcomes.

Conclusion

This chapter has been filled with a variety of strategies that might have challenged you to take up some new perspectives on the usefulness and value of intrinsic motivation and how you can develop it. We encourage you to read through the sidebar on this page, which offers a quick hit list of strategies you can implement into your training. Motivation is a choice, and when you choose to complete a task in a way that exceeds minimal demands, it becomes part of something larger than the immediate activity because it is connected to your larger and higher purpose. Embrace your intrinsic motivation as a life choice and a life mandate. Anything worth doing is worth doing well. Make the decision to be self-motivated because you want to improve, grow, develop, and achieve. It's your choice, so choose wisely.

CHAPTER 9

The Three Cs of Performance Success

One of the areas in which coaches, managers, bosses, and leaders seem to struggle most is motivation: motivation of athletes, motivation of employees, motivation of peers, and motivation of clients. There are two primary reasons that motivation is such an important mental skill:

> **The ability to conquer oneself is no doubt the most precious of all things that sports bestows.**
>
> Olga Korbut, gymnast for the Soviet Union and four-time Olympic gold medalist (1972, 1976)

1. *Motivation is the fuel.* It does not matter that you have a high-performance car if you do not have fuel in the tank. Fuel is what makes the car run and perform to maximum capability and capacity. The same is true for motivation: It serves as the "fuel" for success. To improve, to sustain output, and to succeed in your domain of interest, you must be motivated.

2. *Motivation is variable.* Clients, athletes, and high performers on the same team, in the same sport, at the same competitive level, or in the same performance domain are motivated for a variety of reasons and may experience different levels of motivation at different times in their careers. Performers are constantly dealing with the tug that makes it easier to *get done* rather than to *get better*, so every performer can benefit from learning how motivation works.

In chapter 8, we outlined many of the factors that influence intrinsic motivation as well as several strategies (e.g., reinforcement, feedback) that might help someone become motivated from within to pursue their goals. Internal motivation is the ideal entry point into the conversation about motivation.

This chapter builds on what was discussed previously, but now we build on those earlier concepts with the aim of helping you better understand *why* people are motivated to act and *how* to support sustained engagement. In other words, we will discuss how and why people are moved to action so that you can learn ways to harness your own motivational power, direct your motivation, and sustain your motivation even in the face of failure and grueling challenges.

Learn to Fuel Yourself

If motivation is the fuel, then you need to know what type of fuel you need, when to stop to add it, how much you need, and why it is required to drive your own car. Being able to motivate yourself to train when it would be easier to take the day off, or being able to motivate yourself to perform to capability when the previous efforts have been unsuccessful—to be self-determined in your quest for excellence—is the ultimate goal.

Many people function in the sphere of what we call *passive improvement*. They attend practice or go to work five days per week year after year after year. Certainly, they will improve that way. How could they not? Practicing anything frequently and over time is the surest way to increase capability. Medical students improve through studying and then increase their skills during residency as they complete rounds and observe their mentor interacting with patients. People will get better any time they practice or train. But that is not an example of self-determined behavior; it is an example of passive improvement. Passive improvement is important. It does help and it does matter. For example, you would certainly prefer to have a surgeon who has graduated medical school and successfully completed all required medical training. But, when a person goes to school, shows up to work, or attends practice, they are being told what to do, how to do it, and when to do it. It requires very little active participation or self-directed decision-making on their part. They simply show up and get better by going through the process identified for them and directed by someone else. However, there is a next level of improvement, practice, and motivation that requires a different set of questions. These questions focus on what a person actively brought to the practice table, so to speak. *What did they initiate? What did they actively bring to the table?* They will improve simply by doing what they are told to do, but it is a passive process directed by and dependent on someone else.

Active improvement, on the other hand, requires you to demonstrate self-determined behavior. You must be locked into what you are doing and why you are doing it. It is better for long-term, higher, and sustained development when you are focused on a specific area of improvement, and you hold yourself accountable to specified standards. You need to create self-referenced and appropriate metrics to periodically test your performance and ensure that you are progressing and refining your technique. As businessperson and seven-time *New York Times* best-selling author Harvey Mackay noted, "It doesn't matter whether you are pursuing success in business, sports, the arts, or life in general: The bridge between wishing and accomplishing is discipline." Active improvement is what results from your consistent, self-directed actions. It is what occurs when you are actively pursuing your growth and working to enhance your performance (see figure 9.1).

This cycle of active improvement demonstrates that motivation is dynamic. It is perpetual. It requires ongoing maintenance and examination. And ultimately, it is self-sustaining. The remainder of this chapter outlines strategies for becoming self-determined, for taking an active role in your progress, and in so doing, learning how to support your own adaptive and sustained engagement (Horn and Smith 2020) with your chosen pursuits. A great deal of research about

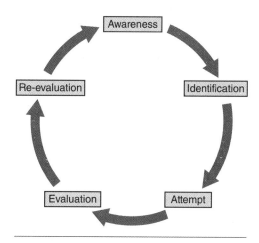

FIGURE 9.1 Active improvement cycle.

motivation shows how it affects effort, persistence, and performance. One of the most useful, practical, and impactful theories of motivation suggests that people are inherently motivated to become competent, to own their choices, and to feel connected to others (Deci and Ryan 1985; 1994; Ryan and Deci 2000; 2017). In this sense, people are proactive in seeking challenges and new experiences to master so they can enhance their lives; however, people can also be vulnerable to fragmented, suboptimal experiences (Deci and Ryan 1985). It is when their three basic needs—competence, choice, and connection—are satisfied that people are more likely to be optimally engaged in their performance domain and will thrive. Now you understand the reason for the title of this chapter: The Three Cs of Performance Success.

Competence

People want to feel competent, to feel like they are skilled at a task, in part because of the collateral benefits they receive from being competent. When they are skilled at their craft, their self-esteem improves, self-concept improves, and self-efficacy improves. They believe in their abilities and skills. People are driven to hone their skills. Soviet gymnast Larisa Latynina, who was the most decorated Olympian (18 medals) in any sport until Michael Phelps (U.S. swimmer) broke her record in 2012, offers a great example of internal drive and quest for competence in the sidebar on pages 146-147.

Competence in any domain is one of the greatest gifts a person can provide to another person or to oneself. Your competence, your skill in a particular area or at a specific task, brings all of the benefits described earlier to the people with whom you are interacting (e.g., teammates, coworkers, employees, clients, patients, students). What if you thought of your training and your work as opportunities to build your competence?

IN THEIR OWN WORDS **A Lesson in Internal Drive**

How did Larisa Latynina, a gymnast from the former Soviet Union, win 18 Olympic medals and become the only gymnast to date to win medals in every event on the program in two separate Olympic Games? How did she sustain her motivation and continue training even after she won her first seven Olympic gold medals?

Latynina was born in the Ukrainian SSR in 1934, and initially dreamed of becoming a ballet dancer. She grew up in poverty and was raised by her single mother after her dad deserted the family when Larisa was 11 months old. He died during World War II. Her mother worked two jobs and never developed the ability to read, so it is often suggested that Latynina grew up an orphan and became self-sufficient early in her childhood. Contrary to popular belief, her dream was not to win at the Olympics; rather, she wanted to make a "better, more beautiful life" through performance. This goal and perspective helped Latynina transition effectively when her ballet school shut down abruptly in her preteen years. Although skilled in ballet, she no longer had the ability to continue her pursuit of excellence in that performance arena when the school closed, and her ballet teachers left the city.

Forced to find another outlet, Latynina found gymnastics and within five years of her transition, at age 16, she became the national gymnastics champion. Two years after that, she entered her first international competition and finished 14th. At 5 feet, 3 inches (1.6 m) tall and 19 years old, Latynina burst onto the gymnastics scene, soon becoming a multiple-time World and Olympic champion. In three Olympic Games, she set the record for the most Olympic medals won at 18 (14 were individual events), a record that held for 48 years. Her performance at the 1956 Olympics marked a shift in the sport away from strength, power, and sustained movements toward an emphasis on beautiful movements and sophisticated choreography.

True to her initial goal and focus, gymnastics and winning awards were not her supreme objectives. Instead, Latynina consistently suggested that it was her desire to create and add beauty to the world that sustained her, that kept her training. And she later added that what set her apart from other competitors was "my desire and a will to win. I had that competitive drive in me." She was so driven for excellence that during one World Championship, Latynina competed and won while pregnant. She waited until after the competition to inform her coach because, as she put it, she did not want him to prevent her from competing and experiencing the success that resulted from her long hours and months and years of training.

In another example of her dedication to competence and not accolades, Latynina did not even know that she had set an Olympic record of 18 medals, 9 of them gold, until she was notified by a reporter in 1979 when an athlete almost surpassed her. Her record stood until 2012 when it was surpassed by American swimmer Michael Phelps. Records were never her goal. She wanted to be the best at her craft and, through that pursuit, to make the world a more beautiful place. Through a series of circumstances, gymnastics became the path through which she could make a difference, and she did.

Based on Sports Illustrated (2012).

Larisa Latynina, one of the most decorated Olympians in history, was clearly driven to be skilled and competent. It did not matter what the craft was, as shown in her transition from ballet to gymnastics. She was driven by her passion for excellence, a dream that likely stemmed from the challenges she experienced as a young person living through the trauma of World War II and the resulting impact on her family and childhood. You do not have to experience the same trauma that this Olympic athlete did to find your own internal motivation. Instead, it is important to extract the relevant lessons and integrate them into your own life. In what ways can you develop competence? How might becoming more competent improve your life and the lives of other people? How then, can you maintain and extend the competence you already possess in your particular achievement domain?

Rather than going for another training run, you could think about how, during this two-minute segment of the run, you are working on your kick or practicing how you will take water at the fourth station during a marathon, for example. Instead of just completing a familiar practice or getting a workout over, you identify a larger goal of extending your competence and capabilities and then measure your increasing progress to higher standards of achievement. With your focus on competence, the countless jumps you attempt at the ice rink become a way to get better at pointing your toes or improving your landing. When you target specific competence extensions in each training session or drill or task at work, then your motivation for completing the task changes. It is no longer sufficient to just get it done. Instead, you are attending to specific elements of the task and finding specific examples of how you have improved. That type of focused and specific recognition of improvement can sustain your energy and effort as you notice and celebrate incremental gains.

And what if, as an employer or boss or leader in your respective industry, you thought of your work with others in terms of helping your clients or employees become more competent? For example, a basketball coach could think of teaching ballhandling skills to athletes to increase their personal agency and competence—they can select which of those moves they might need to implement to create space between themselves and the defender. And the more moves you teach them and then help them select the appropriate move, the more competent they will feel in those situations. Do more than simply teach skills to employees, think of finding areas in which they need to develop competence. Then engage in techniques and evaluation and refinement that will improve the depth and breadth of their perceived competence. An added benefit is that doing so might improve your relationship with your teammates, coaches, instructors, students, employees, and other performers with whom you work and interact.

It is possible that your feelings of competence might differ based on the area in which you are performing. No one is equally competent in every area of performance. For example, you might feel capable as a surgeon but less sure of your abilities to answer patient questions during rounds as a surgical resident. Or you might feel confident in your abilities as a defender but less competent on the offensive end. Tennis players might feel competent in their second serve but less sure of their ability to volley. What is important is that you identify areas where you are competent and work to strengthen your strengths. Then you can apply that process to the next domain. It's amazing how different it feels to practice and perform with a strengths-based focus. In this way, competence can be developed and then extended to new areas. But as we suggest in chapters 8 and 14, competence takes time and requires daily commitment to stick with it and to improve through the challenging times. U.S. soccer legend Mia Hamm said it like this: "I am building a fire, and every day I train, I add more fuel. At just the right moment, I light the match." The quest for competence and for improvement can be a driving force in your life. Identifying what you want to be excellent in and in what areas you need to develop competence is an important initial step in channeling your inner drive and building your fire. Then go to work. Once you have earned authentic competence, it can rarely be taken away. It is also important to realize that your competence cup is never full. You can always increase it, deepen it, expand it, and apply it in new domains.

Choice

Identifying and owning choices in your life is, perhaps, the most supported and proven way to build internal drive. As a performer, you have to be at the center of your career. This is your career; this is your season; this is your game; this is your practice. You are making decisions in each moment that are either moving you closer to meeting your goals or further away from achievement. If you are lifting weights, think of two exercises that would improve strength in the chest muscles. You could complete repetitions of a barbell chest press or dumbbell chest fly, for example. Each of those lifts targets muscles of the chest, but there are advantages and disadvantages for each. You must be taught how to perform each lift correctly and understand the effect each lift can have on the chest, thereby becoming more capable of making the decision about which lift to use for a particular outcome on your own. And when you are offered a selected-choice opportunity, you will be more intrinsically, or internally, motivated to complete those repetitions to the best of your ability because you made your own decision. Notice the emphasis on selected-choice options. We are not advocating to simply ask a fitness client "What lift would you like to use for chest strength?" Rather, we recommend presenting appropriate and limited choices and then providing the performer the power and agency to choose.

Eight-time Grand Slam champion Andre Agassi has talked at length about how a lack of choice in his life affected his experiences, even as one of the greatest tennis players of all time. His father had dreamed of having a child who would become an elite tennis player, and Andre, the youngest, was the "last hope" for his family (Judge 2017). His father pushed him into the sport, bet on him as a junior player at a Las Vegas tournament, sent him away to a tennis academy at age 13, and continued to force him to play long after Andre quit enjoying tennis. On the court, he had some of the best service returns in the game and owned the baseline during matches. Yet, by his own admission, he suffered from a lack of choice. As acts of rebellion, Agassi defied accepted tennis norms: He sported a mullet haircut, he wore cutoff jeans instead of white shorts during tournaments, he used illegal drugs, and he often yelled at his rivals during matches. Agassi has suggested at different times that his antics, his hair, and his wild clothes were the only things he felt he had control over, and he despised the lack of control in his life. Later, Agassi acknowledged, "It is difficult to say that [tennis] was the right thing for me because the greatest frustration is never knowing what else I would have wanted to do." Now, as he reflects on his life and his tennis career, he notes that he finally "made a commitment to take ownership of my life. I started to get more connected . . . it wasn't about a destination" (Beard 2015). Agassi serves as a cautionary tale about the role of choice in anyone's life. A lack of autonomy can thwart happiness and psychological health, while identifying and owning choices increases motivation and enhances the likelihood for mental health and well-being.

When working with other performers, you can begin adding appropriate options or choices for them as early as they can make decisions (even as young as five years old), but the options have to be developmentally appropriate. For example, a young person playing tee ball might have the option during warm-ups to do their arm circles in the same direction or in the opposite direction. That is a simple, selected choice situation. Young athletes do not get to select which defensive system to run, just as any quality contractor would limit a homeowner's options for new kitchen cabinets to two or three rather than allowing the hundreds of possible combinations that exist at a cabinet store. Choices are important, but the performer needs the knowledge and capabilities to select the most appropriate choice. With elite athletes, the choices presented need to fit the competitive cycle, athletes' capabilities, team requirements, and the competitive schedule. As a person moves up the competitive ladder or the performance hierarchy, both choices and consequences increase exponentially. A variety of considerations must be analyzed in relation to selected choice. Autonomy often involves presenting two viable cognitively and developmentally appropriate options and then empowering the performer to make the best, most appropriate choice. Autonomy is about highlighting people's agency (choice) and their internal desire for excellence and improvement (internal motivation). Provide alternatives that are appropriate to the competitive level and to the individual, and then teach and educate the performer about each option. At that point, you are ready to empower the performer to make their own decision. Each decision should be made based on a rationale and with accurate awareness (and acceptance) of the consequences of each option.

As a performer, you must recognize the amount of agency and choice you possess. Language matters, and your language provides insight into your sense of agency, choice, and approach. When you say "I have to work out today" or "I need to get to this next interview" or "I have another long night of studying ahead of me" or "I have another six o'clock meeting with investors," then your focus is on the never-ending jobs that need to be completed. That language indicates a *have-to* rather than a *want-to* orientation to performance. It reflects an unstated belief that you have no choice to make or decision to implement. That orientation negatively affects your psyche. In each of those examples, there is no sense of choice, no recognition of agency. You are simply completing task after task after task. Instead, you should focus on the choices available to you. Focus on your agency. Focus on the value of the task or activity. Think bigger than one small task completion and extend your motivational gaze to the bigger question of *why* you are engaged in this task.

The research is clear that when you pay attention to your choices, when you recognize and own them, you will feel more motivated and experience more joy. So rather than you *have to* train or *have to* study or attend another meeting or interview, think about how what you are choosing to do is connected to your larger purpose. Why are you choosing to train, study, or attend that meeting? Perhaps, you are training because you have an important meet or event coming up, and you want to stay on track, you are studying because you scheduled your GRE or LSAT for one month from today, and you are meeting because these investors could help you keep your business' doors open. Connecting decisions with a larger vision or purpose can help you engage in behaviors even when you do not feel like doing so on a particular day or at a specific time. Feelings are temporary, powerful forces, but recognizing selected choice opportunities is one strategy for sustaining motivation even when emotions and feelings might be an obstacle. Remember, no one *has* to play their sport, study for their exam, practice their music, lead their company's meeting, or answer questions during an interview. Each of those behaviors is a choice.

Recognize the choices available and make deliberate decisions to focus on why you are choosing to do a particular task. When you own your agency, when you change your lens from *have to* to *want to* or *get to*, you change your whole world. Think of the sunglass metaphor. One pair of sunglass lenses makes your view of the world seem blue, another makes the picture amber, and a third tints the world green. The color of the water did not change. The color of the trees did not change. Your lenses did. And, so, when you focus on the choices available to you and the autonomy you have, then you change your outlook. It is a form of cognitive reappraisal (see chapter 3). You are rethinking, reappraising, and developing a new relationship with what already exists in your life. To practice recognizing and owning your choices, complete the worksheet on this page.

Performer-Centered Implementation Worksheet

Examining Your Own Experiences With Choice

Directions

Reflect on your own performance experiences as you read each question. Then craft a detailed and specific response that acknowledges the value of choice in your own life. Identify the event, the people involved, the exact choices you have or had, and other important elements of the context as you respond to help you re-experience the moment described.

1. Think of examples where you have been given a choice during a performance. Describe one moment when choices were created and offered. How did that feel?

2. Think of examples when you were not given a choice. Describe one moment when you had no choice and no control. How did that feel?

3. Think about your next training session or training block or opportunity to practice your skills. Identify three behaviors or activities in which you will likely engage that create the illusion and the feeling that you have no choice or control in the situation. Then reappraise, restructure, or reframe the situation, this time adding an element of choice. Engage in cognitive reappraisal and turn the task into an autonomous choice. To do this, identify the three behaviors or activities. Then make a list of your options for each task or event (e.g., time, location, people involved, intensity).

4. Pause and recognize the value in the options you have just identified and the decisions you get to make within each daily training segment. For example, the task might be to work out. Identify all your options for working out (e.g., play tennis, run, walk your dog, swim, play pickleball). Once that is selected, you also get to choose when, where, for how long, and at what level you will train.

5. Write down the options you have available to you for each behavior, task, or activity.

From C. Hacker and M. Mann, *Achieving Excellence: Mastering Mindset for Peak Performance in Sport and Life* (Champaign, IL: Human Kinetics, 2023).

Connection

To be self-motivated, you also need to feel connected; you need to experience a sense of belonging and attachment to your goals and to other people. This fact is one reason that team building should be part of each group and every performance pursuit (see chapter 16 for more information on team building). This sense of connection must start with individual performers themselves. You must take responsibility for your personal choices first. Be honest in your self-evaluation and self-appraisal of your competency and goals, and engage in self-compassion when warranted. Connection starts with you. You are the center of the relationship bullseye (see figure 9.2). Who you are influences your interactions with other people. Once you are attached to your own goals and direction, you can work to gain a sense of belonging and build relationships with people who play the same position or compete in the same event, people in the larger sport or performance arena, the local community, and then outward into the larger global community.

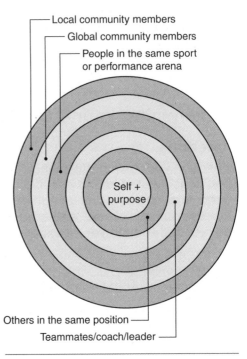

FIGURE 9.2 Circle of connection: relationship bullseye.

Building these connections helps performers stick with training when it is challenging because they are accountable to other people. When NBA superstar Michael Jordan felt exhausted from all of the media attention and pressure he received, he often discussed how his drive was sustained because he wanted his teammates to experience the same success and level of winning that he had enjoyed. His relationships with his teammates, while far from perfect, helped him find reasons to continue when he might have otherwise wanted to take time away from training, take fewer repetitions, or practice less frequently. These connections must be authentic. For example, the Blue Angels, elite pilots and ambassadors of the U.S. Navy, are known for their ability to connect with one another before and after their flight demonstrations. These exchanges between pilots are often described as a primary reason for their success as a group, but they only converse over the mission and over the next demonstration. They are authentically connected to one another because of a shared purpose. It is these types of connections and relationships that we refer to in this chapter. How might you find ways to increase interdependence in your workplace or performance domain? Increasing opportunities for people to interact and work together in authentic ways to complete a task can facilitate people's own motivation.

Feeling connected or related to other people can also help you remember to control what you can control. Once you are connected to someone else and appreciate them for who they are and what unique strengths they bring, you are less likely to try to get them to change or to control or alter their behavior to approximate more closely your own. Instead, you need to allow and encourage each person to perform their best at the skill or task that they are responsible for carrying out. You cannot change how someone else on your team in your position and with your level of expertise behaves. You are not in charge of that element. Instead, it is your responsibility to help them leverage their distinct strengths, talents, and abilities in all of the ways that they are capable. Then you do the same. If everyone in your committee, at your workplace, or on your team does that, if you all find ways to help each other access their own best performance, then you are more likely to meet collective group and team goals. Overall, developing a sense of connection among and between working group (or team) members is essential to motivation. More information on how to specifically facilitate connection and relatedness with others will be provided in chapter 16.

The strength of the self-determination theory rests in its simplicity and ease of use. It means that to be internally driven, people need to own their choices, develop competence, and feel connected to their goals and to other people. When those three needs are met, people are more likely to be self-determined or motivated to engage, to change, and to persevere among setbacks, adversity, and difficulty. Because of its practicality, self-determination models have been applied in a variety of environments. For example, a recent study determined that an at-home lifestyle intervention centered on choice, competence, and connection improved the dietary choices and physical activity behaviors in middle-aged individuals with or at risk of developing metabolic syndrome (Blackford et al. 2016). Recent meta-analysis of the literature since 1970 found that using the self-determination theory to bring about changes in health behaviors (e.g., quit smoking, increase physical activity) was effective in both children and adults across a range of domains (Gillison et al. 2019). These types of interventions and evidence emphasize the wide-ranging, beneficial effects of motivation and demonstrate that every individual—worker, performer, student, parent, child—could benefit from understanding and implementing the core tenets of self-determination theory. The key is to learn how to acknowledge and affirm your own choices, competence, and connection. You must create an environment in which you foster support in each of these areas for yourself. The sidebar on page 154 outlines several strategies that you can implement *right now* to positively affect your motivation and internal drive.

Chalk Talk

Quick Hits for Supporting Choice, Competence, and Connection

☐ Create clear expectations that outline appropriate behaviors and emphasize effort and personal growth and learning.

☐ Seek out and take on 50/50 challenges in which you might be successful 50 percent of the time. Then identify what you learned from the performance or competition.

☐ Identify and recognize your unique strengths.

☐ Own your opportunities to make decisions and choices.

☐ Use language that emphasizes choice and acknowledges self-control (*can* or *want* versus *have to*).

☐ Develop high-quality relationships with a few trusted, high-impact people who support and challenge you to elevate your performance.

☐ Connect with your goals and your dreams daily and ensure that your choices align with your goals.

☐ After training and performances, acknowledge or write down specific, tangible examples of your improvement on a specific task to keep yourself focused on the task and your competence.

☐ Revisit your larger *why* in all your achievement domains.

Goal Orientations and Team Climate

For the past 40 years, psychology and sport psychology researchers (e.g., Ames 1992; Duda 2005; Dweck 1986; Nicholls 1984; Roberts and Treasure 2012) have argued that the environments in which people train and perform play a significant role in the motivation and behavior of that individual. In fact, Ryan and Deci (2017) suggested that the extent to which people are significantly and persistently exposed to autonomy-supportive environments, the more likely they are to take on that type of motivation or orientation to training. How success is defined and recognized in performance environments may also affect performers' motivation.

There are two primary ways that success is defined in performance environments: (1) by outperforming or defeating someone or something else (outcome oriented) or (2) by mastering a task (task oriented). For example, NBA player and Hall of Fame member Allen Iverson, who was often criticized for his tardiness to team meetings and practice, once responded to a reporter's question about his tardiness to practice by pointing out that as a franchise player, he goes out and plays every game like it's his last. He puts forth the effort where he believes it matters, in a game, so he didn't understand the point of talking about practice.

This outcome-oriented sentiment demonstrates that Iverson was motivated by winning and by outperforming people on the court during a game rather than being motivated to perfect his craft. Contrast Iverson's motivation with quotes from Jerry Rice, three-time Super Bowl champion and holder of 100 NFL records, who said, "Today, I will do what others won't, so tomorrow I can accomplish what others can't," or this quote from tennis legend and gender equity icon, Billie Jean King, who won 20 Wimbledon championships: "Champions keep playing until they get it right." As highly successful and elite-level athletes, both Rice and King were known for their attention to detail and motivation to master the task at hand. They both adopted a task orientation to their sport. They were motivated by their ability to grow and learn and master the motor skills required to be successful in their sport.

Laurence Griffiths/Getty Images

To understand motivation and motivated behavior, you must first decide how you define success and failure in honest, real, tangible terms. Are you successful when you record the highest sales of the quarter? Or are you successful when you read and learn strategies to improve the effectiveness of your sales pitch? Are you successful when you beat others in your competitive event? Or are you successful when you master a new technique or element in your sport? Although recording the highest number of sales or winning the most matches is important to everyone, the difference between outcome orientations and task orientations is that people who are task oriented focus primarily on improving from their previous performance. The result or outcome is a byproduct of their consistent improvement. They can be successful then, even if they finish as the second-highest grossing salesperson or the number three team in the league or conference standings. See the differences between a task-involved and ego-involved climate in the following sidebar.

Chalk Talk

Quick Hits for Differentiating a Task-Involved and Ego-Involved Motivational Climate

Task-involved or mastery environment	Ego-involved, results, or outcome-involved environment
Defines success based on individual improvement relative to one's own previous performance.	Defines success based on comparisons with other people or teams (or some performance standard).
Anyone can be successful at every training or practice or workday.	Only a few, highly skilled people or teams can be deemed successful.
Effort and improvement are recognized and rewarded.	Outperforming and defeating others is recognized and rewarded.
Performers are more likely to give increased effort, persist in the face of failure, seek challenging situations and competitors, and perform well when it matters most.	Performers are more likely to give less effort, give up or quit, judge themselves harshly in critical situations, perform poorly in evaluative situations, and avoid challenges.
A focus or priority is to achieve success.	A focus or priority is to avoid failure.

The longer someone trains in their environment, the more likely it will be that they adopt the same orientation to success that was recognized and rewarded. For example, people who perform and work primarily in a task-involved climate are more likely to adopt a task orientation whereby they judge their success based on their own performance and improvement. People can be high in both task orientations and outcome orientations, but most people tend to focus their attention and energy in one area more than the other (Weinberg and Gould 2019). As such, it is both important and preferred to develop a task orientation because these performers give higher, sustained effort, are more likely to persist in the face of failure, challenge themselves with moderately difficult tasks, and have high perceptions of competence. They are more confident than performers who develop an outcome orientation. People who develop an outcome orientation are more likely to struggle in evaluative situations and give up or quit when defeat looks likely. These behavioral differences are significant and make sense given that focusing on the task at hand is within the performer's control. There is always something that a performer can think or do to be successful. On the other hand, with an outcome orientation, the performer cannot control their success because they might face a superior competitor or someone who outperforms them in a particular moment.

One of the issues with an outcome orientation for athletes is the high rate of failure in sport. For example, in softball or baseball, if the only time a player experiences success as a hitter is when they get on base, then even professional athletes in that sport will fail 7 or 8 times out of 10. What about competitive swimmers? Often the goal is to set a new personal record during a season. However, their training schedules are created in ways that prevent them from achieving their physical best until the end of the season. Taking up an outcome orientation, like that taken up by the hitter in baseball or softball, means that the swimmer will almost never experience outcome-oriented measures of success. Instead, developing a task orientation would help the swimmer improve their stroke rate, how they pull through the water, or their recovery stroke, and because of improving each of these elements, it is more likely that the swimmer would continue working hard and be able to celebrate moments of victory on their way to a personal record at the end of the season. While winning is a top goal for any team or individual performer, the best way to bring about that outcome is to focus on mastering each task. Some of the best athletes and performers have adopted this mindset. See the sidebar on pages 158-159 on creating a task-involving climate.

Rather than comparing yourself with other teammates or opponents, compare your current performance with your previous performance standards. Doing so can protect you from the disappointment, frustration, and lack of motivation so common in sport. When you are losing or being outperformed and have an outcome orientation, you cannot be successful. But if you adopt a task orientation, then you retain control over your improvement even when you may not be as skilled as someone else or win on the scoreboard. Focusing on mastering the task helps you stick with your performance and find moments of success even when the overall outcome may not be what you hoped for.

The climate or environment in which you perform also affects the way you define success and motivation. Performers in task-involving climates, those who recognize and reward learning and improvement, tend to exhibit a positive attitude, exert greater effort, and are better able to adapt quickly and efficiently to challenges when compared with performers in ego-involved or results-dominated climates. It is important, then, as a leader (and performer) to carefully construct a productive motivational climate. Any leader can help shape the environment in which they (and others) perform. In the following sidebar, you will see strategies for building an effective motivational climate along with examples.

PUT IT INTO PRACTICE

Creating a Task-Involving Motivational Climate

Coaches and players...

Center the performer

- Involve performers in decisions.
- Offer selected choices.
- Encourage self-directed learning.
- Delegate responsibilities.

Create meaningful, challenging tasks

- Tasks should minimize downtime or waiting in line and maximize participation and opportunities to learn and perform.
- In sport, let athletes play multiple positions; in school, create multiple stations where students can learn the same concepts through different tasks.

Recognize and reward improvement

- Notice and reinforce when a performer tries a new technique and takes a step closer to successful completion of the task.
- Encourage all group members to acknowledge each other's successes—their growth, effort, improvement.
- Deliver feedback that connects the performer with their own sense of joy and satisfaction.

Create small groups based on diverse areas of knowledge, skill, expertise

- Avoid grouping people based on ability or skill level (e.g., first team versus second team in sport).
- Arrange multiple, small groups to work on various elements of the task, and then bring groups together.

Implement feedback that targets growth and improvement

- Encourage performers to self-evaluate.
- Focus on each person's strengths and how they can train to solidify those strengths.
- Focus constructive feedback on what the performer did well and what can be done to improve.
- Once the skill is learned, use feedback sparingly (i.e., talk less: new learners cannot use it effectively yet, and experts can generate their own).

Implement frequent, short training sessions and drills

- Avoid excessive fatigue that will decrease opportunities for improvement.
- Leave performers wanting more.

Adapted from Epstein (1989); Ames (1992).

Conclusion

Throughout this chapter we have outlined strategies for directing your motivation even in moments when it would be easier not to do so. We have focused on strategies that we find to be the most usable, ubiquitous, impactful, practical, and, in some ways, simple so that you can immediately and effectively implement them. The evidence is clear. Becoming a self-determined performer focused on mastering each task at hand will yield active and sustained improvement. You will be more capable of withstanding the challenging times and more likely to embrace and cherish the moments of success. The only question is *Will you do the work?*

CHAPTER 10

Creating an Action Plan

For better and for worse, almost everyone seems to be setting goals in the various spheres of life. Business executives set goals to meet quarterly targets and year-end growth targets; athletes create goals to improve their times, distances, and individual statistics, while musicians set goals to play a difficult concerto.

> Dreams are free. Goals have a cost. . . . Time, effort, sacrifice, and sweat. How will you pay for your goals?
>
> Usain Bolt, Jamaican sprinter, 8-time Olympic champion, 11-time world champion, triple world-record holder (100 meters, 200 meters, 4 × 100-meter relay), 4-time Laureus World Sports Award for Sportsman of the Year

Goals offer direction, motivation, and a guide toward a future accomplishment. Locke and Latham (2002) defined goals as an objective, a pursuit to reach some standard of proficiency within a specified time limit. We set goals for career advancement, professional accomplishments, personal improvement, as well as for relationship satisfaction, among other areas. And for good reason—of all the mental skills, the value of goal setting that is *properly* and *appropriately* conducted is probably one of the most robust findings in the sport psychology literature (and has been for over four decades; see review by Locke and colleagues 1981). Setting goals according to evidence-based standards has been shown to improve performance, increase persistence, direct effort, increase motivation, decrease anxiety, increase confidence, direct attention, and yield overall improved satisfaction and enjoyment (Weinberg and Gould 2019). As professional ultrarunner YiOu Wang said, "You set goals and then over time, if you're consistent and put in the work, those goals are achievable. I get a great sense of confidence and satisfaction when I achieve something" (Wang 2020). To be even more blunt, in their most recent text, Weinberg and Gould (2019) noted that researchers in sport and physical activity settings have proven that appropriately setting goals was useful for novice and expert participants performing over 90 different tasks in 20 countries. Collectively, this evidence suggests that goal setting is one of the most studied and used mental skills. That is the good news.

The bad news is that people are creating goals without using proven, evidence-based strategies. They often create a vision or objective for themselves without developing a plan for achieving their goal. Therefore we titled this chapter Creating an Action Plan. Without a plan, a goal becomes nothing more than a dream. Another mistake people make when they set goals is putting their own, personal, unsubstantiated spin on the goal-setting process. Whether they do so because they do not know the correct techniques or they simply decide not to follow the proven strategies, it is imperative to use all the evidence-based research that explicitly outlines the critical elements of goal-setting effectiveness. Regardless, if people do not know the steps involved in action plans (another name for goal setting) or they are actively shortcutting the process, the result is the same: ineffective goals. Performers are then often perplexed, disappointed, and confused when their goal-setting process does not work.

Following evidence-based goal-setting guidelines is like deciding that you want to make bread and finding a recipe that calls for six ingredients. If you integrate these six ingredients in the right quantities at the right time and bake them for the right length of time, you can expect to consume a delicious loaf of bread. The same is true for setting goals: Follow all the recommended components and you can expect impactful and direct benefit to performance. But if you take that recommended bread recipe and opt to use only four of the six ingredients rather including all six at the outset, then it is highly unlikely that you will end up with a loaf of delicious bread. Many decades ago, the acronym GIGO was popular. It stood for garbage in garbage out. That adage applies to goal setting. If you do not follow all the recommended steps (GI) then you are unlikely to reap the desired outcome (GO). The same result would be expected if you chose to take the bread out of the oven seven minutes early and before the recipe suggests just because that time frame suits your schedule better. By taking the bread out too early, you will likely end up with goo rather than bread. Had you followed the recipe, allowed the dough to rise, and baked the loaf for the full time required, you could expect to eat a nutritious and delicious slice of bread with your meal. In much the same way, you must avoid the temptation to go your own way or eliminate important ingredients as part of your goal-setting program. The purpose of this chapter, then, is to outline appropriate action planning, explain the fundamental principles of goal setting, and offer effective, evidence-based strategies for avoiding or overcoming the common pitfalls you might encounter when implementing action plans.

Setting Effective Goals

Olympic athletes, like most high achievers, commonly set goals to guide and motivate performance. These elite performers would not engage in action planning if they were not sure that setting goals works. Therefore, it is critical to understand just why it does work and which types of goals a performer should set. Learning the *why* of goal setting has the additional benefit of preventing athletes from falling prey to the myriad seemingly persuasive goal-setting programs offered. Scholars hold two perspectives on why setting goals enhances performance, one from a mechanistic perspective and one from a more cognitive perspective. We will address both approaches. Either way, it is important to note that goals both directly and indirectly influence performance.

According to the direct (or mechanistic) view, goals direct performers' attention and effort and foster new learning strategies (Locke and Latham 2002). For example, a lacrosse player's goal to win 80 percent of ground balls requires them to pay attention to maintaining a strong bottom hand at the end of the shaft, pushing their hips forward and down to the ball, angling their stick, and following through when collecting the ball. If an athlete focuses on those subskills, they will be more likely to pick up ground balls more frequently and successfully. Goals also help performers maintain their effort during challenging circumstances. If an undergraduate student has a goal of becoming a medical doctor and is daunted by four years of medical school, then setting goals that break down the program into smaller segments (e.g., semesters, weeks, individual assignments) can help them persist and sustain consistent effort across time. Distance runners and swimmers benefit from goal setting in similar ways when they set a goal for the next lap or 50 meters of a long training session rather than focusing on the entire practice. Finally, according to this mechanistic theory, performers can learn new tactics and techniques through goal setting. For example, a golfer might adjust their putting stance to consistently sink putts from various distances. By targeting each of these performance elements through specific action plans, performers' goals can directly and positively affect performance.

Goals also have an indirect impact on performance (Burton 1983). Burton suggested that the effect goals have on performance depends on how the type of goals being set influence a person's thoughts and feelings, specifically their anxiety, motivation, and confidence levels. For example, if an athlete focuses solely on *outcome goals* (e.g., winning a gold medal, being a top 10 finisher, outpacing a sibling to win the front passenger seat for the car ride), it is more likely that those performers will develop unrealistic expectations for themselves about winning. These unrealistic and outcome-focused goals can result in lower levels of confidence and effort and increased anxiety when unsuccessful. As we have demonstrated in previous chapters, with increased anxiety and lower confidence, poor performance typically follows. Instead, when performers focus on goals they can control, that are process oriented, and that are self-referenced, they are more likely to develop optimal confidence, motivation, and effort (Gould 2020). Using this view of goal setting, prudent lacrosse players would focus on their defensive positioning and staying between their opponent and the goal at least 90 percent of the time rather than setting a goal to prevent their opponent from scoring (an outcome-focused goal). Surgical oncologists would set goals to improve the precision of their incisions rather than thinking about how many lives they hope to save this month. While saving lives or preventing scoring attempts are laudable and desirable preferences, it is setting and reaching their performance goals that increases a person's confidence and decreases anxiety, thus making the preferred outcome more likely.

Understanding the *why*—why goals work—is essential to reaping the benefits. Otherwise, you might fall for any persuasive or new-to-you idea that seems intuitively appealing but is unproven. Both the cognitive and mechanistic theories of goal setting have deep and extensive scholarly support. Quality research and evidence suggest that setting goals can both directly and indirectly affect performance. Research findings also demonstrate that the achievement domain matters, demographic characteristics of the individual matter, and the performance environment matters. The key is in knowing when and how to set effective goals and then apply them appropriately for a specific person in a specific context. You can only apply them in your own life if you understand how goals and action plans work. From both direct and indirect perspectives, you as an athlete, leader, or performer should note that setting goals and creating action plans can enhance performance by directing your attention to the most important elements of the skill and by enhancing your thoughts and emotions (e.g., confidence, motivation, satisfaction). Being aware and knowing what elements of your performance can benefit most from effective goal setting opens the door for you to positively affect any of the four pillars of your sport, namely tactical, technical, physiological, or psychological. You can then direct your attention to confidence or motivation, for example, or to skill improvement or tactical awareness.

Goal Types

There are essential elements of effective goal setting, and before you can implement goals in your life or in a specific achievement domain, you must first be aware of each required component. For one, you need to know what types of goals need to be set for maximum effectiveness. The literature has clearly outlined three important goal types: outcome goals, performance goals, and process goals (Martens 1987).

Outcome Goals

Outcome goals are useful because they require you to identify your intended result. What do you want to accomplish? You may want to finish first in your class, become the best solo climber in the world, or win a World Championship in your sport. Outcome goals set the standard for your performance and are results driven. They are often long-term goals, meaning you hope to accomplish them at the end of a competitive season, across your career, or before the end of your life (think bucket list goals). Most people gravitate toward outcome goals, and they can be useful in setting long-term priorities and serving as motivation during challenging times. World heavyweight champion boxer and social justice leader Muhammad Ali said, "Champions are made from something they have deep inside them—a desire, a dream, a vision." This dream or long-term goal is typically an outcome goal, focused on the desired result. Common outcome goals are to score a goal, to be selected as a starter, to win a court case, or to be chosen as lead soloist. However, this type of goal has been shown to be less effective in consistently improving performance because, at best, performers have only partial control over the outcome, and these goals distract competitors from task-relevant strategies (Burton and Naylor 2002; Martens 1987). Every baseball pitcher wants to win the game, of course, or pitch a no-hitter, but focusing only on that outcome goal prevents a pitcher from focusing on the elements of performance necessary to bring about that outcome, such as the placement of their fingers on the ball or the snap of their wrist after each pitch. In addition, when performers set outcome goals and do not achieve them, perhaps because someone else was more skilled, made a great play, or even caught a lucky break, they are less likely to adjust and continue setting goals in the future.

Performance Goals

Performance goals, on the other hand, are useful before and during training sessions and competitions because they target personal improvement. One of the top speed skaters of her era and one of the most decorated athletes in Olympic history, with five gold medals and one bronze, Bonnie Blair spoke about this type of goal when she said, "No matter what the competition is, I try to find a goal that day and better that goal." Notice she did not mention that her focus was on winning gold or being the best in the world. She might have had those outcome goals, but each day she identified one area to improve. Basketball players might, for example, set a performance goal to shoot 10 more shots from the wing on Tuesday than they shot on Monday. Performance goals are self-focused and completely controlled by the athlete. But even these goals can increase anxiety if they are the only type of goal that a performer sets (e.g., expecting every new performance to be a personal record or a personal best) (Weinberg and Gould 2019).

Process Goals

The third type of goal, *process goals*, highlights procedures, strategies, and techniques that a competitor needs to engage in if they want to perform a task well. In curling, the lead player might think "push" just before they release the stone down a sheet of ice, and a sweeper might set a goal of targeting proper hand placement so they can reduce friction better and help the rock move straighter. These are process goals that help direct the attention of the performer. Like performance goals, process goals are particularly useful before and during training sessions and competitions.

Common Goal-Setting Errors

A common error in goal setting is that performers often implement goals only before competition. Instead, goals should be set before, during, and after both practice and competition. They should be set daily and weekly and over the course of a year or season. It is also important to set all three types of goals: outcome, performance, and process. As a minimum threshold, performers should set at least five process or performance goals for every outcome goal set. Doing so allows individuals to create a vision or long-term objective for their performance while spending most of their focus and attention targeting specific elements of their technique or strategies and improving their personal performance in every session. In this way, process and performance goals allow the competitor to focus on elements they can control (e.g., their effort, their response to competitive challenges, their attitude, their motivation, their technique).

Each of these types of goals can also be considered objective goals that people use to target and approach a desired outcome explicitly and specifically. Subjective goals are, on the other hand, general statements usually about having fun or doing your best. Some research has proven that objective goals are better for athletes than subjective goals because they are measurable and specific, and a performer knows when they have succeeded or failed to reach their selected standard. The goal-setting literature is clear that "do your best" goals are contraindicated for athletes because they are too general and lack measurement capability. But when applied to new exercisers, those same "do your best" goals seem to work better than specific, process goals, which can be defeating and can negatively affect motivation and confidence. Subjective goals are also useful for athletes learning a new sport or a new skill because they help them focus on effort, work rate, and learning new strategies rather than focusing primarily on outperforming others or on errors in their technique so common in early learning stages. In addition, research in business management suggests that subjective goals help workers improve productivity and clarify their values (Weinberg and Gould 2019). For elite athletes, however, competing in the World Championships or Olympic Games, it is best to transform subjective goals to an initial outcome goal and then work back to construct several process and performance goals needed to achieve the outcome goal. The image of the goal-setting process resembles a staircase. Performers know where they are starting, and they know where they want to go. So, they need to construct the connecting steps necessary to get to the top. Those connecting steps are built with process and performance goals.

For people who are working in groups or competing on teams, setting goals as a group or team and implementing individual goals are equally important. Group goals foster collective efficacy and effort (Widmeyer and DuCharme 1997). Collective efficacy, simply stated, refers to the strength of belief members have in their collective ability to be successful. In all types of goal setting, it is important to first set long-term goals to establish a specific path forward, and then create short-term goals (individual steps) on the path to facilitate achievement of the long-term goal. When setting goals as a team or group, it is important to encourage all members to contribute and to consistently monitor and provide feedback on individual and collective progress.

Fortunately, there is a simple template for setting goals effectively. The requisite elements of productive goal setting are well established. The next section offers an example of the processes and procedures necessary to reap maximum benefit from setting team or individual goals. See the following sidebar.

Chalk Talk

Quick Hits for Goal Setting

The following are guidelines for goal setting:

- ☐ Use a 5:1 ratio; five performance or process goals per one outcome goal.
- ☐ Set process and performance goals to direct attention effectively before and during training sessions and competitions.
- ☐ Set subjective goals to increase effort, motivation, and confidence, especially for novice performers.
- ☐ Set short-term goals to guide attention to the performance elements that matter most right now.
- ☐ Set long-term goals that recognize priorities and create an overall direction or vision.
- ☐ Set both team and individual goals.
- ☐ *Always* consider the person, the environment, the achievement domain, and the moment when creating and implementing goals.

Summary of Essential Checklist Components

Setting goals influences performance because they increase effort, improve persistence, direct attention, foster new learning strategies, and affect mental states (e.g., anxiety, confidence, motivation). The key is to know which elements to target and then how to implement goals that influence those factors.

Using a variety of goals and implementing evidence-based goal-setting strategies more frequently than other performers do, for example, are key practices for high-achieving performers. But simply knowing the types of goals a performer should set is only part of the process. *Nuance matters.* The achievement domain matters. The characteristics of the individual matter. The environmental factors matter. You must be aware of the personal and situational variables that affect goal-setting guidelines for individuals and for groups. To set goals effectively, you must be able to determine the type of goal, how many goals, and what areas to target for *this performer (or group)*, at *that competitive level*, in *that environment (sport, business, life)* now. When people are not appropriately attending to the essential factors affecting goal-setting guidelines, results are predictable: Metaphorically speaking, we can expect bad-tasting bread, soggy bread, or no bread at all. Even though the rest of this chapter offers a template for setting goals, it is important to emphasize again that you *must* know the personal and situational variables for each person (or group), rather than take a one-size-fits-all approach. You are then able to set more appropriate and impactful goals based on sound goal-setting guidelines and recommended rationale.

Effective Action Plans

Remember, setting goals is important, but to truly influence performance, it is not only important to set goals but also to create a plan for achieving them. It may seem obvious: The point of setting goals is not to set goals. The value in setting goals is to positively affect performance and to provide a road map to get from where you are to where you want to be. Goal setting, or action planning (as we prefer to say), offers a systematic approach to performance enhancement, one in which goals are created, implemented, monitored, evaluated, and reevaluated over time. As Serena Williams, winner of 23 Grand Slam titles, reminds us, high-achieving athletes must "set realistic goals, keep reevaluating, and be consistent." Latham and Locke (1991) coined the oft used SMART goals acronym to describe one goal-setting model. They suggested that goals should be specific, measurable, attainable, realistic, and time bound. Although a variety of scholars have adjusted this acronym over time to include ideas like changing the R to stand for relevant, meaning goals should be personally relevant, or adding an S at the end to emphasize that goals should be self-determined, or wordsmithing actions such as "attainable" versus "action oriented," the consensus is that this acronym is effective in describing essential features of effective goals. In this section, we will not give preference to one acronym over another. Instead, we want you to know the critical elements of action plans and then to decide how best to remember and enact those principles. The significant power is not in the acronym, but rather, it is in the ingredients used to set effective goals. You need to know and understand each ingredient of the process and when and how to use each to create an action plan that is personally relevant and can be reasonably implemented. So rather than strictly adhering to one version of the SMART acronym or another, let's start baking.

Critical Elements of Each Goal

Although you should be setting objective, specific goals rather than general, subjective goals, all types of goals can be effective at one time or another or for one type of person or another. Once you have decided which type of goal you need to create (e.g., long term, short term, objective, subjective, process, performance, outcome), you want to ensure that the goal is measurable. The goal type is dependent on the performer (e.g., beginners should use subjective goals, whereas expert performers should implement objective, process goals). Regardless of goal type, it is essential that every performer clearly know when they have achieved a particular goal. Whether you are setting a goal to make 8 out of 10 free throw attempts in basketball or to decrease from seven to two the number of distracting speech patterns used when presenting to an audience (e.g., "um" or "like") as you practice an upcoming presentation, it should be clear whether or not the goal was achieved. Even subjective "do your best" goals can become measurable. For example, employees can rate their positive attitude at work each day on a numerical scale (e.g., 1 = not positive, 7 = positive each moment at work). Self-rating is one strategy for ensuring that "do your best" goals can be measured (Butt and Weinberg in press).

The goals should be challenging and attainable for you (Moon, Yun, and McNamee 2016). To enhance motivation, performers should be required to exert energy and effort to achieve the goal, yet they should not be so demanding that they cause people to lose confidence or feel anxious. As we have articulated throughout this chapter, knowing yourself and your capabilities as well as those of the people with whom you work is a crucial initial step. As the T in the SMART goal's acronym represents, it is also important for goals to have target dates (i.e., they are time bound). Setting goals with a specified time line ensures that the performer continues to make progress in the direction of their end goal and has a time frame for accountability.

The ways in which we write or share our goals can influence our likelihood of achieving them or not. Although at times it might be appropriate to set goals to prevent negative outcomes (e.g., Don't miss any conditioning workouts this week), most research indicates that creating mastery- or performance-approach goals is ideal (Lochbaum and Smith 2015). By this we mean that competitors should set goals that focus on what they want to have happen rather than trying to avoid what they hope does not occur. Canadian pitcher Danielle Lawrie-Locke set an outcome goal to make the 2020 Canadian national softball team again at 31 years old after having two children. To reach this outcome goal, she could have set goals in which she tried to avoid giving up a home run or tried not to pass a ball during any one appearance. But, instead, setting goals in which she attempted to master her hand placement for her go-to off-speed pitch or finish one more inning than she did in the previous game would be more advantageous and would be more likely to help her achieve her outcome goal. Lawrie-Locke ultimately played for the Canadian women's national softball team, including during the 2020 Summer Olympics, where she helped Team Canada win a bronze medal. Clearly said, it is best to focus on what you want to accomplish and the behaviors you need to engage in to successfully attain your goals.

Another element of performance that Lawrie-Locke highlighted was that having her family—her daughters, in particular—has made her more aware that the goals she sets for herself professionally are being set by her and for her (Stone 2018). When considering whether or not a coach or trainer should set goals for their team or whether a chief executive officer should set targets for specific departments within their organization, the performers, themselves, should be involved in the process. Assigning goals to other people limits their feelings of autonomy and control (two hallmarks of self-determination theory, discussed in chapter 9); whereas, establishing goals for oneself can increase motivation to achieve that goal and enhance satisfaction after goal accomplishment. Each of these action-planning elements is important to consider when people are crafting goals for themselves or when working with others to help identify targets that an individual wants to pursue.

Start With the End in Mind

When creating action plans, it is best to start at the end point (what you want to achieve) and work your way backward to your current level of performance. Normally, you start where you are and build from that point forward. But with goal setting, we recommend that performers work backward. In the sidebar on page 171, a top Canadian runner explains this process in her own words.

Think about the long-term goals for your career, by the time you graduate, or at the end of your life. What do you want to have accomplished? Do you want to be an Olympian, a medical doctor, a civic leader, a soloist, or a corporate executive? *Start there*. Then work backward. Determine honestly where you are right now: You are an undergraduate honors student, an intercollegiate student-athlete, or first chair in your high school band. Here you are. Now, what can you do where you are *right now* that will get you one step closer to your ultimate goal? Just as we discussed in chapter 4 on mindfulness, do *now* well. You cannot become an Olympian overnight, nor are you likely to immediately travel the world

---

The Backward Chain of Goal Setting

Lanni Marchant grew up in London, Ontario, Canada, as the middle child of seven and, like many Canadians, learned to ice skate before she learned most other sports. Few would have guessed she would become Canada's fastest female marathon and half-marathon runner. She picked up the sport as part of her elementary curriculum and used it to cross-train for figure skating.

After running in college and then becoming a criminal defense attorney, she decided in 2012 that she wanted to go to the Rio Olympics. It was decided. She had set her long-term goal. And "my coach and I worked backwards, in terms of how to qualify. We set goals for each season leading up to the Olympic qualifying events." Marchant follows the same action-plan program in life. "For life goals, I'll always keep the [end] target in mind, but I know there might be some different paths and bends in the road to get there." This backward-chaining plan allows her to adjust to changing circumstances and to factors outside of her control while keeping the end goal in sight.

"I am allowed also to change my mind, and in doing so, change my goals to something bigger." It is this perspective that allowed Marchant, the former figure skater and current lawyer, to break the 28-year-old Canadian women's marathon record in 2013 and become one of the fastest distance runners in the nation.

Based on Hannam (2017).

As Marchant's story highlights, when developing a goal-setting program, it is important to start with the long-term outcome goal first, and then create a plan to move from the current level of performance toward the end goal. Unlike most other mental skills that work from the place the performer currently occupies, goal setting requires a person to consider where they want to end their season, training block, or career, and then create their path forward by achieving the steps along the way to the final goal.

---

as a solo performer or get accepted into medical school out of high school. But you can take a physics course, and you can declare your biology or kinesiology major. In addition to the semester-long goals (intermediate), you also have homework right now (short-term goal). You can complete your biology reading. You cannot apply for the corporate CEO position, but you can take the next step. Everyone is usually quite clear stating what they ultimately want. What they generally need to improve on is the backward-chaining process. Stating an intention for long-term goal achievement requires a willingness to invest honestly, fully, and consistently in the backward-chaining process. The subtasks to long-term goal achievement and the steps along the goal path are as unique as every individual. People will claim that they really want "it" but then fail to fully commit to the time, effort, and subtasks necessary to get there. The Olympic trials are not for another two years, but athletes can train

today, and they can establish time targets for next week's race. They can identify their end goal, the long-term goal that is the motivational focus, and then set short-term goals that are self-referenced, challenging but realistic, and time specified and then commit to taking the necessary short and intermediate steps required to achieve their long-term vision.

After people announce their long-term goal, pay attention. Either explicitly or implicitly, they will tell you what they are willing to do to accomplish that goal. Unfortunately, there is often a disconnect between what they are willing to do and what the subtasks require them to do. Performers are committed to engaging in *some* but not all behaviors, so rarely does a performer's choices and behaviors include *all* the requisite steps. Athletes will, for example, prioritize their physical fitness and training—they will work tirelessly to become stronger, fitter, more flexible, and faster—but they may not make an equal commitment toward nutrition, sleep, hydration, or recovery. Then there are athletes who will control their nutrition but not attend equally to their mental toughness. Action plans and goal setting must follow the recommended process in all four pillars of sport (technical, tactical, physiological, and psychological) to be effective. Performers cannot pick and choose which step they will commit to, and which are open to debate or become suggestions rather than behavioral mandates. They must be willing to do the work.

As five-time National Basketball Association (NBA) Champion and 18-time NBA All-Star Kobe Bryant once said during a press conference, "A lot of people say they want to be great, but they're not willing to make the sacrifices necessary to achieve greatness." His willingness to roll up his sleeves and do all the work outlined in each of the steps on his action plan(s) helped Kobe become one of the greatest NBA players of all time. You do not get to decide which steps are requirements and which steps are mere recommendations. *You identify what must be done and you do it.* It is not what you feel like doing or what you have time to accomplish. It does not matter what you prefer or what you are in the mood for today. Instead, you must determine the action plan that is necessary to get you from point A to point B and then fully commit to that requirement. Just like Jamaican sprinter Usain Bolt says, "Goals have a cost. . . . Time, effort, sacrifice, and sweat. How will you pay for your goals?" What have you done (or will you do) to put yourself in a position to reach the outcome goal you want? A key separator between those who set goals and those who accomplish goals is in what they are willing to do to achieve them and the consistency over time in which they will apply those efforts. Most people want the same things. There is no team in an athletic conference that at the beginning of the season yells "Let's finish sixth. Let's finish sixth!" Everyone has a similar terminal objective. It is just that some people are willing to do the necessary work and to stick with the process even in the face of difficulty, setbacks, and adversity and to do what is required. Most of humanity is willing to do the work some of the time or do the work sporadically or do the work until a significant setback occurs rather than make a full commitment to the terminal goal regardless of the sacrifice or setback. Remember, you do not get to pick and choose which elements of goal setting apply to you or to decide which steps to follow. You know now that all elements of goal setting are essential, not some of them. Begin where you are and where you want to go, and then outline the steps needed to create the staircase to get you from where you are now to where you have planned to go. It is that simple, and it is that hard.

Ink What You Think

Once you have established the goals you set and you have an ultimate target or vision in mind, you should, as Dr. Hacker says, "Ink what you think." Write down your goals or type them on a sheet of paper and place them where you can see them multiple times each day. Have them close and visible. Approximately 60 percent of people who set New Year's resolutions in 2019 gave them up before the end of the year and more than 10 percent of people who set these objectives quit trying to achieve their goals by the end of January (Ipsos 2020). Other research has demonstrated that more than 90 percent of New Year's resolutions fail (Vozza 2016). However, more than 70 percent of people who wrote their resolutions down and sent weekly updates to a friend reported that they successfully achieved their goals. It is easy to maintain focus on your goals within the first few days or weeks after you set them, but most goals require months and even years of consistent effort to accomplish. It's not uncommon to experience difficulty finding a parking spot or a treadmill at the local fitness center in January. Predictably, by February parking opens, and by March treadmills are available throughout the day!

In the mundane activities of daily life, it's easy to forget your goals or fail to recognize that the behaviors you engage in today directly affect whether you achieve your long-term goal a year or two later. However, the reality is that you are rarely in a stagnant or neutral position. You are always getting closer or farther from attaining your long-term goals—with each action you take or fail to take. Each choice today has a direct bearing on achievement of your end goal or desire. Writing down goals, creating a contract with yourself, keeping a log of your daily actions, sharing your goal and progress with others, and holding yourself accountable with measurable outcomes—all these strategies can help you accomplish your dreams.

Goal Support

In addition to writing down your goals, it is important to have support from significant others to make goal setting more effective. Remember the New Year's resolution keepers example? People were more likely to keep their resolutions if they wrote them down *and* updated a friend on their progress each week. In fact, of people who created a goal but kept it to themselves, only 35 percent were successful. People need consistent and contingent feedback to encourage progress (Vozza 2016). Contingent feedback refers to feedback that strongly corresponds with the individual's task behavior and thus can be controlled by the person. Performers need to know how they are doing and to have people in their lives who encourage them to stick with it even when their motivation is low, or their circumstances are challenging. Performers who attempt to fuel their bodies more appropriately for competition are more likely to make the improvement if they have a supportive significant other or friend group reminding them of their nutrition goals. The support of significant others is an especially critical factor affecting exercise adherence, and parental support can be crucial to the goals athletes set for their own sport performance. The important people in the goal setter's life should be included in the process so they can provide feedback, reassurance, and encouragement.

Goal Evaluation and Goal Revision

Speaking of feedback, the essential elements associated with goal execution are evaluating and revising goals. Dr. Hacker often says, "Feedback is the breakfast of champions." Performers need specific feedback that helps them recognize progress (or lack thereof) toward their goals. People need accurate, honest, and specific information that pushes them to narrow their goals or to adjust them based on the changing and dynamic environmental demands of which they are a part. Coaches can do this by providing report cards to athletes at the end of each week, with comments and numerical grades relating to the goals each athlete sets for themselves. Physical therapists and strength and conditioning coaches can provide feedback to clients based on how often they completed their at-home exercise routines. These examples provide evidence to the performer about how their behaviors and efforts are affecting their ability to reach their intermediate or long-term goals. Performers should also provide their own feedback by watching their presentations or performances on recordings and looking for key behaviors they engaged in or by self-rating their concentration at the end of a workday or training session. There are also times in which the environment changes (e.g., an injury, new job requirement, change in resources or personnel) make it necessary for performers to reevaluate their goals and to adjust accordingly. For example, during the COVID-19 pandemic, it became clear that the Olympic Games would not be held in Japan during the first summer of the pandemic. As a result, athletes who had set performance goals leading into the Olympic Games needed to reevaluate, reanalyze, and recalibrate to set new goals or to create new timelines for training or select a new international competition to prepare for the Olympics postponed for a year. Failing to do so would set an athlete back in terms of motivation and preparation and make it more challenging for them to cope with the uncertain and uncontrollable demands of a global pandemic.

We have covered a variety of critical elements of effective goal setting (also called action planning). The sidebar on page 176 offers a summary of these strategies for creating effective action plans.

Incorporate each of these strategies into a clear, systematic action plan. Start with the template provided in the sidebar, and then consider the individual capabilities of the performer. Assess that person's capabilities, commitment, motivation, and personal connection to the goal. If you are working with a team or a group, schedule meetings to discuss goal setting and create strategies. Revisit and refer to the goals frequently. At this point, the individual or team or group should be ready to create and implement both individual and group goals. With proper feedback and ongoing reevaluation, performers are in a strong position to successfully attain their stated objectives.

Chalk Talk

Quick Hits for Creating an Action Plan

The following are guidelines for creating an action plan:

- ☐ "Ink what you think." Write down your goals.
- ☐ Set approach goals (rather than avoidance goals) that target ideal thoughts and behaviors.
- ☐ Set challenging goals that are personally relevant and difficult but achievable.
- ☐ Ensure goal support and feedback.
- ☐ Engage in ongoing evaluation and revision of your goals.
- ☐ Make sure your goals are measurable.
- ☐ Start with the end in mind, then create action steps from where you are now to where you want to go.
- ☐ Set self-created goals.
- ☐ Create a timeline for completion for each goal you set.

Motivational Climate

We cannot conclude this chapter without addressing how goal setting fits into the motivational climate. As we have said throughout this chapter, the environment matters. Words matter. Leadership language matters. The motivational climate in which goal-directed behavior occurs matters. We will address team climate in chapter 16; however, for now just know that motivational climate and goal setting are inextricably linked. This climate could occur in any performance domain, not just in sport. Pat Summitt, former University of Tennessee head women's basketball coach, who finished her career with 1,098 wins and eight national championships, said it like this: "Setting up a system that rewards you for meeting your goals and has penalties for failing to hit your target is just as important as putting your goals down on paper." As Coach Summitt alluded to, the environment in which someone sets their goals plays a significant role in determining the success or failure of the performer.

Climates that encourage performers to compare themselves with others or to define winning primarily as finishing first or being the best are common but ill advised. These situations typically encourage people working and competing in these environments to believe success can only occur when they outperform someone else and, therefore, are more likely to establish outcome goals, which are problematic because they are not fully within the performer's control. Athletes, business leaders, and other performers are constantly engaged in social comparison, however. It is common and should be anticipated. This reality makes appropriate goal setting more difficult because performers tend to focus on outperforming someone else rather than focusing on the daily grind of right now.

Instead, if you are a leader in sport or business or a different performance sector, try to create an environment that rewards people for improving and for learning new skills or strategies. Prioritize progress and personal standards of comparison and behaviors that are under the performer's control. It is within these climates that athletes and performers are more likely to establish a mastery orientation to their craft, a goal style where success is based on self-improvement. While someone with a success orientation might benefit from social-comparison goals, especially if they are favored to win, it is more likely that they will experience a loss of confidence and increased anxiety when they fail to achieve their goals. On the other hand, people who are rewarded for self-improvement and committing to self-referenced standards are more likely to benefit from goal setting because they are more likely to set performance and process goals that they can control, that direct their effort and attention, and that help increase their confidence. All those benefits are more likely to lead to enhanced performance. As a leader, be aware of the words you use because they reinforce behaviors, and pay attention to the culture you are creating because it directly affects the goals performers set and contributes to the likelihood of group and individual success.

Conclusion

Goals can and should be set in multiple areas of life. These include fitness goals, performance-enhancement goals, relationship goals, satisfaction or enjoyment goals, academic goals, and goals to improve mental toughness. In this chapter, our intention has been to offer a template for crafting action plans that are rooted in clear and specific research guidelines. There are critical variables to consider, and the goal-setting literature has outlined these factors over several decades. The further you move from incorporating all the critical elements of goal setting, the more you move away from the benefits of goal setting. And, yet, as the saying reminds us, "The devil is in the details." The characteristics of the individual, the competitive level, the environment, and the achievement domain matter. If you can remember both the critical elements of goal setting and the significance of individual and situational factors, then you will develop an action plan worth following.

As a final note, people's ability to believe in themselves and their ability to accomplish their intermediate goals is a major factor in determining whether they will persist until they achieve their ultimate objective. The more experience people have setting goals, the better they are at finding ways to achieve them and to overcome the inevitable setbacks that occur in every meaningful endeavor. It is never too early to teach goal setting, and people are never too young (provided that they are developmentally able) to learn. Teach young people early how to appropriately set goals for themselves.

Just as we know that the other psychological skills discussed in this text are effective, we know that setting goals works. If done correctly by using all the requisite components, action planning will improve performance. The only question remaining is whether you are willing to roll up your sleeves, follow the protocol, and do the work. We believe you can and that you will.

Performer-Centered Implementation Worksheet

Setting Goals

This worksheet is a useful goal card that Dr. Hacker has used with intercollegiate athletes and with national team competitors. It can be completed at the start of each workweek or block of training. The card provides an opportunity for athletes to practice many of the strategies outlined in this chapter, including setting goals in each of the pillars of performance (tactical, technical, physiological, psychological) plus team goals. This card also incorporates a self-rating and evaluation for each goal.

Directions

For each of the pillars of performance, set one goal. Be sure to follow the guidelines for effective goal setting outlined in this chapter. Indicate a completion date for committing to achieving that goal. At the end of the week or training block, evaluate your effort in reaching your goal. Be honest. In the last column, offer a self-rating from 1 to 10 (1 = did not attempt and failed to accomplish the goal, 10 = gave maximum effort and accomplished the goal). Then describe the behaviors you engaged in to attain the goal in each performance area. At the bottom of the goal card is space for you to describe how you might adjust any of the goals listed based on unexpected events, circumstances, or results.

Goal types (four pillars of performance + 1 team)	Goal (specific, objective, performer controlled, measurable, challenging, realistic)	Completion date	Qualitative and quantitative evaluation
Tactical			
Technical			
Physiological			
Psychological			
Team or group			

> continued

Setting Goals > *continued*

Reevaluation and goal revision comments:

_____

_____

_____

_____

_____

_____

_____

_____

_____

_____

_____

_____

_____

_____

_____

_____

_____

_____

From C. Hacker and M. Mann, *Achieving Excellence: Mastering Mindset for Peak Performance in Sport and Life* (Champaign, IL: Human Kinetics, 2023).

CHAPTER 11

Focusing on the Right Things at the Right Time

"Pay attention! Focus! Concentrate!" Have you ever heard a coach or leader shout those words? Or perhaps you have admonished yourself with a similar phrase when you reached the bottom of a page of text unable to recall the information you read. It is no wonder these words are lauded in critical moments of any performance. The ability to concentrate refers to a person's ability to pay attention to what is most important in a given situation (Moran 2004; 2013). Even a brief moment of listening to the crowd instead of a coach, or considering the rain and wind instead of focusing on getting out of the blocks fast, or thinking back to your at-bat in the third inning as you step into the box in the bottom of the seventh, or turning your head when you hear the door to the conference room open rather than listening to the speaker, or countless other examples of ineffective concentration can disrupt your performance and affect the outcome. In fact, attention and concentration may play one of the most central roles in learning and performance (Abernethy et al. 2007). As 11-time NBA champion Bill Russell noted, "Concentration and mental toughness are the margins of victory."

The problem with yelling words like "focus" or "concentrate" to yourself or another performer is that they only recognize what needs to be done, and most people already know that answer. What is missing from the admonition is information on *how* (and *to what*) to direct and sustain attention appropriately. If a performer has not been taught how to concentrate or to effectively shift their attentional focus, then no matter how loud or how intense the verbal reminder is communicated, that person will be unable to focus on the right thing at the right time. Success is determined, in part, by the ability to direct attention appropriately for as long as it is needed and then to shift the focus somewhere else in a moment's notice as the competitive demands change. Rather than tell people what to do, in this chapter, we outline how to sustain appropriate

> **Feed your focus, starve your distractions.**
>
> Unknown

focus and concentration, especially under duress, and how to remain focused and in the moment after an error.

Direct Your Attention

In significant moments, when your best performance is necessary, the ability to control your focus is a critical factor. Developing appropriate concentration is one of the most fundamental skills in peak performance. Pay attention to too many variables or the wrong elements and you might feel too activated to perform well; fix your focus on one element at the exclusion of others and you risk committing significant errors. You must be able to direct your attention where you need it to go and when you need it to be there. For example, as a pianist, you need to be able to see the entire piano when you sit down so that you know where to place your hands to begin playing the sheet music, and yet, while you are playing, your attention must narrow so that you can move your fingers and play both sharps and flats on time and in the correct order. If you are glancing at the entire keyboard, you might strike a note too early or too late. Likewise, if you are thinking about the next stanza before playing the current section, you might make a mistake. In sport, as an outside hitter, you might survey your opponent's side of the court as the setter pushes the ball out to you while you are making your approach, but as you jump into the air, your eyes must be focused on the ball so that you make contact at the exact moment that will send that volleyball careening down the line, unreturnable.

Each person has a finite amount of attention; it is limited. They cannot pay attention to everything in their changing environment all the time, and whether they are a dentist filling a cavity or a student taking an exam or a gymnast sticking a vault, paying attention to the right elements at the right time is essential. A basketball player dribbling down the court cannot pay attention to where their fingers contacted the basketball, how much force they used to push the ball down, and what direction to push it as they continue moving forward. Instead, they need to automate those steps so they can focus on how their defender is playing them and where their teammates are cutting. In other words, they need to free up their attentional space.

To free up attentional space, you must practice the tasks and skills necessary to perform well in your arena to the point that they become automatic. This *overlearning* (Hardy, Jones, and Gould 1996) of a task frees you to take in more or different information. It's also a major reason that practicing the fundamentals of any sport throughout your competitive career is an absolute necessity. In addition, through practice, as you become more of an expert in your craft, you are able to take in more information, filter it quickly, and select which cues are most relevant at that moment (Mann et al. 2007; Moran 2004). For example, a novice tennis player might look at the tennis ball coming over the net as they set up for their next shot, whereas an expert would notice the racket position of their opponent and start moving into position earlier, thus allowing them, as they prepare for their next shot, to glance at their opponent's court coverage and decide where to place their return winner. Because the expert better understands possible tennis movement patterns and can attend to more advanced information (like racket positioning and direction an opponent's hips are pointing), that athlete is able to quickly sift irrelevant from relevant cues and selectively attend to what matters most, thus allowing them to quickly and accurately respond to the situation.

Once you know the situation and the task well enough, you can selectively attend to the most relevant cues. Do you need to be thinking about how to win the next point as you start your serve in tennis, or do you even need to be thinking at all? Or should you be thinking about where your defender is as you jockey for position in a match? To better understand the role of attentional focus on performance, read the story on page 184 from one of the most successful Canadian soccer players of all time, Christine Sinclair.

Selective attention refers to appropriately choosing between task-relevant and task-irrelevant cues. In some scenarios, this attentional focus could be similar to Sinclair's example. In other instances, it might mean choosing between two cues presented at similar times during a performance and responding to the most critical one to positively affect performance. What we know from the literature is that focusing your attention externally and farther away from the body facilitates enhanced performance (Bell and Hardy 2009). A golfer, then, might focus on the flight of the ball, a basketball player might think about the height or arc of the ball rather than the mechanics of the shot, and a libero in volleyball might pay attention to putting the ball right above the setter's head rather than on extending their elbows. The more you focus on yourself or things closest to you (internal and proximal), the poorer your performance (e.g., less efficient movement, poorer overall outcome). This is true for a variety of tasks, including those that focus on balance, accuracy, speed, endurance, and maximum force production (Wulf 2013).

Knowing what and where to focus matters, but without knowing when to redirect your attention away from some elements and toward others, that initial knowledge is incomplete. While it is critical to know the *what* and *where* in terms of attentional focus, you also need to know *how to* shift your attention.

Four Dimensions of Attention

An important initial step in developing the ability to focus appropriately and to shift your attention appropriately and on-demand, is to understand the dimensions of attention (Nideffer 1976; Nideffer and Sagal 2006). Nideffer (1976) found that every performer has a dominant

Locked and Loaded: Christine Sinclair's Ability to Focus on the Task at Hand

As Christine Sinclair, the 35-year-old soccer phenom from Canada, prepared to take the field in a CONCACAF tournament that served as an Olympic qualifier leading up to the Tokyo Olympic Games, she had many thoughts on her mind: Goal scoring records. The pursuit of five rings. Revenge for 2019.

Any one of those dizzying goals could distract her and become an issue for the Canadians. Coming off of a poor end to the 2019 season, Sinclair, who had scored 181 international goals, was poised to break American Abby Wambach's all-time international goal scoring record of 184 in that very tournament. Much of the sports world had been talking about the tournament being *the* moment in which Sinclair would surpass Wambach. Media scrums followed her every move and repeated the same set of questions over and over again: "Christine, how will it feel when you break the record?" "Sinc [her nickname], what are your thoughts about holding the record?" All of this publicity along with the fact that the Canadian team closed out their previous season with three losses out of four matches and desperately needed to earn nine points in this tournament to qualify for the Olympic Games, where Sinclair could compete for a fifth medal, made for a challenging set of circumstances. And yet, Sinclair was focused on the next match.

"It's nice to know that every game is just going to get that much more difficult, that much more important. One thing we pride ourselves on is we know how to grow and build throughout a tournament and we're going to have to do that here," Canada's all-time leading goal scorer and captain Christine Sinclair said. A teammate noted, "I predict that she's going to beat the record in like the first game and then she can focus on the rest of the World Cup. The record is not her goal." Sinclair later confirmed, "To be honest, they're probably looking forward to it more than I am. I know how important this tournament is, and how important each game is, as we move on. I don't want [the goal-scoring chase] to be a focus point for the team." Instead, she adopted a "want a foot, give an inch" philosophy of play, which helped her direct her attention to finding holes in the opponent's defensive formation, looking for ways to create scoring chances and capitalizing on those moments, which, in turn would give the team an opportunity to win and advance to the next round.

Based on Goldberg (2019).

Sinclair did net her 185th goal and become the all-time leading international goal scorer, and she did so in that very CONCACAF tournament in south Texas against Saint Kitts and Nevis, but as she said afterward, she continues living her life "trying to be the best Canadian that I can, in my own way." Sinclair has demonstrated throughout her career that her attention is on each individual match, each minute and moment that she plays, rather than on the media or personal accolades. Had she focused on the goal-scoring record, then when the ball was played to her, she might have been tight or too focused on the record and consequently committed an error. Instead, she played for that moment alone and scored the history-making goal.

attentional style and that at different moments during performances, competitors will likely need to shift their attention in order to be more effective. The four types of attentional focus are broad external, broad internal, narrow external, and narrow internal (see figure 11.1). And different performance situations require performers to access and shift their attention appropriately often using each of the four dimensions at different and specific times throughout the event.

Michael Jordan, one of the best basketball players to play the game, recognized the need to "focus like a laser, not a flashlight." You must be able to focus on the exact elements of the task

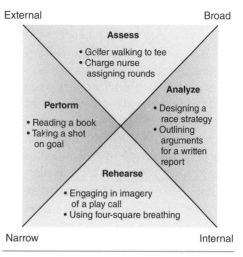

FIGURE 11.1 The four types of attentional focus (broad, narrow, internal, external) intersect to create four quadrants. During each phase of motor skill performance (e.g., assessment, preparation, action, analysis), the performer must shift their focus appropriately.

that require your attention at exactly the right time, and then shift your focus to other elements as the environment changes and demands shift. A swimmer who is preparing for a 100-meter freestyle event might work with their coach in the weeks leading up to the meet to develop a race strategy. That athlete's focus is *broad internal* as they focus on themselves and their race but also consider the entire 100-meter event, their lane assignment, and their competitors. This type of attention is also useful after a performance to evaluate successes, strengths, and areas for growth. Then, as they stand in the waiting area before their race, the swimmer imagines diving into the pool, feeling their hand pulling through the water effortlessly, and finishing the last several strokes without taking a breath to out touch other swimmers and win the event. In this moment, their attention is *narrow internal* as they focus on what it would look like, sound like, and feel like to swim their race strategy. As the announcer calls their event and they walk across the deck to take their position on the block, the swimmer notices their rival is in lane six right next to them and a teammate is on their other side; a smile forms on their face as they assess the situation. Taking their mark on the block, the swimmer picks out a visual point in the pool they want to dive toward once the start signal is given. In these lead-up moments, the performer's attention is *broad external* as they take in the entire environment and analyze information that will help solidify their race strategy. Finally, the horn sounds, and the swimmer dives into the pool. The swimmer uses their cue words to ensure their elbow is high and their kick is strong, taking breaths every third stroke. During performance, attention should be *narrow external*, not focused on competitors or opponents or fan noise. Instead, performers should fully attend to the elements of performance most critical to performing the task.

Athletes and performers are continuously shifting their attention to better concentrate on what matters most in order to perform the task successfully. Seattle Seahawks coach Pete Carroll stated, "Our players learned to compete one snap at a time, one practice at a time, and ultimately, one game at a time. When we focused like that, we were able to achieve our best results and play to our full potential" (Carroll, Roth, and Garin 2011). In his signature direct and succinct style, Coach Carroll summarized Nideffer's findings that different moments in any performance domain require the performer to know each of the attentional styles, to be able to direct their attention appropriately, and sustain their concentration until it is necessary to shift their attention elsewhere.

Becoming Aware of Your Dominant Attentional Style

People who concentrate well can attend to many stimuli without becoming overloaded with information and they can, on time and with purpose, narrow their attention to focus on what matters most. In relation to the attentional dimensions or styles, these performers would score high in both broad-external and broad-internal focusing and be able to effectively shift their focus (Weinberg and Gould 2019). On the other hand, some performers might struggle to block out crowd noise or might be easily distracted during meetings if someone walks in late or readjusts positions in their chair. Novice athletes in particular are known for narrowing their attention prematurely, so much so that they might not see an open teammate or a defender setting up to intercept their next play.

Nideffer (1976) created an attentional assessment questionnaire, called the Test of Attentional and Interpersonal Style (TAIS), which helps people learn their general or dominant form of attention. The questionnaire asks respondents to answer questions such as "In a room full of people, I can keep track of several conversations at the same time" and "When people talk to me, I find myself distracted by my own thoughts and ideas." Responses are then scored on a five-point Likert scale from "never" to "always." The TAIS offers an opportunity to become aware of your generalized attentional style, which is important information because, as will be discussed later in this chapter, in high-pressure moments, people tend to gravitate to their dominant style.

Knowing this information, you could train yourself over time to shift your attention appropriately in pressure-filled competitive situations. This test does not help you learn how to shift your attention but it does offer a baseline of important and individualized information. As with all psychological measurement tools, the results should only provide information that allows you to compare your current performances with previous performances to gain knowledge about how you have improved and what areas continue to need work. They should not be used for selections to teams or for group comparisons or to decide roles or positions.

Because the TAIS measures attention as a general trait and does not account for changes in attentional style in different situations, performers might also benefit from psychophysiological tests, which can be useful in measuring attentional processes across situations (Wilson 2012). For example, by studying heart rhythms during rifle shooting, researchers found that when performers focused attention on external cues like their target rather than on internal cues like their breathing, their heart rate slowed before pulling the trigger, and they tended to be more accurate (Hatfield and Hillman 2001). Not only do these types of tests help people understand what types of attention are useful at different performative moments, in different sports, and for different individuals, when the information is provided to athletes and other performers, it can help them learn how it feels physically when their attention is directed broadly, narrowly, internally, and externally. Then, they can better recognize when they are directing their attention to inappropriate cues and learn to focus on helpful cues. The following sidebar offers takeaways about attention and concentration.

Chalk Talk

Quick Hits for Effective Concentration and Attention

Focus, concentrate, and attend effectively by doing the following:

- ☐ Overlearn the task—through practice—to free up cognitive space so you can attend to multiple performance-relevant cues.
- ☐ Recognize which cues are most important during different moments within a performance or competition.
- ☐ Know your dominant attentional style.
- ☐ Be able to shift attention from broad external to narrow internal, for example, depending on the demands of the situation.
- ☐ Concentrate effectively by focusing your attention on what matters most and sustain attention when it is needed.
- ☐ During performance and executing skills, focus externally.
- ☐ While planning and rehearsing, focus internally.

Improving Concentration

Optimal concentration requires keeping an appropriate focus over time and developing the ability to shift attention to meet changing performance demands (Bernier et al. 2016; Williams and Bhalla 2021). The good news is that *concentration is a skill that you* can *develop*. In this section, we outline various challenges to attentional capacity and how you can train yourself to direct, shift, and focus your attention appropriately.

As Moran (2009) notes, you must first decide to concentrate and then decide to what you will direct your attention. The most productive attentional choice will not happen by chance. The choice is yours. Seven-time Super Bowl champion quarterback Tom Brady put it like this:

> I really don't like leaving much up to fate. . . . If, like me, you're serious about your peak performance, you need to work hard at the things that are within your control. . . . I don't like to focus on negatives or make excuses. I am never a victim. I gain nothing if I get angry or frustrated. You can make life a lot harder for yourself by focusing on negative things in your path or making excuses for why things didn't go your way. Or, you can let them go, learn from them, and become the best version of yourself. It's a choice. It's actually your choice. If I throw an interception or have a bad day or make a bad business decision, by staying in that place, I will just make things worse. Wisdom is about knowing the difference between the things you can control and the things you can't.

Maybe you are delivering your first public speech. You peek around the curtains and see your family in the front row and every seat filled. You can choose to focus on how nervous you are or that you hope you do not embarrass your loved ones or how unsure of yourself you are. Or you can selectively attend to what matters most. You can rehearse your first few lines; you can image yourself speaking confidently and making the crowd smile or laugh; you can focus your attention on the most important elements of your speech and driving home your intended message. Whatever you decide, remember that where your attention is directed, so too is your performance. *It is your choice.* Make it work for you.

Similarly, during performances and competitions, you must decide when you will flip your concentration switch and when you will take a mental break or rest (Moran 2009; Moran, Toner, and Campbell 2019). First, decide what you will direct your attention toward, and then decide when and how to do so. Whether competing in a tournament that lasts multiple days or playing a sport in which the matches might take two, three, four, or even six hours to finish, it is critical for performers to learn when and how to lock on, and conversely when and how to flip the switch to off, allowing for mental rest. These moments of attentional rest might occur between sets or when changing sides of a court or during the first few moments of halftime, but it is your responsibility to identify appropriate moments to turn off your concentration switch and then to learn how to do so consistently and with purpose. One strategy is to develop routines (see chapter 12 for a more detailed explanation of performance routines).

These focus plans involve an athlete or performer being able to identify the environmental cues and the demands of the performance task that require attention and the moments when they can mentally rest and recover. For example, if a player typically grabs their water bottle between sets or when moving to the opposite side of the court, that could become the cue that reminds them to attentionally rest. Or when running a distance event, approaching a water station might cue the runner to switch off for a few seconds whereas passing a light post or mile marker might be a cue to lock on to their arm swing or breathing pattern for the next mile. Some athletes listen to a type of music as they drive to their competition site that is different from the music they listen to in the locker room. This change in music cues them to direct their attention toward or away from the competition. These performance plans should be created and detailed in advance and practiced during training sessions leading up to an event. That way, the performer is not adding yet another drain on their attentional capacity. Instead, these routines are practiced consistently enough that they are automatic, thereby serving as subconscious cues that help the performer maintain desirable and optimal attentional control.

There are also moments during a performance when you need to make decisions to actively distract yourself or, alternatively, to tune in to your physical experience. Studies have demonstrated that elite marathoners tend to use *associative attentional strategies* (e.g., monitor how they feel as they ascend a hill, recognize muscle tension at a particular mile marker, evaluate their heel strike), whereas nonelite runners tend to *dissociate* (e.g., distract themselves with music, think about how good they will feel after the run) during races (Morgan and Pollack 1977). Several studies have indicated that associative strategies are correlated with better or faster performance but that dissociative strategies are particularly useful in decreasing feelings of fatigue and boredom (see review by Brick, McIntyre, and Campbell 2014). Dissociation is particularly useful for nonelite performers who want to stick with a hard training run or adhere to a new exercise program, for example. Associative strategies, like focusing on cadence or arm swing for the next two-minute interval, can help a distance runner maintain a consistent pace through a challenging part of a race. The point here, again, is that multiple strategies can be effective, but the performer needs to know *when, how,* and *for what reasons* they are choosing to implement each strategy. They must attend to the unique demands in each performance situation and understand the nuances of each strategy.

The Importance of Refocusing

In the 2021 NBA playoffs, when asked how his team could get to the conference finals, Utah Jazz guard Donovan Mitchell responded, "It's all about the mental part—locking in, executing, and then responding to adversity when you make mistakes—that's what it's going to come down to" (Todd 2021). If learning how to focus is important, then learning how to refocus—after an error, when you are overactivated, when you are thinking about the past or future (rather than on right now)—is critical for success. You need to be focused in the present moment to perform at your best. You cannot be thinking about what you said when you were introduced to your new boss for the first time while you are being introduced to the new CEO, and you do not want to be thinking about your last penalty kick while you approach the one you are taking right now. You must be engaged in the now, focused on the present. So just as it is important to know where your focus needs to be, you must also understand how to alter or redirect attention away from unwanted distractions. You have to develop both sides of that equation.

One way to stay focused on the present is to focus on what you can control as a performer. When you are focused on the future (e.g., What if I miss this shot? What if I mess up again?) or attending to previous events (e.g., I can't believe I swung at that pitch. I'm such an idiot to make that pass.), you are out of the present moment and often focused on factors that are not within your control. Remember, you have finite attention. If you are paying attention to factors outside of your immediate control, then you have less space to think about what you can influence right now and about what matters most in this moment. Complete the worksheet on page 191 to develop your own refocusing plan.

As part of these refocusing efforts, it is important to direct your attention to where you want it to be rather than trying to avoid what you do not want. Mary Lou Retton, the first American gymnast to win an all-around gold medal at the Olympic Games, referred to this idea when she stated, "Rather than focusing on the obstacle in your path, focus on the bridge over the obstacle." *Ironic processing* suggests that when you try to avoid thinking about or focus on something you don't want to happen, you actually are more likely to bring your attention to that very element (Wegner et al. 1987). We discussed this theory briefly in chapter 3, but it bears repeating here. A popular example of ironic processing occurs when you try not to imagine a white polar bear. *Do not imagine that white polar bear. Avoid the white polar bear analogy.* As you read these words, it is likely that you were actually seeing an image of a white polar bear in your mind. If you spend even longer trying to tell your mind what not to pay attention to, you are using up valuable time and, even more important, attentional focus. You are likely to spend more time than you would otherwise focusing on the very situation, person, event, or outcome

Performer-Centered Implementation Worksheet
Developing a Refocusing Plan

Directions

Look at the following example, and then choose three issues during a performance that are most likely to distract you or negatively affect your focus (e.g., someone from the audience or crowd heckles you; umpire, referee, judge, or official makes a call that negatively affects you or your team; you commit an error at a critical juncture). In the middle column (If this . . .) write what would occur; be as specific as possible. In the third column (Then I . . .) write what you want your response to be and how you will appropriately direct your attention when faced with that situation.

	If this . . .	Then I . . .
Example	Our bus is late to the gym for the game.	I will shorten my warm-up routine. I will do (list behaviors). I will think (list thoughts and phrases to say to yourself). I will feel (list examples of how you want to feel while you are doing your condensed warm-up).

From C. Hacker and M. Mann, *Achieving Excellence: Mastering Mindset for Peak Performance in Sport and Life* (Champaign, IL: Human Kinetics, 2023).

that you don't want to occur. So instead, as Retton acknowledged, rather than trying to avoid what is not helpful, it's better to draw your attention toward the elements, factors, and cues that are most helpful and relevant in a particular moment. For example, rather than trying to block out or ignore crowd noise, drawing your attention to your opponent's midsection or racket or feet would better bring about the performance-enhancing focus you want—to direct and control your attention effectively. This ironic processing phenomenon is one of the many reasons why honestly completing the if-then scenarios created through the worksheet on page 191 can help train the responses you want. The key is to write down where you want your attention to be drawn in less-than-ideal performance situations and then to practice cueing yourself to do just that. Over time, if you are consistent, you will be more likely to refocus effectively and efficiently without much conscious effort.

Aligning Activation With Focus

As we pointed out in chapter 6, when someone is experiencing high levels of cognitive anxiety and physical activation, their attention is often narrowed and more rigid. Learning to control activation levels can be key in developing the ability to focus on the right things at the right time. You can refer to chapter 6 for energy management strategies. A dual relationship exists between activation levels and concentration

such that systematic manipulation of concentration is one way to gain greater control over activation, and alterations in physical activation (or perceptions of anxiety) can help a performer pay attention to the most relevant cues (Nideffer 1976). In this chapter, we highlight the first half of that equation: Directing your attention appropriately can help you manage activation levels, especially in high-pressure moments, and a lack of focus or inability to focus on the right things at the right time can have catastrophic performance outcomes.

In the 1990s, the United States women's national soccer team developed an intense rivalry with the Norwegian women's soccer program. After defeating Norway in 1991 to win the first World Cup, the Americans lost in the semifinals in 1995 to Norway. Later, they would point to their loss of focus, their inability to focus on critical elements throughout the event amid endorsement deal concerns, equipment and personnel issues, and other distractions as a key factor in their momentary demise. You lose concentration when you focus on factors outside your control (Moran 2009). The team's collective inability to focus on what mattered most when it mattered most triggered a cascading and negative effect on their activation levels and, ultimately, on both their individual and collective performance. Targeting their ability to focus and appropriately concentrate then became a major point of performance enhancement during the lead-up to the Olympic Games only one year later. This scenario demonstrates that targeted concentration training and enhancing the ability to direct and maintain attention to appropriate cues can help manage even the most high-pressure situations. As golfing great Jack Nicklaus said, "Concentration is a fine antidote to anxiety."

In sport, the concept of *performance choking* is typically attached to any costly mistake or uncharacteristic error that occurs in critical junctures within the competitive event. While it is certainly true that choking can occur in those moments, the term actually refers to a much more specific experience in which the performer experiences physiological and psychological changes associated with a rapid deterioration in performance in important competitive situations. See the sidebar on the characteristics of choking on page 194.

Often, performers who are *choking* and making poor decisions will say "I didn't even see the defender" or "I can't seem to catch my breath." It might feel as though their field of vision is reduced to the point that they experience what is known as tunnel vision (where the performer feels like they are looking through a telescope and cannot widen their field of vision). Several sport researchers found that as anxiety increases, the "quiet eye" period, the time when relevant cues are processed and movement plans are developed, decreases along with performance (Wilson, Vine, and Wood 2009). As a result of these physical and mental changes, when a person is choking, performance typically decreases and does so

Chalk Talk

Characteristics of choking during competition

Psychological changes	Physiological changes
Internal focus (at the wrong time)	Increased muscle tension
Narrow focus (at the wrong time)	Increased breathing rate
Reduced attentional flexibility (unable to shift attention) often called *tunnel vision*	Increased heart rate
Rigid attention and inappropriate attentional focus (fixated on a single point)	Disrupted timing or rhythm in skill execution

dramatically, meaning their movements are more robotic and less fluid, they might fatigue faster, they tend to rush, and they are more likely to pay attention to irrelevant, unhelpful cues than they are to notice and to lock on to relevant cues.

Choking is an attentional problem in which the performer's movements are no longer automated; they are now thinking about every step in the process. Just as we described earlier in this chapter, the focus often shifts completely internally and to unhelpful cues. This increase in conscious attention means that rather than simply dropping back to pass, the quarterback is now thinking about the pattern of a five-step drop, then consciously attending to each of their possible progressions, thinking about shifting their weight from the back to the front foot, targeting a receiver, and then releasing the football. When an athlete starts to consider each of the steps required to execute their own throwing mechanics, they are much less likely to attend to what matters most (e.g., where the linebackers and safeties are playing, the defensive formation, the timing of receivers' routes; or the time, score, and momentum of the game).

Under pressure, performers revert to their dominant attentional style (Nideffer 1976), regardless of its usefulness in the situation. Instead, as Moran (2009) noted, when performers feel nervous or anxious, it's more important than ever for them to direct their attention outward or externally. Internal attention almost always leads to overthinking and moving from automatic to conscious control, both of which can be disastrous for performance. When performers are under high pressure and an event is important to them, activation and anxiety will almost always increase, and their attention will be affected. These situation-specific responses are normal and expected. For even the highest-level performers, it is not a matter of *if* they will experience a performance choke, it is *when, how often*, and for *how long*. The most important question is, *How will they respond?* So rather than try to avoid choking or pretend that it has never happened, performers should develop the skills and strategies necessary to control their focus and sustain their concentration before the situation arises, especially in high-pressure, competitive moments.

Developing a consistent preperformance routine is one useful strategy for aiding performance, and we will address it in greater detail in the next chapter. Another helpful strategy is to train your instructional self-talk so that you can direct your attention to where you want it to be and to sustain that competitive focus (see chapter 3). Finally, there are simple drills you can practice to train your ability to focus, to shift attention, and to block out distraction.

PUT IT INTO PRACTICE

Shifting Attention Drills

Try these simulations and drills to practice controlling your attention.

Sustaining Focus

Exercise 1

- Use an object that is present during your performance (e.g., hockey puck, gloves, keyboard).
- Hold it in your hands, if possible, and pay attention to how it feels, its color, its shape, and any other identifiable features.
- Set the object in front of you and try to direct your attention to it for as long as possible. Don't be surprised if that attentional focus lasts only a few seconds before your mind wanders to another thought.
- Once you can hold your attention on the object without losing focus for one minute, gradually increase your focus practice in 30-second intervals to four to five minutes. Once consistently successful, start adding distractions (e.g., music, someone clapping next to you, a buzzer sounding).
- This type of focus simulation is particularly useful in sports where vigilance (maintaining attentional focus on a point without much action involved for long periods of time) is important (e.g., out-fielders in softball or baseball must maintain vigilance so they are prepared to respond when a ball is hit in their direction, or goal-keepers in a variety of sports).

> *continued*

Shifting Attention Drills > *continued*

Exercise 2

- Watch the minute hand on a clock and avoid being distracted by the second hand.
- Any time your thoughts wander away from paying attention to the minute hand, bring them back to the specific features of that clock element (e.g., numbers, color, shape).
- Once you can sustain your focus on this object for a designated period of time, begin adding distractions (see exercise 1).
- To begin training your ability to switch or shift your attention, focus on the second hand on the clock for 15 seconds, and then shift your attention to the minute hand for one minute and then to the entire clock for one minute. The key is to ensure that you are focused only on the element you are targeting and no others. Then train your ability to move to the next focal object without holding on to thoughts about the previous clock element or where your attention is moving to next.

It is helpful after each of these simulations or between repetitions to write down all of your thoughts and feelings during the experience. Keep a record or log of how long you were able to maintain focus without distracting thoughts, what you did to redirect your attention once you became distracted, and what the distractions were so you can work to control them in the future.

Switching or Shifting Attentional Focus

Exercise 1

- Play two separate videos on different (but similarly sized) devices that are equal distances from your body.
- The videos should be different in some way (e.g., game film versus favorite television show, highlight video versus professional athlete in the same sport); the exact content contained with the videos or television show is less important. The salient feature of this task is to have two separate devices showing competing videos with sound simultaneously.
- Pay attention to one of the screens. Be sure that you are able to see and hear the commentary or dialogue. Give your undivided attention to that device.
- Shift your attention to the second device, blocking out the noise and the visual and auditory cues from the first device. Now your full attention should be devoted to what is happening during the game or show displayed on the second device.
- Now switch back. Continue this back-and-forth simulation, practicing how you direct your attention where you want it to be when you want it to be there.

- You could set up an alarm sound on your phone to cue you to switch between the two screens.
- Develop and implement instructional self-talk to help direct your attention appropriately.

It can be useful (but not required) to have someone else tell you when to shift so that the amount of time spent focusing on a particular device or screen is outside your control, unpredictable, and unknown.

Exercise 2

- If you are part of a team or group, this second exercise can help you strengthen your ability to focus on one element and block out distractions.
- Select one person and blindfold them.
- Divide half of the remaining team or group and split them up so that half are on the left side of the person and half are on the right side. This creates a tunnel-like atmosphere for the person while giving them enough space to move without contacting or running into anyone else while blindfolded.
- Once the person is blindfolded and the rest of the group is in place, set an object somewhere in the vicinity.
- Half of the team should yell distracting and incorrect cues, and the other half should direct the person appropriately and correctly. The goal is for the person to decipher which group is giving appropriate cues and then to practice blocking out the distracting noise from the other half of the group and successfully find the hidden object.

It is helpful after or between repetitions within each simulation to write down all of your thoughts and feelings during the experience. Keep a record or log of how long you were able to shift your focus, what you did to redirect your attention once you became distracted, how it felt when you were unable to shift your focus or hold it on one screen, and other elements of the experience so that you can view your progress over time.

To be effective as you gain competence with these skills, add stressors and pressure to the simulation. Practicing controlling your attention and using self-talk to direct your focus while systematically and intentionally increasing stress helps you gain confidence in your ability to concentrate on the most relevant cues in moments when it matters most.

Conclusion

Concentration is a significant differentiating factor among successful and less successful performers. Although it is commonly believed that you are simply born to be effective and skilled or ineffective and unskilled attenders, the truth is that this skill can be learned and developed. Your goal is to learn which attentional styles are most useful at different moments in your performance domain, recognize your own dominant tendencies (e.g., moments you tend to become distracted or lose focus), and then train in ways that help you gain repetitions in directing your attention accurately, under control, and at the right time. As you progress in your training, add pressure and distractions so that you can improve your ability to control your attention in moments that matter most. You will make mistakes. You will commit errors. Regaining composure and refocusing will be critical to performing effectively in those moments.

CHAPTER 12

Preperformance Routines

Every performer, athlete, and coach encounters a preevent period—the time just before competition begins when they are preparing their body, mind, and spirit for what lies ahead. In sport, each coaching staff communicates a pregame schedule to the team and includes information such as timing for events like the pregame meal, team and individual meetings, athletic trainer appointments, and travel times. However, it is up to each athlete (and high-level performers in other domains) to intentionally craft their own unique routine within that required and prescribed list of predictable preperformance events. Every performer has time to prepare for a competition and each person has emotions and thoughts leading up to the event. The *only* question that remains, then, is *Will they control their thoughts, affect, and behaviors, or will those elements control them?* A major focus for any competitor and any team should be to develop a consistent and effective performance routine. Identifying, creating, and engaging in specific and purposeful thoughts, feelings, and behaviors during this period are critical for priming desired performance. In this chapter, we explain the significance of these routines and outline how they help people direct their attention appropriately, feel confident and in control, and access their individualized zone of optimal functioning. The importance of these psychological skills is outlined in other chapters; the goal of this chapter is to explain how performers can prime themselves for performance through the use of routines.

> Watch your thoughts;
> they become words.
>
> Watch your words;
> they become actions.
>
> Watch your actions;
> they become habits.
>
> Watch your habits;
> they become character.
>
> Watch your character;
> it becomes your destiny.
>
> Lao Tzu, Chinese philosopher, author of Tao teachings

Routines Cue Your Performance

Everything in sport is based on time or situational cues, so athletes need to similarly cue their minds and bodies to respond to these critical time and situation cues occurring before a performance. If training begins at 4:00 p.m., then performers need to be primed and ready at 4:00 p.m. They cannot afford to "play themselves into" practice or competition. For example, in 2021, in a match against Jamaica, U.S. women's national soccer team player Carli Lloyd scored in the first 23 seconds—23 seconds is all the time it took for a goal to be scored. After a mere 23 seconds, Team Jamaica was trailing the best women's soccer team in the world because of an early goal. Teams and athletes cannot afford to be working themselves into game readiness; if they do, they are likely to find themselves playing from behind. This is not a hypothetical caution or conceptual anomaly; it is a factual reality. We need to be ready from the moment the contest starts until the final second of performance. This necessity is true in sport, in medicine, in business, and in life. Developing and using structured routines before performance has been associated with high-level achievement, the ability of performers to access their preferred performance state, and people's ability to cope with distractions (Boutcher 1990; Lidor and Tenenbaum 1993; Lobmeyer and Wasserman 1986).

A preperformance routine is a sequence of task-relevant thoughts and actions that an athlete engages in systematically (Moran 1996, 177). It involves intentionally planning the process of thoughts, feelings, and behaviors that the athlete prefers before performance. Once created, these routines help people focus on key information and aspects of performance that help prime or cue their minds and bodies for competition. Equally valuable, consistent preperformance routines help prevent athletes from focusing on irrelevant or unhelpful cues such as the magnitude of the moment, the opponents, or myriad internal distractions. French footballer Eric Cantona, who won five English championships (four with Manchester United), did not leave anything to chance with his routine, noting, "Preparation is everything, focus is the key" (Bull 2006). To begin creating a performance routine, use the sidebar on page 201 to identify the critical thoughts, feelings, and behaviors that help bring about your best performance.

Elite athletes and performers understand the thoughts, images, words, and behaviors that are necessary for their best performance as well as those that distract or prevent them from accessing their preferred performance states. As Major League Baseball player Gerald "Buster" Posey recognized, "The benefit of a routine is familiarity. When you step on the field, you know the work you put in is taken care of, and now it's time to go have fun." For each person, those behaviors and thoughts might be different. Stephen Curry, one of the league-leading shooters in the National Basketball Association said,

PUT IT INTO PRACTICE

Best Versus Worst Performances

By examining your best performances and comparing and contrasting them with your worst performances, you can identify the key elements of your ideal performance state. On a sheet of paper, write "best performance" at the top and write down brief responses to the following questions:

- How emotionally charged or activated were you before the performance?
- Did you feel mentally ready or prepared to perform?
- Where were you focused? On what elements?
- How worried were you about losing?
- What were you thinking about before, during, and after the performance?
- What were you saying to yourself during performance?
- How excited or calm were you before the event?
- How tense did you feel?
- How confident were you before the start of the competition?

List and describe any other elements that stood out to you about your best previous performance. For example, what did you do in the locker room or during warm-ups, and what did you think or say to yourself before competition?

Once you have determined the essential precursors to your own best performance, do the same for your worst performance. Rather than simply write the opposite of what you wrote for your best performance, in this instance, skip to the bottom half of the same page and respond to the same list of questions as you think about a specific, previous poor performance or competition.

After you have compared and contrasted both ends of the performance spectrum, identify the most important thoughts, behaviors, and feelings that facilitated or deterred your performance. Use this information to develop a specific performance routine that you can consistently implement before training sessions and competitive events in order to facilitate your performance. Evaluate its effectiveness after each performance and make necessary adjustments. Rate yourself on how consistently you followed your stated and preferred preperformance routine.

Everyone has a pattern of behavior regularly performed in the same manner—teams, players, coaches, fans. Whether it is uniform routines, face paint, or other routines, they play a big role in sport culture. . . . You need those things to settle your nerves, get your mind right, and just be able to relax and focus on what you enjoy, so those routines just help me settle in and appreciate the day and the build-up to game time . . . my game day [routines] are pretty extensive from the time I wake up to the time the game starts. . . . I have pretty much the same breakfast; after shootaround, I take about a two-hour nap; I listen to a pregame playlist in the car on the way to the game, and for the last three minutes, as I pull into any gym or arena, I play the same song. The song changes every year, but it helps me focus that now is "game time." . . . I like to have fun and not take the moments too seriously because it's a long day, and you have to be focused for two-hour games, so I try to have fun and be goofy. (Golden State Warriors 2019)

And for tennis great Arthur Ashe, the goal of his routine was to feel "physically loose and mentally tight." Each performer's routine should be unique to them. Whether they want to feel calm and collected, or they want to be excited and animated before a performance, the key is to create a routine that cues their mind and body that it is game time. These high-achieving athletes clearly recognized the benefit of solidifying their performance routines. In the sidebar on page 203, soccer player Kristine Lilly explains an element of her prematch routine.

Ronald Martinez/Getty Images

Routines allow performers to be in control. Often, people hope for a great performance in the way they hope for nice weather on game day; they wake up and hope or wish to play well. Performance routines remove the guesswork or the uncertainty and inconsistency that is common for many performers and instead help the athlete focus on what they can control and on the immediate, present moment. These routines also help to bring about preferred and consistent self-selected thoughts, behaviors, and feelings. All performers need a routine. Not just athletes but also coaches, CEOs, teachers, physical

---

IN THEIR OWN WORDS **Crafting an Intentional Routine: Kristine Lilly**

In 1996, soccer star Kristine Lilly, "Queen of Caps," and the U.S. women's national team started working with Dr. Hacker. "Nineteen ninety-six was the start of my mental training; 1996 was a year that I remember I believed in it and thought it was an important part of my training. It gave me more confidence and a place to fall back on when things weren't going so well," Lilly recalled.

That year, Dr. Hacker created an audio pregame recording with Lilly's guidance that included music and words that the National Hall of Fame athlete wanted to feel when she played. "For example, phrases like 'I want the ball, run, first touch, take on . . .' things that I wanted to do in the game and feel good about." For her, the music of choice, what she listened to as she prepared for the match, was Enya. As she said, "The combination of the words and music became part of my mental preparation for every game."

Her pregame routine included playing her imagery audio recording while she put her uniform on and one more time right before she took the field. The last action she took was to put her hair in a ponytail before going out on the field. Then she passed with Julie Foudy (and eventually Abby Wambach) at center circle before the formal team warm-ups began. She always completed three jump headers and then high-fived her left back right before the match started. "These preparations were important to me. It wasn't something that was hard. I didn't have to think about it. I just did it. It kept me calm and comfortable."

As Kristine Lilly noted, she specifically picked words or phrases and music that would help her enter her zone of optimal functioning. For her, that meant that she wanted to feel calm and confident, so her performance routine ensured that she was able to create those feelings before competition. Rather than allowing the opponent, the weather, the time of day, the importance of the event, or some other variable to dictate her emotional state or sense of readiness, she controlled her thoughts and behaviors and directed herself in ways that helped her feel calm and comfortable. Also, she noted that her routines did not add thoughts to her preparation or performance; instead, she practiced her routines so much that performing them brought about the very thoughts and feelings that she wanted to experience leading up to the match. From high-fiving specific teammates to the timing of each behavior, every performer should develop routines like Kristine Lilly outlined.

---

therapists, and anyone who performs better in one emotional state (e.g., calm, excited, loose) than another should make decisions in advance of performance about the thoughts and behaviors they want to engage in and that will facilitate the feelings they want to experience before the event. Their routine should not change based on their opponent or the size of the audience or the timing of the event or any number of possible variables that exist for every performance.

Having a routine can also help you identify reasons why you may not have been optimally ready to perform in previous competitions and help you plan or make corrections in your routines to avoid experiencing that issue again. In your last performance, if it took you a few minutes to find your groove or be ready for action, then identify what you did (or did not do) that prevented you from accessing your preferred performance zone the moment the contest began. Becoming aware of each option and decision point you have as a performer leading up to the competitive moment is critical, and to choose carefully and intentionally is an important part of any routine.

Routines—*Not* Superstitions

When initially thinking about constructing a preperformance routine, people sometimes confuse them with superstitions. An example of a superstition is when someone finds a heads-up penny on the way to the event and believes that finding that coin means they will perform well. Another superstition occurs when a performer believes they have to put their uniform on the same side of their body first or eat the same pregame meal or even wear their lucky clothes. Some performers avoid stepping on cracks on the way to the event or take the stairs two at a time as they enter the venue. The problem with superstitions is that the performer is giving up their autonomy, and, worse, they are ceding their control to chance or to actions and behaviors that don't directly affect performance.

Do you believe your performance is mostly *unpredictable* and largely *attributable to luck* or to unknown forces? If so, then you may have developed a superstition or ritual rather than a performance routine. It is okay to have superstitions if you are aware that you are making that choice and it is fun or comforting to do so. For example, if you make it fun (rather than essential or required) to find heads-up pennies on game day, then that's great as long as you also recognize that when no one finds such a penny, that does not mean you are doomed to lose. If you prefer to put your shoes on left foot first, that is perfectly fine, just as long as when something disrupts your focus and you put the right shoe on first, it does not make you feel like you are going to have a bad day at the office or on the field. Superstitions can be fun, funny, and idiosyncratic, but it is important to recognize them as such and avoid relying on them for indications of impending success or failure.

Routines, on the other hand, are examples of cognitive and behavioral cueing; they signal your mind and body that it is time to practice or train or perform. These routines give you *specific, task-oriented guidelines* to facilitate performance and increase the likelihood that you will focus on productive thoughts, helpful emotions, and facilitative behaviors rather than leaving performance up to chance or "magic" superstitions. Routines ensure that you are thinking about what you want to focus on as you are taking in that last bit of fuel at the pregame meal or to ensure that you are feeling strong or powerful or light on your feet as you put on your gear. Routines should be individually created, consistently followed, and designed to put you in control of your performance.

Another significant difference between a routine and superstition is in its flexibility. While detailed and specific to the performer, routines are also adaptable. They can be shortened or elongated when needed. The truth is that while people can control their attitude, their thoughts, their emotions, their behaviors, and their responses to adversity, they do not control every element of the environment. For example, some teams might have a certain amount of time before a competition during the season, but during postseason tournaments or matches, all teams have reduced access to the gym or arena or venue for practice and warm-up. Or a start time for the event might be pushed back. In fact, in 2021, the U.S. Olympic Trials for track and field were twice delayed, first from the afternoon to 8:30 p.m. and then to 11:30 p.m. because of dangerous heat conditions. Or perhaps the lights or electricity in the facility are knocked out by a sudden lightning storm.

Any of these examples could throw you into a tailspin, or you could have planned ahead, knowing that anything is likely to happen, and that something might require you to shorten or lengthen your routine or change the start time of the performance. If you plan which elements to reduce or eliminate and which could be extended, then, when that moment does happen, all that is left to do is make the planned change and confidently adapt. Another benefit of a routine is that after thinking through your performance and developing a routine that allows you to control what you can, there should be less room and fewer factors that could derail your plans.

Unplanned, unpredictable, and uncontrollable variables will occur, so you want to have a response planned for those moments. Relying on superstitions might cause you to feel unhinged or begin to unravel when the unexpected happens, while having a flexible routine allows you to pivot and continue confidently preparing for your performance. Develop your routine, and then plan for traffic on the freeway or when the official does not show or any number of common and unforeseen events. *What will you do? How will you adjust?* Before the 2014 Sochi Olympics, following the advice of the mental skills coach, Dr. Hacker, the general manager and coaching staff for the U.S. women's ice hockey team wanted to have a plan for everything, so they had the lights in the rink intentionally turned off during a training event and required athletes to deal with that unexpected event and still perform to capability. Certainly, those moments are exceptions, but you should have a plan in place so that when disruptions and changes occur—and they will—you are prepared to adjust your routine accordingly and avoid a loss in performance. When that unplanned, unwanted distraction occurs, you make choices about what you will eliminate or truncate in the original plan. Everything becomes a choice and a decision so that you have a feeling of control. You are confident that you have planned for this disruption and are ready to engage your plan, even if it is plan B. The goal is to think about your ability to adapt your plan as a competitive strength. To do so, you must prepare in advance and commit to consistently enacting your routine.

Committing to Consistency

Athletes frequently report that "getting off their routine" or not "coming ready to play" are two common attributes of poor performance. Increasing the consistency of a routine will lead to enhanced performance (Jackson 2003). Unfortunately, many athletes view game day performance much like they do buying a lottery ticket—they wake up and hope it is going to be a winning number. And as a result, they lack a consistent preperformance routine. It changes from contest to contest, opponent to opponent, and location to location. Depending on the time of season, previous performance outcomes, or playing status, performers might create different routines. Inconsistent preperformance routines often lead to inconsistent performances.

In the lead-up to the Tokyo Olympic Games, media coverage of athletes increased. During the 11 months prior, swimmers and gymnasts and track and field athletes trained in relative obscurity, able to focus completely on the task at hand. But, as they moved closer to the qualifying events for their respective Olympic teams, many of these same athletes ended up spending an increasing amount of time on social media reading what the public and sports writers were saying about their performance. It should come as no surprise, then, that performance problems can occur when athletes are required to alter an element of their routine (e.g., engaging with social media differently, interacting with members of the press) for the first time prior to a gold medal performance or the biggest moment of their performance career. These changes to routine can and do have an impact on belief, on preparation, and on confidence, often a negative one. In a different example, if an athlete expects to defeat a lower-ranked opponent, then they might feel more relaxed, talk more in the locker room, and feel more confident before the contest. They might be relaxed and loose when they are typically quiet and focused. On the other hand, when they play an opponent who is challenging—who has defeated them in the past—often, people will watch more game film, review more scouting notes, be more serious and focused in the locker room. The problem here is that the opponent now is dictating whether or not the athlete is consistent in their routine.

In these situations, ask yourself these questions: Is my routine for home games the same or different than for away games? Do I feel, think, and behave the same for the big game as I do for the match against the last-place team or opponent? Do I follow the same procedure if I am starting or if I am coming off the bench? For most athletes, it is the situation that determines their pregame preparation rather than their individual needs and known precursors for peak performance. These different routines trigger your mind differently and might have an adverse effect on technical or tactical execution. How might having these multiple, competing thoughts slow or disrupt the timing of performance? Remember, you have choices; choose wisely.

The number of variables that cause people to change their routines is varied and significant. In the earlier scenarios, creating a different preperformance routine for different situations prevents consistency. People almost always claim they have a preperformance routine, despite consistent evidence to the contrary. Very often, their routine changes based on outside factors. Without consistency, there is no routine. If people inconsistently engage in their routine, how will they know what works? Which thoughts or actions are less effective in positively affecting their performance? If they believe that their thoughts, their behaviors, and their emotions all affect their performance (and they do), then consistently controlling them is an important factor in determining success.

Create Multiple, Specific Routines

Certainly, someone might have multiple performance routines, but each one should be consistent. For example, practice or training or work environments have different performance requirements than competitive or evaluative situations like a game or match or presentation or surgery. Daily training sessions, for example, might occur while someone is also working or attending classes or taking care of children, so how one transitions from daily life into their performance mindset for practice or daily work might be an important part of their routine. Prepractice routines often differ, at least slightly, from precompetition routines. An athlete might start their competitive routine the night before a match or game, whereas the starting point for a practice routine might be driving to the facility or walking into the locker room. The important point is that an athlete should develop routines for *both* practice and competition, and that those individual routines, while different from each other, should be consistently implemented over time.

A third type of routine occurs just before someone needs to perform a closed skill such as a free throw in basketball, a serve in tennis or volleyball, or a penalty kick in soccer. Any particular skill (within the larger sport context) in which the execution is predictable, unchanging, and known and in which the action is almost completely under the control of the athlete is known as a closed skill. More than any other type of skill, closed skills benefit greatly from preperformance routines. These task routines help the performer create rhythm, consistency, predictability, and control, which are necessary for success. Canadian Steve Nash, a two-time NBA most-valuable player and an NBA coach, would practice his shot several times before the referee passed him the ball at the free throw line. Then, once he received the ball, he licked the tips of his fingers and combed his hair out of his eyes before attempting his shot. He completed this preshot routine before every free throw he took in the NBA and averaged over 90 percent success at the foul line over the course of his career.

Rather than relying on numerous outside forces over which you have limited or no control (e.g., the quality of your opponents, whether you start or not, the crowd, the media hype, the field, the weather conditions, or the officiating), you are encouraged to take responsibility for preparing yourself appropriately to reach a peak level of performance each and every time you step into the competitive arena. Your routine cannot be like the weather, changing from one day to the next. Your performance needs to occur on demand. You have to earn that confidence—not hope for that confidence—by implementing your routines day after day, practice after practice, time after time, and situation after situation.

There is also an additive effect to the efficacy of routines when teammates and coaches all adhere to their own plans and respect those of others. If one athlete always warms up with the same teammate, then the positive effect that behavior will have on both people's performance can be additive for the team. So there is a collective commitment and a collective efficacy that occurs when each person is meeting their own performance routine responsibilities. Players need to not only follow their own mental game plan before matches, but they also need to respect and protect their teammates' needs and style. There is an individual and collective sense of responsibility. And any time one person is not engaging in their respective routine, then they are also affecting other teammates who are likely aware of and affected by the change. When that happens, someone is then required to take time, focus, and energy away from their own preperformance routine to get the less consistent teammate back on track. As a performer, you have a responsibility not only to yourself for your routine but also to your teammates and coaches. The sidebar on page 209 offers an example of this collective commitment to adhering to personal pregame routines while also respecting teammates' different but equally important routines.

Recognize and Address Inconsistencies

There will be moments in your career when you or someone on your team for some reason does not engage in a planned and rehearsed routine. There is an obvious moment of inconsistency. Now what? You should not ignore it. You must intervene. Just as there is an additive effect when

Committed to the Fidelity of the Mission: USWNT and Individual Performance Routines

On the U.S. women's national soccer team, it was customary to divide the locker room into different areas. One section became the quiet, more solitary, contemplative space where players might be reading books, preparing their gear or listening to their recorded scripts. Another area was reserved for athletes whose individual performance zone reflected a loud, boisterous, loose, and communal engagement. In this section, athletes might be painting their fingernails, singing, dancing, or jogging around the locker room.

These spaces were separated by whatever distance was available so that athletes who needed and wanted to physically move around and sing before a match could do so without interacting with or disrupting athletes who were quiet, listening to their headphones, or just imagining the upcoming game. This separation honored, acknowledged, and allowed for those individual differences. The team knew and celebrated those differences and took responsibility for protecting each respective space so that every athlete could take control of their own best performances.

On an international trip, just before a match against Portugal, the 20 or 22 members began dividing their locker room so that the training room became the space where the "loud crowd" congregated, and a separate area was designated for the quiet, more introspective, or solitary-focused athletes on the team. What made this day different was that an athlete on the team, who was typically in the quiet group, came into the training room side of the locker room where the loud crowd was preparing for the match. This athlete was listening to her music and quietly preparing for the match while other athletes were singing and dancing around her. Immediately, without prompting, the loud crowd started yelling, "Get out of here! You're raining on our IPZ (individualized performance zone)! We don't want that energy in here!"

Without hesitation the quiet, introspective athlete grabbed her belongings and headed back to the other side of the locker room. Athletes in both groups were then smiling, aware, and ready to play.

In this example, the team demonstrated an understanding that, in order to perform well collectively, they each needed to be able to access their individual performance zone. And to do so, each athlete might need to think or feel or experience something different in the locker room before the match. It is not about creating a mandated and required team or group pregame protocol for all athletes to behave the same way; it is knowing what each person needs in order to perform at their best and then intentionally creating an environment that facilitates, respects, and honors that performance state. The goal is for every athlete to know what they need and then to commit to thinking and acting purposefully and authentically.

Avoid situations in which an athlete does something that is not in line with their best performance zone. For example, avoid situations in which a normally quiet athlete all of a sudden starts telling jokes or dancing with teammates before the match or vice versa. As a result of knowing themselves and their teammates, the USWNT guarded and protected their individual and collective routines and committed to their mission of consistently enacting their own preperformance routines so they could bring about high-level performance with consistency and confidence.

everyone adheres to their routine, there is also a negative effect that accumulates if additional people become affected when someone is out of sync.

In the best-case scenario, you and your team have a plan for what to do when you notice someone off of their routine, and each player is equipped in advance with a way to intervene, similar to the example from the U. S. women's national team on page 209. If you have not planned this response and intervention in advance, the moment it is needed is often too late, and that athlete and team may suffer as a result and fail to perform to potential. You cannot pretend it is not happening or ignore it, and, at a minimum, it is your responsibility to prevent it from having an additional, ongoing, and negative effect on other people who are now having to truncate or disrupt their own routines to help this person. In this instance, it is a matter of team or individual accountability.

By focusing on a personally developed plan—one that is used for all competitions and does not differ greatly between performance opportunities—players can expect to feel a greater sense of confidence and readiness to perform well, but when that has not happened, intervention should occur. Otherwise, they are leaving the successful turnaround or the consequences to chance and, in the meantime, other athletes are likely to be pulled out of their routines to deal with it in some way, directly or indirectly. To intervene, a trusted staff member, a coach, a captain, or a close friend needs to say something that will help that athlete focus on the present moment and remind them of their strengths. The coach could direct their attention to their traditional routine, perhaps by saying "I am here to get you back on track." Or a teammate might say "Let's talk about our player-to-player defense" or "Let's listen to music over the speakers," or they might try to tell a joke. It is essential that each member of the team is aware of their teammates' best performance zone and, when they seem off track, use a strengths-based intervention to direct the athlete's thoughts and attention to what they do well before a performance. Accountability, ownership, and leadership become critical and should be facilitated throughout the season.

Respecting Individuality

Each athlete should make a conscious effort to follow their established routine, which is designed to bring about or replicate their previous best performances. Nothing should be left to chance. Performers are in control of their thoughts, feelings, and behaviors. For some people, these routines start the night before an event, for others, their preparation for performance begins the morning of the competition, and for a third group of people, their routines begin enroute to the event site or venue. The point is that routines can and should be individualized for every performer to help direct their focus on the right things at the right time so they can activate themselves appropriately.

It is important for people to write down their performance routines to add a level or degree of ownership. After completing the Put It Into Practice activity on page 201, fill out the worksheet on page 212 in order to draft your own performance routine. Remember as you complete the worksheet that the goal is to identify the thoughts, feelings, and behaviors you will engage in to bring about your best performance. Your plan should specify what you prefer to think, say, and do in key moments related to your performance domain. It is important to make the plan specific by using time scales or significant, meaningful, and critical moments in the lead-up to competition. Once constructed, *implement*, *evaluate*, and *refine the plan*. Visual reminders can be kept as hard copies (e.g., in kit bags, on lockers) or in electronic format (e.g., on phones, tablets) to cue the start of your routine.

It can be challenging to build routines within teams—to allow individual variations in group or team routines—even when leaders know it is in the best interest of the individual (and team) to do so. Coaches and sport leaders play a significant role in the routines of their athletes. Not only should they encourage performers to identify their ideal performance state and build routines to attain those preferences, but coaches must also ensure that the physical team warm-up matches each athlete's needs without draining their tanks before the competition begins.

Coaches and leaders often like to be in control, and whether they know it or not, they often feel more confident about athletes who have a performance routine that matches their own. So if a leader warms up and acts a certain way, and an athlete warms up and acts that same way, then coaches tend to approve, feel more confident, and prefer that every team member adopts that same approach. Coaches and leaders are much more comfortable when everybody does the same thing in the same way at the same time with the same language, energy, and body language. In other words, they have a narrower zone for acceptance of and confidence in individual preperformance routines. Even though they all want their athletes to be in their best performance states, coaches are not particularly skilled at providing support for a variety of individual routines. As a captain, a leader, a coach, or an integral staff member, it is important to be aware that each athlete has an ideal or preferred performance zone, and therefore the leader needs to create diverse routine options.

Once this awareness is achieved, working to find ways to ensure that each and every athlete is competition ready is crucial. It might be helpful to allow athletes to select their own partners and engage in a warm-up with them, then in small groups, and finally in a small-group activity that approximates the competitive level without draining fitness or cognitive resources. In soccer, that might mean 3 v 3 v 3 small-sided games that cue quick passing in small spaces under pressure so that the thinking and foot skills and the body preparation takes place at match speed. Each athlete does not have to be engaged in the same task for the entire

Create Your Preperformance Routine

As we have indicated previously, some people begin their performance routine the night before or the morning of the performance, and others begin their routine on the way to the event site. There is no right time or best time to begin; your preperformance routine starts when it's best for you! By the time you enter the green room (as a public speaker) or locker room (as an athlete), your routine should be underway. You might prefer to develop a detailed plan, while other people follow a general outline that is loose. The purpose of this worksheet is to help ensure that your routine is personal, purposeful, and successful. It should be meaningful and useful for *you*.

Directions

In the table that follows, review the example provided. These are only a few examples of times or moments that might be important for a performer. You might choose to add your own or eliminate elements of the example that do not fit you or that are less relevant in your performance domain.

Once you have read through the example, write down times and environmental cues that are meaningful to you as you prepare to perform. Then write what you want to say, how you want to feel, and what you are doing physically (behaviors) at each of those time intervals from the moment you begin preparing for your performance until the end of the event.

Time	Environmental cue or event	Behaviors	Thoughts or images	Feelings
8:30 a.m.	Waking up		"I love game day!"	Rested Excited
9:15 a.m.	Preevent meal	Prepare breakfast. Smile.	"Ah, game day."	Calm
10:30 a.m.	Driving to performance venue		"I am prepared and ready."	
10:45 a.m.	Locker room	Change into uniform.	"I am light on my feet."	Excited Nervous
	On-site Warm-up 10 min before event 2 min before event Last 10 seconds At the whistle or start		"I am strong."	

From C. Hacker and M. Mann, *Achieving Excellence: Mastering Mindset for Peak Performance in Sport and Life* (Champaign, IL: Human Kinetics, 2023).

warm-up. Some athletes may need to be on the field, court, ice, track, or in the pool for less time than others. The point is to make sure that when they are engaged in the physical warm-up, it is helping them cue their mind and body for the pressures inherent in the competition rather than creating a performative, choreographed, artistic warm-up that seems to be designed more for the crowd or program notoriety than for athletes' game preparation. Warm-ups are often entire-team functions that focus on looking fancy or being distinct or noteworthy rather than focused on the individual and team preparation for excellence. Ultimately, the physical warm-up that teams engage in before competition should be inclusive of each athlete's routine and also the collective requirements of the sport and needs of the group.

Conclusion

Throughout this chapter, we have encouraged you to create and solidify detailed, purposeful, and flexible performance routines. Your routine should be individualized, and you should practice it consistently both in practice and across competitive demands. Over time and with consistent practice, these unique performance routines should become automated and implemented with little conscious thought. Remember, the purpose of a routine is not to cause people to think more often or to add conscious decision points; instead, routines direct attention, improve focus, and help free people to more consistently access their preferred performance state or competitive zone.

People think thoughts and perform actions but rarely do they do so with both purpose and intention. The goal of this chapter is to help you highlight elements of your performance plans that are consistent and to recognize areas that are inconsistent so you can edit and improve them.

Consider your preperformance routine as part of your actual performance. If all of the elements that you outlined in your preperformance routine (what you think, feel, say, and do) affect your performance, then, really, what you are creating is a performance routine, not merely a *pre*performance routine. That subtle change in language reminds you that you are already influencing performance before you go to bed, when you wake up, when you are traveling to the stadium, or during warm-up. As soon as you begin preparing, you are affecting performance. Be sure that you are in control of and have planned in advance how you want to think, act, and feel. Once you have created and rehearsed your routine, you have to protect it and hone it; every element needs to have a purpose and lead you to be maximally prepared to give your best performance the moment that practice or the contest begins.

CHAPTER 13

Prioritizing Self-Reflection

Throughout this book, we consistently reference the importance of self-awareness and self-regulation. To learn new skills, to change behavior, and to sustain those changes, performers must first become aware of the correction that needs to be made, recognize when the adjustment is needed, and, finally, be able to implement the skill or strategy (e.g., imagery, breath control, self-talk)

> Always ask yourself if what you're doing today is getting you closer to where you want to be tomorrow.
>
> Paulo Coelho de Souza, Brazilian lyricist and author of *The Alchemist*

to bring about the desired change. People must analyze themselves (i.e., self-awareness) and then be capable of managing their thoughts and behaviors moving forward (i.e., self-regulation). Self-reflection is the foundation of that process. Without it, performers are far less likely to become self-aware and capable of self-regulating. As educational reformer John Dewey noted, "We do not learn from experience. We learn from reflecting on experience." This chapter is centered on the components of a reflexive practice and strategies for developing this skill as a performer.

The Value of Feed Forward

The benefits of thinking about one's own thoughts and behaviors, engaging in true reflection, have been well-documented in almost every professional field (e.g., Farres 2004; Johns 2011; Knowles et al. 2007; Osterman and Kottkamp 1993). In business, skilled self-reflection has been associated with increased consistency in planning and decision-making, improved problem-solving capabilities, and sound and efficient adjustments to market changes (Donovan, Guss, and Nasland 2015). Reflective opportunities offered at the end of class helped pharmacy students identify deficiencies in their knowledge, improve their study habits (e.g., increased time spent studying and attending review sessions), and improve performance on summative evaluations (Vinall and Kreys 2020). And in the sport arena, higher-skilled athletes often report greater volumes of self-reflection to help reduce their errors and improve performance (Baker and Young 2014; Locke and Latham 2002; Wilson et al. 2021). A study of adolescent female athletes by van der Sluis and colleagues (2019) found that self-monitoring—reflecting on and regulating their behaviors—predicted time lost to injuries.

Although the evidence is clear on the value of reflection, far too often, performers reflect only after moments of crisis. People critically evaluate themselves *after* the handoff to the anchor leg in the 4 × 100-meter relay during the World Championships is missed, or the team scores an own goal during the World Cup, or a gate is missed during an Olympic slalom event that keeps the skier off the podium. Certainly, it is helpful to engage in reflective work after crucial mistakes and errors. The point, here, is to counter the narrative that reflection is only useful for providing feedback to the performer about what happened. Rather, it may be helpful to think of this information as feed forward information that can be used to correct or enhance future performances. Reflecting in this way can improve self-efficacy, or self-belief, in one's own ability to complete the task, and it should also be used to inform the planning and preparation for the next practice session, training block, or competition. For example, if watching the race film and talking through the dropped handoff leads to a change in technique, then once that technique is mastered, presumably the error would be avoided in the future. Using information gained through reflection to improve future performances can protect and enhance the belief these sprinters have in themselves and in each other as they move from training for the World Championship to training for the Olympic Games later in the year. Reflection can also be useful in building awareness for areas of growth, developing honesty and trust among team members, identifying strengths, setting goals, and evaluating one's own performance. The sidebar on page 217 offers a first-hand account of one elite performer's demonstration of high-level self-reflection. In this retelling of a professional experience, Dr. Hacker, who worked with Mia Hamm and the U.S. women's national soccer team, recounts with precision the effect of Hamm's reflective skills.

As highlighted in Mia Hamm's story, reflection is more than knowing what needs to be done. Most people are aware of which errors they need to correct. Reflection is more than occasionally and randomly thinking through errors and correcting them. True reflection must be intentional, systematic, consistent, and purposeful. That type of self-analysis carries with it a high return on investment.

Defining Self-Reflection

Reflective practice need not occur only after a mistake. Any time performers explore and evaluate their own thoughts, behaviors, and feelings in order to increase self-understanding and to manage their behaviors, they are engaging in reflection (Grant, Franklin, and Langford 2002; Locke and Latham 2006; Osman 2011). More specifically, as Boyd and Fales

IN THEIR OWN WORDS A Retelling of Elite Reflection

Considered by many as one of the greatest soccer players in history and one of the greatest overall athletes in the United States, Mia Hamm was often flooded with questions from reporters after matches. It was common for her to be surrounded by a horde of reporters in the locker room, often asking variations of the same sets of questions without listening to how she had answered a similar prompt previously.

After one match in particular, Mia was sitting in front of her locker; the lights were bright, the mics were on, and a half-dozen reporters were standing directly in front of her and even more standing behind the immediate press group. On this day, people were asking some version of "Mia, what's it like to be the greatest soccer player in the world right now?" Before she could even respond, the next reporter would ask, "Mia, what's it like to carry the weight of the sport on your shoulders?" That was the topic of choice—time after time, a similar question: "What's it like to be the greatest in the world at what you do?"

What people might not be aware of is that Mia Hamm is very honest. She is extremely self-reflective, and she understands the true and the bigger picture. So when Mia listened to yet another iteration of the same question, she paused and reflected. Finally, she said, "When I achieve the fitness of Kristine Lilly, when I have the warrior spirit of Michelle Akers, when I develop the leadership of Julie Foudy and Carla Overbeck, when I have the heading capability to score goals like Tisha Venturini, then come back and talk to me."

She was both clear and specific, and she could have gone through the entire U.S. lineup pointing to the unique skills and capabilities that each teammate possessed. Each teammate had strengths and skills that she wanted to emulate. Each teammate had capabilities in their own game that she wanted to hone, to develop, to improve on. For Mia, this moment was about more than complimenting her teammates, she took the time to self-reflect. She demonstrated not only that she recognized her teammates' skills but also that she was aware of her own areas for growth. She was one of the best players in the world and everyone knew it. But as a high achiever, Mia did not think in those terms. She thought about what was possible—where else could she get better? It was a powerful testament of reflection. Her introspection and awareness had helped her define an internal competitive standard, one that was void of external accolades and media attention. She was mastery oriented and always working to refine her skills. And it was this internal drive, this self-awareness, this self-reflection that made Mia Hamm one of the greatest performers to ever play any sport.

Often, the best athlete on the team or the board-certified surgical prodigy or the CEO of a Fortune 100 company thinks about what they have accomplished. Less often do people consider where they are now versus what is left for them to improve. This story of Mia Hamm demonstrates how her self-reflection made her aware of the distinct growth areas that she could refine and enhance. And if she chose to do so, she knew she would be a better performer. Accurately, effectively, and honestly reflecting on your own performances allows you the opportunity to become aware of your strengths and areas for growth, progress, and development.

(1983) defined it, reflection is "the process of internally examining and exploring an issue of concern, triggered by an experience, which creates and clarifies meaning in terms of self and results in a changed conceptual perspective" (100). This definition is important because it purports that reflection is more than a cognitive or intellectual task. Simply thinking about what happened is not true reflection. It matters and is an important first step, but reflection does not end with becoming more aware of the process or outcome. Instead, it involves thinking about what occurred or what will occur in order to edit or solidify an action and then to *act* on the resulting knowledge.

Reflection is often challenging and sometimes painful. It requires you to be critical of yourself in order to identify areas and strategies for developing your craft. Jesse Owens, who in 1936 was the first American track and field athlete to win four gold medals at a single Olympic Games, believed in the challenge embedded in self-reflection. As he saw it, "The battles that count aren't the ones for gold medals. The struggles within yourself—the invisible, inevitable battles inside all of us—that's where it's at." This struggle is not just for athletes to face. In research over the past several decades, it has become clear that becoming an expert in any performance domain requires consistent work. K. Anders Ericsson, one of the leading researchers in this area wrote, "The journey to truly superior performance is neither for the faint of heart nor for the impatient. The development of genuine expertise requires struggle, sacrifice, and honest, often painful self-assessment. There are no shortcuts" (Ericsson, Prietula, and Cokely 2007). Both of these quotes assert that critical self-reflection is necessary and, in fact, is a separator among high achievers.

Rather than treating self-reflection like the warm-up or cool-down elements of a fitness routine—the parts that are acknowledged as important but rarely performed—we ought to be reflecting on our thoughts and behaviors consistently and over time. One of the greatest coaches of all time, John Wooden, who won 7 national basketball championships in a row and 10 NCAA titles in 12 seasons, said it like this: "Without proper self-evaluation, failure is inevitable." This sentiment is shared by nine-time best-selling author Margaret Wheatley (2007), who noted, "Without reflection, we go blindly on our way, creating unintended consequences, and failing to achieve anything useful." Through goal-focused self-reflection, performers should become aware of their strengths and areas for growth and enact strategies to enhance their experiences (Sanders and McKeown 2008). Asking yourself targeted questions about key decisions and behaviors promotes cognitive flexibility because it requires you to think through alternative strategies. To avoid reflection, to sidestep this process, is to risk coaching or leading or performing the exact same season (or year) every year for the rest of your career. It is *that* significant; high-quality self-reflection is a game changer.

The Blue Angels serve as the U.S. Navy's flight demonstration squadron, and they fly all over the country every year in high-speed shows. They are considered one of the most elite flying teams in the world, often flying upside down within 36 inches (.91 m) from one another at approximately 500 miles per hour (804 km/hour). For perspective, that is akin to flying at a closer distance than your feet are from your head. Most pilots never fly within 10 feet (3 m) of another plane. Suffice it to say, they are a high-performing team. One of the reasons for their success is how they reflect during their postperformance debriefs.

IN THEIR OWN WORDS **Blue Angels Reflection**

The Blue Angels believe, according to former lead solo pilot John Foley, "sustained success requires constant improvement." As part of their process and out of their work together, a former Marine Corps jet fighter instructor and lead solo pilot of the Blue Angels, John Foley, constructed the Diamond Performance Framework, which builds on the lessons and processes developed and enacted by the Blue Angels.

This framework involves elements discussed throughout this book (e.g., focus, preevent planning, self-efficacy). One of the elements of this performance model is an opportunity for reflection. The Blue Angels are known for taking time to debrief together immediately after every performance. It is their process for ensuring that "vital information and important feedback" surfaces and is shared quickly. They consider this reflective event and experience "the most important facet of the performance framework" and argue that every organization, team, class, or other group should embed it in their organizational culture. As the Blue Angels note, while reflection is not a new idea, very "few companies make it a standard practice."

After every practice flight and show, the six elite pilots sit in a room together and talk openly and honestly about the errors or flaws in their flight. Foley notes that for the Blue Angels, the debriefing room is a "special, sacred place" because of their individual and collective commitment to improvement and honesty. The physical room is not the key, any room becomes sacred because of their dedicated and focused approach. They believe that unless they are completely honest about what went well and what needs to be improved, they cannot get better, and for them, that outcome would be unacceptable.

The Blue Angels team believes this process is so important, and they protect their space to such a high degree, that they only select three pilots each year to even begin the process of joining the team. After that invitation, the pilot must agree to train for three months, must demonstrate that they are improving their performance through training, and must show that they understand the team's performance process *before* the others will entertain the idea of accepting the pilot into the team. It is their way of ensuring that the "commitment to improvement mindset" and "culture of excellence" is sustained through generations of the most elite pilots in the world.

> continued

Blues Angels Reflection > *continued*

"The Blue Angels hold a debriefing after every flight, whether it's an air show with thousands of spectators or a practice in the middle of the desert. We always debrief, *no exceptions*."
Based on Foley (2013).

The Blue Angels reflect after every practice and show. They do not wait until an error has been committed to think about their flight patterns or strategies. They make it a consistent part of their daily training routine and intentionally engage in reflection over time as part of their ascent to become the most elite flying squadron in the United States.

Critical Elements of an Effective Reflection

To reflect means to be open to variations in your thoughts, your behaviors, your process, your values, and your experiences. It means that you refuse to shut down or shut off queries about yourself and your decisions. Rather, you remain open to the possibilities and variations that you might become more aware of as you question your strategies and actions. In the next section, we outline the purpose and timing of reflective practice.

Three Levels of Reflective Questions

Self-reflection is a multifaceted process that brings about self-awareness and leads to self-regulation. To become more aware, performers must first attend to and examine their own thoughts, emotions, and behavioral responses. They must reflect. A lack of awareness about strengths and deficiencies in athletes almost always stems from a hyper focus on the outcome. When implemented appropriately, self-reflection can promote self-awareness of the performance process, and help people challenge themselves consistently (Cowden 2017).

There are three levels that the critical, reflective questions you pose should occupy: *technical*, *practical*, and *critical* (Clarke, James, and Kelly 1996).

Technical self-reflection includes questions related to performing specific skills or demonstrating competence, whereas reflecting on thoughts and decisions at the secondary level involves exploring the personal meaning, experience, or perceptions that you might have had during the performance. Finally, you want to make sure that as you reflect, you are critically examining the social and cultural factors that might have prevented or encouraged you to take the action you ultimately chose. For example, you might challenge your habitual practices (e.g., I did it this way because I always have), or you might question the structure of the organization itself (e.g., I did not speak up because junior members of the group are not supposed to talk).

At each level, you explore and sometimes interrogate every moment of your performance, looking for clues that help you understand and evaluate your thoughts and behaviors so you can plan what you might do in the future. For example, a taxi driver might review their strategy of idling at the airport one day as opposed to idling downtown. This performer might examine their number of rides and the total distance of the rides in relation to the cost per hour of idling as they evaluate themselves from a technical perspective. Even better, they could examine whether they have idled downtown before on the same day of the week and at a similar time because part of the reflection value might involve comparing the technical and tactical strategies.

From a practical perspective, the driver would ask themselves questions about the types of interactions with their passengers and how those might have differed from locations away from the airport. Reflecting in this area might also bring up questions about how safe they felt idling near the airport or what their camaraderie with other drivers waiting for passengers entailed. At the critical level, the driver might also examine their tips per distance traveled compared with those of passengers working downtown and think of those differences in terms of economic factors at play. Rather than shut down any of these questions or pathways to different choices, the driver would remain open to each possible strategy. For example, they might decide that tips are a little less in one location, but the practical perceptions and personal experience in one location are so much better that it is worth idling in a place that yields lower tips. Had the driver only reflected on the technical level and examined their tips without thinking through the practical or critical personal elements, then they might make an undesirable decision in the future about where to idle as they wait for the next passenger. Taking this careful, intentional approach each day would help the driver make an informed decision about the best locations in the region to idle based on day and time.

The taxi driver in the example had to know their craft in order to conceive of and then answer the critical, self-reflective questions. To engage in reflection, a performer must understand both the particular task and its unique requirements. Otherwise they risk what is known in psychology as the "double curse of incompetence," also known as the Dunning-Kruger effect, whereby insufficient knowledge yields an inability to accurately assess thoughts, skills, and behaviors (Dunning et al. 2003; Kruger and Dunning 1999). This idea suggests that if someone is not knowledgeable about their profession or performance domain, then they are more likely to evaluate themselves and their actions too positively. An example might be if a coach asks first-year field hockey players to reflect on their effort during a practice drill by showing a thumbs-up (I gave a significant amount of effort) or thumbs-down (I gave very little effort), and they all give a thumbs-up sign. A seven-year-old, first-time hockey player might not be aware of what effort should look like in that drill and on that task; they might believe that running the entire time equated to a productive effort. As a result, they all rate themselves highly even if that assessment is not accurate. In this situation, these athletes are experiencing the "double curse of incompetence" because their lack of knowledge affects not only their performance but also their self-reflection, which limits their ability to improve.

It is critical that as you reflect on each of the three levels—tactical, practical, critical—you view each action taken from multiple angles and perspectives. A former college basketball coach at the University of Oklahoma asked her players to write their perceptions of the game in the locker room immediately after coming off the court. Then, rather than responding to the team emotionally, she would read their reflections and think through all of the possible coaching strategies she could use to respond. Doing so allowed her to better understand the emotions of her team and allowed her to build a plan to help move them forward the next day in practice. In addition, she afforded the student-athletes on her team an opportunity to discover their own strengths and limitations. Encouraging them to self-reflect let the players do the work rather than the coach telling the players what to do all of time. Self-reflection rather than externally imposed assessment is often a more meaningful and effective way to learn. Another example of considering multiple angles and perspectives on reflection comes from Ravizza, Fifer, and Bean (2020). They suggest having athletes write a scouting report on their own strengths and areas for growth. *What would an opponent say about them? What do they want an opponent to say about their play? What do they need to do differently (or the same) to bring the latter about?* Investigating performance from multiple perspectives prevents personal bias and helps create a more holistic, complex, and accurate view of the performance. This reflective process is neither simple nor short; however, when done well, it can be incredibly powerful. The painstaking measures people take now will be worth it as they see the positive impact that reflection can have on their thoughts, behaviors, and future performances.

Timing of Self-Reflection

Self-analysis should always occur after a performance and at the end of the season or competitive event, but it might, when appropriate, occur in action as well. A softball player might quickly reflect on what happened in the field last inning while they are in the dugout watching their teammate at bat, or an ice hockey player might quickly reflect on their last shift once they are off the ice again. Similarly, a surgeon might notice a change in their patient's heart rate or breathing pattern and immediately reflect on their previous decision or actions. These brief moments of self-reflection can be critical in performance; however, they should only be conducted when there is sufficient time to do so. Reflection should not occur while a player is actively defending their opponent or just as they are about to take the handoff from a teammate. As will be mentioned when we discuss mistake routines (chapter 15), reflection should only take place when it is appropriate for a performer's focus to be in the past, not attending to events occurring in the present. If they need to think about what is happening right now, then reflection should wait.

When you reflect *after* a performance, the reflection process should occur immediately (or as close to immediately as possible) after the end of the event. This structure ensures that you can remember with as much vividness and detail as possible what actually occurred. The longer you wait to reflect, the more your memory of the event becomes clouded by your emotions and personal experiences and the less accurate your interpretations will be. Sometimes it seems as though there will never be a good moment to reflect after a success or after a failure. Yet, it is your responsibility to make time and space for reflection. We recommend you develop reflection as part of your postperformance routine. Perhaps it is after you shower postgame, or maybe you reflect with your legal trial team each day during a meal, or you might reflect on your commute home after work. The point is to make sure that you *are* reflecting consistently and intentionally over time.

Reflective Models

"I don't want to be better than you or her or him. I want to be better than I am right now," three-time Olympic gold medal beach volleyball player Kerri Walsh Jennings said. To accomplish that goal and to improve your skills, it is important to think about how you think and act. As psychologist Angela Duckworth says, "When you look at healthy and successful and giving people, they are extraordinarily meta-cognitive. They're able to say things like, 'I totally lost my temper this morning'" (Scelfo 2016). Multiple frameworks, processes, and strategies exist to help performers become more self-reflective, three examples of which we will briefly outline. The point is not to use all three models at once but rather to experiment with each one and spend time with every model, and then decide which one you want to integrate into your training.

Six-Stage Cyclical Model

The first model is one of the earliest structures or outlined processes for people to use when reflecting (Gibbs 1988). It offers a path for examining individual and group experiences. One of the most unique features of Gibbs' framework is that it suggests that reflection is an unending cycle from which a performer or group can learn what went well or what can be improved (see figure 13.1).

Using this model, reflection is viewed as a dynamic process that is constantly changing and adapting based on the reflective

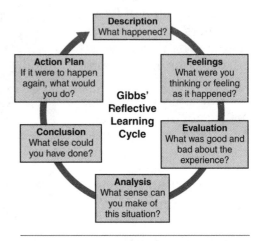

FIGURE 13.1 Gibbs' (1988) cyclical model of reflection.

skills of the performer, the context, and the situation being evaluated. There are six stages in Gibbs' (1988) model:

1. *Description* of the experience
2. *Feelings* and thoughts about the experience
3. *Evaluation* of the experience
4. *Analysis* of the performer's behavior in relation to the task demands
5. *Conclusion* about what was learned and what could be done differently
6. *Action plan* for how the performer would deal with similar situations in the future

Stage One: Description of the Experience

Imagine you are a member of an athletic team, and your program was just eliminated from a preseason tournament or meet. You travel back to your home site and your coach calls a team meeting. During that meeting, you begin to reflect on the experience and plan for upcoming practices. According to Gibbs' model, your team would start by describing the tournament or meet in detail. You would note the location, the time, the opponents, the crowd, and the people in attendance. While every member of the team was present, taking this initial step to describe the environment brings the team back into the atmosphere and reminds them of the nuanced elements that will be useful later in the reflection. *Do not skip this step*. Then the team should describe the purpose (e.g., Why were you there?) and the intended outcome (e.g., What did you want to happen?) as well as the actual outcome. To finish this first step, team members describe what happened by talking about specific key decision-points and actions.

Stage Two: Identification of Feelings

Once the team has identified critical elements of the environment and described what happened during the tournament or meet, the team should begin examining their thoughts and feelings from the time they began the event to the time the competition ended. This could mean a single-day event, or it could mean that they discuss their thoughts and emotions from the moment they left their home site and traveled to the tournament or meet site through multiple heats or games or matches over several days. Often, reflection is best done immediately after each competition but, at times, that is not possible, and Gibbs' structure allows for a larger debriefing session as a single event when those moments occur. In stage two, be as specific and targeted as possible. The team might discuss their thoughts as they walked off the bus, their emotions as they entered the locker room, and their thoughts and feelings as they warmed up before the event. Again, the key is to be honest, accurate, and specific. *How did various athletes feel after a crucial mistake or error? What about at the end of the meet or match or game?* Rather than asking general questions, teams need to discuss their thoughts and feelings in relation to specific and important moments that occurred and that were described in stage one. Through this process, teammates learn how each individual team member prepares for, responds to, and interprets various moments leading up to and during the competition. In this stage, there is also an opportunity for the group to consider what they thought each other might be feeling in a particular moment. Engaging in this dialogue can prevent misinterpretations and help teammates better understand why they behaved in a particular manner.

Stage Three: Evaluation of the Experience

Now it is time to evaluate the event or situation. In stage two, the team worked through their subjective experiences and, in stage three, the goal is to be as objective as possible as each team member is asked to self-assess what went well and what did not go as planned. The team should not be trying to make sense of the experience or attempting to solve any problems *yet*. The goal of the evaluation stage is to identify both the productive and unproductive behaviors and actions of the group and of individuals (i.e., What worked and what did not work?).

Stage Four: Analysis of Behavior

In stage four, the analysis stage, the goal is to make sense of what occurred. The team is now moving away from offering detailed descriptions, evaluating emotional responses, and outlining objective evaluations. Group members are explaining why they believe these decisions or behaviors or outcomes occurred. Before moving to the fifth stage, the team should be clear on why the event happened the way that it did.

Stage Five: Conclusion of Events

In the conclusion stage, the team or group summarizes what they learned from the experience and what they want to take forward with them into the next training session. Specifically, teams outline the thoughts and behaviors they want to repeat, the new skills or strategies they need to learn, and the thoughts or behaviors they are targeting to reduce or eliminate in the future.

Stage Six: Action Plan for the Future

The final stage of Gibbs' model involves developing an action plan. During this stage, teams should set goals to bring about the changes they identified in stage five. It would be helpful to review chapter 10, in which action planning is explained, to ensure success in stage six.

In his famous book *The Last Lecture*, Carnegie Mellon University professor Randy Pausch (2008) said that "educators best serve students by helping them be more self-reflective." As such, several questions are listed in the sidebar on page 227 that can be used during each stage that might be helpful for coaches, captains, and other leaders to consider if they want to lead their team or group through Gibbs' reflective cycle. The goal is not to use every question but perhaps to create a worksheet or journaling opportunity whereby teammates and group members are encouraged to write their self-reflective responses to these critical questions and then discuss them as a group or team.

A strength of this model is that it provides enough structure to serve as a stand-alone process that you engage in as part of a team or group after practices or training sessions. If you plan to use this reflection model with a group or team, however, you should identify a person responsible for charting the success rate for various tasks or changes you are making to your group process. For example, if you change an element of your marketing strategy, then someone in your organization needs to be the

PUT IT INTO PRACTICE

Reflective Cycle In Practice

Description
- What, when, and where did the event take place?
- Who was involved and in attendance? What were their roles?
- What was the outcome of the situation or event?
- What was the intended or desired purpose or outcome?

Feelings
- What were you feeling when X happened?
- What were you thinking after you made a correct decision?
- When you were exhausted, what were you thinking about?
- What do you think your teammates felt after you did X?
- What do you feel about the situation right now?

Evaluation
- What decisions or moments are you most proud of?
- What were the strengths of the team?
- What did you contribute (both positive and negative)?
- What did your teammates contribute (both positive and negative)?
- What did not go as planned?

Analysis (The Why Stage)
- Why did things go well?
- Why did people think or feel the way they did after errors? Or successes?
- Why did a strategy fail?

Conclusion
- What did I or we learn from this situation?
- How could we have made this situation more productive?
- What skills do we need to develop?
- What else could have been done?
- What do we want to keep doing well in the future?

Action Plan
- How will I or we develop the required skills?
- What possible barriers might prevent development?
- How will I or we overcome these barriers or challenges?
- What will I or we do to strengthen our strengths?

person accountable for assessing and evaluating various stages or aspects of the change. That way, when the change process is revisited in your next meeting, you know who will provide the update on the identified change or edit. This is but one model; two other evaluation procedures will be described next. We recommend spending time practicing the Gibbs model first in your next several training sessions or performance events. If you find it helps to identify next steps, then keep with it. If not, return to this chapter to learn about the next evidence-based frameworks you may want to consider.

Three Principles of Reflective Work

Terry (2009) outlined three principles of reflective sport psychology consulting, and these principles can be extrapolated to individual or team performance so that they are useful for any individual reflecting on their craft. The purpose is to help people consider how they are influenced by social and cultural factors and, in turn, how their unique backgrounds might be influencing their interactions and work with other people. These three principles are the hallmark of this approach:

1. Recognize that personal characteristics influence your effectiveness.
2. Understand how you are perceived by others (e.g., teammates, coworkers, opponents, coaches, trainers, athletes).
3. Realize that interpersonal interactions and outcomes depend on your own perspective (e.g., orientation, professional philosophy, theoretical approach).

In sum, this approach suggests that each person brings with them their own unique experiences and backgrounds, and those backgrounds or experiences influence how they see other people and how they interact and perform.

For example, Hacker and Mann (2017) discussed how working with an international team that was from an event-based culture affected how the athletes approached training sessions. If practice was at 9 a.m., but the team was having a prepractice breakfast together and enjoying their time, the athletes might not show up for practice until 9:15 or even 10 because in their culture, being together and experiencing the event and moment as one group was the most important aspect of their day. As a coach or practitioner working with that team, it would be important to understand their personal characteristics. Had the coach or leader not been aware of those elements or not been self-reflective, then perhaps they might have felt angry or upset with a perceived lack of commitment from the team members. This approach does not make excuses for people's behaviors, but it does encourage people to reflect on their own assumptions and biases and how those might color their interpretations and, therefore, their behaviors toward and with other people.

Now think of a similar example, but this time in a different environment. Imagine you are a patient who has been in an orthopedic surgeon's waiting room for over an hour, waiting for your scheduled appointment. No one at the front desk communicates changes, so you begin to believe the doctor is not dedicated to their practice or is incompetent or inefficient or both. As you are called back to the examination room and meet the doctor, you do not trust their recommendations and decide to go elsewhere for another opinion. Certainly, that choice is a possible outcome of that experience. Employing Terry's (2009) principles might lead you instead to question why you are equating the time spent waiting as a sign of incompetence rather than a sign of how busy and popular this doctor is with their patients. As a result, rather than entering the examination room closed off and wanting to leave, you enter the room excited to meet this well-respected doctor. The change in body language, then, might influence how the doctor perceives you as a potential patient and result in the doctor electing to spend more time explaining the injury, the recommended treatments, and the rationale in support of the various options. As a result, you leave the doctor's office feeling heard and respected and more trusting of the medical professional. All of that change can take place in the waiting room by engaging in Terry's reflective principles before your name is called to enter the exam room.

Terry's principles can be used at a moment's notice and once practiced consistently over time, can become as natural as breathing. A decision point arises, an action takes place, and the individual can quickly reflect and assess themselves and then decide how to proceed when in a similar situation. These principles help performers ask: *What do I know? Why do I know it? How do I know it?* (Hertz 1997). Students might ask themselves how their beliefs about math or English are affecting their interactions with their teacher or their study habits, whereas teachers using this approach might ask themselves at the end of each lesson how their own gender or race affected which students they called on in class or who they allowed to answer questions for longer periods of time. Rather than coaches yelling at athletes for questioning them, they might reflect on their own authority preferences and whether or not that matches what this particular athlete needs from a coach in order to perform well. Athletes who integrate these three principles into their reflective practice might ask themselves how their own experiences with anxiety might affect how they snip at their teammates in clutch or crucial moments during a match. This framework provides an opportunity for all performers to reflect on how their knowledge, experience, and background might be influencing their perceptions, interactions, and competitive experiences.

After-Action Reviews (AARs)

At every competitive level, when the competition ends, the planning and preparation *should* immediately begin (again). Extracting the most important and relevant lessons from a previous performance is a critical feature of a postevent routine. After-action reviews (AAR) are often used in military settings and can be useful in other performance domains as well. The goal of an AAR is to offer a structure through which an individual or group can extract the lessons learned and identify best practices for future planning and training purposes. These are the four focal points of an AAR:

1. What was expected to occur?
2. What really occurred?
3. What went wrong and why?
4. What went well and why?

Using this method, individual performers could identify and rate their top three strengths and one area for improvement, compare two performed behaviors with identified, task-related key performance indicators, and write three edits to their process for the future. A tennis player using the AAR method might engage in postcompetition assessment of the moments in which they experienced unproductive self-talk (e.g., I'm going to lose my serve) and behaviors (e.g., racket tossing) as well as be able to target when these thoughts and behaviors were likely to occur and the outcome that resulted. Perhaps they focused on losing a service game when down a break point, and as a result they committed a double fault, thus bringing on the exact outcome they were hoping to avoid. Then, the last step would be to recognize how to train a different approach or response. The worksheets on pages 231 and 232 provide two examples of reflection opportunities using this type of framework.

All of these frameworks work. They are supported by evidence in the literature and have been carried out anecdotally by a cross-section of performers in a wide range of performance domains, including business, sport, and the military. All three models are connected because they provide pathways to learning about yourself as a performer and to developing strategies for improvement going forward. The goal of reflection is to *Know thyself, then to act.* Consider what went well and what could be improved and identify and implement improvement strategies. Each model offers a way to accomplish that task. Experiment with each framework for reflection to find out what works best for you.

Try each model and pay attention to how each method of reflection affects you or your team's performance. Identify areas that will help you recognize measured changes. For example, if you identify a new strategy or skill you need to develop through Gibbs' reflective cycle, then find a

Performer-Centered Implementation Worksheet

This worksheet can become part of your postevent or postperformance analysis routine.

Directions

Write what happened, and then explain the *so what*, or the relevant lesson or lessons learned. In the column on the right, outline the *now what* action plan for moving forward. The key is to ensure that the *now what* elements identified are specific and measurable. As Peter Drucker, a management consultant and author known for his belief that a manager or leader holds a distinct responsibility, said, "If you can't measure it, you can't improve it."

What?	So what?	Now what?

From C. Hacker and M. Mann, *Achieving Excellence: Mastering Mindset for Peak Performance in Sport and Life* (Champaign, IL: Human Kinetics, 2023).

Performer-Centered Implementation Worksheet

Respond to the questions as part of a performance review and evaluation to use for planning.

Directions

For each of the four pillars (+1) listed, identify one element or aspect that you performed, rate yourself in that area, and then describe specifically what you did well and what you need to improve. At the bottom of the worksheet, select one area to target for improvement and write a brief action plan.

Four pillars (+one) reflection	Score (1-10) 1 = performed poorly 10 = best performance	Description of specific areas that went well or need to be corrected
Tactical elements (e.g., race strategy, offensive set, corners, specific defensive alignment, press)		
1.		
2.		
Technical elements (e.g., aspects of a specific skill you perform)		
1.		
2.		
Psychological elements (e.g., emotional control, activation, self-talk, confidence)		
1.		
2.		
Physiological elements (e.g., muscle tension, fatigue, fitness)		
1.		
2.		
Team elements (e.g., communication with teammate, collective efficacy, team response after error, feedback provided to group member)		
1.		
2.		
Action plan		

From C. Hacker and M. Mann, *Achieving Excellence: Mastering Mindset for Peak Performance in Sport and Life* (Champaign, IL: Human Kinetics, 2023).

way to measure improvement in that skill and compare those objective measures with your self-reflections in order to hold yourself accountable for implementation. In other words, now that you have read about each reflection framework, select one to try. Become more familiar with that strategy and integrate it into your practice. Then continue to reflect after practice or competition to ensure that this model or framework is helping you improve. If not, return to this chapter, read about one of the other frameworks, and integrate it into your practice. Repeat this process as long as needed. Remember, reflection is never done. As Gibbs noted, it is an unending cyclical process that you can and should engage in for the rest of your life (1988).

Conclusion

In this chapter, we outlined three distinct self-reflection strategies you could integrate into your post-performance routine. Understand that becoming a reflective performer is more than knowing a collection of techniques and strategies, however. Selecting a framework is valuable and understanding the critical elements of effective reflection is significant. Yet the goal or purpose of the reflection is what matters most. As we have championed throughout this book, to improve performance, people need to become aware of their strengths and areas for growth and then develop the skills and strategies to self-regulate, to manage, and to control their thoughts, behaviors, and emotions. Developing strategic awareness of their thoughts and behaviors is the first step in this process, and self-reflection provides a path (McCardle, Young, and Baker 2019; Zimmerman 2006).

Becoming a self-reflective performer usually involves a change in attitude. You have to be honest with yourself and stay committed to professional and personal development. You must stay open to pursuing new paths and developing novel strategies. Reflection requires you to critically evaluate your own thoughts, emotions, and behaviors. You have to own your actions and investigate whether those decisions were best or if they need to be edited. That process can sometimes be challenging and painful. There will be moments in life and throughout your career when it is easier to avoid honest self-reflection, to run from it. It is in those instances that you will learn whether you have truly cultivated the mindset and the habit of critical self-reflection. If you have, you will benefit as a person and as a performer.

CHAPTER 14

Growing Through Adversity

Trauma, failure, and stress are never welcomed experiences. We certainly do not wish any of you to experience moments of hardship, but we recognize it is an inevitable element of the human condition. In each of your lives, there will be stress. There will be trauma. There will be failure and setbacks. That is true in all performance domains. You will experience failure psychologically, socially, physically, and competitively. No one escapes it. And while you do not hope for nor wish for traumatic experiences, given their inevitability, it is essential to discuss how to cope with and respond to them.

In the face of hardship, you have but a handful of options for a response, and each decision will inevitably change your path forward. Will you get better and grow stronger through your pain or will you quit in the middle of the struggle

> **Believe me, the reward is not so great without the struggle.**
>
> Wilma Rudolph, track and field sprinter, first American woman to win three gold medals in one Olympic Games (1960 Rome)

> **We all have obstacles. The feeling of satisfaction comes by overcoming something.**
>
> Marta, Brazilian soccer player, six-time FIFA World Player of the Year, named Best FIFA Women's Player (2018), two-time Olympic Games silver medalist (2004, 2008), record holder for most goals scored at FIFA Women's World Cup tournaments (17), first footballer to score at five different World Cup events

and perhaps never recover? "Obstacles don't have to stop you. If you run into a wall, don't turn around and give up. Figure out how to climb it, go through it, or work around it," said Michael Jordan, six-time NBA champion and six time NBA Finals Most Valuable Player. Here Jordan is alluding to mental toughness, which is defined as developing an unshakeable belief in your ability to accomplish your goals regardless of obstacles or setbacks (Jones, Hanton, and Connaughton 2002). Jones and his colleagues also recognized that mentally tough performers not only survive under high-pressure conditions but they also often thrive during adversity. Mentally tough people bring their best in the most challenging moments of their lives. They remain in control of their thoughts and feelings and intentionally select their most helpful behavioral responses in the greatest moments of competitive chaos. They keep their shoulders back and their heads up when others might slump forward in defeat. The benefits of mental toughness are numerous. Effective performers are able to remain fully focused on the task at hand under competitive pressure, they can adapt to changing situations quickly and effectively, they are confident, they are in control of their emotions, they are decisive and effective in moments of high anxiety, and they cope better with failure and loss than others. These are the people others want on their team, in their boardroom, trying their case, and performing their surgery.

Mental toughness does not just happen by chance, and it is not required when things are going well, when you are happy, or when the coach is satisfied with your performance. Mental toughness is revealed under pain, adversity, and loss. Mental toughness is required when adversity comes about, when confidence takes a hit, or when outcomes do not go as planned. In this chapter we outline strategies and perspectives that will facilitate mental toughness and contribute to your ability to grow through pain, loss, setbacks, and adversity. Aly Raisman, two-time Olympian and gold medal gymnast, says, "You have to remember that the hard days are what make you stronger. The bad days are what make you realize what a good day is. If you never had any bad days, you would never have that sense of accomplishment!" To develop the recognition that Raisman references so that you can not only endure but also improve through challenge and hardship, the first step is to better understand two related concepts, namely, post-traumatic and stress-related growth.

Post-Traumatic Growth Versus Stress-Related Growth

Stress and failure are common springboards for some people, some of the time, and in some situations. What we mean by this is that failure is not necessary, it is not a requirement for growth or improvement, but it is often the impetus for change. Canadian skier Nancy "Tiger" Greene Raine, a two-time overall FIS World Cup champion (1967, 1968) and Olympic gold medalist (1968), for example, did not score any points for nearly two months before mounting a comeback during the two weeks before winning her first World Cup (Beaudry 1967). Most coaches and experts had counted her out. Greene certainly did not need to go two months without earning a point in order to change her technique and equipment, but those cumulative losses served as fuel that she used to make necessary changes and propel herself to victory in the last race of the season. During moments of adversity, there can be performance improvement. After challenges, opportunities for *post-traumatic growth* (PTG) and *stress-related growth* (SRG) are often available to performers. Some people use these terms interchangeably, but each refers to specific and distinct experiences.

Stress-Related Growth

Adversarial or *stress-related growth* (SRG) is a process of struggling through adversity that propels individuals to higher levels of functioning than existed before the event (Linley and Joseph 2004). It is not comfortable or fun. This improvement does not occur when a person swims with the current or floats on the stream. Ronda Rousey, American mixed martial artist and Ultimate Fighting Championship fighter noted that "[Failure] is the one fear I have to face all the time. Yes, it's uncomfortable, but I'm finally comfortable being uncomfortable." Rafael Nadal, winner of 14 tennis Grand Slam tournaments, two Olympic gold medals, and four Davis Cups with Spain, says it like this: "Accept the mistakes because . . . you need to keep going after the mistakes. That's the only way" (Tignor 2019). Both athletes underscore the significant role that stress-related growth has played in their career ascension in their sport. SRG is a process of struggling through adversity rather than skating through it. It requires a performer to swim upstream against the current and recognize that through that difficult process, they are now capable of functioning at a higher level than they might have been without the adversity, setback, or stress.

Post-Traumatic Growth

Closely related to SRG, *post-traumatic growth* (PTG) refers to changes that are important, essential, and transformative (Tedeschi and Calhoun 2004). Rather than returning to baseline after a traumatic experience, PTG yields a deeply profound sense of improvement or growth. Tedeschi and Calhoun (2004) would argue that adverse events are critical to our development; they motivate us to move beyond the status quo and exceed our previously identified limits or standards. The Japanese art of Kintsugi is a visual representation of the process of post-traumatic growth. When pottery breaks, many artists discard the vessel, but traditional Kintsugi artists honor the cracks, repairing them with lacquer and dusting them with gold. They do not shrink from the brokenness or hide the cracks of the vessel. Rather, people who practice this traditional Japanese artistry identify and accentuate the beauty of the restored piece. Here the metaphor is clear: What can break us might make us stronger *if* we recognize the moment and then engage in the behaviors that will bring about growth and improvement.

When Surviving Is Enough

It can be tempting, with all of the stories of redemption and growth presented throughout this book, to believe that struggle is necessary for success. That to thrive, you must experience significant failure. We do not subscribe to such an ideology. Certainly, failure is both likely and inevitable, and as we have pointed out, there are strategies you can practice and implement in order to springboard from moments of hardship to the experiences that lead to the benefits of stress-related or post-traumatic growth. However, you do not need to fail or to lose or to experience a troubling health diagnosis, for example, to live your best life or perform at a high level. For many cancer patients, a cancer diagnosis is the trauma or the stress that spurs them to clarify their priorities and values or motivates them to achieve unmet accomplishments. For them, the trauma of a cancer diagnosis served as a defining moment in which they both grew and evolved as individuals. But you do not need to be diagnosed with cancer to run your first marathon or to travel to Antarctica. You do not need a cancer diagnosis to prioritize family or cut back on work hours. We want to acknowledge that you could learn these lessons and commit to living a fulfilled life without a traumatic health diagnosis or painful loss. Stress is neither a requirement, nor is it essential to live your best, purpose-driven life.

This chapter outlines several ideas for "extracting the relevant lessons" (a common phrase Dr. Hacker uses with clients when confronted with loss, difficulty, or setbacks) so that you can grow through adversity, but we also want to make clear that sometimes surviving is the most heroic response to trauma. Young children who are living through daily trauma at home and people who have experienced sexual assault or faced a life-threatening diagnosis—for people in these circumstances or who encounter other unnamed traumatic situations—the best, and perhaps only, option available to them is to survive and live through another day. We recognize there are moments of trauma and stress for which thinking about a "lesson learned" or how to "grow through it" might not be ideal or even the most salient issue at that time. Further, it is inaccurate to believe that, for an experience to have worth or meaning, you must evolve or improve or develop in some tangible way. Sometimes, the *only* thing to do is to find a way to make it through the trauma.

We have outlined remarkable stories of stress-related growth and post-traumatic growth. Yet, we do not want to romanticize pain or trauma. Remember the following:

- Moments of stress, failure, or trauma are *not* necessary in order to grow, evolve, or thrive.
- When facing stress, failure, or trauma, sometimes what there is *to do* is to survive. When that is the case, hear us: *It is enough*.

Mental Toughness Moments

In a vast majority of situations and in most of the competitive challenges you will encounter, growth is possible. It is an option. Through the remainder of this chapter, strategies for recognizing and improving through setbacks and failures are offered.

Growth must be an intentional and active pursuit. The first step in this process is to recognize and name the moment. Dr. Hacker has coined the term *mental toughness moments* (MtM), which are events or situations in which you have the opportunity to grow through your struggle or thrive through the daily grind. Acknowledging your MtM creates distance between yourself and the event. Instead of being passive and focusing on the feeling of hardship or fear or defensiveness, it is better to become an active agent in your own story. There is little value in not recognizing your MtM or to not naming it immediately. You might be delayed because you feel too much emotion or shock related to the trauma, but the sooner you can name it ("This is an MtM for me"), the quicker you can begin your journey. When you recognize the moment and name it, take a breath. Pause. Everything you think or say or do from that point forward will be infinitely more impactful than if you did not recognize it as a mental toughness moment.

Names and labels matter because they direct behavior. In sport, it is the equivalent of talking about trying to run an offense in a ball sport (e.g., baseball, softball, soccer, tennis, basketball, volleyball) without using a play call. In a timeout, a coach will not spend time talking about where each player should move or cut or be in a specific moment; they will say the name of the play or offensive set. Immediately, when the coach calls the name or number of the set piece, athletes begin imagining their role in that play or offensive set.

Once you name your mental toughness moment, then you can take the next action. You have choices to make, and each of those decisions will take you down one path or another and, by default, away from a different path. As Dr. Terry Orlick writes in *In Pursuit of Excellence* (2016), performers must "docide" rather than "decide." What he means is that you must decide to act, to do, to behave according to the outcome you hope to experience. An important element associated with naming your MtM is to realize that the future is not yet written. Just because you are injured or were cut from a team roster or erred during a performance does not mean you are doomed to this new plight forever. Similarly, every injured athlete or person who does not receive the promotion may not recover or grow or get better. After the trauma or stress occurs, the rest is unwritten and undetermined. It is up to you. You must do certain things and avoid other behaviors. For some athletes, being cut from a team is unexpected, traumatic, and an event they never recover from. For others, like Crystal Dunn of the USWNT, they name their MtM and move quickly to their comeback plan (see the sidebar on page 240).

Once you name the mental toughness moment as Crystal Dunn chose to do by calling deselection from the national team an opportunity, then you have new behavioral options in front of you. As an athlete, you do not need to lose or perform badly or be cut from the team to learn and improve, just as teachers or workers do not need a poor performance

USWNT and NWSL Star Crystal Dunn's Story of Redemption

As a soccer player, Crystal Dunn is considered a phenom. She has the ability to play multiple positions on the pitch and dominate from any one of them. After playing at powerhouse University of North Carolina (UNC) for famed coach Anson Dorrance, Dunn was the overall first pick in the National Women's Soccer League (NWSL) and started 19 games as a rookie. She had already won a U-20 World Cup in 2012 and a national championship in 2013 with UNC. But in 2015, her soccer career hit a crossroads. She was one of the last players cut from the U.S. women's national soccer team (USWNT) that year.

> I took it pretty hard . . . hearing you aren't good enough or your coach doesn't value you enough was a hard pill to swallow, but . . . it was an opportunity to me to reinvent myself. That's how I took that year. I had a clean slate. I had an opportunity to be the player and visualize the player I wanted to be, and I think that was also the year that I really honed and embraced my versatility.

That year was a mixed bag of emotions for Dunn; she started the year with a devastating national team deselection and ended the season by winning the Golden Boot award and earning the MVP title in the NWSL.

> Looking back on that year, it was so pivotal because, for the first time, I had to make a decision and decide who I want to be and what I wanted to be part of my legacy. I had to dig deep within myself and not look for someone else to pick me up. Of course, I had tons of support, but it was so important to look at myself and visualize who I wanted to be. . . . I wanted to be a great teammate and the hardest-working player on the team and lead by example. That's the year when I started to feel those traits within me.

> For anyone who has ever gone through a tough situation, it really starts with you. It starts with knowing these tough times don't last and you can bounce back and you can reinvent yourself and come back even better. Since 2015, I can honestly say that I've gotten better every year.

Based on Hacker and Dorrance (2021).

It would have been easy for Dunn to let go of her dream of making the national team. At a time when everyone around her would have understood her desire to quit or lose motivation or blame the coach, she took a different approach. Crystal Dunn made a different decision. She had been very successful doing what she had been doing to that point in her career, but she took what was initially a traumatic moment in her life, a devastating deselection, and turned it into an opportunity to challenge herself to grow and get better. She took control of her story rather than allowing herself to blame others or quit. She focused on what she could control; she believed in the capabilities she had inside to separate herself from the pack, and she did just that. When the next World Cup arrived, Dunn was not only selected for that roster, she also was a full-time starter and eventually helped lift the World Cup trophy.

evaluation to reflect on their job performance. But often, people are not ready to take in the lesson until the loss, the trial, the bad evaluation, or the court trial goes awry. The lesson was always available to the performer, but the trauma or stress shines a laser beam on it and opens up the performer to look at themselves or the situation differently. Sometimes success fosters complacency and comfort, but it doesn't have to.

Here are some of the most common mental toughness moments in sport:

- Chronic or acute injuries
- The loss of a starting position or change in position
- A significant performance error
- Deselection or being cut from a team
- Criticism from significant others
- Event criticality (e.g., postseason offers different stressors from preseason or early season)
- Personal or family disruptions before a performance or competition

Think about the last time you experienced criticism from someone. The common reaction is to feel like that person does not know what they are talking about, to feel defensive, or to deny the potential truth in the critique. Mentally tough athletes, however, recognize honest criticism as a mental toughness moment, reflect on their performance, and use the guidance to improve (Jones, Hanton, and Connaughton 2002).

Business scholar and expert Adam Grant emphasizes the importance of treating unpleasant feelings and discomfort as teachable moments. Rather than avoiding those often-unwelcome feelings and emotions, recognize that regret and guilt can become a good teacher so that you make wiser decisions next time. Certainly, each of these mental toughness moments is hard to take on, and they are all hard to struggle through and find your way, but if you persevere, you gain valuable experience and engage in post-traumatic growth. Doing so, working through the pain and disappointment, is the key to determining whether or not you get better at your craft. Most people think that being successful occurs when you stack or string multiple successes together, but more often than not, you reach the top of the achievement mountaintop by struggling and failing and overcoming adversity time and time again. Winston Churchill describes success as "the ability to go from failure to failure with great enthusiasm." Step one, then, is to recognize the mental toughness moment and name it. Once you label it, you can no longer ignore it. Now what?

Identify and Connect With Trusted Confidantes

Each athlete and performer has both individuals and groups of people with whom they interact regularly. The list may include current or past teammates, coaches, and support staff. Increasingly, clubs, teams, and organizations are hiring mental skill coaches to complement the technical and tactical staff and to support athletes. Other performers have cowork-ers, office mates, direct reports, and bosses as well as access to services offered by the human resources department. Those people can serve as excellent resources during mental toughness moments, but not all mem-bers in a direct performance environment are equally helpful. Family members and friends, often in their desire to be supportive, become "yes" people. They try to support athletes and performers by agreeing with how wrong the situation was or how unfairly someone was treating them. When performers face a MtM, it is more critical than ever to seek advice from people who can appropriately understand and direct them toward facilitative decisions, emotions, and choices. Blaming others does not make them better. Complaining about circumstances does nothing to change the situation. People who simply agree with the anger, hurt, frustration, or feelings of loss without also offering alternative decisions and choices that foster growth, enhanced capability, or productive emo-tional coping are not the best voices to rely on in difficult circumstances. We encourage athletes and performers to be more selective in the people they choose to include in the mental toughness moments. It's reasonable to need support but not helpful to simply disconnect from the situation or avoid personal reflection and evaluation.

Remember, the future is not yet written and the choices you make today are likely to become the greatest indicators of the options that exist for you going forward. Seek people who will both understand and guide you. Listen to folks who understand your particular performance domain and who can offer tangible guidance for productive strategies going forward.

One of the factors that Crystal Dunn credits for her success in bouncing back from not being selected as a member of the U.S. soccer team was the wise counsel offered by her trusted mentors, coaches, and former teammates. She did not mention that she wallowed in self-pity with them, but that she reached out for guidance and direction. Although outside the purview of this book, social support is a common strategy identified in the health psychology literature as a way to help people successfully cope with poor health outcomes or diagnoses or to change behavior, for example.

The key is to reach out to people who will help and guide you, not people who will blindly support you without analysis or a standard. Those are often different groups of people. Social support, in this sense, does not mean that you are looking for people who will allow you to complain or blame or deny the issue at hand. You want to reach out to people who will give you space to react and then encourage you to take the next, productive step forward, to behave in ways that will bring about positive change. This advice may also mean that your support comes from external resources like books or videos or from religious leaders or former coaches or bosses—anyone or anything that will help guide and direct behaviors that will lead to growth and development.

You might also be in a position like Carla Overbeck found herself in during the 1999 Women's World Cup to support someone else through their mental toughness moment (see the following sidebar). Overbeck provides an excellent example of how to offer social support to a teammate during a competitive moment of adversity.

IN THEIR OWN WORDS **Carla Overbeck—A Captain's Story**

During the 1999 Women's World Cup, Team USA was playing Germany in the quarterfinal match with 70,000 people in the stands and millions watching on television. It was quite possibly the largest stage the U.S. team had ever played on. The crowd was loud, and it was difficult to hear during this highly contested game with their rival. During the match, defender Brandi Chastain miscommunicated with the keeper, which resulted in an own goal (Chastain kicked it into her own net).

After it happened, Chastain was devastated and Overbeck noted, "I ran over to her because I wanted to be the first person that she heard from, the first voice reassuring her that this one will be okay." She went on to tell her teammate, "We have a freaking great team, and we're going to win this game. You just need to forget about it. It's over. You can't do anything about it. Forget it and we're going to frickin' win."

At halftime, head coach Tony DiCicco considered subbing Chastain, but Overbeck said the team needed her and that, other than the massive error of an own goal, she was playing well. She reminded her coach that she and the team believed in Chastain and that she would play well in the second half.

Later in the match, as a defender, Chastain scored the game-tying goal, and Team USA went on to win the match. She, according to Overbeck, "made the difference . . . she had the unbelievable drive to keep her head in it . . . and I just made sure I got to her first and reminded her we needed her and that she was a great player."

Based on Hacker and Dorrance (2021).

Team captain Carla Overbeck recognized the mental toughness moment and took a strengths-based approach to reassure her teammate that she would have a moment of redemption and that she needed to keep herself mentally prepared. Her support helped Brandi Chastain not only survive that difficult moment but also come back and score a critical and decisive goal in the match.

While initially this story might seem like it contradicts the point made earlier about social support, it reinforces it. Overbeck did not tell her teammate that the error was acceptable. But in that moment, time for analysis did not exist. She needed Chastain to bounce back and move forward, so she offered support by reminding her that, although it was a significant error, she was skilled and playing well and that the team was good enough to overcome the error if they stuck together. In that moment, the team captain offered an example of support that reinforced Chastain's strengths and allowed her to advance to the next moment where she could be a difference maker for the team.

Responses, Not Reactions

Once you have named your MtM, you can cultivate your responses. When experiencing stress or trauma, there are only three options: (1) Never return to your previous form, (2) struggle and toil and return to previous performance levels, or (3) come back better than before. You do not have 30 options, you have 3. There is no guarantee which of the three will occur. It is neither stress nor trauma that creates growth. You do not improve simply because you experienced challenges or difficulties in your life. *Growth is not linear, and it is not guaranteed, but it is available to you.*

Once you have named the mental toughness moment, you must choose your response. Notice the word *choice*; not your reaction, but your *response*. There is a subtle yet significant difference in that language. Physical therapists and athletic trainers are well aware of the difference between pain threshold and pain tolerance. Pain threshold refers to the lowest point at which a person feels or experiences pain and is similar for almost every person. When we put our hand on a hot stove or feel a papercut on our index finger, we all report those experiences as painful, and our thresholds are similar. However, pain tolerance refers to the highest amount of pain we can endure, and it is unique and individualized. Each person can tolerate a different amount or level of pain. It is highly variable and might be affected by gender, previous experiences, family background, culture, varying situations, and other factors. Similarly, an emotional or behavioral *reaction* is instantaneous, usually involves little thought, and is universal. In sport, when someone loses, it hurts. When someone makes a mistake at work, they are bothered by it. A student loses all of their written files right before class or an important presentation, and their ego and emotions take an immediate hit. The most common reactions are denial, defensiveness, and emotional upheaval. Reactions are immediate and universal. On the other hand, like how much pain a person can tolerate, *behavioral and emotional responses* are chosen, unique to the individual, variable, and trainable.

Imagine you are writing the practice plan, creating a new physical education unit, creating the rehabilitation program for a client, or crafting a paper or speech that you will deliver at an upcoming meeting or presentation. Now imagine your electronic device gives out or you become distracted by a child or pet entering your room and you close out of the document without saving it first. In that one second, you lose all your work—your notes are gone, your examples lost—it is all deleted. In that moment, what will you do?

You might initially react by telling everyone you know and anyone who will listen how unfair it is and how untimely this event is. You might even yell or scream. In fact, everyone would likely feel that way initially and for at least a moment. Reactions, remember, are universal. However, the length of time you stay in that reactionary place is individualized. It is up to you. You could call 10 people and spend five minutes complaining to each one about how you lost your work. Or you could begin again. You could begin the long and difficult but necessary process of reconstructing your lost data. Reactions will occur immediately. If your doctor comes in and gives you a cancer diagnosis, your immediate reaction might be to think that you will die. That reaction is not unique to you; it is universal. It is often what is expected. The problem is that reactions lack proper reasoning and analysis and often lead to less-than-desirable choices, behaviors, and outcomes. For example, in ice hockey when an opponent attempts to provoke an athlete, a common reaction is to want to fight or engage in a behavior like hooking or high sticking to send a message to the opponent that they cannot intimidate you. However, that reaction is exactly what the opponent wants. Now the retaliating player is sent to the penalty box. On the other hand, a solid hip check at the appropriate time is a planned response that sends the same message and denies the opponent the intimidation effect and is done in a way that keeps the player out of the penalty box, on the ice, and in the game.

Responses are volitional decisions that you have control over. You did not get to choose that you lost all of your work and preparation when you became distracted or your computer shut down; you did not select a cancer diagnosis, and you did not elect to have your opponent attempt to intimidate you. But you can choose your response. Instead of complaining, throwing a tantrum, pouting, withdrawing, or being upset, you can select a response that allows you to stay in the game, to advance, and to move forward. Sometimes, the best response is to skate away from the opponent who is attempting to provoke you on the ice. Other times, it might be a well-timed hip check. If you tend to experience somatic anxiety, you might need to practice the energy management techniques presented in chapter 6 as part of your preferred response during difficult situations. Or you might plan playtime with your children or play fetch with your puppy after work or go for a long run to distract yourself and reduce your negative reactions from a poor performance. Any of these are appropriate responses if they bring about the desired outcome. And the moment you implement these responses, change becomes possible, growth can occur, and improvement can happen.

There is one key behavior that performers could engage in that would improve their ability to cope with adversity in the moment: *Keep things in perspective*. The mistake was not fatal, and it does not have to invade other aspects of their life or hijack their emotions. They would do well to compartmentalize the error or setback, but people often allow mistakes to be pervasive and to carry them into future endeavors. For example, a student-athlete earns a failing grade on an exam and then swims poorly in their meet later that evening because they can't shake the jolt of a bad grade. That person allowed their emotions from one performance domain to pervade or encroach on another. They should not allow that to happen.

Technotr/E+/Getty Images

Recognize when pervasiveness is starting to occur. Have a plan for that event. One error or mistake does not mean that the rest of the game has to go poorly. Just because something goes poorly in life does not mean that you must bring that negativity onto the field, the pitch, the court, or the track or into the pool. Make different decisions. Choose a different response. In addition to compartmentalizing effectively, to keep things in perspective, it is important to remember that circumstances change and that the future is not yet written. Just because you are experiencing hardship now does not mean that you will never experience success or that life will always be harder for you. Trauma and adversity are not permanent. These moments will pass, and, if you keep the current issue or challenge in perspective, you will be more likely to recognize opportunities to work on yourself and to hone and expand your skills.

That is not to suggest that by choosing your responses carefully you will stop the negative reactions from occurring. Reactions are immediate and nearly universal. Your goal, however, is to shorten the amount of time you spend in that reactionary space and quickly access your intentional, self-selected behavioral response. The fastest way to get to your preferred response is to identify and train it in advance. In the heat of the moment, when mental toughness is required, it is often difficult to think clearly or effectively beyond your immediate reaction. And in the moment, that reaction feels normal, warranted, and familiar. It may feel good or appropriate in the moment, but it will not help you grow. You must recognize that some behaviors and ways of thinking and choices will increase the likelihood of growth, and some will decrease the likelihood of improvement. The best time to recognize these differences and select the most appropriate response is *before* the emotionally charged moment occurs. Therefore, it is important to plan and to prepare a response in advance of the mental toughness moment you might face. As you learned in chapter 6, in moments of stress, you revert to your most familiar, practiced, and unconscious behaviors even though they are not always helpful. The familiar adage that "practice doesn't make perfect; rather, practice makes permanent" applies. Train how you want to respond in practice before those responses are needed in the height of competition. Train your response the way you train your physical skills, through thoughtful, intentional repetitions as outlined in the following sidebar.

Performer-Centered Implementation Worksheet

Training Your Preferred MtM Response

Use this worksheet to become aware of your *typical reactions* to common stressful, difficult, or challenging experiences in your performance domain and to plan and train your self-selected *responses* before those MtMs occur.

Directions

Identify three of the most common mental toughness moments in your domain (use recent or familiar examples from your own career for ideas) and write them in the first column. Next, outline your typical reaction (i.e., how do you typically feel or behave in those moments) and the typical outcome (e.g., you earn a technical foul, your team has to play a person down, you lose a client, your significant other becomes upset).

To the right of the black bar, write your preferred MtM response (i.e., what is the best possible response in this moment) and the preferred outcome that response would likely yield. All responses should be as detailed and specific as possible.

In completing this worksheet, you are planning your response to common or likely stressors and difficult experiences (e.g., loss, deselection, performance error). Now you must practice your preferred MtM responses by using imagery (see chapter 5) to create the specific mental toughness moments in your mind and then implementing your preferred MtM response. Over time, this training will lead to your preferred response becoming your dominant response so that when, not if, this event occurs, you will be ready to engage and implement your planned, intentional, and preferred behavioral and emotional response.

> *continued*

Training Your Preferred MtM Response *> continued*

Mental toughness moment (event or situation)	Typical reaction (emotional and behavioral)	Typical outcome	Preferred MtM response	Preferred outcome
1.	1.	1.	1.	1.
2.	2.	2.	2.	2.
3.	3.	3.	3.	3.

From C. Hacker and M. Mann, *Achieving Excellence: Mastering Mindset for Peak Performance in Sport and Life* (Champaign, IL: Human Kinetics, 2023).

Extract the Relevant Lessons

Another major element of post-traumatic or stress-related growth occurs when people commit themselves to extracting the relevant lesson. Mistakes, setbacks, and an entire host of negative experiences can be transformed into teachable moments of growth, development, and progress when each is analyzed with an eye toward discovering a useful lesson that can come out of the difficulty. A useful lesson (or two or three) is always revealed in intensely negative or difficult situations. But you must look for them.

How Are You Equipped to Handle Setbacks and Disappointments?

It is up to you to make the connection between the event, situation, or difficulty and the opportunity it provides for learning a valuable lesson and for ways in which it contributes to your personal growth. In 2020, everyone in the world experienced trauma in the form of the COVID-19 pandemic. And then in 2021, some students were more excited than ever to return to in-person learning, and athletes could not wait to return to practice and competition. It is likely that students and athletes had grown accustomed to that access of opportunity and unconsciously took it for granted. Everyone could have been grateful for their in-person working environments or daily interactions with friends and family members without the abrupt halt to "normal" life brought on by COVID-19. For many people, the pandemic inspired renewed gratitude that they had not experienced before the pandemic. People appreciated teachers more. People appreciated close friends and family members who helped them cope with the unexpected challenges. People appreciated simple pleasures and freedom so often taken for granted. Still others experienced a new appreciation for life or greater clarity about important relationships, or they discovered newfound personal strengths or experienced spiritual renewal.

How Did You Grow Through the Experience?

These stressors and traumatic moments do not have to be relegated to disconnected dots on the timeline of your life. Rather, you can choose to make the connection between facing unexpected challenges and your ability to respond, successfully cope, and even thrive. Explicitly connect the dots so that you become more aware of and own your growth and development. Probing questions that coaches, bosses, teachers, and other leaders can ask performers to help them connect the dots between adversarial situations and their personal development are found in the sidebar on page 250.

Performers need to become more aware of what they are doing well to cope and grow in moments of adversity and, equally important, what they could do to better prepare or respond to the next setback or challenge. To improve awareness, leaders have to model and encourage critical self-reflection and the questions in the sidebar can enhance that skill (see chapter 13 for more

PUT IT INTO PRACTICE

Growth Through Adversity Analysis

The following are probing questions to help performers connect traumatic events, recognize their growth, and develop their mental toughness:

1. What did you learn from this experience (both positive and negative)?
2. What could you have done differently?
3. What could you do to better deal with this (and other) setbacks?
4. What can you do right now to help maintain confidence and self-belief?
5. What can you do next time to help better manage behaviors and emotions?
6. Is there anyone you can reach out to who could help next time?
7. What thoughts, decisions, emotions, or actions helped you manage this setback?
8. How can you apply the lessons learned to other events, situations, or challenges?

information on self-reflection). Identify what happened, what went well, what could be improved, and then, and only then, move forward.

What Did the Adversity or Trauma Mean for and to You?

It is also important to impart or give meaning to the situation or event. For example, Mothers Against Drunk Drivers is an organization that was formed when a mother lost her child to drunk driving. The founder ascribed meaning to an otherwise horrible and needless trauma and in so doing, she helped pass legislation that made it less likely similar events would occur in the future. Similarly, to increase the likelihood for growth to occur from trauma or stress, performers need to make meaning of the adversity, to give it value and purpose beyond the suffering and pain. No one wishes or hopes for an injury, but that forced time away from their performance domain can provide space for creativity, provide more time to watch film and target areas for improvement, or allow them to develop other leadership skills that will serve the team. As we have consistently mentioned, it is not the trauma or the stress that yields growth. However, people can improve through those moments, if they recognize them as mental toughness moments, implement their chosen responses, and reframe or reconstruct the adversity they faced by giving it purpose and meaning.

Reclaim Your Agency

It is possible to acknowledge that an unwanted test result, criticism from a coach or boss, or a divorce is painful and difficult and also that each of those moments have meaning, purpose, and a lesson to extract. Certainly, they did not have to occur, but now that they have, recognizing that you can control your behavioral responses presses you into action. You reclaim your agency when you recognize the choices available to you and decide to act in ways that will bring about growth. Your decision to ascribe meaning to the stress or trauma does not mean that you believe it was necessary or even that it was good or welcomed, but sometimes out of horrible circumstances, we can become more aware of our values and priorities in all areas of our lives, not just in a particular performance domain. It can feel bittersweet (good coming from bad) but is so often true. When you remember the adage "tough times don't last, but tough people do," you can marshal your resources and begin the important process of stress-related growth. The point of this chapter is to convey that trauma and stress are inevitable parts of life. No one wants to experience these moments, but they inevitably will occur. Every single person will experience their mental toughness moments.

Given that truth, remind yourself that there are only three options—get better, never recover, or return to previous levels—and that you have the resources, capability, and fortitude to choose behaviors and options that are most likely to help you transition from survive to thrive. You can extract the relevant lessons and help yourself grow through the struggle. And we encourage you to revisit many of the strategies outlined earlier that are listed in the following sidebar to help you chart your own path of growth through adversity.

Chalk Talk

Quick-Hit Reminders for Growing Through Adversity

☐ Recognize the trauma, stress, adversity, or failure.

☐ Name it as a mental toughness moment (MtM).

☐ Seek appropriate support.

☐ Train your response and move beyond reactions.

☐ Extract the relevant lesson.

Conclusion

We hope you are leaving this chapter with the knowledge that there is nobility in both surviving the struggle and in growing through difficulties. Remind yourself that it is common in life for people to point to periods of adversity and difficulty when asked about the events that helped shape them. There is wisdom in that type of response. Adversity, especially that which occurs in athletics, is frequently fuel for greatness. The purpose of this chapter is to highlight strategies you can integrate into your life to ensure that the most challenging moments in life become salient reinforcers that are catalysts for growth and transformation. When you experience what Dr. Hacker calls a *mental toughness moment* (MtM), name it, and then roll up your sleeves and get to work. The decisions and actions you take next will either take you down a path that accelerates or impedes your growth in your career, personal life, social interactions, and other performance domains. As Julie Foudy, former team captain of the U.S. women's national soccer team, two-time FIFA World Cup champion, two-time Olympic gold medalist (1996, 2004), Golden Blazer recipient (2015), first woman to win the FIFA Fair Play Award (1997), notes, "You decide your path, your attitude, your approach to every day. You wake up with that choice" (Foudy 2017). Trauma and stress will happen. The decision about how to respond is yours. Implement the tools and strategies offered in this chapter and integrate them with the other mental skills outlined in this book, and you will grow and expand your capabilities to meet the moment and grow through your struggle.

CHAPTER 15

Bouncing Back

To compete and to perform in any achievement domain is to commit errors. Often people believe that mental skills training is only about developing the psychological tools to perform at their best, and while it is certainly fun when they are performing at their best, the truth is that most of the time they are recovering from failures. A recurring theme in this book has been to provide strategies to help people give as much of themselves during less-than-ideal moments as possible and to learn how to regroup and move forward from errors as quickly as possible. This skill set and a competitive mindset are so important that we have not only referenced it throughout the book but also dedicated two chapters to it. This chapter is an extension and refinement of chapter 14 and offers additional strategies for persevering through challenges and overcoming mistakes. The focus now is on how performers can rebound from those errors quickly and continue performing at a high level.

In this chapter, like chapter 14, we offer several strategies and encourage you to think of them as ingredients for success or puzzle pieces to complete the competitive picture. They are all important and are most effective when used in combination. To add only one piece would bring you closer to completing the puzzle but adding all of the pieces is needed to create a more cohesive and complete picture. No one piece is more important than another, yet without each element, the puzzle is incomplete. Similarly, each strategy in this chapter is important for your performance and should be considered

> Whether in running, business or anything else, there are moments that feel like the most immense failures, but that's where the good stuff happens. That's where you test the self-belief you're trying to build.
>
> Megan Roche, MD, five-time U.S. national ultrarunning champion, six-time member of U.S. world ultrarunning team

> I've failed many times in my life and career and because of this I've learned a lot. Instead of feeling defeated countless times, I've used it as fuel to drive me to work harder. So today, join me in accepting failures. Let's use them to motivate us to work even harder.
>
> Phil "Lefty" Mickelson, American professional golfer, 45 PGA Tour wins, six major championships

a critical element for your performance toolbox. For example, fostering grit is important, but without implementing mistake routines, you will be less likely to persevere through errors when it's time to, or if you do try, you will be less effective. Even Angela Duckworth, the noted psychologist who popularized the term *grit*, acknowledged, "When we are talking about what [people] need to live lives that are happy and healthy and good for other people, it's a long list. . . . Grit is on that list, but it is not the only thing on the list" (Young 2018). Similarly, developing a growth mindset is essential for recognizing the value of a mistake routine and implementing it effectively. As you read through the chapter, pause and consider how, when used in combination, each new strategy might help you to more effectively overcome setbacks and recover from mistakes on your performance journey. In addition, we urge you to move beyond the "bumper slogan" reality in today's sport world, where overused phrases are given as pep talks and cheerleading chants. Statements like "Believe in yourself" or "You can do it" might be offered with sincerity, but they don't provide much sustained fuel for a person's competitive fire. As much as anything, this text is meant to challenge you to develop a deeper, more thorough and complex understanding of each outlined strategy. The power of each skill is in the intricate and nuanced details that we describe.

Grit

Much has been said about the approach Rafael Nadal, winner of 14 Grand Slam singles titles, takes to tennis. After a recent tournament victory, Nadal remarked, "I don't have a better feeling because I won, 6-0, 6-2, 7-5, than if I won, 6-4 in the fifth honestly. . . . Maybe it's a little bit more beautiful to win 6-4 in the fifth than winning in straight sets, no?" (Clarey 2020).

This Nadalian perspective, as some have dubbed it, allows him to find value and meaning in the suffering. The challenge, the difficulty, is actually what intensifies the joy. The truth is that every competitor knows what Nadal is describing. If you play long enough, if you've faced a significant number of competitive challenges, if you strive for something bigger than one game or one event, and if you are moving toward a greater purpose, then you are bound to encounter setbacks and obstacles along the way. Examples are endless: You do not get the job offer you really want, you are passed over to assist on a surgery, you get cut from the team, you suffer a season- or career-ending injury, you get a poor test result from your medical provider, or you are rejected from a top-tier graduate program. What separates the most successful performers from their less successful peers is their ability to stick with it, to persist, and to hang on. Because they know that if they do, if they can hang on for one second longer than their opponent, then they are one second closer to their next victory. As Dan Gable, considered one of the greatest amateur wrestlers and freestyle and folkstyle wrestling coaches in American history, said, "Gold medals aren't really made of gold. They're made of sweat, determination, and a hard-to-find alloy called guts." Everyone enjoys performing on their version of a game day. It is why we all do what we do. Surgeons enjoy being in the operating room more than they enjoy completing rounds, field hockey players like being on the field during a match more than they enjoy the day-in and day-out grind of practice, musicians enjoy concert performances, and playwrights live for opening night at the theater. But the seeds of greatness are planted during the daily grind. Everyone flocked to watch *Hamilton* in cities across the world, but very few had the opportunity to see how much it required for Lin-Manuel Miranda to complete the musical. J.K. Rowling proudly (now) touts that she was turned down by 12 publishers before finding success with the Harry Potter book series. *Embrace the struggle. Embrace the grind.* That is what leads to success.

Grit refers to a person's "tendency to sustain interest in and effort toward very long-term goals" (Duckworth et al. 2007; Duckworth 2016). Since 2006, Duckworth has explored why, despite having the same talent, intelligence, and resources, some people accomplish much more than others. Grit is really about stamina, stamina in the direction or pursuit of your interests. As Duckworth notes, "If you are working on different things but all of them are very hard, you're not really going to get anywhere. You'll never become an expert" (Martin 2016). Grit is more than sustained effort. You have to know what you are pursuing and then invest yourself completely and over time. That is the type of directional effort, or stamina, that grit intends. *That* is what separates the most elite people in their respective professions from their less elite peers. Grit is the quality or characteristic that allows people to maintain their focus and work rate for years upon years over the course of their life. It is a shared characteristic of high achievers in a variety of fields from Nobel laureates to Olympic athletes.

Establish a Passion

The first step in developing *grit* is to identify and establish a passion for something. What is your purpose and how passionate are you about achieving it? You must decide what you want, to be in touch with your purpose to the point that you develop enough passion and enough love that you will stay committed to it regardless of the hardships you will encounter. And to be clear, you will encounter hardships. Don't make the mistake of believing that having a passion for something means that you won't have to suffer or that you will always be happy or that you will never feel as though you are working hard. Nothing could be further from the truth. Terry Fox, a Canadian athlete, humanitarian, and cancer research activist is a paragon of grit and an example of the importance of identifying your purpose and passion (see sidebar on page 256).

Terry Fox: A Paragon of Grit

Even as a child, as Terry's mother, Betty, recalled, he stacked wooden blocks tirelessly and enjoyed games that lasted for long periods. He even played table hockey by himself because, rather than setting up a single game, Terry devised a long, complicated season schedule in which he played for both teams to keep the season going. These qualities of persistence and passion would later serve him well.

Terry was highly influenced by his high school basketball coach, Bob McGill, who told his team, "If you want something, you work for it, because I'm not interested in mediocrity." Terry went on to become a standout high school basketball player and distance runner and later played basketball in one of the premiere programs in Canada at Simon Fraser University. He was developing a passion for sport and exercise and wanted to become a physical educator. Little did he know, his passion would soon take a different path.

At 18 years of age, Terry Fox was diagnosed with osteosarcoma, and his right leg was amputated soon after. He had to learn to walk again. And over time Terry began to run again. And run he did. Just two and a half years after he lost his leg to cancer, Terry entered the Prince George to Boston Marathon. Although he finished last, he proved to himself that he had strength and stamina. His diagnosis did not stop his pursuit of excellence; he continued running and won three national championships in wheelchair basketball in Vancouver.

As he continued to run, the idea formed in his mind to use his passion for athletics to help bring awareness and funding to cancer research. In 1980, just seven months after finishing his first marathon, Terry Fox began a cross-country run as part of his Marathon of Hope project for cancer research and funding. Although Terry died in 1981, for each of the past 40 years, the Terry Fox Run has taken place in 25 countries and is the largest one-day fundraiser for cancer research. All of this success and impact came from one man who defied odds and used his passion and perseverance to make a difference for others. As Terry often said, "Dreams are made possible if people try."

Based on Teotonio (2008); The Terry Fox Foundation (2021).

The life of Terry Fox demonstrates the role that passion and purpose can play in someone's life. While many people might have been distraught at the diagnosis of cancer and the prospect of a life that would seemingly be unfulfilled, Terry knew that he needed to find a way to bridge his two passions: first sport and later funding cancer research. His passion fueled his perseverance and, regardless of the obstacles, Terry committed to using his abilities to help others and to help fund the fight against cancer.

If you have not found your purpose and your passion yet, then keep sampling. Try new sports; work in a variety of settings (e.g., outdoors, indoors, in a hospital, at a desk). You need to try novel tasks before you narrow your options. You have likely been asked from the time you were in elementary or primary school what you were going to "do" when you grew up. We require young people to artificially narrow their career or professional aspirations early and then wonder why, as young adults, they change their undergraduate major on average three times over the course of their college career. Then, nearly two-thirds of college graduates suggest they would change what they studied if they could go back to school and make the decision all over again (Johnson 2020; National Center for Education Statistics 2013).

In sport, specialization is an all too common practice that has significant and consistent consequences. We hear the stories of child prodigies but fail to realize that for every name we know, there are thousands of other early-specialization athletes we will never know. From a research and performance standpoint, the push toward early specialization is a major issue and ongoing cause for concern. Although 97 percent of professional athletes believe playing multiple sports was crucial for their success, and despite knowing that highly specialized youth sport athletes are three times more likely to experience serious overuse injuries, almost 70 percent of collegiate athletes in the United States report having specialized in a single sport during their childhood or early adolescence (Buckley et al. 2017; Donahue 2019). Narrowing interests at a young age is likely to leave many without a passion or purpose well into adulthood. The two most common reasons for this are the high prevalence of burnout and injuries.

If you are looking for your purpose, then set a goal to try new positions, to take up novel tasks, and to sample a variety of physical activities. Part of developing grit is finding where you excel and what you enjoy. Don't assume that your early selections are necessarily the enduring ones or believe that early success as a youth necessarily translates to long-term success as an adult or in more senior-level performance domains.

Persevere Over Time

Duckworth suggests that once they have established their purpose and passion, gritty people also demonstrate perseverance over time in pursuit of their long-term goals. Most people think that once they have identified their passion and decided to pursue it, their path will be linear, a straight line from where they are now to their final destination. But rarely is this expectation accurate. Instead, the journey often requires changing directions multiple times, starting and stopping, waiting for longer than anticipated, sprinting uphill, and zigzagging for years and years and years.

Any worthy pursuit requires you to zig and to zag. As we outlined in the previous chapter, you will encounter setbacks and trauma in your life. It is not a matter of *if*, but rather *when* and *how often*. Not infrequently, the grittiest decision you can make is to withdraw (see chapter 14); however, this chapter is about sticking it out and persevering. You were not born knowing how to work hard, how to discipline yourself, how to accept critical feedback, or how to overcome challenges and setbacks. Those skills must be taught, developed, and strengthened.

Many of the psychological skills already mentioned in this text will help you become grittier. For example, you must construct productive self-talk to aid in developing a grit mindset. Telling yourself "I stick with it" or "I was made for this challenge" is one way to cultivate grit. Rather than reminding yourself of another obstacle you must overcome, tell yourself that when life gets hard, you get tougher. Thinking of previous obstacles you have successfully overcome serves as a reminder of how you to want to behave in the current challenge. Then, when you get through those tough moments, reflect. Start with the recognition that "It did not break me," and then examine what plan or strategy you used to get through it. Did it work? What did you learn from it that you can use next time so you can move through the challenge even faster? You also want to remind yourself again to "be where your feet are." Duckworth refers to this process as WOOP. Identify your wish (W) or purpose and your intended outcome, identify and imagine the best possible outcome (O), recognize major obstacles (O) or setbacks you might experience, and then develop and revise your plan (P) for getting around those obstacles. However, even when using WOOP strategies, you will encounter challenges, so preparing for them and then executing your plan when the anticipated obstacles occur is key to your success.

Planning ahead allows you to focus on the current moment, which is another key factor in perseverance. Stop thinking about what career you want to move into, what the next position will be, or the next championship you want to win, and instead, focus on right now. What are you doing right now to get better? If you want to be the best at your position, in your sport, or in your profession, then practice long enough and hard enough that you develop your skills in your current position to the best of your ability. Focus on the now, and perform in the now. Then let the next step in your path or journey unfold. Wynton Marsalis, the world's first jazz artist to perform and compose across the full jazz spectrum and composer of a violin concerto and four symphonies, has described how he had to learn to, in the words of Dr. Hacker, "do *now* well." As a child, Marsalis wanted to be successful, but he was scared to fail and did not want to practice as a result. He wanted to attend his private lessons with his music instructor and then improve under their direction. What he later learned was that to "systematically practice and go through your deficiencies, that is what makes you a better musician, and once I got over the fear of practicing, I became a better musician" (Joy2Learn Foundation 2013). Marsalis' plan was to be a successful musician, but he needed to focus on the *now*. He knew his purpose and had developed a passion for music, but he did not have the necessary perseverance. Practice was hard. He made mistakes, and those mistakes and negative evaluation made him afraid to stick with it. He wanted to avoid practicing. Then, at the age of 12, he figured it out. He needed to create a plan and stick with it, day in and day out, for years. Then he could excel. And, as one of the world's leading jazz musicians of his time, he has done just that (Joy2Learn Foundation 2013). As Duckworth has said, "Grit is living life like it's a marathon, not a sprint."

Resilience

If grit is about developing a sustained, consistent effort through struggle toward your goals and dreams, then resilience is about developing an ability to bounce back after the struggle, after the failure. According to the American Psychological Association (2012), resilience is "the process of adapting well in the face of adversity, trauma, tragedy, threats or significant sources of stress—such as family and relationship problems, serious health problems or workplace and financial stressors." As Dr. Hacker has often mentioned in her work with clients, it is important to learn to "adjust and adapt, adjust and adapt." Canadian ice hockey phenom Hayley Wickenheiser said, "Many times I had to dig deep and perform. All of that adversity helped me and drove me to want to be the best." That is exactly how we want every performer to feel—like the errors, the adversity, and the challenge propelled them to their next victory.

miljko/E+/Getty Images

Identify Opportunities for Resilience

An important element of developing resilience is to understand what it means to bounce back. *What does that look like? What does that sound like?* We need to know the strategies involved in developing resilience. Read the story in the following sidebar about how Dr. Hacker challenged the U.S. women's ice hockey team to bounce back from adversity.

IN THEIR OWN WORDS A Bounce Back Story

Before the 2014 Winter Olympic Games in Sochi, Russia, the U.S. women had beaten the Canadian ice hockey team in the World Championships the year before and again in a run-up competition to the Olympics. The rivalry was intense and often ended in one-goal victories or overtime celebrations for one country or the other. Now it was time for the Olympic Games, and everyone was expecting the familiar rematch between Team USA and Team Canada. In Olympic ice hockey, competition begins in pool play, then there are crossover games between teams in various pools, and finally, teams move on to the medal rounds. In the third game of the pool play round, the United States faced Canada. It was considered the last game of the preliminary rounds and, as such, would not affect either team's chances of winning a gold medal. But, as is always the case between these two teams, the stakes were high, the pressure was intense, and a collateral objective was to send a message to the other squad because they were likely to clash again for the gold medal.

The United States was coming off of a 3-1 victory over Finland and a 9-0 rout of Switzerland. The Canadians had defeated Finland 3-0 and Switzerland 5-0. Both teams were feeling good, but the United States was particularly confident coming off the ice against Switzerland, and everything seemed to be clicking for them. The final round of pool play was the much anticipated USA-Canada matchup. From the moment the puck dropped, it was a back-and-forth contest. However, Team USA made errors in the neutral zone, committed uncharacteristic turnovers, and were penalized for reckless decisions that cost them the game. Canada won 3-2. All of a sudden, in one game, the emotion of Team USA changed. It was a difficult loss, even though from a gold medal perspective, nothing had changed: Team USA was not in a better position nor were they in a worse position. Winning the gold medal was equally probable for both teams. But it did not feel that way to the athletes or the coaches. Doubt crept in. The United States often felt they "owned Canada" in events outside the Olympic Games, but that Canada seemed to "have their number" during the Olympic Games. Some members of the team might have been thinking "here we go again" after that loss in the prelims. Either way, they had another game in a few days, and they needed to bounce back and bounce back quickly.

Every athlete has talked about and heard about the importance of bouncing back. However, it is one thing to say it and another to see what is required and then engage in strategies that will lead to resilient action. As the mental skills coach for Team USA, Dr. Hacker asked the general manager for a small, solid rubber ball that would rebound quickly when dropped from any height and a soft, squishy ball that would not bounce. Dr. Hacker wanted to provide a visual, tangible metaphor that would ignite the team's resilience. The entire team met in front of their residence in the Olympic Village. Dr. Hacker took the solid rubber ball in one hand and the squishy, nonbouncing ball in the other and held them up, with arms extended in front of her. She said, "Here are two competitors, two teams. One went through an unexpected, unanticipated emotional loss. And so did the other." She asked them to look at each ball. There was no discernable difference in the height of the drop or the overall shape of either object. Then she dropped both balls. One bounced and the other splatted on the ground, landing flat with no rebound.

At that moment, Dr. Hacker asked the team to describe what they observed. Athletes responded, "One hit the ground and splatted," "One hit the ground and bounced," "same speed," "same distance to the ground." One by one the athletes detailed the event. As they did, Dr. Hacker added, there were only two variables: the drop (the failure, the loss), which both objects experienced, and the constitution or individual makeup of each ball and the resulting action. That was it. Everything else was the same. Then she asked Team USA: *What are you made of?* And she dropped the balls. *How will you respond to the drop?* Then she dropped the balls again. *What is your response to hitting the ground?* Then she dropped the balls again. Each time the balls dropped, one splatted flat on the ground and the other bounced immediately back to its starting place. That exercise made the visual point that each player on the team had a choice, in that moment, in how they would respond to their moment of Olympic adversity. In the next game, four days after the loss that threatened to derail them, Team USA rebounded and defeated Sweden 6-1.

That lesson stuck with the team for the rest of the tournament. When they faced moments of adversity, they asked themselves and each other, "What are you made of? Are you the squishy ball or the bouncy ball?"

In using a metaphor or analogy, the ego is avoided, and because it is not personal, people's defense mechanisms are not energized or activated. Instead, the recipient, in this case, Team USA, could focus on the message. In this example, after a moment of defeat during the high-stakes event of the Olympic Games, the team had to respond, they needed to bounce back, and they had to do so almost immediately. The ball drop scenario offered an authentic, visual representation of what was needed. The physics involved highlighted the choice that each player on the team had to make in order to bounce back. Sometimes we all need to be reminded that when we face a setback, we have two choices: to metaphorically splat on the ground and let it ruin us or to immediately bounce back and start again.

Whether you are performing at work, as a parent in your own home, as a significant other in your relationship, as an athlete in your sport, or in some other performance area, setbacks are coming. Moments of failure lie ahead on your journey. You can be certain of that fact. Athletes know it and corporations know it. In fact, Google has recognized the importance of resilience for their employees and how important it is to both develop it and train it and has launched a TEA Check-In Guide to help employees develop resilience. Google encourages people to check in on their thoughts (T), their energy (E), and their attention (A). The check-in can be done individually or with groups or teams of employees, and the guide offers strategies for bouncing back, similar to strategies outlined in this chapter, if there are issues in any of those three areas. This is one example of how elite performers and companies are starting to focus on resilience and how it can be built intentionally over time.

Certainly, you will have an emotional response to adversity and to errors. That response is both normal and expected, but it is ineffective to stay in that space. It is not useful. To stay in the feeling space associated with the error or adverse situation is a poor use of psychological, emotional, and physical energy. Instead, it is time to respond (rather than react) and to engage in strategies that will help you bounce back. As boxer Floyd Mayweather said, "I don't fold . . . great athletes perform better under pressure, so put pressure on me." And gender equity icon and tennis legend Billie Jean King often said, "Pressure is a privilege." You want to welcome the pressure and stress involved in overcoming obstacles placed in front of you. Remind yourself, whether everything feels like it is going well or the world feels like it is caving in on top of you, that you are in control, that you have decisions to make, and that you were made for this moment.

In other words, to be resilient, you need to be *optimistic* and *adaptable*. Remain flexible. Dr. Hacker reminds clients to "adjust and adapt" and to combine that phrase with a little swagger or dance move to regain confidence, to smile, and to stay in the moment. No matter the competitive challenge, you have a plan for that, and you can successfully "adjust and adapt" and do so as needed. Let's use an example from golf. If you are up four strokes heading into the back nine, here's what you want to be thinking:

- I have them right where I want them.
- I love playing with the lead.
- I am strong and capable.
- I control the match.
- They have to chase me.

In the next tournament, as you head to the back nine, you look up and you are much lower on the leaderboard, down by six strokes. Here is what you want to be thinking:

- I have them right where I want them.
- I love playing from behind.
- They will never see me coming.
- I control the game.
- Here I come. Watch me go to work.

You want to be flexible and open to performing well under any condition. Pressure exists in each of those scenarios. Some people claim they prefer to perform when they are not expected to succeed and others believe they play well from in front. The truth is that you can be resilient, and you can play well from either position. Rarely does life (or a competitive event) unfold as planned. Stop acting like your performance will always happen as you drew it up. Instead, be optimistic; trust yourself and your capabilities. You have performed well across a range of situations before and can do so again. People who are flexible are better able to adapt because they look for and seek opportunities for learning and growth. Every competitive challenge is viewed as a valuable competitive opportunity to face adversity or the pressure of the moment and to succeed. When success is not the outcome, then those experiences are opportunities to learn and to grow.

Learn to Bounce Back Quicker

Another important aspect of resilience is learning how to bounce back from errors. As track icon Wilma Rudolph said, "Nobody goes undefeated all the time." In fact, if you are pushing the boundaries of your capabilities, then you are going to make mistakes and you are going to fail. At whatever moment in the day you are reading this chapter, you have likely already committed at least one mistake. And it was neither the first error of your life nor the last of the day. So when you make a mistake, stop swearing and acting out and stomping around. The mistake is normal; it is common. You are not the first person to make that error, and it is not going to be your last. The entire time you are circling the drain of negativity and wallowing in your own self-pity, the rest of your team is playing a person down. Regardless of the performance domain, if you are stuck in the past, then your current students are not learning new material, the other nurses are having to cover patients for you, or another trial lawyer is stepping in to deliver your closing remarks. You are hurting the team, and you are preventing yourself from moving forward. Errors are inevitable. Swiss tennis player Roger Federer, one of the greatest players of all time, identified his four principles for success: (1) learn quickly, (2) understand the message, (3) develop an old-school work ethic, and (4) when you lose, learn. Rather than trying to avoid them, why not learn the skills to cope with mistakes effectively and efficiently and keep moving forward? It is to this point that we turn our attention.

Maltz (1960) theorized that humans are like thermostats. Similar to how a thermostat turns the furnace or air-conditioner on or off to regulate the temperature of the house, humans try to self-correct when they make a mistake or commit an error. If you take a shot on goal that goes wide left, it is likely that you will self-correct to the right on your next shot. Sue Bird, standout point guard for the Seattle Storm, recently published a social media post about this exact issue. She missed her three-point shot from the left corner, wide left. It hit the side of the backboard—a rarity among elite basketball players. Rather than sulk, she rebounded and shot again, this time making the shot. She self-corrected. In the span of three or four seconds, she exemplified what Maltz explained. In her post, she laughed at her shot and said, "I was seeing that third-rim. Had to fix my vision." Even LeBron James commented on her post, acknowledging that he, too, had recovered from similar errors. What is unique about professional athletes is not that they don't make mistakes: That is mundane; it is ordinary. What sets them apart is that they are deliberate in their response in those moments. Sue Bird, like many basketball players before her, could have pouted or failed to hustle back on defense or blamed a teammate for a poor pass in response to her first shot attempt. Instead, she rebounded the ball, made the correction, and took another shot at the hoop. *That* is the type of player you want on your team; *that* is the type of player you want to become.

If mistakes are normal, even inevitable, then you better develop a *mistake routine* and commit to implementing it. A mistake routine is a behavior paired with a correction that allows you to stay in the moment. Let's start with an example from the workplace. Imagine that you are attending your first office function as a new member of a company and call one of your bosses by the wrong name. You can get stuck in that moment and be unable to hear anyone else introduce themselves as you replay the mistake over and over, or you can implement a mistake routine and stay focused on the task. We are not telling you to ignore the error. Mistakes should not be ignored, but there are productive ways to handle them, and both how and when are important considerations. Of course, it's not ideal that you did not remember your boss' name, but a mistake routine helps professionals (and athletes) direct their attention to what matters most and engage in productive, chosen, and purposeful behaviors.

Every mistake routine involves two elements: (1) a physical action and (2) a mental correction. The physical action is created to mark the end of the mistake. It should be a meaningful, authentic behavior. For example, soccer players might pull on their socks or pull their shin guards up, football players might pick up a blade of grass and toss it onto the field, volleyball players might adjust their knee pads, swimmers might dunk their goggles between events or grunt as they take a breath during a race. After swinging at a bad pitch, major league baseball player Aaron Judge steps outside of the batter's box, picks up dirt, and throws it in the air before stepping back in the box. Soccer star Julie Foudy learned how to snap an elastic band she wore on her wrist. It is best when these physical actions are related to behaviors that performers already engage in. That way, the routine is already established and is familiar to each athlete. The second aspect of a mistake routine is to extract the relevant lesson. There is always a lesson to be gleaned, a correction to be made. See examples of mistake routines on page 265. The purpose of a mistake

Teaching Three Mistake Routines

Flush It

The idea with this routine is that it is important to flush a mistake or error. A toilet is flushed immediately after use, and whenever that action is required, no one dwells on the contents of the flush or revisits the contents with multiple teammates or friends and family members. We too should flush mistakes—learn from them and move one. Stop thinking about them throughout the day or ruminating over them with friends. That moment is done and over. Flush it.

- When the mistake occurs, determine what the relevant lesson is, make the adjustment in your mind, and then flush it.
- Some NFL and MLB teams have kept small, nonworking toilets on their sidelines and in their dugouts to visually remind everyone to flush their mistakes.
- Youth sport teams have created a flush it signal to hold each other accountable and, when an error is committed, they pretend they are flushing a toilet to signify that mistake or error is over and the next play is right now.

Fudge, Fix, Focus

This is a technique that Dr. Hacker implemented with the national team.

- When a mistake happens, you say to yourself "fudge" or whatever fudgelike word resonates with you!
- The immediate follow-up step is to fix it. Remind yourself not of the error, but of the correction (e.g., head down, lock the ankle, follow through to target, take a breath, stay balanced).
- Once you have fixed the error, then you focus. Focus on the next play, the shoelaces, the racket, the strings, the ball. Wherever your attention should be, whatever the next responsibility is, that is where you should direct your focus.

Park It

This is another technique that Dr. Hacker implemented with the USWNT

- Imagine you are driving to the mall or your favorite place to shop. The purpose of going to the mall is to shop, not to park your car. You might take a picture of your parking place so you remember where it is when you are ready to head home.
- When you start walking into the shopping mall, you don't keep checking on your car. You don't walk a few feet, turn around, and check to see if the car is still there. You don't keep revisiting where it is. The point of the trip is to go shopping, so you park your car, you know where it is, and you will come back to it when it is time.

> continued

Teaching Three Mistake Routines > *continued*

- Do the same with mistakes. You don't want to forget about a mistake; you want to "park it," because what is important is *this moment, this game, this responsibility.* Park it. Play the game. Perform. Then go back and analyze the mistake.
- Analysis could also quickly happen during a dead ball, during a timeout, at halftime, between presenters, at the end of a meeting, in the dugout between innings, or in other moments that allow space to reflect and analyze what happened and what could be done differently.

routine is to help performers stay connected with the current moment and to immediately let go of the past (mistake). Yes, it was a mistake, and, yes, that error indicates that a change is required going forward. Athletes must figure out what that lesson is and focus on the correction. They must focus on what they want *to do* rather than on what they did wrong. However, once the correction or lesson is identified, it is time to move on. A mistake routine is just that, it is a routine that, when practiced, can be implemented effectively after an error is committed to help a performer stay in the only moment that matters: the one happening *right now.*

There are times during competition when analysis and corrections are inappropriate. For example, if you just attempted a pass and it was intercepted by the other team, then you do not have time to analyze that play in the moment. In ice hockey, when your shift might only last for 30 to 60 seconds, you do not have three minutes available to dedicate to correcting an error. On the surgical table, when a patient is coding, you cannot stop and think about how you might have corrected the sequence of your suture technique. In these pressure-filled moments, it is important to know how to set aside the error and continue performing the most important and needed task at hand. Then you can (metaphorically speaking) pick it up and analyze it at a more appropriate time (see the park it strategy on page 265). This park it strategy, in particular, has helped professional and Olympic athletes develop resilience.

The Importance of Yet

Now that we have established that struggle is not only normal, but it can also be useful, we turn our attention to a concept that has gained massive attention over the last few decades: a *growth mindset* (Dweck 2008). Dweck (1986; 2008) and Dweck and Yeager (2019) have studied the impact of children's and adult's beliefs on their motivation and achievement. These scholars identified two distinct mindsets that students adopted: growth mindset and fixed mindset. They found that when children believed they could increase their intellectual abilities and focused on effort and trying new strategies, they were more likely to succeed over time. This belief, called a *growth mindset*, refers to the idea that you can develop and improve if you implement appropriate, targeted effort and strategy (Dweck 2016). People with a growth mindset believe that their skills come from hard work and that there is always room to develop. They view their effort as essential to their success and are looking for feedback so they can improve their skills and strategies. This type of mindset stands in sharp contrast to what Dweck calls a *fixed mindset*, in which a person believes their knowledge, talent, and skills are static, inherent, and unchangeable (Dweck 2016). Individuals with a fixed mindset get defensive when they receive feedback because it feels like a personal attack on who they are as a human being. They try to avoid challenges and often blame others or feel discouraged when they fail at a task (see the following sidebar to differentiate a growth versus fixed mindset). A growth mindset has been associated with people embracing

Chalk Talk

Quick Hits for Differentiating Between a Fixed and a Growth Mindset

What do you believe?

Growth mindset	Fixed mindset
Challenges help me grow.	When I'm frustrated, I give up.
What am I missing?	I'm not any good at this.
I like to try new things.	I prefer to stick with what I know.
I can learn anything.	I'm smart.
I'll use some of the strategies I have learned.	I give up.
Is this really my best work?	This is good enough.
I'll figure out what they do and try it out.	I'll never be as good as they are.
This may take some time and effort.	This is too hard.
I'm on the right track.	I'm awesome at this.

challenges, persisting in the face of setbacks, seeing effort as the path to mastery and achievement, learning from criticism, and finding lessons in the success of others (Dweck 2016).

Almost all performers at some point in their career begin to recognize the importance of a growth mindset. Olympian and triathlete Sarah True remarked, "For too long, I just believed you're either good at something or you're not. . . . I spent a lot of time not being nice to myself—just holding myself to unrealistic standards. That can become really toxic. . . . I [had] to see myself as a work in progress instead of just deeply flawed." In the growth mindset literature, failure is painful, but it does not define you as a performer. It is something to face and learn from. Someone with a growth mindset might ask, "Why hide deficiencies or try to prove your worth when you could get busy getting better?"

As human beings, our very survival has depended on our ability to overcome challenges, to face and overcome defeat, to persevere, to adjust and adapt, and to improve through trial and error. Our ancestors would not have survived long if they had foraged for one day and, unable to find food, refused to look again, announcing instead "I am not a good gatherer; someone else will have to bring food to the family." You might read that sentence and laugh, knowing how ludicrous it sounds. And yet every day, students announce "I am not a writer" and "I am not good at public speaking." Athletes tell themselves, their teammates, and their coaches that they are not skilled at X or Y all the time. Those examples are equally as useless and unhelpful as the one about our foraging ancestors. Human beings can and do learn from failure, and they can sustain their effort over time. But to do so, they must develop a growth mindset. They must first believe they can improve before they deliberately enact strategies that will bring about personal or career development.

When confronting a critic of her grit theory, Duckworth demonstrated a growth mindset. As part of a dissertation, a doctoral student of sociology wrote that the way Duckworth described grit evoked a bootstrap mentality (anyone can achieve anything if they work hard enough) that ignored structural poverty and other institutional barriers that might prevent some people from achieving preferred outcomes. Rather than shut down the conversation, Duckworth, who had dedicated much of her professional life to studying this concept, chose instead to listen to the feedback and even joined the student's dissertation committee so that she could learn and become more aware of potential holes in the theory and areas that required further investigation. Imagine embracing and incorporating a strong critique of your life's work. Anyone in that position would have an emotional reaction, but Duckworth did not stay in that space. She resisted the emotional trap and sought more information, and she stayed open to development, learning, and growth. It is this openness to critique and commitment to identifying strategies for improvement that are the hallmarks of a growth mindset.

Recognizing Effort *and* Strategy

The popularity of growth mindset literature over the past few decades has had a positive effect on people's lives. However, a significant and potentially deleterious misconception has also emerged, one that suggests encouraging and focusing on effort and improvement are all that matter. Instead, as Dweck points out (2008; Dweck and Yeager 2019), the process and learning from successful and less successful strategies is critical to achievement. It is not enough to put posters about effort and growth on the wall or write down moments of your own effort achievements. Coaches, teachers, and employers have bought into a simplistic version of the growth mindset and often say "Don't worry; you'll get it if you keep trying" or "Great effort! I love that you went for it." Certainly, effort is necessary and essential, but it is not the only requirement of a growth mindset. Emphasizing effort without an effective strategy is a mistake that is eerily similar to that which we made in previous generations when we provided participation trophies. In that case, showing up equated to giving effort. In fact, Dweck (2015) commented that what keeps her awake at night is fearing that the mindset concepts, which developed as a counter to the failed self-esteem movement, would be used to perpetuate that same philosophy. Performers need a broad repertoire of effective strategies they can employ to learn and improve. It is good to try, but to give effort without thinking about what strategies worked or did not work does little more than improve self-esteem. Self-reflection and situational analysis are equally critical elements.

A growth mindset does not mean that anyone can accomplish anything they want; it is not a self-belief model, and it is not cheerleading for yourself or someone else. Instead, a growth mindset is about generating multiple strategies for success and being willing to do the work, sustained over time to bring about change and greater competence. The value of Dweck's (2016) work is in the details. Performers benefit from developing a growth mindset because it encourages them to recognize the solutions that are useful and accurate, and it encourages them to always be willing to generate and implement new remedies or strategies for problems that have yet to be mastered.

Absolutely, appreciate the work you have put in so far, but, if you have not yet solved the problem, then ask yourself what you have tried, how it worked out (or not), and what you can try next. Imagine you are trying to solve a math problem but cannot seem to find the solution: What have you tried and what you can you try next? Now, think about trying to get past a pressing defense in basketball or racing a mile against an opponent you have not defeated before. *What did you try before? What else can you try? How will you change your approach? What else do you need to practice? Where do you need to practice?* That is the magic sauce. Developing the appropriate belief system or mindset is like a noun in a sentence. It matters, but without a verb, the sentence is incomplete. You must believe that you can improve, develop, and grow, and then you need to identify actionable steps that will bring about that growth (see the following worksheet).

Performer-Centered Implementation Worksheet

Developing a Growth Mindset After Adversity

The purpose of this worksheet is to help you develop a growth mindset when faced with setbacks, rejection, or failure.

Directions

Answer the following prompts as completely as possible.

1. Think of a moment when you experienced a significant failure or setback. Describe that moment in detail: What happened? When did it occur? Where did it take place? Who was involved? Why was it a failure? How did it occur?

2. Using the example you described in the first prompt, describe three strategies you could have implemented that might have led to a different outcome or result. Answer the question "What could I do differently?" Identify who, what, when, where, how, and why for each strategy. Be as specific as possible.

3. Write down at least one person from whom you could solicit feedback for each of the strategies you identified and identify one question you might need answered before you implement this new technique or strategy.

From C. Hacker and M. Mann, *Achieving Excellence: Mastering Mindset for Peak Performance in Sport and Life* (Champaign, IL: Human Kinetics, 2023).

Conclusion

For people to develop grit, Duckworth (2013) says that they need to cultivate a growth mindset. We, along with others, argue that grit and resilience are the necessary ingredients required to build and sustain a growth mindset. Perhaps both perspectives are true. The important point for performance is that, to sustain effort toward long-term, even lifelong, pursuits, to persist through challenges and long periods without great success, and to bounce back from setbacks efficiently, *you need to cultivate a growth mindset, be gritty, and develop resilience.* Remember, these are not personality traits that you either have or don't have. You were not born gritty and resilient, believing you can grow and improve. Instead, as with all of the cognitive strategies in this book, these are skills that you can develop with consistent, systematic practice over time. And like with all skills, you will get better at each one with practice. Life will get hard, and when there is significant time and distance between your achievements, you might be tempted to give up. In this and the previous chapter, you have learned strategies for sticking with it and staying the course. Hold on. In those moments, as Hall of Fame basketball coach Pat Summitt said, "Left foot, right foot, breathe." Trust that you have the grit, the resilience, and the mindset to meet the challenge in front of you. Do *now* well. Be where your feet are.

In this chapter, we also make explicit our belief that many ideas of value are at risk of becoming too general and too simple and sounding more like cheerleading phrases than calls to action. In that case, the platitudes and bumper sticker slogans are just common words and phrases and, often, ineffective. Avoid the temptation to take an impactful quote or an easy-to-read concept and use it to either justify your current behaviors or think that by name dropping or term dropping, you are on the cutting edge of mental skills training. Instead, learn the specific, layered, and often nuanced requirements of each mental skill and strategy. In other words: *Read the fine print*. Then commit to acting in accordance with the evidence-based principles underlying each technique.

CHAPTER 16

Highlighting We Before Me

When Sue Bird was announced as one of the flag bearers for the United States during the 2020 Tokyo Olympic Games, she responded, "Anything I get is because of everyone around me." During the same Olympic Games, after Team Canada defeated the U.S. women's national soccer team (USWNT), Jessie Fleming talked about how special the win was as a member of that specific team: "It's really special to get to contribute to the win. There's a group of players on our team who have worked on this for 20 years. Seeing them cry after that match means so much." Each of these quotes from athletes demonstrates the significance of the team in both collective and individual achievements. Teams can also be important in holding individuals accountable to their purpose and goals. For example, following the second set of the gold medal game, the U.S. women's volleyball team reminded each other to slow down. Setter Jordyn Poulter said,

> Chemistry is a verb.
>
> Dr. Colleen Hacker, FNAP, CMPC, six-time Olympic Games coaching staff member, mental skills consultant

> Relationships with people are what it's all about. . . . You have to realize it takes a group to get things done. . . . You have to make players realize you care about them, and they have to care about each other and be interested in each other. Then they start to feel a responsibility toward each other. Then they want to do for each other (Boudway 2018).
>
> Gregg Popovich, head coach of the San Antonio Spurs, who has won the five NBA titles under his direction

> You can be so dialed in, so focused, that you forget to enjoy this moment, enjoy the fact that we're playing in a gold-medal match. Enjoy that we're beating one of the best teams in the world as a group, with the people that we love. So, just toward the end, I think we were really trying to stay in the moment with each other. (Chrös McDougall 2021)

The influence of group dynamics on performance is not limited, however, to team sports. NASCAR drivers talk about the importance of the pit crew, golfers share credit with their caddy, and last year teams from NASA and the European Space Agency joined forces to complete work on a spacecraft. Positive group interactions have also been shown to improve adherence to exercise programs (Spink and Carron 1992). Group dynamics and team cohesion clearly have an impact on performance in a variety of achievement domains.

While often used synonymously, groups and teams are not the same. Teamwork is a dynamic process that requires collaboration among team members to effectively complete both individual and collective responsibilities and maximize the likelihood of success (McEwan and Beauchamp 2014). A group might form to achieve a common or shared task and immediately dissolve thereafter, but teams are created and maintained through intentional acts over time. And unlike groups, who interact and share a similar task, teams hold four distinct characteristics: (1) a collective sense of "we" or unity, (2) each member knows their role and responsibility, (3) established, structured lines of communication, and (4) rules and norms that guide member behavior (Weinberg and Gould 2019). In this chapter, we outline the team development process and identify strategies and behaviors that help facilitate group effectiveness.

Developing a Group Into a Team

One of the main points from this chapter is that groups and teams are formed through intentional actions; they don't just happen by chance. The most effective and high-functioning teams are made of a collection of individuals that have all decided to think and behave in ways that help them form strong bonds and perform at a high level. What you need to be aware of about teams are the predictable stages, cycles, or shifts that each will likely experience. There are critical challenges and similar issues that might arise and knowing what stage or shift your team is in can help you prepare for these moments and respond with clarity and effectiveness.

As groups prepare to complete a task, whether that is ensuring that the restaurant is ready to open on time, the patient is woken up every two hours to take their medicine, or an athletic team is readying for a new season, they are likely to move through four stages, according to Tuckman (1965): forming, storming, norming, and performing.

Stage One: Forming

In the *forming* stage, team members are getting to know one another and often assess each other's strengths and weaknesses. People are trying to figure out if they belong in the group and to identify their role. It's important to remember that in this first stage, individuals are strangers to one another and have been selected to be on the team or nominated for this particular task. It might seem like the team is functioning well because there is a lack of conflict, but that reality is deceptive because in the norming stage, people are typically sticking to safe topics to be polite or collegial and to avoid rather than work through issues. Early on in this initial stage, it is important to establish expectations and criteria for success.

Stage Two: Storming

Once individuals have established group membership and roles have been identified, they enter the *storming* stage, which is marked by conflict. People resist their roles and the leader's expectations; they do not want to be subsumed by the team. Individuals still see themselves as separate from the group, and they may feel anger or hostility when their wants or needs are not met. Some members actively push back either in the open in words or actions or behind the scenes with a small group of like-minded teammates.

Stage Three: Norming

If groups can stay together through this stage, the *norming* stage is where cooperation and unity emerge, and conflicts are reduced (Weinberg and Gould 2019). Here, norms are established for the group. What are the expectations and how is this team or group different from others? Tony Gustavsson, coach of the Australian women's national soccer team, tweeted, "This team has passion and belief and what lives in this team is this never-say-die attitude [which] means we connect with our heart." This exemplifies the team's standard of excellence and defines how the team thinks, behaves, and performs. As norms are embraced, rather than competing for status, people start to feel like they are part of the team and recognize that, if they accept their roles and work together, they can accomplish their goals.

Stage Four: Performing

In the *performing* stage, team members actively and explicitly work together to solve problems and test new ideas (Weinberg and Gould 2019). This stage is defined by well-established and accepted roles and more stable relationships among individuals within the team. Individuals defer to the team's needs, and the group ensures that everyone is recognized for their unique efforts. This remark by soccer player Mia Hamm, two-time Olympic gold medalist and two-time World Cup champion, illustrates how an individual might feel when their team is in the performing stage: "I am a member of a team, and I rely on the team, I defer to it and sacrifice for it, because the team, not the individual, is the ultimate champion. . . . Goals have never defined me as a player.

What has defined me is my impact on the team. If that means passing or playing defense to win, I'll do it."

Although Tuckman's four stages are considered a linear approach to group development, meaning that each group will progress through the stages in a known and predictable order, they are not guaranteed. Some groups may never enter the *performing* stage, for example, and may stay in the *storming* stage for the entire season or the entire year. Teams may move very quickly into the norming stage, while other teams, for a variety of reasons, never make it out of the forming stage, and their group may dissolve sooner than expected. See the sidebar on page 277 for a few strategies that might help ensure that your group resolves the common issues in each stage swiftly and effectively.

All groups go through these stages. It is true for families, sport teams, and organizations. It is expected. It is normal. It is predictable. There are also relational shifts that occur within each group or team throughout the development process. These shifts do not occur linearly, but rather, members of the group shift back and forth between them like a pendulum. Specifically, feelings of unity and cohesion ebb and flow, as do conflicts. For example, when a new group is formed for a project at work, feelings of unity might be high initially, but as the group begins to work together and individuals compete for rank, responsibility, or recognition, cohesion might decrease. Then, as those issues are resolved, unity and commitment to the group rise until individuals begin to feel like their effort or work is going unnoticed or is underappreciated. The point is that members of the group and the leaders must remain vigilant to the dynamic interactions within the group or team. The image of a pendulum swinging back and forth as the environment changes (e.g., a string of failures or losses, a change in roles or positions) might be helpful. Each member of the group must remain attentive to how their coworkers and teammates respond to changing demands and intervene when needed to ensure collective progress and achievement.

Know and Accept Your Role

An important element of any effective team is to create a structure in which roles and responsibilities are clear and accepted by each individual. There are two types of roles: formal and informal (Mabry and Barnes 1980). *Formal roles* are dictated by the nature of the sport or organization and are often communicated or assigned by the leader of the group (e.g., point guard in basketball, lead attorney in a court case), whereas *informal roles* evolve organically from interactions among teammates (Weinberg and Gould 2019). Some people will serve as the comedian to keep the team or group light, and others will serve as the social or event planner who ensures the team or group spends quality time together outside of their work or performance environment. Some members of the group

Chalk Talk

Quick Hits for Strategies to Address the Four Stages of Team Development

Stage of development	Key issues encountered	Key strategies to resolve
Forming	Unclear expectations Unsure of affiliation or belonging Avoidance of controversial or challenging topics	Devote time to quality introductions and time together. Communicate goals and objectives. Implement clear evaluation process.
Storming	Resistance to group and leader Competition Anger, frustration, hostility High interpersonal conflict Lack of participation Decrease in performance	Establish clear roles for each group member. Consistently and objectively communicate standards. Provide frequent feedback on individual and group efforts.
Norming	Confidence and acceptance of role Demonstrated commitment to the group Support of one another among members Collaboration	Recognize individual efforts when behaving or engaging with their role. Recognize team and group efforts.
Performing	Individuals who don't defer to the team Ineffective teamwork to solve problems Inconsistent performance	Celebrate successes. Recognize individual efforts and contributions. Encourage collective decision-making.

will be serious and quiet while others are likely to be loud and outgoing. Informal roles can have either a positive or negative effect on the team.

To improve a team's effectiveness, people must understand and accept their roles. Research has demonstrated that to be effective in each role, you must first understand four aspects of it: (1) the breadth and depth of your responsibilities, (2) required behaviors to carry out your responsibilities, (3) how you will be evaluated, and (4) the consequences of not fulfilling your role or responsibilities (Beauchamp et al. 2005). The most effective athletic teams are those comprising people who each bring their unique strengths and talents to the team as opposed to having a team made up of the same type of player (or personality) with similar strengths. When people know and accept their roles, they are more satisfied, have less anxiety, and view their team as cohesive and effective (Benson, Eys, and Irving 2016; Bosselut et al. 2012; Eys et al. 2003). To ensure role clarity, leaders need to be proactive and consistent in their messaging. Conflicts typically occur when there is an unclear message or a changing message about what a person's role is supposed to be for that group or for that specific task. It is exceedingly difficult for anyone to accept a role if they are unsure of what it is. Roles need to be defined and then consistently communicated across multiple messaging platforms (e.g., media, practice fields, in games, private conversations) and multiple sensory displays (e.g., visually on bulletin boards in the locker room, auditory through conversations and consistent feedback). See the sidebar on page 279 for examples.

The Role of the Group Member in Role Acceptance

At times, group conflict can occur when a person knows their role but does not accept it. An athlete wants to start and views themselves as a starter, but their formal role is as a reserve player. Beyond sport, an elementary school teacher may want to be the leader of their grade-level team but is not elected to serve in that position. Role acceptance is important for enhancing group structure and performance (Benson et al. 2013). Each individual needs to believe that they could be the margin of victory and that their efforts, unique skill, and contributions matter. Every single person in the group or member of the team needs to have that belief about their role. They should believe that they can do as well, or even better, at performing a particular role than anyone else. But the rules or the structure of the organization or sport might not allow for everyone to play the same role. For example, in soccer, only 11 people can play on a side at the same time. There might be as many people formally in reserve roles as there are people on the field. Similarly, there can only be one first chair in an orchestra even though there are many worthy and talented musicians. Someone has to be in the second-chair position. As a member of a team, everyone must separate the rules and the structures that regulate sport from their personal value or capability.

Next, consider your legacy. At some point, your tenure with that group, team, or organization will come to an end. At some point, you will no longer work at your current place of employment. At some point, you will retire from your sport. You will change hospital affiliations or the

PUT IT INTO PRACTICE

Strategies for Communicating and Clarifying Roles

Butcher Paper Role Identification
From 1996 to 1999, the U.S. women's national soccer team used this exercise to clarify roles by drawing on butcher paper their positions during set pieces and identifying each person's responsibilities during each moment of the play. After the exercise, the butcher paper was posted in the locker room.

1. Have group members write down their top three responsibilities.
2. What is their role today?
3. You want each person to know their job and to do their job.

Numbers Game for Proactive Communication
Use this process to schedule monthly sessions to meet with individuals to talk about their role and how well they are performing in it, and discuss other elements of performance or life outside of the performance domain. This exercise is easy for teams because players wear uniforms with numbers.

1. Use their jersey number for the corresponding days during a month and meet with them on that day. For example, if a player wears number 24, meet with them on the 24th of each month to touch base, talk about their role and how well they are performing in it, and discuss other elements of performance or life outside of the performance domain.

2. If a team member wears a number that exists outside of the number of days in a month (e.g., 44 or 50), pick a digit from their number (e.g., 4 or 5) and meet with them on the fourth or the fifth.

3. If you work with a team or group that does not have numbered jerseys or uniforms, assign each group member a date to meet or have them select their own date.

school where you teach or learn. It's helpful to consider how you want to be remembered. *What do you want your legacy to be?* Because you must live that legacy consistently and act in accordance with it daily, it is not easy to embrace a role that you prefer not to hold. But do you want your legacy on that team to be that you were constantly unhappy with playing time or that you were frustrated with your role in the organization? Think carefully about your professional epitaph, so to speak. What would members of your team write about you for your epitaph? How will they remember you?

The reality is that there is often a disconnect between what people think they are, what their role is, what they are doing, and how they are really behaving. Typically, people see themselves in more charitable, understanding, forgiving, and positive terms. So, when they are struggling to accept their formal role, they should identify the structural issues at play, and then act in accordance with what they want as their legacy. In the following sidebar, we outline two examples of how elite athlete leaders set the standard through acts of service and in so doing, likely made it possible for others to accept roles that they might not have otherwise embraced.

IN THEIR OWN WORDS **Elite Athlete Leadership Archetypes**

When the U.S. women's national soccer team arrived at a hotel after an international flight, team captain Carla Overbeck carried teammates' bags to their hotel rooms. "I'm the captain, but I'm no better than anybody else. I'm certainly not a better soccer player." Less known to the public, her teammates, like goalkeeper Briana Scurry, viewed Overbeck as the "heartbeat of that team and the engine. Everything about the essence of the team—that was Carla" (Walker 2017).

Rafael Nadal made headlines when, as the number two tennis player in the world and 19-time Grand Slam singles champion, he swept his own clay courts after practice rather than leaving it to one of the academy staff members. This habit of sweeping his court after training began in his childhood and is a behavior he has maintained to date. As he reported to Real Madrid TV, "For me, it is a good example of overcoming passion for what you do and commitment to your professional front."

Based on Prakash (2020); Walker (2017).

Leaders sweep the courts. Leaders carry the bags. You cannot talk about effective teams or groups without also talking about the role of leaders. In these two examples, Nadal and Overbeck lived their legacy through consistently chosen behaviors; they set the standard and created a template or a path that made it possible for their teammates to then accept their roles—whether they were satisfied with them or not. They led through their actions. Some people label these actions as examples of servant leadership.

When people embrace their role, the team becomes greater than the sum of its parts. As Dr. Hacker (2018) wrote in an article for the Positive Coaching Alliance, "1 + 1 = 3. We are stronger together." When group members embrace a legacy where their goal is to play for something bigger, to play for the team, and to make a teammate look good, then the outcome can be superior to what any individual could have accomplished on their own. Take the example of Canada's women's soccer team, who after 20 years of heartache and disappointment, defeated the U.S. team in the 2020 Tokyo Olympic Games.

Christine Sinclair, the Canadians' captain, noted that, "I was just sitting there thinking how proud I am of this team. . . . It's a very unique group. It's a special group and I'm so proud to be a part of it."

She was also candid while talking about *not* going for bronze again: "Back-to-back bronzes, we were kind of sick of that," Sinclair said. "And this team, I mean, wow, what a performance, what a fight. Just so proud of our team, and one more to go" (Sadler 2021).

Balancing Me and We

The most effective and successful groups adopt a team-first mentality, and they also recognize and celebrate the wide range of important team behaviors and skills that each member brings with them. There is a beautiful tension and synergy between uplifting, refining, and cultivating the individual at the same time that you extend, refine, and celebrate the team. Both sides of that equation need to be nurtured concurrently. When the two sides are out of balance—when the individual becomes more important than the team or conversely when all the focus is on the team as a whole and individual contributions are ignored—then conflict is sure to occur.

The U.S. women's national soccer team offers one example of how to intentionally develop consistent recognition of individual behaviors that contribute to group outcomes. In the lead-up to the 1999 World Cup, Dr. Hacker, the team's mental skills coach, created a bulletin board where players posted examples of their teammates' behaviors that helped them feel better, play better, and feel connected to the team. For example, someone might write "Mia ran over and gave me a high five after scoring a goal" or "During a water break, Foudy told me I was an important leader on the team." The noted actions were lifted up visibly to all teammates. They were publicly shared on the Put-Up Board, and this offered a personal and authentic way to move from simply knowing privately that a teammate positively affected someone to actively celebrating specific examples of team-first behaviors. Everyone knows that it is important to say that every role matters and that every person is important, but we often do not actively live in accordance with those stated values. As a coach or leader, you might consider creating a version of a put-up board and post practical, tangible examples of how individuals on the team contributed to the collective goal or mission and to each other. Remember Dr. Hacker's recognition that "Chemistry is a verb."

As the quote at the beginning of the chapter signifies, chemistry requires action. You must "do" chemistry in the same way that you "do" a relationship. If you only "have" a relationship, you should be worried. You must actively engage in that relationship and do so daily to keep it nourished, growing, and sustained. You have to choose to invest in it. In the same way, you do not "have" a team or an organizational culture. It must be an explicit part of training and practice, and each member of the team must demonstrate their ongoing and individual commitment each day, consistently over time. You must turn the goal of team or group cohesion into a series of daily verbs, a series of daily decisions to act. Both the individual and the group have to be invested. You must recognize the unique demands of each side of that equation, and then you must actively, consistently, and appropriately invest in both sides. As Rudyard Kipling (1899) wrote, "For the strength of the pack is the wolf, and the strength of the wolf is the pack."

It is not easy to balance both the individual and the team, but when it is done well and right, individuals are more satisfied, and the group is more likely to function at a high level. The effects are palpable. When the USWNT won the World Cup, Briana Scurry was the starting goalkeeper and the only goalkeeper to have played every minute of that tournament. And the first people running to her after the final whistle were the reserve goalkeepers. They took collective pride in her success and in the team's success. When roles are clear and embraced by everyone, it eliminates questions of whether or not to celebrate the success of another team member. There is none of that. Teams celebrate the accomplishment of each person because each person contributed their distinct and unique skill set to help make the outcome possible. Those experiences only happen when people target both sides of the equation (individual and team) and recognize, understand, value, and invest in both.

When athletes struggle to embrace their formal roles, leaders need to address this disconnect directly rather than complaining or criticizing it in private or in small cliques. "I think I should be a starter." "I think I should be a leader or a captain." Yes! Encourage those thoughts; do not argue with them. Remember, it is healthy and advantageous for each member of the team to believe they can be the starter or the leader of the group. You want to clearly communicate, however, that you have decided on their formal role for now and provide rationale based on facts and evidence. Encourage team members to consider the evidence you provide in light of the team or group rather than personalizing it. For example, just because one player holds superior vision, or another person is really fast, does not mean that the player who is struggling to accept their role as a reserve does not also possess those skills. As the leader, it is your responsibility to identify and make clear your values and priorities. Perhaps you value one particular skill set over another that a different person on the team possesses. Own that. Be honest about those preferences. It does not mean that the player in front of you is not skilled or not capable or not equally talented, it simply means that as a leader, you prioritize one capability over another. In sport, you might value speed over technical skill. In business, you might value customer relations over budgetary focus. Either way, you must be clear on your personal core principles and be able to state them with clarity and consistency.

Value Individual Contributions

You want every player to chase or work toward the role of a starter or of a playmaker while also embracing their current position. It is important, then, to both explain your core principles and rationale as well as remind team members of how they are contributing to the collective whole and find unique ways to acknowledge and reward those important behaviors and contributions. Recognize the authentic individual strengths and skills that everyone brings to the collective good and help each person become more aware of these characteristics and behaviors as well. At the corporate level, employees are often aware of the actions or behaviors they could engage in that would cause them to lose favor with their boss, yet they are less likely to recognize what they could do to make themselves more desirable and beneficial to the company. Simply doing their job is a neutral act. They should be doing their job. It's the threshold minimum. Showing up for work or practice is an expectation. Help performers recognize what they can do daily to contribute to the team environment over and above their minimum job description. The worksheet on page 284 offers one way to encourage group members to focus on what they are bringing to the team.

Being part of a group and, therefore, working and performing in close proximity are important but not sufficient for building an effective team. Even sharing a common task is not enough to create cohesion. It is required of course, and it is important, but it is not enough. How many people live in the same house or work in the same office but are not actively invested in the group or in the various relationships? Proximity cannot be passive. Instead, you must actively cultivate and take on specific behaviors and actions to develop into a cohesive group. Each member of the group must engage in these and be actively supportive of one another. Along these lines, social support has been related to increased feelings of cohesion among group members (Weinberg and Gould 2019). Researchers have identified several types of social support that can improve team cohesion (Rees 2007). When discussing how leaders might work with a group member who is struggling to accept their role, they might have been providing emotional-challenge support, asking the indi-

Performer-Centered Implementation Worksheet

Making Chemistry a Verb: Addressing the "+1" Pillar of Performance

+1 of the Four Pillars

This worksheet is an extension of the four pillars worksheet in chapter 10. You might choose to combine that worksheet with this one so that you are consistently balancing the equation (individual + team).

Directions

Each member of the group or team should respond to the following questions at the beginning of each week of the competitive year or season.

1. List three *observable* individual actions you can take that would actively and positively contribute to team (or group) chemistry.
2. List three examples where the team itself (or individuals on the team) made a positive contribution to you or to someone else as a member of the group.

From C. Hacker and M. Mann, *Achieving Excellence: Mastering Mindset for Peak Performance in Sport and Life* (Champaign, IL: Human Kinetics, 2023).

---

vidual to question and evaluate their attitudes and feelings. There might also be times when, for example, a coworker is struggling to assert their voice on a topic and another team member offers reality-confirmation support to affirm their feelings and encourage them to speak in the next meeting. We have provided examples throughout this chapter of ways for teammates to offer task-appreciation support as well, which can be used to support a person's efforts. We have highlighted specific behaviors from the sport psychology literature, and each is a viable option for investing in a team's culture. If members want to develop an effective group or team, consistently engaging in these behaviors over time will make that goal a reality.

A Note on Social Loafing

Even when groups or teams form, it is possible that one or more individuals within the group might engage in social loafing, which occurs when people put forth less than their best effort. This phenomenon, later called the Ringelmann effect, was first proven when, as the number of people pulling on a rope increased, the incremental gains in the amount of weight pulled did not increase (Weinberg and Gould 2019). As more people join or participate in the group, the more likely it is that someone will attempt to hide or give less than their best. Of course, this idea of social loafing is less likely when people engage in the active and positive behaviors we have outlined in this chapter. However, social loafing becomes an issue when individual group members are unsure of how to contribute or feel like their contributions are unimportant or go unrecognized. As a result, the individual might feel less invested in the team or in contributing to the group. It can also occur because of volitional deference. Simply stated, volitional deference occurs when someone holds the view that "If someone else is going to do the work, then I do not need to do it as well."

To prevent social loafing, recognize and reward the individual contributions of each team member consistently. Each person on the team or in the group should be aware of what they bring to the group that is unique and take pride in that knowledge or skill (more information on how to help people identify their unique talents and skills will be presented in chapter 17). In addition, make individual contributions known and visible to others so that people do not feel like their work is anonymous. Research on swimmers has indicated that these athletes swam faster in relay events when their individual splits were announced and slower when their splits were not announced publicly (Weinberg and Gould 2019). When possible, break larger groups and teams into smaller subgroups that work on a task or practice together. Both large-group and small-group work is useful so that people feel connected to each other and can see the big picture. These behaviors can help prevent or at least reduce the likelihood that social loafing will occur on your team.

Enhancing Cohesion Through Team Building

Often, when people think of group dynamics or group development, they assume we are talking about team building. It is true that building a team is part of this process, but it is only one element. Cohesion is a much larger concept that refers to the forces that act on individuals to remain part of the group (Festinger, Schacter, and Back 1950). Any group or team might achieve *task cohesion*, which refers to the degree to which people work together to achieve common goals and objectives, and *social cohesion*, which is the degree to which people enjoy working together and with each other (Weinberg and Gould 2019). You can have neither, or your team can achieve one without the other, but the greatest joy, satisfaction, and performance occurs when both are present. In 2014, when Canada defeated the United States and won Olympic gold in women's ice hockey, the U.S. team appeared to have higher social cohesion even though the Canadian team was victorious. On the other hand, in 2018, Team Canada was close socially but lost the gold to Team USA. Social cohesion helps, but it does not guarantee success. Task cohesion is closely associated with performance success, whereas social cohesion affects the experience of individual group members but does not always determine performance outcomes.

In some ways, leaders must make peace with discontent. As we outlined through Tuckman's (1965) work at the beginning of this chapter, conflict will occur among group members. It is normal and predictable and should be expected. Anecdotally, almost half of all teams or groups might have or experience some conflict that is unifying to them. For example, a college sport team might unite over their distrust or dislike of a head coach. Or a different team might unite over what they perceive as lack of respect from the media or their opponents. So, it is important to understand that what facilitates cohesion does not mean everyone will get along or even like each other at every moment. Cohesion does not necessarily mean harmony. When we discuss team-building strategies, we are not suggesting that these efforts will eliminate conflict.

One way to facilitate both task and social cohesion on teams and among group members, however, is to engage in carefully designed and appropriately led team-building activities followed by a formal debriefing process. Here we are not talking about walking over hot coals in your bare feet or parachuting out of an airplane together. We are not referencing team breakaway events spent at remote cabins, campsites, or the beach. Nor are we talking about working through an escape room experience together or mock Army Ranger events. Certainly, individuals might feel closer or more connected through these experiences, but that is irrelevant when it comes to task cohesion. Teams do not bond, they build. Glue bonds: teams build. You need to build team cohesion through intentional, purposeful, educationally designed, and evidence-based team-building sessions. Martin, Carron, and Burke (2009) conducted a meta-analysis (a statistical analysis of all of the studies performed in this area) and found that team-building interventions positively affected performance and were particularly helpful in individuals' perceptions of performance and satisfaction with their experience on the team. Two organizations are known as leaders in crafting educational programming that can facilitate team building: Project Adventure and Training Wheels. If you want to learn more about team building and how to develop cohesion through team-building sessions, we recommend their work.

It is important to note that a process is involved in team building, and multiple approaches in the sport psychology literature help to explain how leaders can and should conduct these sessions. The most adopted approach (Carron and Spink 1993; Carron, Spink, and Prapavessis 1997) involves three initial stages during which leaders learn about group dynamics and strategies to develop team cohesion and specific team-building protocols. Then, in the fourth stage, the *intervention stage*, the actual team-building session occurs. We highlight the three stages in advance of the actual team-building session to emphasize that team building is more than a collection of fun activities. Done right, team building is about implementing experiential learning opportunities that challenge group members and target a specific element of group dynamics that will facilitate cohesion. As we have outlined throughout this chapter, team building is but one of many strategies and behaviors that leaders and group members can engage in that build cohesion. Each of these behaviors should help create group norms, identify individual roles and responsibilities, foster team distinctiveness, recognize and reward individual contributions and efforts, and cultivate appropriate communication and interaction among group members. Along those lines, we end this chapter with a final activity (see the worksheet on page 288) to differentiate your team or group from others by helping your group create a core theme or mission statement.

Conclusion

Throughout this chapter, we have offered stories, anecdotes, and research to help you create and maintain group cohesion over time. Cohesion is dynamic. It is essential that every member of the group is committed to and invested in daily behaviors that will cultivate a productive team or group environment. Remember, investment in both the team and the individual will improve the effectiveness of the group. You need to feel you are a unique and valued member of the collective. Without consistency of effort and deliberate, targeted actions, you are leaving your performance and enjoyment to chance. We hope that in reading this chapter and implementing these tools and strategies you will be well on your way to reducing conflict and facilitating productive collaborations among group members. This example perhaps summarizes the effect of building a successful team:

When geese fly in a V formation, they add 71 percent greater flying range than if each bird flew alone. As each bird flaps its wings, it creates an uplift for the bird immediately following. When the head goose is tired, it rotates back in the wing and another goose flies point. They even honk from behind to encourage those up front to continue their work and speed. And, when a goose becomes ill or is wounded and falls out of formation, two other geese fall out with their team member to lend help and protection.

Let us all work to develop a community in which we lift each other, take turns doing the heavy lifting, encourage our teammates' efforts, and support each other during challenging times.

Crafting a Mission Statement or Core Theme

A mission statement articulates the purpose of the group or team and can serve as a unifying feature. To create an effective mission statement, think of *what* your group, team, or organization does; *how* it does it; and *why* it does it. The three key elements of a mission statement are (1) statement of vision, (2) statement of core values, and (3) a statement of the big picture goal or objective. Keep any mission statement short—think one sentence or a few words—and inclusive of the range of tasks and people that might join the group in the future.

Directions

Use the following prompts and examples to help create an effective mission statement.

1. List up to five core themes for your group or team.
2. Identify one reason that completing these tasks or achieving these objectives is important.
3. Use your core themes to create a mission statement. Refer to the examples that follow.

Example mission statements:

1. *Pete Carroll, NFL coach of the Seattle Seahawks, refers to their team's mission statement as "Always compete."*
2. *The Canadian Olympic Committee's mission statement is "To lead the achievement of the Canadian Olympic Team's podium success and to advance the Olympic values in Canada."*
3. *Nike's mission statement is "To bring inspiration and innovation to every athlete in the world." (The company also mentions "If you have a body, you are an athlete.")*

From C. Hacker and M. Mann, *Achieving Excellence: Mastering Mindset for Peak Performance in Sport and Life* (Champaign, IL: Human Kinetics, 2023).

CHAPTER 17

Inclusive Excellence

The quote from Nneka Ogwumike helps identify the focal points of this chapter. This chapter adds to and complements chapter 16, which focused on strategies for developing effective teams and groups. Creating an inclusive climate, one in which each member of the team is aware of their unique skills and talents and valued for their contributions to the mission, is essential for developing high-performing teams and groups. The first half of this chapter is dedicated to connecting diversity, equity, and inclusion efforts with performance and offering strategies for building inclusive environments in sport, in work, and in life. The second half of the chapter focuses on the ways in which social justice is now interconnected with athletic pursuits. To be an athlete or coach in the 21st century is to consider your role in the bigger picture of local, regional, national, and global issues. Rather than dividing yourself into two people—athlete or performer on the one hand and human being on the other—integrating these identities is becoming an increasingly important part of successful and enjoyable experiences in sport. As such, the second half of the chapter centers on lessons gleaned from exemplars like the 1999 U.S. women's national soccer team to help you learn how to navigate the related challenges and opportunities you might encounter in your career.

> I haven't always been this comfortable speaking about my personal thoughts and convictions; but, as time has gone on, I've realized that speaking up is better than not saying anything. . . . A lot of what we've done as WNBA players has been directly related to changes that we may never experience. . . . That's what legacy is. And, that's what people talk about when you break up glass ceilings.
>
> Nneka Ogwumike, WNBA champion, WNBA MVP (2016)

Making the Case for Diversity and Inclusion

There are many definitions for *diversity*, *equity*, and *inclusion*. Although these terms are used interchangeably, we caution you to avoid conflating these concepts. Before we begin to outline why you should care about diversity, equity, and inclusion as a performer in your performance domain, it is important to define what *we* mean by diversity and inclusion in this text.

Diversity

Diversity refers to the richness of human differences, including (but not limited to) socioeconomic status, race, ethnicity, gender, personality, language, sexual orientation, religion, body size and shape, as well as physical and mental abilities (Hurtado et al. 1999). Rather than considering diversity as a simple construct, here it is espoused as an essential component of the human experience. Considering diversity in this way makes what Martusewicz, Edmundson, and Lupinacci (2020) argue in their book seem accurate and true: that diversity is "the condition of difference necessary to all life and creativity" (22). Take NBA Hall of Fame players John Stockton and Karl Malone, for instance, who have two of the most different personalities and are from wildly different backgrounds. Stockton is a quiet, reserved, out-of-the-spotlight, white point guard from Spokane, Washington. Malone is a flashy, aggressive, power forward from Summerfield, Louisiana, who loves the spotlight and identifies as African American. Polar opposites in many respects, these two acknowledged and respected the unique strengths they each brought to the game and combined to form one of the best pick-and-roll duos in NBA history. Recognizing that each person in the executive suite or on the medical school board or athletic team is a unique individual is an important initial step. The knowledge that each person's unique background affects their eye contact, body language, interpretation of feedback, and other aspects of communication on a team or in a group matters. However, it is only the first step in the process of inclusive excellence. To stop here would be like stepping into the blocks before a race and deliberately *choosing* to stay there when the start signal sounds.

Equity

An equitable performance environment is one in which various advantages and disadvantages are recognized and acknowledged. The World Health Organization defines equity as "the absence of avoidable or remediable differences among groups of people, whether those groups are defined socially, economically, demographically, or geographically." For example, in sport, the term *sport stacking* refers to cultural and social factors that make it more likely that athletes of color are located predominantly in certain positions or in certain sports (Smith and Leonard 1997). Rather than assuming that athletes of color only want to be running backs in football, for example, or are less interested in sports like ice hockey or lacrosse, leaders in an equitable environment would recognize the barriers that might result in fewer athletes of color in certain athletic positions or sports and then attempt to actively reduce or remove those barriers. An equitable restaurant would ensure that the tables and chairs for patrons were appropriate for a variety of body sizes and were accessible to people who use wheelchairs or assistive devices.

Research has found that female job candidates were deemed less competent and less worthy of being hired, and, when hired, were offered a lower starting salary even though their resumes were identical to those of male candidates (Moss-Racusin et al. 2012). Equitable work and sport environments are not those in which each person is given equal accommodations; rather, equity requires recognition of unequal conditions and a commitment to correcting the underlying factors causing the imbalance.

Inclusion

It is not enough to admit that difference exists or even to ensure that each person can participate; we must integrate and include diverse and, at times, conflicting voices and ideas from people who have a range of life experiences. Doing so will lead to more complex and thoughtful race strategies, game plans, play calls, and other performance-related decisions. Inclusion efforts ensure that every member of a diverse group or club or team feels welcomed and participates in key decisions. They are not simply sitting at the table or represented in the room. Rather, each person's input is sought and even required, and their talents are leveraged in pursuit of the group's goal. Creating an inclusive environment could mean seeking players' input on a specific strategy for a match or race, or it could occur when an orthopedic surgeon consults with another medical expert in a different specialty on a treatment plan. Inclusive environments are both *diverse* and *just*, and yet neither diversity nor equity necessarily guarantees inclusion. See the sidebar on page 292 for a summary of how diversity, inclusion, and equity differ, as well as examples of each term. The latter half of this chapter is dedicated to offering tools and strategies for inclusion.

To function at our highest levels individually and collectively, we need diverse, inclusive, *and* equitable performance environments. McCleary-Gaddy (2019) further clarified the importance of each of these efforts through the analogy of being invited to a dance. She noted, "'Diversity' is the invitation to the party . . . 'inclusion' is being asked to dance . . . [and] 'equity' is providing transportation for those that do not have a ride" (1443). In other words, recognizing diversity is important for ensuring that people are represented, but without inclusion and equity, without voice and opportunity to make a difference, we have fallen short. And as a result, our companies, our teams, and our organizations may be less effective and successful—a point to which we will return throughout this chapter.

High-performing teams and groups, on the other hand, are composed of a variety of people (diverse) that are each integrally involved in the decision-making process (inclusive) and who work together to ensure that each person is positioned in ways that allow them to bring their unique talents with them (equitable or just) to the performance domain. To

Chalk Talk

Quick Hits for Differentiating Diversity, Inclusion, and Equity

Inclusion	Examples
Integrating and leveraging each group member's unique physical and intellectual capabilities in pursuit of the organization's goals	The most gender-diverse company in the world, DNB Bank in Norway, ensures that almost 40% of the top four layers of management positions are held by women, including the CEO.
	The International Coordinating Committee of World Sports Organizations for the Disabled (ICC) was created in 1982 by four separate organizations (and later became the International Paralympic Committee) to ensure all policies and strategies for the Paralympic Games were inclusive.

Diversity	Examples
The representation of a variety of identities and cognitive and physical abilities in one group or team or organization	More than 150 languages are spoken in the Seattle, Washington, public school district.
	55% of all staff members are women at Sodexo, a food services and facilities management company.

Equity	Examples
A process that ensures each member has an opportunity to engage, invest, and contribute to the mission or goal of the group	Changing sports equipment and uniform rules to allow for religious differences (e.g., allowing Muslim women to wear a hijab).
	Ensuring COVID-19 tests and vaccines are free in order to remove the barrier of cost.

accomplish this goal and to become an inclusive, high-performing team, everyone must commit to these goals. As Colin Kaepernick, a former NFL quarterback who received the 2017 Sports Illustrated Muhammad Ali Legacy Award, said during the 2018 W.E.B. Du Bois Medal award ceremony given by Harvard University and Hutchins Center Honors, "I feel it's not only my responsibility, but all of our responsibilities as people that are in positions of privilege, in positions of power, to continue to fight for them and uplift them, empower them. Because, if we don't, we become complicit in the problem" (Hutchins Center Honors 2018).

The Cognitive Diversity Coefficient

There is a moral and social argument for diversity, equity, and inclusion efforts as well as a performance one. Every person deserves the opportunity and the right to participate and engage in a variety of professional contexts. In this chapter we focus on the idea that including people with a range of backgrounds and capabilities is essential for high performance. Companies with more ethnically and culturally diverse executive teams are 33 percent more likely to financially outperform less diverse peers, and companies with executive teams with more gender diversity outperform less diverse peers financially by 21 percent (McKinsey 2018). In the United States, creating more equitable workplaces through policies in the 1960s that increased the number of white women and Black Americans entering the workforce has helped explain 25 percent of the country's gross domestic product according to a new study by Hsieh and colleagues (2019). It is not that those workers were not available before the 1960s, but rather, that through diversity, equity, and inclusion efforts over the past seven decades, the United States has made better use of its existing and available talent pool.

Research has consistently demonstrated that increased diversity promotes creative thinking, increases knowledge, enhances self-awareness, increases adaptability, and improves satisfaction and enjoyment (Chamorro-Premuzic 2017). Specifically in education, research has shown that students in the most diverse classes demonstrated increased engagement, active thinking, motivation, and intellectual skills (Gurin et al. 2004). In addition, a study conducted by the Union of European Football Associations (UEFA) Champions League from 2003 to 2012 found that players represented 50 nationalities. As they examined the effect of diversity on performance, they found that the effectiveness of different styles of play, training methods, skills, organization of players, strategies for set pieces, and communication all increased as the diversity of the team (measured by linguistic distance) increased (Ingersoll, Malesky, and Saiegh 2014). The word is out: Diversity improves performance in business, in sport, and in life. A study by Deloitte found that 78 percent of global human resources and business leaders believe diversity and inclusion offer a competitive advantage, and almost 40 percent of those leaders believe the advantage is significant (Bourke and Dillon 2018).

Simply creating more diverse teams and groups does not necessarily yield these outcomes alone. Rather, the results are by-products of an inclusive environment in which the diverse and unique capabilities of people are leveraged effectively for the good of the group. It is important to recognize that there are different types of diversity, two of which we will highlight: representational and cognitive (see figure 17.1). Representational, or demographic, diversity is what most people think about when the word *diversity* is mentioned. It is an identity-based conceptualization of diversity that recognizes difference based on demographic factors such as religion, age, size, ethnicity, gender, sexual orientation, and race, among others (de Anca and Aragon 2018).

Cognitive diversity, on the other hand, refers to differences in thinking styles, problem-solving skills, communication patterns, work styles, personality, risk tolerance, and interests and values (Jones-Rooy 2019). Increasing cognitive diversity is often what is associated with

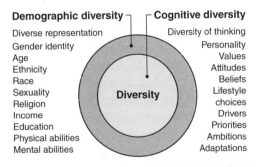

Demographic diversity

Diverse representation
Gender identity
Age
Ethnicity
Race
Sexuality
Religion
Income
Education
Physical abilities
Mental abilities

Cognitive diversity

Diversity of thinking
Personality
Values
Attitudes
Beliefs
Lifestyle choices
Drivers
Priorities
Ambitions
Adaptations

Diversity

FIGURE 17.1 Diversity types. Cognitive and demographic diversity represent two types of diversity that are important to consider when creating inclusive and equitable performance environments.

increased creativity and productivity among teams and groups. It is the opposite of groupthink, which is a phenomenon marked by less-than-ideal decisions and performances that occur when people feel compelled to conform to the majority viewpoint (regardless of their personal views) or value coherence above all else. In sport, rather than thinking there is only one way to play a particular defensive scheme, as the UEFA study indicates, having a team comprising players from different regions might increase the number of ways that athletes could play the defensive scheme from their position. And, if through inclusive strategies, coaches could help those athletes integrate their unique playing styles and problem-solving abilities for the good of the team, then it might create an even more dynamic and effective defensive system.

Cognitive diversity is often, but not always, related to identity or representational diversity. Certainly, representational diversity matters. It helps explain how Althea Gibson paved the way for Serena and Venus Williams to play tennis and how their collective and individual success spurred the next generation of girls and women of color like Coco Gauff and Naomi Osaka to become champions on the Women's Tennis Association circuit. Now, consider how the gender or age of a woman in her first stint as a head coach of a men's professional sport might affect her game strategy, delivery of feedback, and nonverbal body language, among other elements of her leadership style. Serving as the first woman to lead a men's major professional sports team could serve as an opportunity for other young girls and women to see themselves in similar positions (*representational diversity*), yet it is the effect her identities exert and how they inform her thought processes and coaching behaviors that might be most impactful for the athletes she coaches and their performance (*cognitive diversity*).

Thinking of diversity only in terms of demographics can be limiting and frustrating because identities often, but do not always, yield different perspectives or behaviors. Just because someone practices a particular religion does not mean that they will share all of the same beliefs with others from a similar religious background, nor does it mean they will not share similar values with people from other religions. Increased representational diversity is likely to yield increased cognitive diversity and, therefore, more complex, accurate, and holistic performance responses, but that is not always the case. *Diversity is not deterministic. Diversity is dynamic.* Both of these types of diversity are important, but it is cognitive diversity that helps directly explain why and how diversity affects performance and increases the likelihood of a successful performance. The best way to enhance the cognitive diversity of any team or group is to create a demographically diverse and inclusive environment in which each person feels valued and recognized for their individual contributions to the team.

Developing Inclusive Excellence in Performance Domains

Often, people claim to value diversity and understand its importance, yet fail to behave in ways that demonstrate their beliefs and commitments. Physical educators and coaches, for instance, "value diversity but struggle to implement culturally responsive pedagogy" or teaching strategies (Columna et al. 2010). It is in trying and struggling and getting it wrong and committing to doing better next time that we ultimately move toward more inclusive performance spaces. In this section, we offer strategies for achieving inclusive excellence. This list will not be exhaustive but will provide ideas for challenging your thoughts and biases and behaviors.

Cultivating Cultural Competence

Denying or ignoring culture in physical activity and sport contexts can result in decreased participation, alienation and distress, and reduced physical performance (Blodgett et al. 2011; McGannon and Schinke 2013). On the other hand, learning about the barriers and challenges that Tatyana McFadden faced on her journey to 17 Paralympic medals or how Perdita Felicien became an Olympic hurdler for Team Canada after growing up in poverty could help create a more inclusive performance environment for everyone. It is impossible to understand performers' psychological states and behaviors without becoming aware of the social and cultural context in which they live and work and perform.

Whether you are a teammate, a boss, or a coach, developing knowledge not only of the performance domain but also of your own identity-based experiences and those of your employees, teammates, and coworkers is imperative. In addition, working to grasp how those experiences affect each group member's interpretations and behavioral responses is critical.

Develop Cultural Awareness

The first step in this process is to become *culturally aware* that each member of your team holds multiple intersecting identities and that each of those identities has shaped their experience, their values, and their beliefs. For example, an article written by Hacker and Mann (2017) described a mental skills coach working with a national team from a cultural background different from hers, and the expectation for timeliness became a point of concern. The mental skills coach expected the team to arrive for practice at the exact start time, but this team was late. Only through reflection and developing cultural awareness was the sport psychology consultant able to recognize that her expectation of time stemmed from her experiences living in a time-based culture, whereas the athletes lived and performed in an event-based culture that taught them time was secondary to the experience of togetherness and that one event did not end until everyone agreed to move to the next event. A culturally blind approach, where all people were treated the same regardless of their background, might have led this consultant to punish the group or to be upset with the members of the team and thus silence the athletes (Schinke et al. 2012). It is important for each performer to develop cultural awareness in order to better understand themselves and their teammates. Use the worksheet on page 297 to practice cultivating awareness of yourself and others.

Develop Cultural Competence

The second step in this process is to develop *cultural competence* and an understanding of how diversity can affect interpersonal dynamics. As stated earlier, the UEFA study (Ingersoll, Malesky, and Saiegh 2014) found that athletic teams composed of players from various regions in the world experience performance benefits. However, without careful and intentional demonstration of cultural competence over time, these differences and this diversity among athletes can be detrimental to communication and to performance. One such example comes from a team playing in the National Women's Soccer League, a professional league in the United States (Hacker and Mann 2017). On this team, women from Asia, South America, and North America all competed together; however, several of these athletes were performing in their second, or even third, spoken language. As a result, their teammates who were native English speakers were becoming frustrated with the delay in processing verbal commands and responses on the field. Although coaches had encouraged athletes to be patient with one another and to be aware of the player's circumstances, tension was mounting early in the season. A culturally competent approach to this problem included putting each team member in an alternative competitive situation (unrelated to soccer) and requiring them to perform by learning words in a language system with which

Investigating Biases

The purpose of this activity is to help the performer become more aware of their own cultural assumptions and biases and to understand how those assumptions can affect their interpretations and behavioral responses.

Directions

Respond to the questions openly and honestly. Be as specific and detailed in your responses as possible.

1. Think of one time in the last three days (at practice, at work, at home) when a misunderstanding or argument occurred with a teammate, coach, friend, coworker, employer, or significant other. Then respond to the questions below:

   a. What happened?

   b. Who was involved?

   c. How did you think, feel, and behave?

   d. What, from your own background and experiences, motivated or drove your thoughts, feelings, and behaviors? What beliefs, assumptions, or experiences were they based on?

   e. How did the other person behave or respond?

   f. What, from their background and experiences, might have motivated their behavior or response?

   g. How might you interpret (similarly or differently) this situation in the future?

   h. Are there alternative explanations for this event or interaction?

   i. In the future, what would you do the same? Differently?

2. Think of a time in the last three days when you were misunderstood (at practice, at work, or at home) and an argument or misconception occurred with a teammate, coach, friend, coworker, employer, or significant other. Now respond to the following questions:

   a. What happened?

   b. Who was involved?

   c. How did you think, feel, and behave?

   d. What, from your own background and experiences, motivated or drove your thoughts, feelings, and behaviors? What beliefs, assumptions, or experiences were they based on?

   e. How did the other person behave?

   f. What, from their background and experiences, might have motivated their behavior or response?

   g. How might you interpret (similarly or differently) this situation in the future?

   h. Are there alternative explanations for this event or interaction?

   i. In the future, what would you do the same? Differently?

From C. Hacker and M. Mann, *Achieving Excellence: Mastering Mindset for Peak Performance in Sport and Life* (Champaign, IL: Human Kinetics, 2023).

they were unfamiliar (Hacker and Mann 2017). As a result, each athlete felt and developed empathy for what it must be like for their peers and teammates to perform under competitive pressures and demands while communicating in a second or third language. This example demonstrates the importance of cultural competence in sport settings. When preparing for a business meeting across the world, a culturally competent executive would study the nonverbal forms of expression that signal respect or demonstrate agreement or displeasure. Doing so could provide the critical difference between closing a deal or failing to sign on for a project that the company was providing.

Engage in Critical Reflection

There is an important note of caution, however, when developing cultural competence: Culture is not a fixed concept. Instead, it is dynamic and changing. As you learn about a particular geopolitical, economic, or historical moment, you must also be careful to not assume it affects each person living in that culture the same way. Avoid generalizing or applying all elements of a culture to every person that possesses a similar identity. Finally, to become a culturally competent performer, you need to be *reflective* and to engage in ongoing critical self-assessment and growth. As 10-time NCAA champion basketball coach John Wooden often recalled, "It's what you learn after you know it all that counts." No one ever outgrows the need to become more aware of what drives their thoughts, emotions, and behaviors and that of others. (Refer to chapter 13 for reflection strategies.)

Identifying Inclusive Behaviors

Along with developing cultural competence, performers need to also exhibit specific behaviors that are likely to enhance feelings of inclusion within a team or group. Each person needs to feel that they are unique and also that they belong. They need to know what skills or knowledge they bring to the group that no one else does and they need to understand how those skills and capabilities contribute to the larger mission or goals. Simone Biles, who earned the World Championship all-around title five times and is considered one of the best gymnasts of all time, was often teased for her body size. As a young performer, coaches told her that she was too muscular and that her body was too big to succeed in the sport. She recently admitted that the negative comments about how she looked in a leotard and even in casual pants has affected her emotions and performance. Biles struggled to find her place in a sport that seemed not to recognize her unique talents. Now, a decade later and with seven Olympic medals, she recently said, "It's my body and it does incredible things" (Brar 2020). This story demonstrates the impact of owning your own capabilities and understanding how they help you accomplish your goals or move your organization forward. People can be successful in a range of sports and performance domains with a variety of identities, cultural backgrounds, and body sizes and shapes. To compete at a high level, they must be aware of their strengths and those of their teammates and coworkers, and each person must recognize and celebrate how their individual capabilities fuel collective achievement. Using strategies offered in this text, such as the three Cs (competence, choice, and connection) outlined in chapter 9, a performer can cultivate a sense of uniqueness and a sense of belonging, both of which are crucial in an inclusive environment.

Every person has implicit biases in which they create immediate subconscious beliefs about other people—their teammates, competitors, and leaders. These thoughts carry significant, even if unintended, consequences. In becoming an inclusive leader in sport and other performance domains, people must become aware of these thoughts and how they affect behavior and performance and then train themselves to counter these biases and microaggressions. Cherng (2017) found that English teachers viewed their classes as too challenging and too difficult for Latino and African American students. These students were called on less often in class and given less or easier homework, and as a result, rather than improving performance, students of color (BIPOC: Black, Indigenous, people of color) scored 0.2 GPA points lower than their white peers in English classes. In psychology, this relationship between a person's thoughts and someone else's behaviors and performance is called the *Rosenthal effect* (Rosenthal and Jacobson 1968). People's biases can become a self-fulfilling prophecy as they subconsciously engage in behaviors that are likely to bring about the very result they initially assumed would happen. When a new athlete joins a team and the returning players assume that because that athlete is Black she will be fast and athletic, the returning players may be less likely to run their fastest speed in the next conditioning drill, or they might be more likely to ask the new member of the team to practice in certain speed-dependent positions in pickup games. As a result, the newcomer learns what is expected of them and thus gains additional reps in the very skills that teammates already expect of them. It is likely, then, that the athlete might develop greater speed and quickness in ways that match teammates' biased expectations. Although this example is less controversial, there are plenty of examples in a variety of performance domains in which the Rosenthal effect (also called the Pygmalion effect) can lead to much more harmful consequences. What we hope performers will take away is that monitoring how much attention and corrective feedback they give to team members will affect their beliefs about themselves and their own behaviors. It is important for leaders to control their behaviors to such an extent that they ensure equitable response time, positive nonverbal behaviors, and that skill-related challenges are provided equally to each member of the team.

Deloitte, a multinational professional services network with offices in over 150 countries and territories around the world, offers a diversity and inclusion maturity model, whereby they explain how a company or team can move from a compliant group to one that believes that diversity, equity, and inclusion should be integrated and woven into the daily practices of each valued member of the group (Bourke and Dillon 2018). The key element requires the entire organization to become involved in these efforts, to engage in the behaviors outlined earlier, and to work together to become a high-performing, diverse-thinking team with a shared sense of purpose.

Lessons From Exemplars

Equity and inclusion work occurs through continuous, sustained effort over time. It often starts with one or two people who are initially vilified, and then slowly their work is recognized and inspires more people to get involved. People are not born changemakers or "inclusifiers." Often, their actions are spurred when they recognize a need in society, in their workplace, or on their team. Tommie Smith won the 200-meter gold medal at the 1968 Olympic Games and raised his black-gloved fist in the air with teammate John Carlos on the awards podium in protest of racial injustice in the United States.

The very act of pursuing excellence and reaching the pinnacle of their sport can make a difference for the next generation of performers. For example, take Marta, who in 2021 became the first footballer to score in five straight Olympic Games. Fellow Brazilian soccer legend and changemaker, Pele, remarked:

> Your achievement means much more than a personal record. This moment inspires millions of athletes from so many other sports, from all over the world, who fight for recognition. Congratulations on your trajectory. Congratulations, you are much more than a football player. You help build a better world with your talent, in which women gain more space. (AFP 2021)

Slowly over time, these change agents learn new skills and tactics that help them to overcome barriers that others could not and to access new heights of achievement and impact. When acclaimed WNBA player Becky Hammon became the first woman to become a full-time assistant coach in the NBA, she noted,

> I'm a little uncomfortable with people saying "trailblazer" . . . because I know somebody else blazed the trail for me to even have the opportunity to play basketball. I never want to lose sight of the women who came before me and laid the groundwork for me to be able to walk through this door. (Cunningham 2015)

Change is neither fast nor linear. As a result, we end this chapter by recognizing two separate, distinct movements toward inclusion and justice in sport. Both of these movements were sparked decades earlier, and the line of connection was often overlooked by many until recently. They are poignant examples of the efforts we have touted throughout this chapter, and they are exemplars from which we can all learn as we continue to perform in our respective achievement domains.

The first example of diversity, equity, and inclusion efforts sustained over time occurred in the sport of track and field at the Olympic Games. Many people remember the resistance that John Carlos and Tommie Smith demonstrated in the 1968 Olympic Games in Mexico City, but there was another athlete at that Games representing Team USA in track and field who also took a stance for diversity, equity, and inclusion that was unpopular. Wyomia Tyus set a world record and became the first person to win 100-meter titles in consecutive Olympic Games. She did this while wearing dark blue (as close to black as she could find) shorts as a sign of protest against the racism she experienced as a Black woman from Jim Crow Georgia (Longman 2021). Her shorts were distinct from the official white shorts sanctioned by the United States Olympic Committee and that her two American teammates wore in the same race. Calling it her "contribution to the protest for human rights," she said, "It made the statement that I needed. . . I was doing it for what I believed in, that it was time for a change" (Longman 2021). She credited her coach for helping her and her teammates take a stand, stating:

> It used to be, you know, and still is, that athletes should be athletes, not doing anything else. We're also human. We also have feelings. We also have rights. We also should be able to express those rights. [Coach Temple] used to tell us, "It doesn't matter how many gold medals [you win] or how many times you go to the Olympics. When you come back home, you're still going to be Black, and you're still going to be a woman". . . . He would always say to us that track will open the door; education would keep the door open. He made us believe in ourselves and believe that we could make a difference. (Thompson 2020)

Tyus' story of activism mirrors that of Smith and Carlos, and she later denounced the ousting of her two countrymen and dedicated her relay gold medal to them. It also supports the fact that female athletes of color have long advocated for diversity, equity, and inclusion around the world. Tyus later became instrumental in the formation of the Women's Sports Foundation, and her efforts became part of a pivotal turning point as Black women in the United States began recognizing their fight for equity as being tied to experiences of both their gender and race (Longman 2021).

Fast-forward to the 2019 Pan American Games when American hammer thrower Gwen Berry bowed her head and raised her fist after winning her competition to signal her protest against police brutality and also her support of the Black Lives Matter movement. Berry said, "I feel there is a direct connection between us. It's unfortunate we don't hear these stories. So often, women are overlooked. We bear the biggest burdens" (Longman 2021). Track athlete Noah Lyles raised his fist in the air as well at a meet the following year to protest the death of Jacob Blake (Thompson 2020). This legacy of activism shows that a single person's decision to take a stand to, as Tyus indicated, "Speak up and speak out," can plant seeds in the minds and hearts of the next generation to continue the work of advocating for inclusion (Longman 2021).

The United States women's national soccer team (USWNT) offers another same-sport legacy of fighting for inclusion. In 1991, the USWNT won the first Women's World Championship (it wasn't yet called the World Cup) and yet they were flying in middle seats on airplanes, seated next to and sometimes in the smoking sections, staying in substandard hotels, and receiving $10 per day without salary (Shulman 2019). The women on the team loved representing their country, but they knew they had to stand up for future generations. By 1995, nine of the team's top players chose to sit out of camp as part of their contract dispute. They were nervous, but captain Julie Foudy reminded them, "This is gonna make a difference. . . . We have to stay in it now. Because if they start pulling us apart, then we're done" (Shulman 2019). Unified, just before the 1996 Olympic Games began, the team was awarded new contracts from the United States Soccer Federation. Since then, the USWNT has become the best in the world, winning four FIFA World Cups and four Olympic gold medals, and they have been ranked number one by FIFA for 10 of the last 11 years (Goodman 2019). They have achieved this performance success while continuing to fight for gender equity in their sport. The USWNT sued the United States Soccer Federation 95 days before the team's first World Cup match in France in 2019, claiming "purposeful gender discrimination." In relation to her efforts, Alex Morgan has said,

> I had this dream of being a professional soccer player, and I never knew it entailed being a role model, being an inspiration, standing up for things I believe in, standing up for gender equality. But now I don't know a world where I just play soccer. It goes hand in hand. (Goodman 2019)

It started with the 1999 USWNT (commonly referred to as the 99ers) using their platform to work toward changes like better pay, better uniforms, and better stadiums. The current iteration of the USWNT is committed to extending those efforts as they too seek gender equity. What is most impressive about these efforts is that the leaders intentionally introduced a sense of social responsibility to any newcomer on the team. As Megan Rapinoe said, "We try, first of all, education. We break down the inequities. We tell them: This is why we are choosing to take a stance and we try to show specifically how it affects each individual player, but then also the team as a whole" (Goodman 2019). That consistent leadership thread has helped the team's collective diversity, equity, and inclusion efforts across generations of performers. As interesting and important as these stories are, what we hope to show is that the best chance for creating change and for creating a more inclusive performance environment for everyone occurs through thoughtful, principled, and sustained effort. Sometimes this spans decades. See the following sidebar for a list of strategies that can be extracted from these exemplars in sport and applied in your own performance domain.

PUT IT INTO PRACTICE

Reflections From an Insider

These strategies come from reflections offered by Dr. Hacker, who served as a mental skills coach and member of the coaching staff for the U.S. women's national soccer team and the U.S. women's national ice hockey team as each team sought pay equity in their sports. These reflective suggestions are useful for anyone in a variety of performance domains but are particularly poignant for athletes and teams that are currently or will someday pursue equity and inclusion.

Develop a Vision

As a performer, you have to be able to see beyond this moment, beyond this sport. It can often be all consuming to spend your life honing your craft; it can be challenging to look at how your thoughts and behaviors contribute to and shape the larger culture. As a high-level performer, you are worried about the next practice, the newcomers nipping at your heels, and how to stay at your current level or ascend to the next. But both the 1999 USWNT and the 2018 U.S. women's ice hockey team were able to look through a larger lens and develop a greater vision about how they wanted to leave the game for the next generation.

Cultivate Leadership and Mentorship

It matters who gets the microphone. For these two teams, the captains took the reins. For the USWNT that meant Julie Foudy and Carla Overbeck, and for the U.S. hockey team, that was Meghan Duggan. Each was a respected, powerful leader who recognized the situation, the opportunity, and the potential. They kept everyone focused on the bigger "why," beyond their place or performance on the team and beyond the next practice or competition. The commitment to be in a fight for equality and inclusion can be a powerful organizing and galvanizing experience, and these leaders were able to articulate that vision during team meetings, at team meals, on the bus, and with both the media and fans. They led from the front, and they mobilized people around the vision and around issues much bigger than their performance.

> continued

Reflections From an Insider > *continued*

In addition, both of these teams were actively mentored by the athlete activists who came before them. That leadership through mentorship is important because people need to learn from others who have been there before and have stood where they are standing now, who have endured the inevitable difficulties and setbacks, and who have made a significant and lasting difference. For the USWNT, it was tennis legend and women's sport advocate Billie Jean King. Julie Foudy was instrumental in guiding the efforts of the U.S. women's national ice hockey team, and she—along with others—helped bring in Billie Jean King to mentor the team as well.

Use Your Power and Platform to Leverage Relationships

You have to control the narrative. You have to understand the issues, understand who the essential and necessary allies for change are, and understand how to convey messages and through what medium. This requires sophisticated, concerted efforts; otherwise, the message is viewed merely as ungrateful athletes complaining about something. The message has to be more than pointing out problems or grievances. It has to be more than observation. Allies have to see these efforts as part of a larger, systemic issue and be able to articulate that vision to the public. The message has to get out and resonate with people from various backgrounds and experiences. Both of these teams planted seeds along the way. For example, the USWNT from 1996 to 1999 stayed late to answer media questions and signed autographs until they were forced to ascend the bus stairs. They knew that they need to connect with their grassroots supporters. They had to make themselves available to their potential allies in order to cultivate their shared understanding, investment, and receptiveness. It was an example of using the current reality to shed light on the inequities and issues standing in the way of excellence. In 1996 and 1999, we [USWNT] were doing hundreds of clinics *for free* in cities all over the United States. The team rode a bus for 14 hours from one site to the next, and then got off the bus and talked to crowds and fans for hours. That helped drive connection, buy-in, and support as more and more people began to feel invested and personally affected by the women on the team. Reporters also respected their factual, consistent, and principled perspective and, as a result, they covered both the team and their fight for equality. Developing rapport and then leveraging those relationships was key to the success of both of these teams during their historic and transformative movements in sport.

Be Relentless

No one outside these teams fully knew about the myriad sleepless nights, the heated meetings, the personal sacrifice. Each team had to shoulder the responsibility and carry the baggage of that exhaustion, frustration, anger, loss, or disappointment all the while performing at the highest level in sport. It required relentless, unwavering effort. The teams would practice and then could not get cold water to rehydrate or warm water for showers or would have to fly commercial and in middle seats when the men's team chartered planes for games. The players had to not only endure those stark differences, but they also had to summon the means to thrive competitively. Then they had to relive the inequality as they told the story over and over, thousands of times to try to get the message across to fans, leaders, media, and the general public. They were committed to the story, the message, and the need for change. Everyone had to be relentless in connecting all of the stories. Everybody needed to recognize the facts, what was at stake, and how these efforts would affect the future of these sports. Everyone had to be relentless in telling the story. What the public perhaps doesn't fully understand is that in order to have any chance of success, they all had to be committed to the message: morning, afternoon, and night, 24 hours a day, seven days a week.

Continue to Perform at a High Level

Nobody would have blamed the U.S. ice hockey team for losing after coming into the World Championship training camp a mere two days before the start of competition. But they had so much cohesiveness, so much collective efficacy, so much belief in each other and the importance of their message, that the adversity may have proved to be a competitive advantage. The team had a fire in their souls. They knew their fight was for the future of their sport and for future generations and that they had to win it all to have the greatest impact. There is no coach who can motivate a team to greater heights. There is no opponent that can engender that resolve. They were playing for their lives, and they were playing for something much greater than themselves.

> continued

Reflections From an Insider > *continued*

Likewise, there was a fine line between how much the team laughed and had fun and the immense pressure they felt in the 1999 World Cup. They had to win that World Cup for the story to end like it did. And that is exactly what the team did. Billie Jean King could not have just played well against Bobby Riggs, right? You feel the need to win and to be successful in your performance domain while you fight for diversity, equity, and inclusion. In some ways, and I hate to say it, but you often have to win for people to listen.

At the same time, a team can never say they have to win. It cannot be solely about outcome because the pressure would bury anyone. I do not remember any player saying—publicly or privately—that they *had* to win, but I am 100 percent sure that every person on both of those teams knew they needed to be successful on the field or on the ice in order to have maximum impact. The diversity, equity, and inclusion fight was always a part of their performance. It was always integrated. They were not fighting for equality in one compartment of their lives and then playing their sport on the world stage in another compartment of their lives. Performance and inclusion efforts were inextricably linked. The team needed to perform at a high level in order to be game changers for the next generation in their sport. And they knew it.

Conclusion

It is tempting to believe that diversity, equity, and inclusion efforts are different or separate from performance. What we have tried to demonstrate in this chapter is that they are, in fact, explicitly linked. To perform at a high level, both personally and collectively, awareness of the cultural diversity present on your team and making intentional decisions to include a range of voices and perspectives are required. We do not mean to imply that this process is easy or without problems. Instead, we remind you that it is dynamic, messy, challenging, and full of errors. As acclaimed poet and speaker Maya Angelou noted:

> "Equal rights, fair play, justice, are all like the air; we all have it or none of us has it. That is the truth of it." She also reminds us that "You may encounter many defeats, but you must not be defeated. In fact, it may be necessary to encounter the defeats so you can know who you are, what you can rise from, how you can still come out of it."

The pain, the failure, the fear of saying the wrong thing—they are all necessary as teams work together to create a climate in which each individual feels valued and brings their unique skills and capabilities for the good of the group.

CHAPTER 18

Career and Life Transitions

The truth is that everyone will experience multiple transitions during their life. Even Tom Brady (professional American football player at 43 years old), Oksana Chusovitina (oldest Olympic gymnast, who competed in 2020 at 46 years old), or Jaromir Jagr (professional hockey player at 49 years old) will eventually face the end of their competitive athletic careers. The question is not whether people will experience a transition but whether they will be prepared for the inevitability of that experience. There are stories of athletes who have fared well in retirement and those who have struggled to succeed either in their personal lives or in their new achievement domain. After she transitioned from international, elite competitions in 2015, Abby Wambach, one of the world's best soccer players, started WOLFPACK Endeavor to develop and train high-achieving female leaders in the corporate world. On the other hand, Brett Favre, the only NFL player to win three consecutive MVP awards, came out of retirement three times before ending his football career for the final time in 2011. Like many athletes, he struggled to know when and how to make the transition.

Elite performers in any performance domain are also elite planners. The ability to create detailed mental preparation plans and consistently implement those routines is the hallmark of performance excellence (Gould and Maynard 2009). These competitors are detail-oriented

> Now it's time for the next chapter. I have new dreams and aspirations. And I want new challenges.
>
> Derek Jeter, five-time World Series champion, five Gold Glove Awards, and member of the exclusive 3,000-hit club

> When I retired, I did not have enough money to retire for the rest of my life. I needed to figure out something else to do—not just because I wanted to make the world a better place, but out of need. People are like, "Oh wow, you won gold medals, and World Cups, and you played on the Women's National Team—you're famous, and you're going to be rich forever." It's one of the most frustrating things. . . . But the truth is, when you retire at 35, you have to plan for the next 40, maybe 50 years. I'll be retired from soccer for way longer than I ever was able to earn any money [in it].
>
> Abby Wambach, retired USWNT (United States Women's National Soccer Team) forward, highest all-time goal scorer for the national team and second in international goals, two-time Olympic gold medalist, World Cup champion

people who plan, often to the minute, their preevent routines and preevent meals, yet these same athletes often avoid planning for critical life and career transitions. Retirement and discontinuation of their competitive careers are sometimes viewed like injuries (or even worse). Canadian and NBA star Steve Nash once said, "Sport retirement is really like a death" (Stankovich 2014). Athletes rarely speak this candidly in public, but it is a feeling that many people experience. Some people have come to the inaccurate conclusion that planning for long-term transitions, progressions, and retirement somehow indicates that people are not fully present and committed to their current team, career, or sport. That notion is akin to telling performers not to prepare in advance to execute a motor skill. Can a field goal kicker, for example, work on a prekick routine or plan and still be ready to kick or punt? Absolutely. They can and they do. Can faculty members enjoy teaching their classes and still consider whether or not this school or university is where they should retire from or evaluate their financial retirement investments? Yes, and they do. Some might argue that by answering those questions, people might be able to maintain an even greater focus and presence free from worry, anxiety, or fear about the future.

In reality, people need to plan for possibilities, and they should, in fact, plan for eventualities. Transitions will happen. Being prepared for the inevitability of change is critical for success in both current and future achievement endeavors. In this chapter, we outline some of the challenges that occur during career transitions and offer strategies for preparing for the certain realities people experience.

The Role of Identity in Transitions

A transition occurs when an event leads to a change in self-belief or worldview in a way that also brings a change in behavior (Schlossberg 1981). These are turning-point phases in a performer's life that include demands that must be coped with and managed effectively (Alfermann and Stambulova 2007). Often, transitions are viewed as being forced or externally controlled as a result of a career-ending injury, age-related ending of a career, termination of a contract, or deselection from a team. While any of these events would lead to significant personal and professional disruption, Samuel and Tenenbaum (2011) proposed that career-changing events (e.g., deselection from the team, junior-to-senior competitive levels, sign-and-trade deals) are transitions as well because these events have the potential to destabilize careers, require implementation of effective coping strategies, and bring significant alterations in beliefs and behaviors. In this sense, each performer will encounter multiple transitions throughout their careers (and their lives) and would be wise to prepare so they can adapt to the changes quickly and successfully.

To successfully cope with a significant transition, performers need to be aware of the common processes involved in times of significant change. Alfermann and Stambulova (2007) offer one such model for consideration that explains the transition process as coping with demands (challenges) and using relevant coping strategies in light of personal and environmental resources and barriers (see figure 18.1). Someone's success in transition is defined by their improved performance in sport or other achievement domains and satisfaction with those efforts and pursuits, and it is determined by their ability to cope with demands and use effective coping strategies.

Athletic Identity

Many factors might limit a performer's resources or affect their coping strategies. In this chapter, we focus on the role of a strong and pervasive *athletic identity*. Many athletes struggle with career transitions because their identities are so strongly rooted in sport, in their position as an athlete, or in their shared group membership and identity. Transitions can prompt identity changes that can be disruptive, like when a high school athlete is not afforded the opportunity to play at the college level or when a professional athlete retires. Athletes spend a significant amount of their time and energy training and preparing for competition.

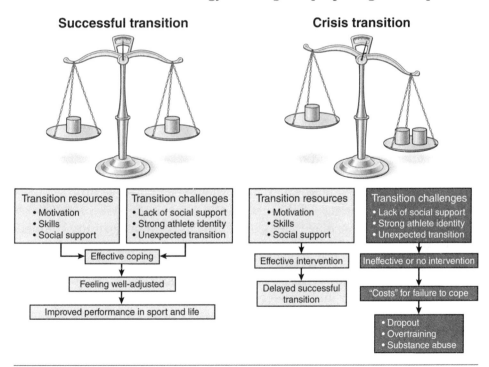

FIGURE 18.1 Athletic career transition model.

Adapted from Alfermann and Stambulova 2007.

Because of their devotion to athletics, sport performers might be delayed in exploring other interests beyond sport or developing a broader range of the critical skills necessary for success in the workplace or in life outside of sport. In fact, developing a strong *athletic identity*, which we define as the degree to which a person identifies with the role of an athlete, is related to enhanced sport performance.

Once an athlete, for example, sees and values themselves as an athlete first, they begin to behave in ways that are consistent with that social group and shared identity (Tajfel and Turner 1979; Strachan and Whaley 2013). However, a strong athletic identity has also been connected with more challenges when transitioning out of sport participation and difficulty adjusting (Alfermann, Stambulova, and Zemaityte 2004; Brewer, Van Raalte, and Linder 1993; Horton and Mack 2000). Strongly adhering to a single identity, such as being an athlete, is useful when pursuing that singular goal or working in that specific environment, but we are increasingly becoming aware of how detrimental an athletic identity can be during subsequent life transitions if it is an all-consuming personal view in which being an athlete overshadows other personal and professional identities and interests. It is crucial, then, to ensure that athletes construct a self-view that integrates multiple identities based on cultivated skills and personal capabilities and interests.

When a parent transitions from having children in the home to all of the children living and working outside of the home, we have terms and words for that transition. We call those parents empty nesters, and a significant amount of literature exists to guide the transition from active parenting to helpful guide for adult children. Many strategies are offered to help parents prepare for what they might think and feel and the new behaviors and changes that might accompany a transition from raising children to becoming a parent of adults. However, athletes are either an *athlete* or a *former athlete*. We would never call parents of adult children *former parents*. Many drawbacks are associated with identifying an identity as *former*. In the case of athletes, *former athlete* implies that the athletic part of their being no longer exists when, in reality, athletes never lose the elements or characteristics that made them identify as an athlete in the first place. They are shifting from performing competitively as an athlete to a different level or type of competition or sport or a different career altogether. It is important for athletes to ensure that they view sport and their athletic performance as one of several areas of achievement and impact rather than as an all-consuming and singular identity. Athletes are human beings first and are also people pursuing their passion and achievement in sport. Golfer Rory McIlroy put it like this:

> I've always talked about trying to separate who I am as a person and who I am as a golfer—and sometimes that's hard because it

is our livelihood and it's what we do. But at the end of the day, just because you hit a few bad golf shots and miss a few putts, it doesn't change who you are as a person. (Langmann 2021)

Simone Biles put it another way in a Tweet during the 2020 Tokyo Olympics: "The outpouring of love & support I've received has made me realize that I'm more than my accomplishments and gymnastics which I never truly believed before."

Identity Integration

While athletes are often rewarded for dedicating their lives to their sport, it should not be viewed as a badge of honor to develop a single identity. In fact, if a transition disrupts your ability to perform in that domain, often called a *crisis transition*, then the outcome can be catastrophic (Stambulova 2017). Some athletes might experience subclinical symptoms like decreased self-esteem, overtraining, or emotional discomfort, whereas other athletes will experience clinical issues such as depression, anxiety, or substance abuse (Stambulova 2017; 2021). Any of these issues could lead to premature dropout or other negative consequences that warrant professional clinical intervention. Developing an athletic identity is helpful when it is viewed as one identity among several others and is integrated within a broader range of identities.

Similarly, in a business setting, imagine working on the same project for your company for a significant amount of time and then one day the boss walks in the room and tells you that you are off of this specific project, and now your assignment is on a different, completely unrelated project. You may have been working for months, even years, on this initial project, and you have developed an identity in that role. Now you have been separated from that role, that identity and, in this case, without your input or control. It feels jarring. You might feel disrespected, like all of your work went unnoticed or unrecognized or was undervalued. You might even lose motivation. If you hold a single identity too tightly and allow one identity to become all consuming, you are at risk for adding challenges during life transitions.

Every performer should consider career-changing events such as being deselected from a team, changing positions midcareer, or enduring an injury that limits performance for a period of time as fertile training ground for personal reflection and reevaluation. These moments offer opportunities to check in with yourself to ensure that you are cultivating an integrated and more expansive sense of self in which you derive joy and satisfaction from multiple identities and roles. In addition, at the micro level, these transitions offer opportunities to practice developing coping skills that allow you to adapt to the required demands quickly and efficiently. In her Barnard College commencement address in 2018, famed soccer player Abby Wambach described such a situation and how she used it to her benefit. Although she had netted more international goals than any other soccer player—male or female (Christine Sinclair has since broken the record)—and served as the national team cocaptain, it was decided during the 2015 World Cup that she would not start the remaining games of her last World Cup (Reilly 2018). Although she was disappointed and frustrated by being benched, she began to lead from her new position as a reserve and, after becoming World Cup champions, her teammates told her that her vocal and relentless belief in them from the bench carried them to the victory (Reilly 2018). She had to productively respond to the transition. She had to—in the moment and on the spot—implement the leadership skills she had developed in service to a new role. And in 2018, she reminded the Barnard graduates that they could "lead from the bench."

Eventually, like Wambach, you, too, will need to apply these skills on a grander scale as you retire from one performance domain and transition into a new area of achievement. As Wambach learned in that transition and later explained, "Soccer didn't make me who I was. I brought who I was to soccer. And I get to bring who I am wherever I go. . . . Ask yourself, who do I want to be? Because the most important thing I've learned is that what you do will never define you; who you are always will" (Reilly 2018).

Expanding Your Vision, Expanding Your Role

Embracing and adapting well during transitions is similar to the process we discussed in chapter 14 for successfully coping with adversity: You need to recognize, name, and address the transition. It can feel freeing and reduce the stress and pressure associated with the change once you have identified it and labeled it. If you listen to athletes who at some point during their competitive career became parents, without fail they say how healthy it was for them and what a great perspective it provided. Track athlete Allyson Felix, for example, has spoken about how the birth of her daughter, Camryn, helped her find her voice as an advocate for women's health and drove her to push for equality for women in and out of sport (Fox 2021). Rather than focusing on practice or replaying all of their errors after competition, parent performers frequently talk about how their child helped them gain balance and a better, healthier perspective on competition. British diver Tom Daley, just before and again during the Tokyo Olympic Games, said, "I want to make my son proud" (Browne 2019). After being one of the premier divers in the world for more than a decade, it was his transition into fatherhood, he said, that helped him access new heights of achievement and eventually win his first gold medal in 2021. He added,

> I took four months off with my family because I now have a son. It changed my perspective on a lot of things, including training and diving. For me being able to train and dive is all the more important now because I have someone that I want to make proud. . . . Before [my son] was around, I would come home and be thinking about diving and all the things that I could have done better. When I get home now, there's this little face with his hands reaching towards me, and I'm instantly taken away from the diving pool. (Browne 2019)

Rather than subtracting from focus and training, these performers demonstrate that holding multiple identities and developing a broader picture of themselves aided their performance. They became more balanced and were better able to cope with adversity. Similarly, transitions do not have to take away from your resolve, investment, or motivation to achieve. Handling the small transitions well is like depositing money in the bank for the future. You will continue to face transitions. You need resources and skills to draw on and implement immediately so that you can adapt quickly, efficiently, and effectively. Start by naming the transition and recognizing it for what it is: an opportunity to either develop or to implement personal skills and resources to successfully navigate the inevitable changes inherent in your performance career.

Harry How/Getty Images

A second critical point is that successfully managing a transition does not mean that you are simply swapping out physical achievement domains. When an ice hockey player retires and then begins to play roller hockey, that is not necessarily a transition into a new achievement domain. When an elite athlete retires and then begins training for a marathon, while it might feel like positive coping or effectively adapting during a transition, it can often serve as a way to delay the process. It's important to examine the reasons for adopting or investing in a new achievement domain. If it is done to substitute one activity for another without focusing on authentic growth, an interest, or personal development, the activity might serve as a distraction rather than a transition.

Change is hard but recognizing that fact and then seeing yourself as part of a bigger constellation of identities and capabilities is a critical initial step. See the following sidebar for examples of athletes who have flourished in retirement because they were aware of both their responsibilities and their possibilities and of the impact they could achieve in a greater and expanded role.

IN THEIR OWN WORDS Legacy Building After Athletic Retirement

The USWNT players have developed a reputation for their continued efforts to push the United States Soccer Federation to treat their female athletes equitably. They have discussed their actions as being part of their collective legacy as members of the program and team.

It is fitting, then, that upon retirement from their international playing careers, many of the athletes have banded together to form the first women-led ownership team in professional sport when they invested in Angel City FC. The 33-person ownership group includes more than a dozen former U.S. players, including Julie Foudy and Mia Hamm.

Once Mia Hamm and Julie Foudy signed on, they immediately emailed other teammates and U.S. players who lived in or had connections to the Southern California region where the team would be based. Their vision was to lay the foundation for greater impact and outreach and to create the mechanism for other women to follow in the future. In this way, women would be in charge of securing the ownership and viability of their own professional sports teams rather than relying on the most common structure in which women's sports are often attached to a men's professional league, organization, or team.

Based on Lewis (2020).

This example from the USWNT demonstrates the importance of developing a greater vision for yourself beyond that of a performer. Rather than solely focusing on playing or competing, these women performed on the field and learned to leverage those successes and the media platform they created to change the world—both in and out of sport. The same can be true for any performer. In what way are you using your talents and skills in pursuit of your larger life's purpose? When you can authentically and confidently answer this question, you can begin to apply the same skills you crafted as a performer to other achievement domains available in your life.

There are numerous transitions any performer will face throughout their career, and they are labeled or defined differently based on their predictability. Normative transitions, for example, are relatively predictable and based on a person's development in sport and life (e.g., transition from high school to college or from active player to retirement). Non-normative transitions are less predictable (e.g., injury, deselection from a team; Stambulova 2021). If not prepared, people experiencing these types of transitions can struggle to cope and may even resort to harmful coping mechanisms (e.g., substance abuse, eating disorders). Ensuring they are aware of the resources available during these times of non-normative transitions is essential for adequate and successful coping. The third type of transitions are quasi normative transitions, which are somewhat expected but for which the timing or other elements might be unexpected, such as a promotion at work or moving to a residential high-performance center to train as an elite athlete (Stambulova 2017).

Performers may even experience these transitions concurrently, which can create additional demands on their time, energy, and resources as they attempt to anticipate the changes that could influence them in the future while remaining focused on the demands of their current achievement domain. For predictable transitions like career retirement, it is essential to plan ahead. We know that when an athlete retires, they are likely to go through four phases: (1) planning for athletic retirement, (2) career termination, (3) start of the postathletic career, and (4) reintegration into society (Reints 2011). So beginning this process ahead of the termination or retirement phase of the process is likely to yield faster and more positive adaptations (see the following sidebar for an example).

IN THEIR OWN WORDS **Viewing the Last Competition as a Grand Culminating Experience**

April Ross entered the Tokyo Olympic Games knowing that it was likely her last beach volleyball appearance on the Olympic stage. She had won a bronze and a silver medal and was focused on the gold, but this time felt different. In possibly her last Olympic tournament, it was the successes and failures, the doubts and the joys that provided her with a unique perspective.

In some ways, she had been preparing for this moment, this transition, for more than a decade. During her sophomore year of college, her mother passed away, and she struggled with the transition brought on through that family loss. After some time, she said, "It really came down to: If my mom was still here, how would she want me to be reacting? Would she want me to be doing all of this [irresponsible stuff] or would she want me to be responsible and uphold the values that she instilled in me, which were taking care of school, giving my all to volleyball, and taking care of myself? So it was just a shift in perspective, and it was really powerful for me."

> continued

Viewing the Last Competition as a Grand Culminating Experience > *continued*

Ross began tracking her schedule, including her classes and workouts, she set a strict nighttime and wake-up routine, and cooked healthy foods. In the next two years, Ross led her team to back-to-back NCAA championships and was named the nation's top collegiate volleyball player her senior year at the University of Southern California.

"It definitely changed the trajectory of my college career and played a big part in my future success," Ross said. It was the lessons and skills she developed during this transition that grounded her as a professional athlete when she made the move from indoor volleyball to beach volleyball and again when she began to climb onto the Olympic stage. Now she is more at peace with her career than ever before, adding, "The only things we can control are our attitudes and our preparation. The gold medal is the 'vision,' but it is not the end all, be all of everything in life, and we'll be OK no matter what."

Based on Witham (2021).

April Ross used a transition earlier in her life to learn and develop skills that put her in position to perform well in the 2020 Tokyo Olympics, where she won a gold medal with teammate Alix Klineman. Consider how, in your life, you might have previously experienced transitions that might help you prepare for retirement, career changes, or other life transitions in the future.

Forced Versus Voluntary Transitions

It is important to understand that performers who experience forced transitions such as those caused by injury, illness, or deselection may struggle more than those who experience voluntary transitions (Martin, Fogarty, and Albion 2014). Forced transitions and voluntary transitions are not the same experience. Age, injury, and deselection are three of the most common forms of forced transition in sport. It is particularly important that athletes and nonsport performers alike be aware of the potential challenges they might encounter during a forced transition and develop an awareness of their own skills and capabilities to cope so that when they experience an unexpected, forced transition, they can implement their knowledge and skills effectively and successfully (see the worksheet on page 317).

The worksheet is meant to help you when you are facing a forced transition. Choice, connection, and competence (see chapter 9) are important skills to use in these moments. If you have been cut or deselected from a team, for example, there is nothing you can do to alter that forced outcome. Of course you are likely to initially feel upset, frustrated, angry, or hurt. Those emotions are common and expected. But you do not have to stay in that negative space forever. You can choose to effectively transition into a new achievement domain or to pursue a different path within the same sphere. It is at this point that you need to reframe the experience

Performer-Centered Implementation Worksheet

Use this worksheet when you are experiencing a forced transition (as a result of age, deselection, injury, or another factor outside of your control). Usually, when people are forced into a transition, they feel a loss of control and a drop in internal motivation or drive.

Directions

Answer the following questions honestly and thoroughly. This will help you to be more aware of the choices you have control over and what you can do to keep moving forward.

1. What are three examples of things that you are now able to do that you could not do or did not enjoy before this transition?

2. What do you love to do? Where do you derive joy? What are your sources of satisfaction? What environments do you enjoy the most? What type of people do you enjoy spending time around?

3. What do you view as one of your most significant accomplishments?

4. What are the skills required of you and the characteristics you possess that allowed you to achieve in the domain in which you are currently experiencing a transition?

5. What is one decision or area you have control over right now? And what decision could you make in that area that would help you feel happier, more content, and more satisfied with this transition? (For example, perhaps an injury has made it difficult to continue training for marathons. However, through physical therapy, you have gained more joint flexibility than you ever had before.) What other activities could you engage in that would help you be active and enjoy life? Or, using the marathon example, are there other activities available that could allow you to exhibit your enhanced flexibility and enjoy that experience? Planning to engage in that type of physical activity might be a decision you could make rather than staying frustrated with not being able to run as fast or as far as you previously could.

6. What is a goal you have for yourself in this or a new achievement domain?

From C. Hacker and M. Mann, *Achieving Excellence: Mastering Mindset for Peak Performance in Sport and Life* (Champaign, IL: Human Kinetics, 2023).

and focus on what you can control and what you can do right now. You do have a choice. You do have power. The decisions and power you exert will come with different consequences.

With voluntary transitions, however, especially with voluntary retirement, having the power and control to plan for and dictate your retirement is often a rare gift. You can think of it as a prize for being excellent at your craft. Not every performer will experience that luxury. Few will, in fact. So if you are able to be in control and are able to choose the timing of your own departure from sport (or other achievement and performance domain), recognize the value and benefit of that significant opportunity. Then, engage in the internal work necessary to become aware of the skills you developed as an athlete (or other high-achieving performer) and how those same qualities can help propel you to success in your next endeavor. The next section will help you to accomplish this task.

Redeployment of Athletic Skill Sets

Any transition is challenging; it will often be difficult and is often life altering. All performers develop transferable skills in their primary performance domain that can be used in other areas. For example, athletes may have developed the ability to perform under pressure, compartmentalize their focus or priorities, or commit themselves to one goal or purpose for a long period of time. In his retirement speech, Pro Football Hall of Fame quarterback Peyton Manning remarked, "I revere football. I love the game, so you don't have to wonder if I'll miss it. Absolutely. Absolutely, I will. . . . There were other players who were more talented but there was no one who could out-prepare me. And, because of that, I have no regrets." It was his ability to prepare that he relished. He knew that his commitment to hard work was a significant part of his Hall of Fame career. It is that type of personal and career awareness that will continue to benefit him as he makes the transition into retirement from football.

Similarly, there are times when you, as a performer, will benefit from taking stock of the knowledge and skills you are either gaining or already possess and consider how those same skills can be useful to you later. Perhaps it is your dogged determination or your ability to endure long preparation hours in pursuit of your goals that are your strengths. Think about the skills you already possess. Think about the characteristics you have refined and developed to achieve in your current position. Recognize them, own them, and then be ready to apply them in different performance arenas. Use the worksheet on page 319 to honestly and comprehensively identify some of your transferable skills.

Performer-Centered Implementation Worksheet

Identifying Transferable Skills Forged Through Transition

Directions

Before you respond to the following prompts, consider a moment of adversity that you recently experienced. Then respond to each question as honestly and specifically as possible.

1. Describe a moment of adversity you recently faced and what you learned from it.

2. How are you using the skills that you developed during that moment of adversity right now in your life? Or how might those already-developed skills serve you moving forward?

3. What are the top three skills or characteristics that you possess that have helped you succeed as an athlete or performer? Think beyond the Xs and Os of sport.

4. What are two examples of how these skills will help you take on a new challenge you might face in a different performance domain?

From C. Hacker and M. Mann, *Achieving Excellence: Mastering Mindset for Peak Performance in Sport and Life* (Champaign, IL: Human Kinetics, 2023).

Conclusion

We hope all performers grow to feel the way that NBA legend Kobe Bryant described upon his retirement:

> There is beauty in that. I mean it's going through the cycle . . . of growth, of maturation. There's no sadness in that. I mean I had so many great times, right? I see the beauty in not being able to blow past defenders anymore. I see the beauty in getting up in the morning and being in pain because I know all the hard work that it took to get to this point. So, I'm not sad about it. I'm very appreciative of what I've had.

To achieve the same peace and understanding that Bryant described, you need to prepare for your own transitions—both expected and unexpected. In this chapter, we laid the groundwork for strategies to help you examine the skills and characteristics you have developed and already possess and how you might apply them in other achievement domains. Transitions are inevitable, but how you cope with and adapt to the changing demands is volitional and up to you. This chapter is only the starting point. If you are experiencing a transition or know you will be in the near future, we encourage you to look through the resources offered in the appendix for more information. Rather than waiting, begin the work now.

Learning More

In this book, we have used examples, stories, athlete testimonials, statistics and research evidence, application-focused exercises, reflective questions, and quotes to help explain the major psychological skills that define peak performance. We attempted to be both specific and broad so that you could make this book your own. As we pointed out in the introduction, psychological skills are one of the four pillars of performance. NBA star Steph Curry stated, "My mind is where every challenge that I have ever faced has been won or lost." The concepts and models presented in each chapter are fundamental to enjoyment, improvement, and success in any domain.

> **The potential for greatness lives within each of us.**
>
> Wilma Rudolph, first American woman to win three gold medals in track and field at the same Olympic Games

> **Commit yourself to lifelong learning. The most valuable asset you'll ever have is your mind and what you put into it.**
>
> Albert Einstein, German-born theoretical physicist

The research offered in the previous 18 chapters is clear and compelling: Mental skills training works. Whether you are competing at the youth sport level, preparing for a meeting, training for the Olympic Games, studying for the LSAT or medical board exam, raising a child, or trying to improve your sales in the next quarter, the psychological skills in this book will help you accomplish your goals. But, just like physical skills, psychological skills require consistent, intentional training done over time. You will need to dedicate yourself to improving in one area at a time. Then when you have mastered your current mental skills focus, you move on to the next. Think of it as a "rinse and repeat" process. Not everyone will choose to engage in this work, but those who do can expect to reap the benefits. College football coach Nick Saban noted:

> It's not human nature to be great. It's human nature to survive, to be average, and to do what you have to do to get by. That is normal. . . . It's the special people that can stay focused and keep paying attention to detail, working to get better, and not be satisfied with what they have accomplished. (Tuscaloosa Fitness n.d.)

These strategies work, provided you are willing to work the strategies, skills, and techniques. The only remaining question is whether or not *you* are willing to do the work required. Choosing to read this text shows that you already are willing to engage in sharpening your mental skills repertoire. We hope that the text provides a blueprint for pursuing and achieving excellence in whatever achievement domain you pursue.

This book can be read in order, from the first chapter to last, and we recommend that approach upon initial reading. However, each chapter has been designed to be distinct and able to stand alone when needed. Thus, as you move forward in your career or as you change careers, and as you experience moments of success and inevitable setbacks, you can turn to the chapter that best fits your need in *that* moment. In six months or a year and even in the many years to follow, you will be a different performer, and the performance demands in your life will surely change. Those changes are normal and expected. You should, in fact, be a different performer. Over time, you are more likely to have struggled and persevered through unexpected challenges and adversity. Our hope is that you will have developed and refined your psychological skills so that what was useful and needed this year or in this moment might soon become an area of strength, and a technique or strategy that seemed less important or useful upon first reading eventually becomes a targeted area for growth. Through training and refining your performance, new areas and issues will surely emerge that you will need to address. At some point, you will be a veteran who needs to read through the career transitions chapter again, and the very next year you might be a newcomer in a new performance domain who needs to read other chapters related to confidence and self-talk. Chapters can be read and reread to help you successfully navigate new positions, life transitions, regressions. You can also read them during moments of ascension and success at the highest ranks in your field. We wrote this book in a way that allows each chapter to serve as a resource for each new experience you encounter on your performance journey. It is not only warranted but recommended that you reread and revisit this content throughout your life. We challenge you to not simply read over the worksheets, but to actively apply, engage with, and complete each exercise as you continue to evolve and progress as a competitor or high-level performer in your own achievement domain.

Remember, performance excellence is a lifelong pursuit. The road to success should always be under construction. If you are involved in an achievement domain, be it sport, work, or life, you will need to work on and train your mental toughness. Accordingly, as you reach the end of this book, we want you to think of it as a jumping-off point to learn more about the skills and strategies you have read about here. Toward that end, we have provided several resources to help you learn more, grow more, invest more, and practice more as you refine and deepen your craft.

> In life, unlike chess, the game continues after checkmate.
>
> Isaac Asimov, American writer and biochemist

Resources

To continue learning in areas related to sport psychology and performance psychology, we have created a list of resources. Each of these meets the same rigorous standards we held ourselves to throughout the writing of this book. By that, we mean they highlight evidence-based, applied strategies that can help people across a variety of performance domains to pursue excellence and enjoy their journey.

Books

Advances in Sport and Exercise Psychology, Fourth Edition, by Thelma S. Horn and Alan L. Smith (2021)

Applied Sport Psychology: Personal Growth to Peak Performance, Eighth Edition, by Jean M. Williams and Vikki Krane (2021)

Biofeedback and Mindfulness in Everyday Life by Inna Khazan (2019)

Coaching for the Inner Edge by Robin S. Vealey (2005)

Doing Exercise Psychology, Sixth Edition, by Mark B. Andersen and Stephanie J. Hanrahan (2015)

Foundations of Sport and Exercise Psychology, Seventh Edition, by Robert S. Weinberg and Daniel Gould (2018)

Peak Performance: Elevate Your Game, Avoid Burnout, and Thrive With the New Science of Success by Brad Stulberg and Steve Magness (2017)

Psychology of Sport Injury by Britton W. Brewer and Charles J. Redmond (2016)

The Mindful Athlete: Secrets to Pure Performance by George Mumford (2016)

Academic Journals

Case Studies in Sport and Exercise Psychology

Journal for the Study of Sports and Athletes in Education

Journal of Applied Sport Psychology

Journal of Contemporary Athletics

Journal of Sport Psychology in Action

Modern Athlete and Coach

Related Professional Organizations

Association for Applied Sport Psychology

Canadian Sport Psychology Association

International Society of Sport Psychology

National Alliance for Youth Sports

National Council of Youth Sports

North American Society for the Psychology of Sport and Physical Activity

Positive Coaching Alliance

SCAPPS (Canadian Society for Psychomotor Learning and Sport Psychology)

STOP (Sports Trauma and Overuse Prevention) Sports Injuries

Women's Sports Foundation

Websites

www.zoneofexcellence.ca/index.html

www.mindfulnesscds.com

https://mbsrtraining.com

https://changingthegameproject.com

www.aspeninstitute.org/tag/youth-sports

BIBLIOGRAPHY

Abernethy, Bruce, Jonathan P. Maxwell, Richard S. W. Masters, John van der Kamp, and Robin C. Jackson. 2007. "Attentional Processes in Skill Learning and Expert Performance." In *Handbook of Sport Psychology*, edited by Gershon Tenenbaum and Robert C. Eklund, 245-263. West Sussex, England: John Wiley and Sons.

AFP. 2021. "Pele hails 'much more than footballer' Marta after Olympics landmark." The42. July 21, 2021. www.the42.ie/pele-marta-brazil-5502122-Jul2021.

Albert V. and Kevin S. Spink. 1992. "Group Cohesion and Adherence in Exercise Class." *Journal of Sport and Exercise Psychology*, 14, no. 1: 78-86.

Alfermann, Dorothee, and Natalia B. Stambulova. 2007. "Career Transitions and Career Termination." In *Handbook of Sport Psychology*, edited by Gershon Tenenbaum and Robert C. Eklund, 712-733. West Sussex, England: John Wiley & Sons.

Alfermann, Dorothee, Natalia B. Stambulova, and A. Zemaityte. 2004. "Reactions to Sport Career Termination: A Cross-National Comparison of German, Lithuanian, and Russian Athletes." *Psychology of Sport and Exercise*, 5, no. 1: 61-75. https://doi.org/10.1016/S1469-0292(02)00050-X.

American Psychological Association. 2012. "The Road to Resilience." https://uncw.edu/studentaffairs/committees/pdc/documents/the%20road%20to%20resilience.pdf.

Ames, Carol 1992. "Classrooms: Goals, Structures, and Student Motivation." *Journal of Educational Psychology*, 84, no. 3: 261-271. https://doi.org/10.1037/0022-0663.84.3.261.

Anderson, Ruth, Stephanie J. Hanrahan, and Clifford J. Mallett. 2014. "Investigating the Optimal Psychological State for Peak Performance in Australian Elite Athletes." *Journal of Applied Sport Psychology*, 26, no. 3: 318-333. https://doi.org/10.1080/10413200.2014.885915.

Anuar, Nurwina, Jennifer Cumming, and Sarah E. Williams. 2016. "Effects of Applying the PETTLEP Model on Vividness and Ease of Imaging Movement." *Journal of Applied Sport Psychology*, 28: 185-198. https://doi.org/ 10.1080/10413200.2015.1099122.

Atkinson, John W., and J. O. Raynor. 1974. *Motivation and Achievement*. Washington, D.C.: V. H. Winston & Sons (Wiley).

Baccellieri, Emma. 2020. "Pirates Mental Skills Coach Bernie Holliday on How to Master Mindfulness. *Sports Illustrated*. July 1, 2020. www.si.com/mlb/2020/07/01/bernie-holliday-mental-skills-coaching-mindfulness-techniques.

Baker, Joseph, and Bradley Young. 2014. "20 Years Later: Deliberate Practice and the Development of Sport Expertise." *International Review of Sport and Exercise Psychology*, 7, no. 1: 135-157. https://doi.org/10.1080/1750984X.2014.896024.

Baldock, Lee, Sheldon Hanton, Stephen D. Mellalieu, and Jean M. Williams. 2021. In *Applied Sport Psychology: Personal Growth to Peak Performance*, 8th ed., edited by Jean M. Williams and Vikki Krane, 210-243. New York: McGraw-Hill.

Bandura, Albert. 1977. *Social Learning Theory*. Englewood Cliffs, NJ: Prentice-Hall.

Bandura, Albert. 1997. *Self-Efficacy: The Exercise of Control*." New York: W. H. Freeman.

Beard, Alison. 2015. "Life's Work: An Interview with Andre Agassi." *Harvard Business Review*, October 2015. https://hbr.org/2015/10/andre-agassi.

Beauchamp, Mark R., Steven R. Bray, Antony Fielding, and Mark A. Eys. 2005. "A Multilevel Investigation of the Relationship Between Role Ambiguity and Role Efficacy in Sport." *Psychology of Sport and Exercise*, 6: 289-302.

Beaudry, Michel. 1967. "All or Nothing." *Skiing History*. April 20, 2021. www.skiinghistory. org/sites/skiinghistory.org/files/22-25_ma17_greene_kj_final.pdf.

Bell, James J., and James Hardy. 2009. "Effects of Attentional Focus on Skilled Performance in Golf." *Journal of Applied Sport Psychology*, 21, no. 2: 163-177. https://doi. org/10.1080/10413200902795323.

Benson, Alex J., Mark A. Eys, and P. Gregory Irving. 2016. "Great Expectations: How Role Expectations and Role Experiences Relate to Perceptions of Group Cohesion." *Journal of Sport and Exercise Psychology*, 38, no. 2: 160-172.

Benson, Alex J., Mark A. Eys, Mark Surya, Kimberley Dawson, and Margaret Schneider. 2013. "Athletes' Perceptions of Role Acceptance in Interdependent Sport Teams." *The Sport Psychology*, 27, 269-280.

Bernier, Marjorie, Christian Trottier, Emilie Thienot, and Jean Fournier. 2016. "An Investigation of Attentional Foci and Their Temporal Patterns: A Naturalistic Study in Expert Figure Skaters." *The Sport Psychologist*, 30, no. 3: 256-266. https://doi. org/10.1123/tsp.2013-0076.

Blackford, Krysten, Jonine Jancey, Andy H. Lee, Anthony James, Peter Howat, and Tracy Waddell. 2016. "Effects of a Home-Based Intervention on Diet and Physical Activity Behaviors For Rural Adults With or At-Risk of Metabolic Syndrome: A Randomized Controlled Trial." *International Journal of Behavioral Nutrition and Physical Activity*, 13, no: 13. https://doi.org/10.1186/s12966-016-0337-2.

Blodgett, Amy T., Robert J. Schinke, Brett Smith, Duke Peltier, and Chris Pheasant. 2011. "In Indigenous Words: Exploring Vignettes as a Narrative Strategy for Presenting the Research Voices of Aboriginal Community Members. *Qualitative Inquiry*, 17, no. 6: 522-533. https://doi.org/10.1177/1077800411409885.

Bosselut, Gregoire, Colin D. McLaren, Mark A. Eys, and Jean-Philippe Heuze. 2012. "Reciprocity of the Relationship Between Role Ambiguity and Group Cohesion in Youth Interdependent Sport." *Psychology of Sport and Exercise*, 13, no. 3: 341-348. https://doi. org/10.1016/j.psychsport.2011.09/002.

Boudway, I. 2018. "The Five Pillars of Popovich." *Bloomberg Businessweek*. January 10, 2018. https://www.bloomberg.com/news/features/2018-01-10/the-five-pillars-of-gregg-popovich.

Bourke, Juliet, and Bernadette Dillon. 2018. "The Diversity and Inclusion Revolution." *Deloitte Review*, 22: 82-95.

Boutcher, Stephen H. 1990. "The Effect of a Pre-Shot Attentional Routine on a Well-Learned Skill." *International Journal of Sport Psychology,* 18, 30-39.

Boyd, Evelyn M., and Ann W. Fales. 1983. "Reflective Learning: Key to Learning From Experience." *Journal of Humanistic Psychology*, 23, no. 2: 99-117. https://doi. org/10.1177/0022167883232011.

Brar, Faith. 2020. "Simone Biles Shares Why She's 'Done Competing' With Other People's Beauty Standards." *SHAPE*. February 12, 2020. www.shape.com/celebrities/news/simone-biles-body-shaming-beauty-standards.

Brewer, Britton W., Judy L. Van Raalte, and Darwyn E. Linder. 1993. "Athletic Identity: Hercules' Muscles or Achilles Heel?" *International Journal of Sport Psychology*, 24, no. 2: 237-254. https://doi.org/10.1080/10413209308411316.

Brick, Noel, Tadhg McIntyre, and Mark J. Campbell. 2014. "Attentional Focus in Endurance Activity: New Paradigms and Future Directions." *International Review of Sport and Exercise Psychology*, 7, no. 1: 106-134. https://doi.org/10.1080/1750984X.2014.885554.

Browne, Ken. 2019. "What Drives Tom Daley: 'I Want to Make My Son Proud.'" July 14, 2019. https://olympics.com/en/news/what-drives-tom-daley-fatherhood.

Buckley, Patrick S., Megan Bishop, Patrick Kane, Michael C. Ciccotti, Stephen Selverian, Dominique Exume, William Emper et al. 2017. "Early Single-Sport Specialization: A Survey of 3090 High School, Collegiate, and Professional Athletes." *Orthopaedic Journal of Sports Medicine*, 5, no. 7: 1-7. https://doi.org/10.1177/2325967117703944.

Bull, Steve. 2006. *Game Plan: Your Guide to Mental Toughness at Work*. West Sussex, UK: Capstone Publishing Limited.

Bullock, Maggie. 2019. "Abby Wambach Wishes She Didn't Buy All Those Watches and Cars." *The Cut*. March 28, 2019. www.thecut.com/2019/03/abby-wambach-soccer-player-more-money-pay.html.

Burton, Damon D. 1989. "Winning Isn't Everything: Examining the Impact of Performance Goals on Collegiate Swimmers' Cognitions and Performance." *The Sport Psychologist*, 3: 105-132.

Burton, Damon D., and Sarah Naylor. 2002. "The Jekyll/Hyde Nature of Goals: Revisiting and Updating Goal-Setting in Sport." In *Advances in Sport Psychology*, 2nd ed., edited by Thelma S. Horn, 459-499. Champaign, IL: Human Kinetics.

Butt, Joanne, and Robert S. Weinberg. In press. "Goal-Setting." In *Routledge International Encyclopedia of Sport and Exercise Psychology*, edited by Dieter Hackfort and Robert Schinke. New York: Routledge.

Butterworth, Liam. 2019. "Eliud Kipchoge's Sub-Two-Hour Marathon Record Sparks Debate Over Runner's Shoes." ABC News. Last modified October 19, 2019. https://www.abc.net.au/news/2019-10-19/outrage-over-kipchoges-mechanical-advantage-marathon-shoes/11619856.

Carden, Lucas, and Wendy Wood. 2018. "Habit Formation and Change." *Current Opinion in Behavioral Sciences*, 20: 117-122. https://doi.org/10.1016/j.cobeha.2017.12.009.

Carlin, John. 2006. "Most Bonito." *The New York Times*. June 4, 2006. https://www.nytimes.com/2006/06/04/sports/playmagazine/most-bonito.html.

Carroll, Pete, Yogi Roth, and Kristoffer A. Garin. 2011. *Win Forever: Live, Work, and Play Like a Champion*. London, UK: Penguin Book Group.

Carron, A. V., K. S. Spink, and H. Prapavessis. 1997. "Team Building and Cohesiveness in the Sport and Exercise Setting: Use of Indirect Interventions." *Journal of Applied Sport Psychology,* 9, no. 1: 61-72. https://doi.org/10.1080/10413209708415384.

Chamorro-Premuzic, Tomas. 2017. "Does Diversity Actually Increase Creativity?" *Harvard Business Review*. June 28, 2017. https://hbr.org/2017/06/does-diversity-actually-increase-creativity.

Cheng, Wen-Nuan Kara, Lew Hardy, and David Markland. 2009. "Toward a Three-Dimensional Conceptualization of Performance Anxiety: Rationale and Initial Measurement Development. *Psychology of Sport and Exercise*, 10, no. 2: 271-278. https://doi.org/10.1016/j.psychsport.2008.08.001.

Cherng, Hua-Yu Sebastian. 2017. "If They Think I Can: Teacher Bias and Minority Student Expectations and Achievement." *Social Science Research*, 66. https://doi.org/10.1016/j.ssresearch.2017.04.001.

Clarey, Christopher. 2020. "Rafael Nadal Routs Novak Djokovic at the French Open to Catch Roger Federer." *The New York Times*. October 11, 2020. www.nytimes.com/2020/10/11/sports/tennis/nadal-french-open.html.

Clarke, Brenda, Chris James, and Jan Kelly. 1996. "Reflective Practice: Reviewing the Issues and Refocusing the Debate." *International Journal of Nursing Studies*, 33, no. 2: 171-180. https://doi.org/10.1016/0020-7489(95)00045-3.

Columna, Luis, Timothy D. Davis, Lauren J. Lieberman, and Rebecca Lytle. 2010. "Determining the Most Appropriate Physical Education Placement for Students with

Disabilities." *Journal of Physical Education, Recreation, and Dance*, 81, no. 7: 1-60. https://doi.org/10.1080/07303084.2010.10598506.

Comaneci, Nadia. 2009. *Letters to a Young Gymnast*. New York: Basic Books.

Connaughton, David, Sheldon Hanton, and Graham Jones. 2010. "The Development and Maintenance of Mental Toughness in the World's Best Performers." *The Sport Psychologist*, 24, no. 2: 168-193. https://doi.org/10.1123/tsp.24.2.168.

Cowden, Richard G. 2017. "On the Mental Toughness of Self-Aware Athletes: Evidence from Competitive Tennis Players." *South African Journal of Science,* 113, no. 1/2: 1-6. https://doi.org/10.17159/sajs.2017/20160112.

Cumming, Jennifer, and Richard Ramsey. 2009. "Imagery Interventions in Sport." *Advances in Applied Sport Psychology: A Review*, edited by Stephen D. Mellalieu and Sheldon Hanton, 5-36. London, UK: Routledge.

Cumming, Jennifer, and Sarah E. Williams. 2012. "The Role of Imagery in Performance." In *Handbook of Sport and Performance Psychology*, edited by Shane Murphy, 213-232. New York: Oxford University Press.

Cunningham, Lillian. 2015. "Becky Hammon's Path to the NBA." *The Washington Post*. January 22, 2015. www.washingtonpost.com/news/on-leadership/wp/2015/01/22/becky-hammons-path-to-the-nba.

Das, Andrew. 2021. "U.S. Women's Soccer Team Routs New Zealand." *New York Times*, July 23, 2021. https://www.nytimes.com/live/2021/07/23/sports/olympics-tokyo-updates.

Davidson, Richard J., and Garry E. Schwartz. 1977. "Brain Mechanisms Subserving Self-Generated Imagery: Electrophysiological Specificity and Patterning. *Psychophysiology*, 14, no. 6: 598-602. https://doi.org/10.1111/j.1469-8986.1977.tb01207.

de Anca, Celia, and Salvador Aragon. 2018. "The Three Types of Diversity that Shape Our Identities." *Harvard Business Review*. May 24, 2018.

Deci, Edward L., and Richard M. Ryan. 1985a. "The General Causality Orientations Scale: Self-Determination in Personality." *Journal of Research in Personality*, 19: 109-134.

Deci, Edward L., and Richard M. Ryan. 1985b. *Intrinsic Motivation and Self-Determination in Human Behavior*. New York: Plenum.

Deci, Edward L., and Richard M. Ryan. 1994. "Promoting Self-determined Education." *Scandinavian Journal of Educational Research*, 38, no. 1: 3-14.

Deci, Edward L., and Richard M. Ryan. 2000. "The 'What' and the 'Why' of Goal Pursuits: Human Needs and the Self-Determination of Behavior." *Psychological Inquiry*, 11: 227-268.

Diggins, Jessie. 2021. "Falun Frolicking and Ulricehamm Hammering." February 15, 2021. https://jessiediggins.com/falun-frolicking-and-ulricehamn-hammering.

Donahue, Joe. 2019. "Impacts of Early Sport Specialization." *Positive Coaching Alliance Blog*. July 17, 2019. https://positivecoach.org/the-pca-blog/impacts-of-early-sport-specialization.

Donovan, Sarah J., C. Dominik Guss, and Dag Nasland. 2015. "Improving Dynamic Decision Making Through Training and Self-Reflection." *Judgment and Decision Making*, 10, no. 4: 284-295.

Driskell, Tripp, Steve Sclafani, and James E. Driskell. 2014. "Reducing the Effects of Game Day Pressures Through Stress Exposure Training." *Journal of Sport Psychology in Action*, 5, no. 1: 28-43. https://doi.org/10.1080/21520704.2013.866603.

Duckworth, Angela L. 2013. "Is It Really Self-Control: A Critical Analysis of the 'Marshmallow Test.'" *Society of Personality and Social Psychology Connections*, 39, no. 7: 843-855. https://doi.org/10.1177/0146167213482589.

Duckworth, Angela. 2016. *Grit: The Power of Passion and Perseverance.* New York: Scribner/Simon & Schuster.

Duckworth, Angela L., Christopher Peterson, Michael D. Matthews, and Dennis R. Kelly. 2007. "Grit: Perseverance and Passion for Long-Term Goals." *Journal of Personality and Social Psychology*, 92, no. 6: 1087-1101. https://doi.org/10.10370022-3514.92.6.1087.

Duda, Joan L. 2005. "Motivation in Sport." In *Handbook of Competence and Motivation Performance*, 8th ed., edited by Andrew J. Elliot and Carol S. Dweck, 318-335. New York: Guilford Press.

Dunning, David, Kerri Johnson, Joyce Ehrlinger, and Justin Kruger. 2003. "Why People Fail to Recognize Their Own Incompetence." *Current Directions in Psychological Science*, 12: 83-87. https://doi.org/10.1111/1467-8721.01235.

Dweck, Carol S. 1986. "Motivational Processes Affecting Learning." *American Psychologist*, 41, no. 10: 1040-1048. https://doi.org/10.1037/0003-066X.41.10.1040.

Dweck, Carol S. 2008. *Mindset: The New Psychology of Success*. New York: Ballantine Books.

Dweck, Carol S. 2015. "Carol Dweck Revisits the 'Growth Mindset.'" *Education Week*. September 22, 2015. www.edweek.org/leadership/opinion-carol-dweck-revisits-the-growth-mindset/2015/09.

Dweck, Carol S. 2016. "What Having a 'Growth Mindset' Actually Means." *Harvard Business Review*. January 13, 2015. https://leadlocal.global/wp-content/uploads/2016/12/Dweck-What-Having-a-%E2%80%9CGrowth-Mindset%E2%80%9D-Actually-Means-HBR.pdf.

Dweck, Carol S., and David S. Yeager. 2019. "Mindsets: A View from Two Eras." *Perspectives on Psychological Science*. February 1, 2019.

Epstein, Joyce L. 1989. "Family Structures and Student Motivation: A Developmental Perspective." In *Research on Motivation in Education: Goals and Cognitions*, edited by Carol Ames and Russell Ames, 259-295. New York: Academic Press.

Epstein, Mark. 1995. *Thoughts Without a Thinker: Psychotherapy from a Buddhist Perspective*. New York: Basic Books.

Ericsson, K. Anders, Michael J. Prietula, and Edward T. Cokely. 2007. "The Making of an Expert." *Harvard Business Review*. July-August, 2007. https://hbr.org/2007/07/the-making-of-an-expert.

Eys, Mark A., Albert V. Carron, Steven R. Bray, and Mark R. Beauchamp. 2003. "Role Ambiguity in Sport Teams." *Journal of Sport and Exercise Psychology*, 25, no. 4: 534-550. https://doi.org/10.1123/jsep25.4.534.

Farres, Laura G. 2004. "Becoming a Better Coach Through Reflective Practice." *BC Coach's Perspective*, 6: 10-11.

Festinger, Leon, Stanley Schacter, and Kurt Back. 1950. *Social Pressures in Informal Groups: A Study of Factors in Housing*. New York: Harper.

FIFA. 2020. "McLeod: Mindfulness Would Have Completely Changed My Career." FIFA. October 21, 2020. www.fifa.com/who-we-are/news/mcleod-mindfulness-would-have-completely-changed-my-career.

Foley, John. 2013. "Glad to Be Here: Lessons in High Performance from the Blue Angels." *Leader-to-Leader Executive Forum*. https://higherlogicdownload.s3.amazonaws.com/CORENETGLOBAL/f2d6ddf2-66f5-4042-b2ea-71e165781e82/UploadedImages/Articles/Glad+to+be+here+Lessons+in+high+performance+from+the+Blue+Angels.pdf?fbclid=IwAR04fjo1MsGmoGzn_VOKPxn0WVBPGMi_jhcnnMHAGQgAjGlukiC0gY5aGFI.

Foudy, Julie. 2017. *Choose to Matter: Being Courageously and Fabulously YOU*. Los Angeles, CA: ESPNW.

Fox, Michelle. 2021. "Allyson Felix Strives for Olympic Gold and Equality for Mothers – 'There is Still a Really Long Way To Go.'" CNBC. July 12, 2021. www.cnbc.com/2021/07/12/allyson-felix-strives-for-olympic-gold-and-equality-for-mother-athletes.html.

Frank, Cornelia, William M. Land, Carmen Popp, and Thomas Schack. 2014. "Mental Representation and Mental Practice: Experimental Investigation on the Functional Links Between Motor Memory and Motor Imagery." *PLoS One*, 9, no. 4: e95175. https://doi.org/ 10.1371/journal.pone.0095175.

Freidel, Nick. 2020. "Miami Made the Jimmy Butler Gamble That Chicago Never Could." ESPN. September 21, 2020. www.espn.com/nba/story/_/id/28672481/miami-made-jimmy-butler-gamble-chicago-never-could.

Fyodorov, Gennady. 2012. "Interview–Olympics–Latynina Roots for Phelps to Break Her Record." *Olympic News*, July 18, 2012. www.reuters.com/article/oly-gymn-latynina-adv9/interview-olympics-latynina-roots-for-phelps-to-break-her-record-idUKL6E8II-FUW20120718.

Gabriele, T.E., C.R. Hall, and T.D. Lee. 1989. "Cognition in Motor Learning: Imagery Effects on Contextual Interference." *Human Movement Science*, 8, 227-245.

Gardner, Frank L., and Zella E. Moore. 2004. "A Mindfulness-Acceptance-Commit-ment-Based Approach to Athletic Performance Enhancement: Theoretical Consider-ations." *Behavior Therapy*, 35: 707-723. https://doi.org/10.1016/S0005-7894(04)80016-9.

Gibbs, Graham. 1988. *Learning by Doing: A Guide to Teaching and Learning Methods*. Oxford, UK: Further Education Unit.

Gill, Diane L. 2000. *Psychological Dynamics of Sport and Exercise*. Champaign, IL: Human Kinetics.

Gillison, Fiona B., Peter Rouse, Martyn Standage, Simon J. Sebire, and Richard M. Ryan. 2019. "A Meta-Analysis of Techniques to Promote Motivation for Health Behavior Change From a Self-Determination Theory Perspective." *Health Psychology Review*, 13, no. 1: 110-130. https://doi.org/10.1080/17437199.2018.1534071.

Goff, Steven. 2019. "'Winning by Any Means Possible,' U.S. Grinds Past Spain to World Cup Quarterfinals." *The Washington Post*. June 24, 2019. www.washingtonpost.com/sports/2019/06/24/uswnt-spain-world-cup.

Goldberg, Jamie. 2019. "Goal Scoring Record Secondary as Christine Sinclair Focuses on Leading Canada to World Cup Success." *The Oregonian*. June 5, 2019. www.oregonlive.com/portland-thorns/2019/06/goal-scoring-record-secondary-as-christine-sinclair-focus-es-on-leading-canada-to-world-cup-success.html.

Golden State Warriors. 2019. "Rituals: Stephen Curry." Video, 5:56. www.youtube.com/watch?v=FOd7HTemROA.

Goodman, Lizzy. 2019. "The Best Women's Soccer Team in the World Fights for Equal Pay." *New York Times*. June 10, 2019. www.nytimes.com/2019/06/10/magazine/wom-ens-soccer-inequality-pay.html.

Gould, Daniel. 2020. "Goal Setting for Peak Performance." In *Applied Sport Psychology: Personal Growth to Peak Performance*, 8th ed., edited by Jean M. Williams and Vikki Krane, 189-209. New York: McGraw-Hill.

Gould, Daniel, Christy Greenleaf, and Vikki Krane. 2002. "Arousal-Anxiety and Sport Behavior." In *Advances in Sport Psychology*, edited by Thelma S. Horn, 207-236. Champaign, IL: Human Kinetics.

Gould, Daniel, and Ian Maynard. 2009. "Psychological Preparation for the Olym-pic Games." *Journal of Sports Sciences*, 27, no. 13: 1393-1408. https://doi.org/10.1080/02640410903081845.

Grant, Anthony M., John Franklin, and Peter Langford. 2002. "The Self-Reflection and Insight Scale: A New Measure of Private Self-Consciousness." *Social Behavior and Personality: An International Journal*, 30, no. 8: 821-835. https://doi.org/10.2224/sbp.2002.30.8.821.

Gross, Mike, Zella E. Moore, Frank L. Gardner, Andrew T. Wolanin, Rachel Pess, and Donald R. Marks. 2018. "An Empirical Examination Comparing the Mindfulness-Acceptance-Commitment Approach and Psychological Skills Training for the Mental Health and Sport Performance of Female Student Athletes." *International Journal of Sport and Exercise Psychology*, 16, no. 4: 431-451. https://doi.org/10.1080/1612197X.2016.1250802.

Guardado, Maria. 2019. "Carli Lloyd Had a Dream That She'd Score 4 Goals in the World Cup Final." Last modified January 17, 2019. www.nj.com/soccer-news/2015/07/clairvoyant_carli_carli_lloyd_had_a_dream_that_she.html.

Gurin, Patricia, Jeffrey S. Lehman, Earl Lewis, Eric L. Dey, Sylvia Hurtado, and Gerald Gurin. 2004. *Defending Diversity: Affirmative Action at the University of Michigan*. Ann Arbor, MI: University of Michigan Press.

Hacker, Colleen M. 2018. "Adopting an Olympian's Mindset: 5 Principles." Positive Coaching Alliance. https://devzone.positivecoach.org/resource/article/adopting-olympians-mindset-5-principles.

Hacker, Colleen M., and Anson Dorrance. 2021. "Coaching Mentally Tough Athletes: Are They Born or Made?" Paper presented at the United Soccer Coaches National Convention, January 2021.

Hacker, Colleen M., and Mallory E. Mann. 2017. "Talking Across the Divide: Reflections and Recommendations for Context-Driven, Cultural Sport Psychology." *Journal of Sport Psychology in Action*, 8, no. 2: 76-86. https://doi.org/10.1080/21520704.2017.1287144.

Hanin, Y. L. 1997. "Emotions and Athletic Performance: Individual Zones of Optimal Functioning Model." *European Yearbook of Sport Psychology*, 1, 29-72.

Hannam, Lisa. 2017. "Canadian Marathoner Lanni Marchant on How to Set Goals Like an Athlete." *Best Health Magazine*. Last modified August 30, 2017. www.besthealthmag.ca/article/lanni-merchant-goals.

Hardy, James, Craig R. Hall, and Lew Hardy. 2005. "Quantifying Athlete Self-Talk." *Journal of Sports Sciences* 23: 905-917. https://doi.org/10.1080/02640410500130706.

Hardy, Lew, Graham J. Jones, and Daniel Gould. 1996. *Understanding Psychological Preparation for Sport: Theory and Practice of Elite Performers*. West Sussex, England: John Wiley and Sons.

Harter, S. 1978. "Effective Motivation Reconsidered: Toward a Developmental Model." *Human Development*, 1: 34-64.

Hatfield, Brad, and Charles H. Hillman. 2001. "The Psychophysiology of Sport: A Mechanistic Understanding of the Psychology of Superior Performance." In *The Handbook of Sport Psychology*, 2nd ed., edited by Robert N. Singer, H. A. Hausenblas, and Christopher M. Janelle, 362-388. New York: John Wiley and Sons.

Hatzigeorgiadis, Antonis, Evangelos Galanis, Nikos Zourbanos, and Yiannis Theodorakis. 2014. "Self-talk and Competitive Sport Performance." *Journal of Applied Sport Psychology* 26: 82-95. https://doi.org/10.1080/10413200.2013.790095.

Hatzigeorgiadis, Antonis, Nikos Zourbanos, Evangelos Galanis, and Yiannis Theodorakis. 2011. "Self-Talk and Sport Performance: A Meta-Analysis." *Perspectives on Psychological Science* 6: 348-356. https://doi.org/10.1177/1745691611413136.

Hatzigeorgiadis, Antonis, Nikos Zourbanos, and Yiannis Theodorakis. 2007. "The Moderating Effects of Self-Talk Content on Self-Talk Functions. *Journal of Applied Sport Psychology* 19: 240-251.

Hays, Kate. 2017. "The 80% Edge: What Do You Do When You Need to Perform and You're Not At Peak?" May 13, 2017. *Psychology Today*. www.psychologytoday.com/us/blog/the-edge-peak-performance-psychology/201705/the-80-edge.

Hayslip, Bert, Trent A. Petrie, Mae M. MacIntire, and Gretchen M. Jones. 2010. "The Influences of Skill Level, Anxiety, and Psychological Skills Use on Amateur Golfers' Performances." *Journal of Applied Sport Psychology*, 22, no. 2: 123-133. https://doi.org/10.1080/10413200903554281.

Hertz, Rosanna. 1997. *Reflexivity and Voice*. Thousand Oaks, CA: Sage.

Holmes, Paul S., and Dave Collins. 2001. "The PETTLEP Approach to Motor Imagery: A Functional Equivalence Model for Sport Psychologists." *Journal of Applied Sport Psychology*, 13, no. 1: 60-83. https://doi.org/10.1080/10413200109339004.

Horn, Thelma S., and Alan L. Smith. 2020. *Advances in Sport and Exercise Psychology.* 4th ed. Champaign, IL: Human Kinetics.

Horton, Robert S., and Diane E. Mack. 2000. "Athletic Identity in Marathon Runners: Functional Focus or Dysfunctional Commitment?" *Journal of Sport Behavior*, 23, no. 2: 101-120.

Hsieh, Chang-Tai, Erik Hurst, Charles I. Jones, and Peter J. Klenow. 2019. "The Allocation of Talent and U.S. Economic Growth." *Econometrica*, 87, no. 5: 1439-1474.

Hunt, Vivian, Lareina Yee, Sara Prince, and Sundiatu Dixon-Fyle. 2018. "Delivering Through Diversity." McKinsey and Company. January 18, 2018. www.mckinsey.com/business-functions/organization/our-insights/delivering-through-diversity.

Hurtado, Sylvia, Jeffrey F. Milem, Alma Clayton-Pedersen, and Walter Allen. 1999. "Enacting Diverse Learning Environments: Improving the Climate for Racial/Ethnic Diversity in Higher Education." *ASHE-ERIC Higher Education Report*, 26, no. 8: 1-140.

Hutchins Center Honors. 2018. W. E. B. Du Bois Medal Ceremony. Video, October 11, 2018. https://www.youtube.com/watch?v=Kca69p0CveU.

Ingersoll, Keith, Edmund J. Malesky, Sebastian Saiegh. 2014. "Diversity and Group Performance: Evidence from the World's Top Soccer League." Presented at the American Political Science Association Conference: Washington, D.C. July 30, 2014.

Ipsos Survey. 2020. "Public Poll Findings and Methodology." Ipsos, Inc. www.ipsos.com/sites/default/files/ct/news/documents/2020-12/urban_plates_-_nyr_survey_key_findings_12-8-2020.pdf.

Jackson, Robin C. 2003. "Pre-Performance Routine Consistency: Temporal Analysis of Goal Kicking in the Rugby Union World Cup." *Journal of Sports Sciences*, 10: 803-814.

Jacobson, Edmund. 1938. *You Can Sleep Well; The ABCs of Restful Sleep for the Average Person.* New York: Whittlesey House, McGraw-Hill.

Jain, Manoj. 2015. "A Doctor Puts His Mind to Mindfulness." *The Washington Post.* October 19, 2015. www.washingtonpost.com/national/health-science/a-doctor-puts-his-mind-to-mindfulness/2015/10/19/d191fc48-57c3-11e5-8bb1-b488d231bba2_story.html.

Johns, Christopher. 2011. *Guided Reflection: A Narrative Approach to Advancing Professional Practice*, 2nd ed. Hoboken, NJ: Wiley-Blackwell.

Johnson, Reece. 2020. "New Survey Finds Most College Grads Would Change Majors." *Best Colleges.* www.bestcolleges.com/blog/college-graduate-majors-survey.

Jones, Graham, Sheldon Hanton, and David Connaughton. 2002. "What Is This Thing Called Mental Toughness? An Investigation of Elite Sport Performers." *Journal of Applied Sport Psychology*, 14, no. 3: 205-218. https://doi.org/10.1080/10413200290103509.

Jones-Rooy, Andrea. 2019. "Three Types of Diversity." *Medium.* June 6, 2019. https://medium.com/@jonesrooy/three-types-of-diversity-d34ea9689183.

Joy2Learn Foundation. 2013. "Wynton Marsalis: Wynton—Discipline and Practice." Video, 1:31. www.youtube.com/watch?v=3BSSCOtuz0E.

Judge, Shahid. 2017. "Andre Agassi Opens Up: From Dealing with His Father to Managing Fatherhood." *The Indian Express*, updated January 19, 2017. https://indianexpress.com/article/sports/tennis/andre-agassi-memoir-revisited-from-dealing-with-his-father-to-managing-fatherhood-4480881.

Kabat-Zinn, Jon. 1982. "An Outpatient Program in Behavioral Medicine for Chronic Pain Patients Based on the Practice of Mindfulness Meditation: Theoretical Considerations and Preliminary Results." *General Hospital Psychiatry*, 4: 33-47. https://doi.org/10.1016/0163-8343(82)90026-3.

Kabat-Zinn, Jon. 2013. *Full Catastrophe Living: Using the Wisdom of Your Body and Mind to Face Stress, Pain, and Illness*. New York: Bantam Dell.

Kaiseler, Mariana, Jamie M. Poolton, Susan H. Backhouse, and Nick Stanger. 2017. "The Relationship Between Mindfulness and Life Stress in Student-Athletes: The Mediating Role of Coping Effectiveness and Decision Rumination." *The Sport Psychologist*, 31, no. 3: 1-30. https://doi.org/10.1123/tsp.2016-0083.

Karageorghis, Costas I., Peter C. Terry, Andrew M. Lane, Daniel T. Bishop, and David L. Priest. 2012. "The BASES Expert Statement on Use of Music in Exercise." *Journal of Sports Sciences*, 30, no. 9: 953-956.

Kipling, Rudyard. 1899. *The Jungle Book*. New York: Century Co.

Knowles, Zoe, David Gilbourne, Victoria Tomlinson, and Ailsa G. Anderson. 2007. "Reflections on the Application of Reflective Practice for Supervision in Applied Sport Psychology." *The Sport Psychologist*, 21, no. 1: 109-122.

Krane, Vikki, Jean M. Williams, and Scott A. Graupensperger. 2021. "Mental Training for Performance Enhancement." In *Applied Sport Psychology: Personal Growth to Peak Performance*, 8th ed., edited by Jean M. Williams and Vikki Krane, 159-175. New York: McGraw-Hill.

Kremer, Andrea. 2014. "Tom Brady Still Driven Entering 15th NFL Season with Patriots." *NFL Network*. September 7, 2014. www.nfl.com/news/tom-brady-still-driven-entering-15th-nfl-season-with-patriots-0ap3000000389333.

Kruger, Justin, and David Dunning. 1999. "Unskilled and Unaware of It: How Difficulties in Recognizing One's Own Incompetence Lead to Inflated Self-Assessments. *Journal of Personality and Social Psychology*, 77: 1121–1134. https://doi.org/10.1037/0022-3514.77.6.1121.

KSN News. 2018. "Lindsey Jacobellis Emphasizes Optimism, Not Heartbreak, After Another Olympic Miss." *KSN.com*. Last updated February 16, 2018. https://www.ksn.com/news/lindsey-jacobellis-emphasizes-optimism-not-heartbreak-after-another-olympic-miss/.

Kudlackova, Katerina, David W. Eccles, and Kristen Dieffenbach. 2013. "Use of Relaxation Skills in Differentially Skilled Athletes." *Psychology of Sport and Exercise*, 14, no. 4: 468-475. https://doi.org/10.1016/j.psychsport.2013.01.007.

Langmann Brady. 2021. "Rory McIlroy on Mental Health, Naomi Osaka, And How He Overcame His Lowest Moments." *Esquire*. June 25, 2021. www.esquire.com/sports/a36820863/rory-mcilroy-mental-health-interview.

Latham, Gary P., and Edwin A. Locke. 1991. "Self-Regulation Through Goal Setting." *Organizational Behavior and Human Decision Processes*, 50: 212-247.

Latinjak, Alexander Tibor, Miguel Torregrosa, and Jordi Renom. 2010. "Studying the Effects of Self-Talk on Thought Content With Male Adult Tennis Players." *Perceptual and Motor Skills*, 111: 249-260. https://doi.org/10.2466/02.05.28.PMS.111.4.249-260.

Latinjak, Alexander, Nikos Zourbanos, Victor Lopez-Ros, and Antonis Hatzigeorgiadis. 2014. "Goal-directed and Undirected Self-talk: Exploring a New Perspective for the Study of Athletes' Self-talk." *Psychology of Sport and Exercise*, 15, no. 5: 548-558.

Laumann, Silken. n.d. "About Me." https://www.silkenlaumann.com/about-silken.

Lepper, Mark R., and David Greene. 1975. "Turning Play Into Work: Effects of Adult Surveillance and Extrinsic Rewards on Children's Intrinsic Motivation." *Journal of Personality and Social Psychology*, 31, no. 3: 479-486.

Lepper, Mark R., David Greene, and Richard E. Nisbett. 1973. "Undermining Children's Intrinsic Interest With Extrinsic Reward: A Test of the 'Overjustification' Hypothesis." *Journal of Personality and Social Psychology*, 28, no. 1: 129-137.

Lewis, Samantha. 2020. "Angel City FC's Ownership Model Could Shape the Future of Women's Sport." ESPN. November 4, 2020. www.espn.com/soccer/united-states-nwsl-womens-league/story/4221096/angel-city-fcs-ownership-model-could-shape-the-future-of-womens-sport.

Lidor, Ronnie, and Gershon Tenenbaum. 1993. "Applying Learning Strategy to a Basketball Shooting Skill: A Case Study Report." In *Physical Activity in the Lifecycle: The 1993 FIEP World Congress Proceedings*, edited by Ronnie Lidor, D. Ben-Sira and Z. Artzi, 53-59. Netanya, Israel: The Zinman College of Physical Education at the Wingate Institution.

Linley, Alex P., and Stephen Joseph. 2004. "Positive Change Following Trauma and Adversity: A Review." *Journal of Traumatic Stress*, 17, no. 1: 11-21. https://doi.org/10.1023/B:JOTS.0000014671.27856.7e.

Lobmeyer, DeAnn L., and E. A. Wassermerman. 1986. "Preliminaries to Free Throw Shooting: Superstitious Behavior?" *Journal of Sport Behavior*, 9, no. 2: 70-78.

Lochbaum, Marc, and Chad Smith. 2015. "Making the Cut and Winning a Golf Putting Championship: The Role of Approach-Avoidance Achievement Goals." *International Journal of Golf Sciences*, 4: 50-66. https://doi.org/10.1123/ijgs.2015-0001.

Locke, Edwin A., and Gary P. Latham. 2002. "Building a Practically Useful Theory of Goal-Setting and Task Motivation: A 35-year Odyssey." *American Psychologist*, 57, no. 9: 705-717. https://doi.org/10.1037/0003-066X.57.9.705.

Locke, Edwin A., and Gary P. Latham. 2006. "New Directions in Goal-Setting Theory." *Current Directions in Psychological Science*, 15, no. 5: 265-268. https://doi.org/10.1111/j.1467-8721.2006.00449.x.

Locke, Edwin A., Karyll N. Shaw, Lise M. Saari, and Gary P. Latham. 1981. "Goal-Setting and Task Performance." *Psychological Bulletin*, 90: 125-152.

Longman, Jere. 2021. "A Quiet Demonstration and a Long Shadow." *New York Times*. June 17, 2021. www.nytimes.com/2021/06/17/sports/olympics/wyomia-tyus-athlete-protests-racism.html.

Mabry, Edward A., and Richard E. Barnes. 1980. *The Dynamics of Small Group Communication*. Hoboken, NJ: Prentice-Hall.

MacMullan, Jackie. 2019. "Rise Above It or Drown: How Elite NBA Athletes Handle Pressure." *ESPN*, May 29, 2019. https://www.espn.com/nba/story/_/id/26802987/rise-drown-how-elite-nba-athletes-handle-pressure.

Maltz, Maxwell. 1960. *Psycho-cybernetics*. New York: Penguin Random House LLC.

Mann, Derek T.Y., A. Mark Williams, Paul Ward, and Christopher M. Janelle. 2007. "Perceptual-Cognitive Expertise in Sport: A Meta-Analysis." *Journal of Sport and Exercise Psychology*, 29, no. 4: 457-478. https://doi.org/10.1123/jsep.29.4.457.

Mannion, Joe. 2020. "Mindfulness in Sport." In *Applied Sport Psychology: Personal Growth to Peak Performance*, 8th ed., edited by Jean M. Williams and Vikki Krane, 334-357. New York: McGraw-Hill.

Martens, Rainer. 1987. *Coaches' Guide to Sport Psychology*. Champaign, IL: Human Kinetics.

Martin, Jeffrey J. 2002. "Training and Performance Self-Efficacy, Affect, and Performance in Wheelchair Road Racers." *The Sport Psychologist*, 16, no. 4: 384-395. https://doi.org/10.1123/tsp.16.4.384.

Martin, Lisa Anne, Gerard J. Fogarty, and Majella J. Albion. 2014. "Changes in Athletic Identity and Life Satisfaction of Elite Athletes as a Function of Retirement Status." *Journal of Applied Sport Psychology*, 26, no. 1: 96-110. https://doi.org/10.1080/10413200.2013.798371.

Martin, Luc J., Albert V. Carron, and Shauna M. Burke. 2009. "Team Building Interventions in Sport: A Meta-Analysis." *Sport and Exercise Psychology Review*, 26: 136-153.

Martin, Rachel. 2016. "Forget Talent, Success Comes From Grit." *National Public Radio*. May 1, 2016. https://www.npr.org/2016/05/01/476346709/forget-talent-success-comes-from-grit#:~:text=DUCKWORTH%3A%20Grit%2C%20in%20a%20word,-really%20going%20to%20get%20anywher.

Martusewicz, Rebecca A., Jeff Edmundson, and John Lupinacci. 2020. *EcoJustice Education*, 3rd ed. Oxfordshire, UK: Routledge.

McCardle, Lindsay, Bradley W. Young, and Joseph Baker. 2019. "Self-Regulated Learning and Expertise Development in Sport: Current Status, Challenges, and Future Opportunities." *International Review of Sport and Exercise Psychology*, 12, no. 1: 112-138. https://doi.org/10.1080/1750984X.2017.1381141.

McCleary-Gaddy, Asia. 2019. "Be Explicit: Defining the Difference Between the Office of Diversity and Inclusion and the Office of Diversity and Equity." *Medical Teacher*, 41, no. 12: 1443-1444. https://doi.org/10.1080/0142159X.2019.1597261.

McCracken, Lance M., and Kevin E. Vowles. 2014. "Acceptance and Commitment Therapy and Mindfulness for Chronic Pain." *American Psychologist*, 69, no. 2: 178-187. https://doi.org/10.1037/a0035623.

McDougall, Chrös. 2021. "Jordan Larson's Final Spike Sends U.S. Women's Volleyball Team to First Olympic Gold Medal." *Team USA News*. August 8, 2021. www.teamusa.org/news/2021/august/08/jordan-larsons-final-spike-sends-us-womens-volleyball-team-to-first-olympic-gold-medal.

McEwan, Desmond, and Mark R. Beauchamp. 2014. "Teamwork in Sport: A Theoretical and Integrative Review." *International Review of Sport and Exercise Psychology*, 7, no. 1: 229-250. https://doi.org/10.1080/1750984X.2014.932423.

McGannon, Kerry R., and Robert Schinke. 2013. "My First Choice Is to Work Out at Work; Then I Don't Feel Bad about My Kids: A Discursive Psychological Analysis of Motherhood and Physical Activity Participation." *Psychology of Sport and Exercise*, 14, no. 2: 179-188. https://doi.org/10.1016/j.psychsport.2012.10.001.

McGrath, Joseph E. 1970. *Social and Psychological Factors in Stress.* New York: Holt, Rinehart, and Winston.

Mizuguchi, Nobuski, Kazuyuki Kanosue, and Hiroki Nakata. 2012. "Motor Imagery and Sport Performance." *The Journal of Physical Fitness and Sports Medicine*, 1 no. 1: 103-111. https://doi.org/10.7600/jpfsm.1.103.

Moon, Dal-Hyun, Joonkoo Yun, and Jeff McNamee. 2016. "The Effects of Goal Variation on Adult Physical Activity Behavior." *Journal of Sports Sciences*, 34, no. 19: 1816-1821. http://dx.doi.org/10.1080/02640414.2016.1140218.

Moran Aidan P. 1996. *The Psychology of Concentration in Sports Performers: A Cognitive Analysis*. Hove, England: Psychology Press.

Moran, Aidan. 2004. "Attention and Concentration Training in Sport." In *Encyclopedia of Applied Psychology*, edited by Charles Spielberger. Amsterdam, Netherlands: Elsevier.

Moran, Aidan. 2009. "Attention in Sport." In *Advances in Applied Sport Psychology*, edited by Stephen D. Mellalieu and S. Hanton, 195-220. New York: Routledge.

Moran, Aidan. 2013. *Sport and Exercise Psychology: A Critical Introduction*, 2nd ed. London, UK: Routledge.

Moran, Aidan, John Toner, and Mark Campbell. 2019. "Attention and Concentration." In *Sport, Exercise, and Performance Psychology*, edited by Angus Mugford and J. Gualberto Cremades, 233-250. New York: Routledge.

Morgan, William P., and Michael L. Pollack. 1977. "Psychologic Characterization of the Elite Distance Runner." *Annals of the New York Academy of Sciences*, 301, no. 1: 382-403. https://doi.org/10.1111/j.1749-6632.1977.tb38215.x.

Moss-Racusin, Corinne A., John F. Dovidio, Victoria L. Brescoll, Mark J. Graham, and Jo Handelsman. 2012. "Science Faculty's Subtle Gender Biases Favor Male Students." *Proceedings of the National Academy of the Sciences of the United States of America*, 104, no. 41: 16474-16479. https://doi.org/10.1073/pnas.1211286109.

Murphy, Shane, Doug Jowdy, and Shirley Durtschi.1990. "Report on the U.S. Olympic Committee Survey on Imagery Use in Sport." In *Foundations of Sport and Exercise Psychology,* edited by Robert S. Weinberg and Daniel Gould, 293. Champaign, IL: Human Kinetics.

Nash, Steve. https://sportmedbc.com/news/don%E2%80%99t-choke-%E2%80%9Cjust-breathe%E2%80%9D-%E2%80%93-dr-david-cox-helps-steve-nash.

National Center for Education Statistics. 2013. *The Condition of Education.* https://nces.ed.gov/pubs2013/2013037.pdf.

Nicholls, John G. 1984. "Achievement Motivation: Conceptions of Ability, Subjective Experience, Task Choice, and Performance." *Psychological Review*, 91, no. 3: 328-346. https://doi.org/10.1037/0033-295X.91.3.328.

Nideffer, Robert M. 1976. "Test of Attentional and Interpersonal Style." *Journal of Personality and Social Psychology*, 34: 394-404.

Nideffer, Robert M., and Marc-Simon Sagal. 2006. "Concentration and Attention Control Training." In *Applied Sport Psychology: Personal Growth to Peak Performance*, edited by Jean M. Williams, 382-403. New York: McGraw-Hill.

Nirell, L. 2013. "Wisdom 2.0's Compassionate, Chaos-Reducing Brand of Leadership." *Fast Company*, February 28, 2013. www.fastcompany.com/3006293/wisdom-20s-compassionate-chaos-reducing-brand-leadership.

O, Jenny, and Krista J. Munroe-Chandler. 2008. "The Effects of Image Speed on the Performance of a Soccer Task. *The Sport Psychologist*, 22, no. 1: 1-17. https://doi.org/10.1123/tsp.22.1.1.

Orlick, Terry. 2016. *In Pursuit of Excellence*, 5th ed. Champaign, IL: Human Kinetics.

Orlick, Terry, and John Partington. 1988. "Mental Links to Excellence." *The Sport Psychologist*, 2, no. 2: 105-130. https://doi.org/10.1123/tsp.2.2.105.

Osman, Kamisah. 2011. "The Inculcation of Generic Skills Through Service Learning Experience Among Science Student Teachers." *Procedia – Social and Behavioral Sciences*, 18: 148-153. https://doi.org/10.1016/j.sbspro.2011.05.022.

Osterman, Karen F., and Robert B. Kottkamp. 1993. *Reflective Practice for Educators: Improving Schooling Through Professional Development*. Newbury Park, CA: Corwin Press.

Pausch, Randy. 2008. *The Last Lecture*. New York: Hyperion.

Peterson, Christopher, and Martin E. P. Seligman. 2004. *Character Strengths and Virtues: A Handbook and Classification*. Oxford, UK: Oxford University Press.

Prakash. 2020. "Rafael Nadal Sweeps the Courts After His Practice Session." *Tennis World*. July 19, 2020. www.tennisworldusa.org/tennis/videos/Rafael_Nadal/89598/rafael-nadal-sweeps-the-courts-after-his-practice-session.

Privette, Gayle. 1983. "Peak Experience, Peak Performance, and Flow: A Comparative Analysis of Positive Human Experiences." *Journal of Personality and Social Psychology*, 45, no. 6: 1361-1368. https://doi.org/10.1037/0022-3514.45.6.1361.

Ramsey, Richard, Jennifer Cumming, and Martin G. Edwards. 2008. "Exploring a Modified Conceptualization of Imagery Direction and Golf Putting Performance." *International Journal of Sport and Exercise Psychology*, 6, no. 2: 207-223. https://doi.org/10.1080/1612197X.2008.9671862.

Rapaport, Dan. 2021. "Collin Morikawa's Best Tips for Being a Better Ball-Striker." *Golf Digest*, July 19, 2021. www.golfdigest.com/story/collin-morikawa-instruction-tips-magazine.

Ravizza, Kenneth, Angela Fifer, and Eric Bean. 2021. "Increasing Awareness for Sport Performance." In *Applied Sport Psychology: Personal Growth to Peak Performance*, 8th ed., edited by Jean M. Williams and Vikki Krane, 176-188. New York: McGraw-Hill.

Ravizza, Kenneth, Angela Fifer, and Eric Bean. 2020. "Increasing Awareness for Sport Performance." In *Applied Sport Psychology: Personal Growth to Peak Performance*, 8th ed., edited by Jean M. Williams and Vikki Krane, 278-290. New York: McGraw-Hill.

Rees, T. 2007. "Influence of Social Support on Athletes." In *Social Psychology in Sport*, edited by S. Jowett and D. Lavallee, 224-231. London: Human Kinetics.

Reilly, Katie. 2018. "'Make Failure Your Fuel.' Read Soccer Star Abby Wambach's Barnard Commencement Address." *Time*. May 17, 2018. https://time.com/5281711/abby-wambach-barnard-commencement-2018-speech.

Reints, A. 2011. "Validation of the Holistic Athletic Career Model and the Identification of Variables Related to Athletic Retirement" (doctoral thesis). Vrije University Brussels, Belgium.

Rivera, Joe. 2021. "Tom Brady Documentary: Full Schedule for ESPN 'Man in the Arena' Series Covering All 10 Super Bowls." *Sporting News*, November 11, 2021. https://www.sportingnews.com/us/nfl/news/tom-brady-documentary-espn-man-in-the-arena-schedule/6f3lutipa2hp1bo3yze6ip5cr.

Roberts, Glyn C., and Darren Treasure. 2012. *Advances in Motivation in Sport and Exercise*. 3rd ed. Champaign, IL: Human Kinetics.

Roche, Megan, and David Roche. 2020. "Dr. Megan Roche and David Roche on Running, Coaching, and Finding Your Why." Interview by David Swain. Prokit, May 4, 2020. https://theprokit.com/posts/dr-megan-roche-and-david-roche-on-running-coaching-and-finding-your-why.

Rosenthal, Robert, and Lenore Jacobson. 1968. *Pygmalion in the Classroom: Teacher Expectation and Pupils' Intellectual Development*. New York: Holt, Rinehart, and Winston.

Roure R., C. Collet, C. Deschaumes-Molinar, G. Delhomme, A. Dittmar, and E. Vernet-Maury. 1999. "Imagery Quality Estimated by Autonomic Response is Correlated to Sporting Performance Enhancement." *Physiology and Behavior* 66: 63-72.

Ruiz, Montse C., John S. Raglin, and Yuri L. Hanin. 2017. "The Individual Zones of Optimal Functioning (IZOF) Model (1978–2014): Historical Overview of Its Development and Use." *International Journal of Sport and Exercise Psychology*, 15, no. 1: 41-63. https://doi.org/10.1080/1612197X.2015.1041545.

Rumbolt, James L., David Fletcher, and Kevin Daniels. 2012. "A Systematic Review of Stress Management Interventions With Sport Performers." *Sport, Exercise, and Performance Psychology*, 1, no. 3: 173-192. https://doi.org/10.1037/a0026628.

Ryan, Richard M., and Edward L. Deci. 2000. "Intrinsic and Extrinsic Motivations: Classic Definitions and New Directions." *Contemporary Educational Psychology*, 25: 54-67. https://doi.org/10.1006/ceps.1999.1020.

Ryan, Richard M., and Edward L. Deci. 2017. *Self-Determination Theory: Basic Psychological Needs in Motivation*. New York: Guilford Press.

Sadler, Emily. 2021. "'We Never Want to Lose to Canada': U.S. Players, Media React to Canada's Win." Sportsnet. August 2, 2021. https://www.sportsnet.ca/olympics/article/never-want-lose-canada-u-s-players-media-react-canadas-win/.

Samuel, Roy D., and Gershon Tenenbaum. 2011. "How Do Athletes Perceive and Respond to Change-Events: An Exploratory Measurement Tool." *Psychology of Sport and Exercise*, 12, no. 4: 392-406. https://doi.org/10.1016/j.psychsport.2011.03.002.

Sanders, R. L., and L. McKeown. 2008. "Promoting Reflection Through Action Learning in a 3D Virtual World." *International Journal of Social Sciences*, 2: 50-58.

Scelfo, Julie. 2016. "Angela Duckworth on Passion, Grit, and Success." *The New York Times.* April 8, 2016. www.nytimes.com/2016/04/10/education/edlife/passion-grit-success.html.

Schinke, Robert, Kerry R. McGannon, William D. Parham, and Andrew M. Lane. 2012. "Toward Cultural Praxis and Cultural Sensitivity: Strategies for Self-Reflexive Sport Psychology Practice." *Quest*, 64, no. 1: 34-46. https://doi.org/10.1080/00336297.2012.653264.

Schlossberg, Nancy K. 1981. "A Model for Analyzing Human Adaptation to Transition." *The Counseling Psychologist*, 9, no. 2: 2-18. https://doi.org/10.1177001100008100900202.

Schultz, Johannes H., and Wolfgang Luthe. 1969. *Autogenic Therapy. Vol. I: Autogenic Methods.* New York: Grune & Stratton.

Schwartz, Tony. 2013. "How to Be Mindful in an 'Unmanageable' World." *Harvard Business Review.* February 27, 2013. https://hbr.org/2013/02/how-to-be-mindful-in-an-unmana.

Selk, Jason. 2009. *10-Minute Toughness: The Mental Training Program for Winning Before the Game Begins.* Columbus, OH: McGraw-Hill.

Shulman, Ken. 2019. "'Let's Move on This:' The '99 U.S. Women's National Team's Fight For Equality." Only a Game. June 7, 2019. www.wbur.org/onlyagame/2019/06/07/lilly-foudy-lockout-world-cup-team-usa.

Skottnik, Leon, and David E. J. Linden. 2019. "Mental Imagery and Brain Regulation – New Links Between Psychotherapy and Neuroscience." *Frontiers in Psychology*, 10, no. 779: 1-14. https://doi.org/10.3389/psyt.2019.00779.

Smetana, Jessica. 2020. "Crystal Dunn and the Art of Adaptation." *Sports Illustrated.* October 8, 2020. www.si.com/.amp/soccer/2020/10/08/crystal-dunn-uswnt-courage-the-unrelenting?__twitter_impression=true&s=03.

Smith, Earl, and Wilbert M. Leonard II. 1997. "Twenty-Five Years of Stacking Research in Major League Baseball: An Attempt at Explaining this Reoccurring Phenomenon." *Sociological Focus*, 30, no. 4: 321-331.

Spink, Kevin S., and Albert V. Carron. 1993. "The Effects of Team Building on the Adherence Patterns of Female Exercise Participants." *Journal of Sport and Exercise Psychology*, 15, no. 1: 39-49.

Sports Illustrated. 2012. "With Her All-Time Record Set to Fall, Little-Known Latynina Looks Back." July 10, 2012. https://www.si.com/olympics/2012/07/10/larisa-latynina-michael-phelps-olympic-medals-record.

Stambulova, Natalia B. 2017. "Crisis-Transitions in Athletes: Current Emphases on Cognitive and Contextual Factors." *Current Opinion in Psychology*, 16: 62-66. https://doi.org/10/1016/j.copsyc.2017.04.013.

Stambulova, Natalia B. 2021. "Athletes' Careers and Transitions." In *Applied Sport Psychology: Personal Growth to Peak Performance*, edited by Jean Williams and Vikki Krane, 519-541. New York: McGraw-Hill.

Stankovich, Chris. 2014. "Steve Nash says 'Sport Retirement like a Death.'" The Sports Doc Chalk Talk. May 16, 2014. https://drstankovich.com/steve-nash-says-sport-retirement-like-a-death.

Stoker, Mike, P. Lindsay, Joanne Butt, M. Bawden, and Ian Maynard. 2016. "Elite Coache' Experiences of Creating Pressure Training Environments for Performance Enhancement." *International Journal of Sport Psychology*, 47, no. 3: 262-281.

Stone, Larry. 2018. "Husky Legend Danielle Lawrie Pitching Again With Hopes of Making the 2020 Olympics." *The Seattle Times.* May 12, 2018. www.seattletimes.com/sports/uw-huskies/husky-legend-danielle-lawrie-pitching-again-with-hopes-of-making-the-2020-olympics.

Strachan, Shaelyn M., and Diane E. Whaley. 2013. "Identities, Schemas, and Definitions: How Aspects of the Self Influence Exercise Behavior." In *Routledge Handbook of Phys-*

ical Activity and Mental Health, edited by Panteleimon Ekkekakis, 212-223. London, UK: Routledge.

Suinn, Richard M. 1980. "Psychology and Sport Performance: Principles and Applications." In *Psychology in Sports: Methods and Applications*, edited by R. M. Suinn, 26-36, Minneapolis, MN: Burgess.

Tajfel, Henri, and John Turner. 1979. "An Integrative Theory of Intergroup Conflict." In *Organizational Identity: A Reader*, edited by Mary Jo Hatch and Majken Schultz, 56-65. Oxford, UK: Oxford University Press.

Tedeschi, Richard G., and Lawrence G. Calhoun. 2004. "Posttraumatic Growth: Conceptual Foundations and Empirical Evidence." *Psychological Inquiry*, 15, no. 1: 1-18. https://doi.org/10.1207/s15327965pli1501_01.

Teotonio, Isabel. 2008. "Survivor's Grit Inspires Runners." *Toronto Star*. September 15, 2008. www.thestar.com/life/health_wellness/nutrition/2008/09/15/survivors_grit_inspires_runners.html.

Terry, Peter C. 2009. "Strategies for Reflective Sport Psychology Practice." In *Cultural Sport Psychology*, edited by Robert J. Schinke and Stephanie J. Hanrahan, 79-89. Champaign, IL: Human Kinetics.

The Terry Fox Foundation. 2021. "Terry's Story." https://terryfox.org/terrys-story/.

Thomas, Owen, Sheldon Hanton, and Ian Maynard. 2007. "Intervening With Athletes During the Time Leading Up to Competition: Theory to Practice II." *Journal of Applied Sport Psychology*, 19, no. 4: 398-418. https://doi.org/10.1080/10413200701599140.

Thompson, Rachel. 2020. "Wyomia Tyus' Olympic Protest Resonates 52 Years Later." NBCSports. August 27, 2020. https://olympics.nbcsports.com/2020/08/27/wyomia-tyus-protest-olympics/.

Thrive Global. 2016. "How Andre Iguodala Trains His Body, Mind and Soul." Video, 4:23. https://m.facebook.com/thriveglbl/videos/225771667844659.

Tignor, Steve. 2019. "It Wasn't Rafael Nadal's Body That We Underestimated—It Was His Mind." *Tennis*. November 15, 2019. www.tennis.com/news/articles/it-wasn-t-rafael-nadal-s-body-that-we-underestimated-it-was-his-mind.

Tod, David, James Hardy, and Emily J. Oliver. 2011. "Effects of Self-Talk: A Systematic Review." *Journal of Sport and Exercise Psychology*, 33: 666-687. https://doi.org/10.1123/jsep.33.5.666.

Todd, Sarah. 2021. "Deseret News – Talent and Skill Account for a Lot but Donovan Mitchell Wants to Win the Mental Battle Through the Playoffs." *JazzFanz*. May 30, 2021. https://jazzfanz.com/threads/deseret-news-talent-and-skill-account-for-a-lot-but-donovan-mitchell-wants-to-win-the-mental-battle-through-the-playoffs.148023.

Tolle, Eckhart. 2010. *The Power of Now*. Vancouver, BC, Canada: Namaste Publishing.

Tseng, Julie, and Jordan Poppenk. 2020. "Brain Meta-State Transitions Demarcate Thoughts Across Task Contexts Exposing the Mental Noise of Trait Neuroticism." *Nature Communications*, 11, no. 3480. https://doi.org/10.1038/s41467-020-17255-9.

Tuckman, Bruce W. 1965. "Developmental Sequence in Small Groups." *Psychological Bulletin,* 63: 384-399.

Turner, Martin J., and Jamie B. Barker. 2014. "Using Rational Emotive Behavior Therapy With Athletes." *The Sport Psychologist*, 28, no. 1: 75-90. https://doi.org/10.1123/tsp.2013-0012.

Tuscaloosa Fitness. n.d. "How Nick Saban Motivates and Inspires Champions." www.tuscaloosafitness.com/post/how-nick-saban-motivates-and-inspires-champions.

van der Sluis, Alien, Michel S. Brink, Babette M. Pluim, Evert A.L.M. Verhagen, Marije T. Elferink-Gemser, and Chris Visscher. 2019. "Self-Regulatory Skills: Are They Helpful in the Prevention of Overuse Injuries in Talented Tennis Players." *Scandinavian Journal of Medicine and Science in Sports*, 29, no. 7: 1050-1058. https://doi.org/10.1111/sms.13420.

Van Raalte, Judy L., Andrew Vincent, and Britton W. Brewer. 2016. "Self-Talk: Review and Sport-Specific Model." *Psychology of Sport & Exercise*, 22, no. 1: 139-148. https://doi.org/10.1016/j.psychsport.2015.08.004.

Van Raalte, Judy L., Lorraine Wilson, Allen Cornelius, and Britton W. Brewer. 2018. "Self-Talk in a SCUBA Diving Context." *The Sport Psychologist*, 32: 244-247. https://doi.org/10.1123/tsp.2017-0091.

Vealey, Robin S., and Melissa A. Chase. 2008. "Self-Confidence in Sport: Conceptual and Research Advances." In *Advances in Sport Psychology*, 3rd ed., edited by Thelma S. Horn, 54-80. Champaign, IL: Human Kinetics.

Vealey, Robin S., and Samuel Forlenza. 2020. "Using Imagery as a Mental Training Tool in Sport." In *Applied Sport Psychology: From Growth to Peak Performance*, 8th ed., edited by Jean M. Williams and Vikki Krane, 244-277. New York: McGraw-Hill.

Vinall, Ruth, and Eugene Kreys. 2020. "Use of End-of-Class Quizzes to Promote Pharmacy Student Self-Reflection, Motivate Students to Improve Study Habits, and to Improve Performance on Summative Examinations." *Pharmacy*, 8: 1-9. https://doi.org/10.3390/pharmacy8080167.

Vine, Samuel J., and Mark R. Wilson. 2010. "Quiet Eye Training: Effects on Learning and Performance Under Pressure." *Journal of Applied Sport Psychology*, 22, no. 4: 361-376. https://doi.org/10.1080/10413200.2010.495106.

Vozza, Stephanie. 2016. "The Secrets to Keeping Your New Year's Resolutions." *Fast Company*. February 5, 2021. www.fastcompany.com/3066648/the-secrets-to-keeping-your-new-years-resolutions.

Walker, Sam. 2017. *The Captain Class: A New Theory of Leadership*, 132-152. New York: Random House.

Walks, Matt. 2016. "The Little-Known Story Behind Allen Iverson's 'Practice' Rant." ESPN. May 10, 2021. www.espn.com/nba/story/_/id/29143112/the-little-known-story-allen-iverson-practice-rant.

Wang, YiOu. 2020. "Ultrarunner YiOu Wang: Learning Consistency and the Pursuit of Excellence." Interview by David Swain. Prokit, January 16, 2020. https://theprokit.com/posts/yiou-wang-learning-consistency-the-pursuit-of-excellence.

Wegner, Daniel M., and Ralph Erber. 1992. "The Hyperaccessibility of Suppressed Thoughts." *Journal of Personality and Social Psychology*, 63: 903-912. https://doi.org/10.1037/0022-3514.63.6.903.

Wegner, Daniel M., David J. Schneider, Samuel R. Carter, and Teri L. White. 1987. "Paradoxical Effects of Thought Suppression." *Journal of Personality and Social Psychology*, 53, no. 1: 5-13. https://doi.org/10.1037/0022-3514.53.1.5.

Weinberg, Robert S., and Daniel Gould. 2019. *Foundations of Sport and Exercise Psychology*, 7th ed. Champaign, IL: Human.

Weinberg, Robert S., and Daniel Gould. 2019. *Foundations of Sport and Exercise Psychology*, 7th ed., 174-209. Champaign, IL: Human Kinetics.

Weinberg, Robert S., and Daniel Gould. 2019. *Foundations of Sport and Exercise Psychology*, 7th ed., 287-293. Champaign, IL: Human Kinetics.

Weinberg, Robert S., and Daniel Gould. 2019. *Foundations of Sport and Exercise Psychology*, 7th ed., 336-360. Champaign, IL: Human Kinetics.

Westlund-Stewart, Nicole, and Craig Hall. 2016. "The Effects of Cognitive General Imagery Use on Decision Accuracy and Speed in Curling." *The Sport Psychologist*, 30, no. 4: 305-313. https://doi.org/10.1123/tsp.2016-0001.

Wheatley, Margaret J. 2007. *Finding Our Way: Leadership for an Uncertain Time*. San Francisco, CA: Berrett-Koehler Publishers.

Widmeyer, W. Neil, and Kimberly DuCharme. 1997. "Team Building Through Team Goal Setting." *Journal of Applied Sport Psychology*, 9, no. 1: 97-113.

Williams Jean M., and Jennifer Bhalla. 2021. "Concentration and Strategies for Controlling It." In *Applied Sport Psychology: Personal Growth to Peak Performance*, edited by Jean M. Williams and Vikki Krane, 314-333. New York: McGraw-Hill.

Williams, Jean M., and Colleen M. Hacker. 2020. "Cognitive Techniques for Building Confidence and Enhancing Performance." In *Applied Sport Psychology: Personal Growth to Peak Performance*, 8th ed., edited by Jean M. Williams and Vikki Krane, 278-290. New York: McGraw-Hill.

Williams, Sarah E., and Jennifer Cumming. 2012. "Athletes' Ease of Imaging Predicts Their Imagery and Observational Learning Use." *Psychology of Sport and Exercise*, 13: 363–370. https://doi.org/10.1016/ j.psychsport.2012.01.010.

Wilson, Mark R. 2012. "Anxiety: Attention, the Brain, the Body, and Performance." In *Oxford Library of Psychology*, edited by Sean M. Murphy, 173-190. Oxford, UK: Oxford University Press.

Wilson, Mark R., Samuel J. Vine, and Greg Wood. 2009. "The Influence of Anxiety on Visual Attentional Control in Basketball Free Throw Shooting." *Journal of Sport and Exercise Psychology*, 31, no. 2: 152-168. https://doi.org/10.1123/jsep.31.2.152.

Wilson, Stuart G., Bradley W. Young, Sharleen Hoar, and Joseph Baker. 2021. "Further Evidence for the Validity of a Survey for Self-Regulated Learning in Sport Practice." *Psychology of Sport and Exercise*, 56: 1-10. https://doi.org/10.1016/j.psychsport.2021.101975.

Witham, Hannah. 2021. "For April Ross, Tokyo Olympics are the Pinnacle of an Enlightened Journey." *Just Women's Sports*. July 22, 2021. https://justwomenssports.com/for-april-ross-tokyo-olympics-are-the-pinnacle-of-an-enlightened-journey.

Wood, Wendy, and David T. Neal. 2007. "A New Look at Habits and the Habit-Goal Interface." *Psychological Review*, 114, no. 4: 843-863. https://doi.org/10.1037/0033-295X.114.4.843.

Woodman, Tim, Matthew Barlow, and Recep Gorgulu. 2015. "Don't Miss, Don't Miss, D'oh! Performance When Anxious Suffers Specifically Where Least Desired." *The Sport Psychologist*, 29, no. 3: 213-223.

World Health Organization. https://www.who.int/health-topics/health-equity#tab=tab_1.

Wulf, Gabriele. 2013. "Attentional Focus and Motor Learning: A Review of 15 Years." *International Review of Sport and Exercise Psychology*, 6, no. 1: 77-104. https://doi.org/ 10.1080/1750984X.2012.723728.

Young, Jeffrey R. 2018. "Angela Duckworth Says Grit Is Not Enough. She's Building Tools to Boost Student Character." *EdSurge On Air*. April 20, 2018. www.edsurge.com/news/2018-04-20-angela-duckworth-says-grit-is-not-enough-she-s-building-tools-to-boost-student-character.

Zettle, Robert D., and Steven C. Hayes. 1986. "Dysfunctional Control by Client Verbal Behavior: The Context of Reason Giving." *The Analysis of Verbal Behavior*, 4, no. 1: 30-38. https://doi.org/101007/BF03392813.

Zimmerman, Barry J. 2006. "Development and Adaptation of Expertise: The Role of Self-Regulatory Processes and Beliefs." In *The Cambridge Handbook of Expertise and Expert Performance*, edited by K. Anders Ericsson, Neil Charness, Paul J. Feltovich, and Robert Hoffman, 705-722. New York: Cambridge University Press.

INDEX

Note: The italicized *f* and *t* following page numbers refer to figures and tables, respectively.

A

abbreviated five-to-one breathing 109
ability to concentrate 181
acceptance and commitment therapy 49
action plans. *See also* goal setting
  description of 161-162
  effective 168-175
  end-based approach to 170-173
  in Gibbs' model 224*f*, 226-227
  guidelines for creating 176
  peak performance pillars and 172
  summary of 177-178
activation
  anxiety and 88-93
  breath control for 103, 108
  control of 91-95, 192
  focus and 192-197
  levels of 90
  perception effects on 93, 95
  physical symptoms of 90
  positive self-statements for 103
  reducing of 103-104, 105-122
  self-regulation of 91
  strategies for 103-104
  stress and 88-93
  tunnel vision caused by 91
activation behaviors 104
activation-control techniques 4
active improvement 144-145, 145*f*
active progressive relaxation 110, 116
adaptability 262
adversarial growth 237
adversity
  analysis of 250
  coping with 245
  emotional response to 262
  growing through 251-252
  growth mindset after 270
  meaning from 250
  mental toughness in 236
  performance improvements during 236
  summary of 252
affect 73
affirmations 36-38
after-action reviews (AARs) 230-233
Agassi, Andre 149
agency, reclaiming of 251
Ali, Muhammad 36, 165
all-or-nothing thinking 98, 101

All-Star 173
American Psychological Association 259
anticipatory self-reinforcement 132-134
anxiety
  activation and 88-93
  breath control for 108
  cognitive 116
  cognitive state 95
  competitive 90-91
  definition of 90
  management of 88-98
  performance affected by 90-91
  "quiet eye" period affected by 193
  somatic state 95
  somatic symptoms of 106
  state 95, 97
  stress and 88-93
  tunnel vision caused by 91
Ashe, Arthur 1, 14, 202
associative attentional strategies 189
athletes
  control by 60
  rest and recovery 60
athletic identity 309-311
athletic skill sets 318-319
attention
  associative strategies 189
  dimensions of 183, 185-186
  directing of 182-187
  dissociative strategies 189
  drills for practicing 195-197
  finite amount of 182, 190
  internal 194
  overview of 181-182
  selective 183
  shifting of 186
attentional focus 185*f*, 185-187, 196-197
attentional focusing 4
attentional style 186-187, 194, 198
attitude 1, 233
attributional training 139-141
attributions 137-142
auditory vividness 74
autogenic training 117-118
autonomy 149, 170
autonomy-supportive environments 154
awareness. *See also* self-awareness
  nonjudgmental 51-52, 59-60
  present-moment 53, 56

B

Bannister, Roger 7-8
baseline 22
behavior(s)
  analysis of 226-227
  anticipatory self-reinforcement and 133
  cue for 135-136
  focusing on 22
  inclusive 298-300
  self-determination theory for changing of 153
  self-determined 144
  self-talk and 30
  thoughts and 30*f*
behavioral responses 244, 251
believing in yourself. *See* self-belief
Berry, Gwen 301-302
bias 222, 297, 299
Biles, Simone 298, 311
Bird, Sue 263-264, 273
Blair, Bonnie 165
blaming 142, 242
Blue Angels 219-220
Bolt, Usain 1, 161, 173
bouncing back from errors 263-266, 270
Brady, Tom 32, 188, 307
breath control 103
breathing
  abbreviated five-to-one 109
  diaphragmatic 108
  exercises for 108-109
  five-finger 64
  focusing on 57-58, 101, 108
  four-square 109
  one-to-five 109
broad external focus 185-186
broad internal focus 185-186
Bryant, Kobe 126, 173, 319
Buddhism 46
Butler, Jimmy 12

C

calmness. *See* relaxation/relaxation training
Cantona, Eric 200
Carlos, John 300-301
Carroll, Pete 186, 288
catastrophizing 40
Chastain, Brandi 243
chemistry 282, 284
choice 148-151, 154
choking 193-195
Clarke, Peter 99
coaches
  goal setting by 170
  mastery experiences facilitated by 19
  performance routines 211
  self-efficacy affected by 18
cognitive anxiety 116
cognitive behavioral therapy (CBT) 48-49, 54
cognitive defusion 51-52
cognitive diversity 293-295, 294*f*
cognitive diversity coefficient 293-295
cognitive flexibility 218

cognitive reappraisal 151
cognitive restructuring 40-42
cognitive skills 68-69
cognitive state anxiety 95
cohesion, team 284-287
collective efficacy 166-167, 208
Comaneci, Nadia 9
communication, mindful 48
competence 145-147, 154
competency 126
competition. *See also* performance
  after-action reviews 230-233
  analysis and corrections during 266
  choking during 194
  concentration during 188
  focus during 236
  situation-specific responses 195
  warm-ups for 213
competitive anxiety 90-91
complete relaxation 106
concentration
  ability to concentrate 181
  in competitions 188
  improvements in 188-189
  optimal 188
  in performances 188, 197
  as skill 188
  tips for effective 187
confidantes 241-243
confidence. *See* self-confidence
connection 152-154
contingent feedback 174
control
  activation 91-95, 192
  description of 170
  routines for establishing 202
core theme 288
Courtney, Kate 45
COVID-19 pandemic 175, 249
crisis transition 311
critical reflection 298
critical self-reflection 221-223, 249
criticism 241
Crosby, Sidney 128
cues
  for behaviors 135-136
  situational 200
  for thought stoppage 39
cultural awareness 296
cultural blindness 296
cultural competence 295-298
cultural diversity 306
Curry, Stephen 200, 202, 321

D

Daley, Tom 312
debriefing 225
Deloitte 293, 300
demographic diversity 293-294, 294*f*
diaphragmatic breathing 108
DiCicco, Tony 66, 243

Diggins, Jessie 99
disappointments 249
discipline 144
dissociative attentional strategies 189
diversity
  cognitive 293-295, 294*f*
  definition of 289
  demographic 293-294, 294*f*
  examples of 292
  exemplars of 300-303
  in high-performing teams and groups 291
  representational 293-295, 294*f*
Dorrance, Anson 240
double curse of incompetence 221
doubt. *See* self-doubt
Duckworth, Angela 224, 254-255, 258-259, 268, 270
Duggan, Meghan 303
Dunn, Crystal 239-240, 242
Dunning-Kruger effect 221
Durant, Kevin 40
Dweck, Carol 266-269
dysfunctional self-talk 39-40

E
Ederle, Gertrude 1
efficacy
  collective 166-167, 208
  self-. *See* self-efficacy
effort 269-270
ego-involved motivational climate 156
80 percent probability decisions 23
electroencephalography (EEG) 71
emotional responses 244, 262
emotional state 20-21
empty nesters 310
energy management 87-104
equity
  description of 290-292
  exemplars of 300-303
  reflective suggestions for 303-306
errors
  bouncing back from 263-266
  emotional response to 262
  focusing on 11, 27
  refocusing after 190
  responding to 17
  self-correction of 263-264
  self-reflection after 216
European Space Agency 274
experience(s)
  description of 224-225, 227
  evaluation of 225-227
  growth from 249-250
  positive 42
  vicarious 18, 24-25
external imagery 72-73

F
failure 157, 236-238
Favre, Brett 307
Federer, Roger 263

feedback 130, 174, 299
feed forward 215-216
feelings
  choices versus 150
  focusing on 21-22
  identification of 225, 227
  prioritizing of 73
  as teachable moments 241
Felix, Allyson 312
first-person language 17
five-finger breathing exercise 64
fixed mindset 267
Fleming, Jessie 273, 281
flexibility 205, 218, 263
focus
  ability to 182, 184
  activation and 192-197
  attentional 185*f*, 185-187, 196-197
  on breathing 57-58, 101, 108
  broad external 185-186
  broad internal 185-186
  narrow external 186
  narrow internal 185
  present-moment 47, 47*f*, 57, 59-61, 190, 258
  refocusing 190-192
  self-confidence and 12
  sustaining of 195-196
focus plans 189
forced transitions 316-318
formal roles 276, 280, 282
forming stage 274-276
Foudy, Julie 252, 264, 281, 302-304, 314
four-square breathing 109
Fox, Terry 255-256
functionally equivalent images 70-75
functional magnetic resonance imaging (fMRI) 71

G
Gable, Dan 254-255
garbage in garbage out (GIGO) 162
gender diversity 293
Gibb's six-stage cyclical model 224-228, 230
Gibson, Althea 294
goal(s)
  accomplishment of 172
  achieving of 174
  action plans for 161-162. *See also* action plans
  critical elements of 169-170
  definition of 161
  evaluation of 175
  feedback on 174-175
  intermediate 178
  learning strategies and 163
  long-term 164, 167, 170-172, 174
  New Year's resolutions as 173-174
  objective 166, 169
  outcome 163-166
  performance 165-166
  process 165-166
  purpose of 161
  revision of 175

goals *(continued)*
  short-term 167, 172
  SMART 168-169
  subjective 166, 169
  summary of 177-178
  support for 174
  writing down 169-170, 173-174
goal orientations 154
goal setting. *See also* action plans
  backward chain of 170-173
  benefits of 161-162
  by coach 170
  end-based approach to 170-173
  errors in 166-168
  evidence-based strategies for 168
  experience in 178
  goal accomplishment versus 172
  guidelines for 167
  learning about 178
  life areas for 177
  mechanistic theory of 163-164
  for motivation 169
  motivational climate and 176-177
  peak performance pillars and 164, 172
  performance benefits of 162-163
  precompetition 166
  purpose of 168
  as team 166
  worksheet for 179-180
"good enough" plan 100-102
Google 261-262
Gordon, Aaron 49
go-to plan 99-100, 102
Greene Raine, Nancy "Tiger" 236
grit
  critics of 268
  definition of 255
  examples of 254-256
  growth mindset and 270
  passion and 255-257
  perseverance and 257-259
  self-talk and 258
grit mindset 258
group. *See also* team
  cohesion of 284-287
  diversity, equity, and inclusion in 291, 293
  goal setting as 166
  mission statement for 288
  norms for 275
  roles in 276-284
  social support in 283-284
  team development stages 274-277
  team-first mentality of 281
  team versus 274
growth
  post-traumatic 236-237, 249
  stress-related 236-237, 249-251
  through adversity 251
growth mindset 266-270
Gustavsson, Tony 275

H
habit(s) 135-137, 142
habit cycle 135
habit loop 135-136
Hamm, Mia 14, 148, 216-217, 275, 281, 314
Hammon, Becky 300
Hanin, Yuri 96
hardships 235
high achievers 126
Holliday, Bernie 56
Honnold, Alex 18

I
Iapoce, Anthony 87
identity
  athletic 309-311
  cognitive diversity and 294
  integration of 311-312
Iguodala, Andre 49
image(s)
  control over 74
  emotional correlates of 68
  functionally equivalent 70-75
  multisensory 67, 73-75
  symbolic 75
imagery
  buy-in of 76-77
  cognitive skills improved with 68-69
  consistency in practicing of 70
  daily uses of 69
  definition of 65
  emotional components of 68
  environmental components of 67
  examples of 66, 76-77
  external 72-73
  of frequent or anticipated skill 82-83
  gustatory element of 74
  implementation of 77-79
  internal 72-73
  memories and 67
  motivation affected by 68-69
  neuroimaging studies of 70-71
  olfactory elements of 74
  physiological components of 68
  practicing of 3-4, 77-78
  psychological uses of 69
  real-time conducting of 73
  reasons for using 68-69
  senses in 73-74
  sensory components of 67
  of signature strength 84-85
  statistics regarding 65
  timing of 73
  uses of 68-70
  visualization versus 67-68, 77
  vividness of 73-74
  when to use 69-70
imagery scripts 78-79, 118-121
imagery training
  emotion in 68
  examples of 66

external environment in 74
in performance psychology 81, 83, 85
physical practice in 67
relaxation uses of 118-121
script used in 78-79
sessions 78
in sport psychology 80-85
worksheets for 80-85
implicit biases 299
inclusion 289, 291-292
inclusive behaviors 298-300
inclusive excellence
  cultural competence 295-298
  exemplars of 300-303
  inclusive behaviors 298-300
inconsistencies, in routines 208, 210
individualized zones of optimal functioning
    (IZOF) model 96-98
informal roles 276
In Pursuit of Excellence 100, 239
instructional self-talk 32-35
intermediate goals 178
internal attention 194
internal imagery 72-73
intrinsic motivation 126-129, 141-143
ironic processing 51, 190, 192
irrational thinking 40-42
"I" statements 17, 37
Iverson, Allen 155

J
Jackson, Phil 53
Jacobellis, Lindsey 40
James, LeBron 4, 264
Jennings, Kerri Walsh 224
Jeter, Derek 306
Jordan, Michael 1, 69, 126, 152, 185, 235
Joyner-Kersee, Jackie 125
judgments 58

K
Kabat-Zinn, Jon 46-47
Kaepernick, Colin 292
kinesthesis 73-74
King, Billie Jean 53, 155, 262, 304, 306
Kintsugi 237
Kipchoge, Eliud 8, 27
Korbut, Olga 143

L
language 28
Latynina, Larisa 145-147
Laumann, Silken 126-128
Lawrie-Locke, Danielle 169-170
leadership 280, 303-304
legacy 278, 280, 314
Lemieux, Mario 1
Letters to a Young Gymnast 9
leveraging of relationships 304-305
Lewis, Carl 104
Likert scale 186
Lilly, Kristine 78, 202-203
Lloyd, Carli 3, 66, 200

loafing, social 284-285
long-term goals 164, 167, 170-172, 174
luck 87-88, 204

M
Malone, Karl 290
Manning, Peyton 318
Marchant, Lanni 171
Marsalis, Wynton 258-259
Marta 235, 300
mastery experiences 18-20, 24-25
Mayweather, Floyd 262
McFadden, Tatyana 295
McIlroy, Rory 310-311
McLeod, Erin 48
medical issues 47
memories 67
mental correction, of mistakes 264, 266
mental fitness 4
mental rehearsal 69, 73
mental skills training
  cognitive behavioral therapy approach to 48-49
  description of 124, 321
  examples of 3
  importance of 5, 13
  mindfulness-based approach to 48-54, 54*t*
  in preparation 15
  self-awareness. *See* self-awareness
  self-confidence 7
  self-regulation. *See* self-regulation
  traditional approach to 50-51, 53, 54*t*
mental toughness
  adversity and 236
  characteristics of 235-236
  definition of 235
  description of 7
mental toughness moments (MtM)
  confidantes as resources during 241-243
  description of 238-239
  keeping perspective during 245-246
  naming of 239, 244, 252
  reactions to 244-246
  relevant lessons from 249-251
  responses to 244-248, 252
  social support during 242-243
  sport examples of 241
mentorship 303-304
meta-analysis 286
Mickelson, Phil "Lefty" 253
mindful communication 48
mindfulness
  behavioral element of 60
  benefits of 53, 57-58
  cognitive defusion 51-52
  cognitive element of 60
  critiques of 59-60
  daily integration and practice of 53, 56, 61
  definition of 46-47
  examples of 48
  exercises for 63-64
  goal of 61

mindfulness *(continued)*
  history of 46-48
  implementation of 54-61
  judgments during 58
  medical issues and 47
  mental skills training based on 48-54, 54*t*
  multitasking versus 60-61
  nonjudgmental awareness 51-52, 59-60
  nonsport applications of 52-53, 58-59
  peak performance through 49, 54
  practicing of 54-61, 63-64
  present-moment awareness through 56
  present-moment focus of 47, 47*f*, 57, 59-61
  roots of 46-48
  self-awareness and 53, 55
  simplicity in 58-61
  summary of 61
  uses of 45
  worksheet for 63-64
mindfulness-based stress reduction (MBSR) program 47
mind-to-muscle relaxation 106, 116-121
mission statement 288
mistakes 263-266
Mitchell, Donovan 190
modeling 18-19, 24-25
momentary relaxation 106, 116
Morgan, Alex 302
Morikawa, Collin 3
motivation
  attributions effect on 139
  ego-involved climate 156
  environment effects on 154
  high achievers 126
  imagery effects on 68-69
  intrinsic 126-129, 141-143
  life pursuits driven by 125
  reasons for importance of 143
  rewards effect on 129-130
  task-involved climate 156-159
  variable nature of 143
motivational climate
  ego-involved 156
  goal setting and 176-177
  task-involved 156-159
motivational self-talk 34-36
multisensory images 73-75
multitasking 60-62
muscle-to-mind relaxation 106-116
music 104

N
Nadal, Rafael 237, 254, 280
Nadalian perspective 254
Naeher, Alyssa 27
nap 100, 102
narrow external focus 186
narrow internal focus 185
NASA 274
NASCAR 273
Nash, Steve 4, 208, 308

National Basketball Association (NBA) 12, 40, 69, 126, 152, 155, 173, 190, 200, 290
National Women's Soccer League 296
negative feedback 130
neuroimaging 70-71
New Year's resolutions 173-174
nonjudgmental awareness 51-52, 59-60
non-normative transitions 315
normative transitions 315
norming stage 275-276
norms 275
nutrition 3

O
objective goals 166, 169
Ogwumike, Nneka 289
one-to-five breathing 109
optimistic 262
Orlick, Terry 100, 239
outcome goals 163-166
outcome orientation 157-158
Overbeck, Carla 243, 280, 303
overlearning 182
overthinking 194
Owens, Jesse 218

P
pain threshold 244
pain tolerance 244
Pan American Games 301-302
passion 128-129, 255-257
passive improvement 144
passive progressive relaxation 116
past performance accomplishments 18-22, 24-25
peak performance
  in challenging situations 1
  definition of 1
  examples of 1
  mindfulness approach to 49, 54
  technical aspects of 2
peak performance pillars
  goal setting and 164, 172
  physical 3
  psychological 3
  tactical 2-3
  technical 2-3
  training of 5
  worksheet 284
Pele 300
perception 11, 93, 95, 124
perfection 101
performance. *See also* competition
performance(s)
  affirmations effect on 36-38
  anxiety effects on 90-91
  best 201
  concentration in 188
  consistency in 92
  events before 199
  goal setting effects on 163
  outcome orientation to 157-158
  personal factors that affect 11

routines effect on 195, 200-204
self-confidence effects on 8-10
self-reflection after 223
self-talk and, relationship between 30-38, 43
situational factors that affect 11
task orientation to 155, 157-158
worst 201
performance choking 193-195
performance environments 154-155
performance goals 165-166
performance psychology 81, 83, 85
performance state, ideal 201
performance success
choice in 148-151, 154
competence in 145-147, 154
connection in 152-154
defining of 154-155, 156
performing stage 275-276
perseverance 257-259
persuasion, verbal 16-18, 24-25
PETTLEP model 71-73, 72*t*
Phelps, Michael 1, 145-146
physical, environment, task, timing, learning,
emotion, perspective model. *See* PETTLEP
model
physical action, for mistakes 264
physical conditioning 14-15, 17
physical pillars 3
physiological states 20-21, 24-25, 30
planning ahead 258
poor performance 206
Popovich, Gregg 273
Posey, Gerald "Buster" 200
Positive Coaching Alliance 281
positive experiences 42
positive feedback 130
positive self-statements 103
positive self-talk 31
positron emission tomography (PET) 71
postperformance routines 223, 231-232
post-traumatic growth (PTG) 236-237, 249
Poulter, Jordyn 273
practical self-reflection 221
praise 130
precompetition routines 207
preferred state 95-98, 121
preferred zone 98-103, 121
preparation
elements of 15
mental skills training 15
physical conditioning 14-15
self-confidence and 14
self-confidence plan 15
thought stoppage 39, 44
preperformance events 199
preperformance routines. *See* routines
prepractice routines 207
present moment
awareness of 53, 56
focus on 47, 47*f*, 57, 59-61, 190, 258
nonjudgmental awareness of 55

staying in 55-56
pressure 263
process goals 165-166
productive thoughts 39-40, 42, 44
progressive muscular relaxation (PMR) 110-116
progressive relaxation 110-116
Project Adventure 286
psychological pillar 3, 6
psychological skills training 49, 51
psychological state
imagery effects on 69
language and 28
purpose, passion and 128-129
purposeful self-talk 38
Pygmalion effect 299

Q
quasi normative transitions 315
"quiet eye" period 193

R
Raisman, Aly 236
Rapinoe, Megan 302-303
reactions 244-246
reflection. *See* self-reflection
reflective practice 216
refocusing 190-192
relaxation/relaxation training
autogenic training for 117-118
benefits of 124
breathing exercises for 108-109
complete/total 106
description of 105-106
imagery training for 118-121
implementation of 121-124
mind-to-muscle techniques 106, 116-121
momentary 106, 116
muscle-to-mind techniques 106-116
on-demand 124
progressive 110-116
timing of 123
relentlessness 305
representational diversity 293-295, 294*f*
resilience
bouncing back from errors 263-266
definition of 259
growth mindset and 270
opportunities for 260-263
responses
behavioral 244
definition of 245
emotional 244
to hardships 235
to mental toughness moments 244-248, 252
rest and recovery 60
retirement 308
Retton, Mary Lou 190, 192
rewards
implementation of 130
intrinsic motivation and 129
motivation effects of 129-130
for self-improvement 177

rewards *(continued)*
  self-reinforcement 131-132
Rice, Jerry 155
Riggs, Bobby 306
Ringelmann effect 284-285
Roche, Megan 47, 253
role(s)
  acceptance of 278-281
  communicating and clarifying of 279-280
  expansion of, in transitions 312-316
  formal 276, 280, 282
  informal 276
  on team 276-284
Roll, Rich 105
Ronaldinho 66
Rosenthal effect 299
Ross, April 315-316
Rousey, Ronda 237
routines
  for achievement setting 142
  benefits of 204-205
  changing of 206-207
  coach's approach to 211
  concentration and 189
  consistency of 206-210
  control and 202
  creating of 212
  definition of 200
  efficacy of 208
  familiarity created with 200
  flexibility of 205
  goal of 202
  inconsistencies in 208, 210
  individual 209-211, 213
  for mistakes 264-266
  multiple 207-208
  performance affected by 195, 200-204, 213
  postperformance 223
  precompetition 207
  prepractice 207
  summary of 213
  superstitions versus 204-206
  task-specific 207-208
  team 211
  unforeseen events managed with 205
  worksheet for 212
  writing down 211
Rudolph, Wilma 235, 263, 321
Ruggiero, Angela 128
Russell, Bill 181

S
Saban, Nick 321
Scurry, Briana 282
selective attention 183
self-appraisal 152
self-awareness
  definition of 5
  mindfulness and 53, 56
  of preferred state 95-98
  of self-confidence 13

self-reflection for 220
  of self-talk 38
self-belief. *See also* self-efficacy
  examples of 7-8
  fluctuations in 11
  perceptions of 11
  protective quality of 7
  strengthening of 14-21
self-composure 27
self-confidence
  behavioral outcomes of 22
  building of 13-14, 24-25
  changes in 10
  culture for building 17
  definition of 9
  development of 10-14, 17
  drops in 13, 13*f*
  factors that affect 11
  focus and 12
  high levels of 13, 13*f*
  importance of 7
  lacking of 23
  levels of 11, 11*f*
  performance affected by 8-10
  physical conditioning and 14-15, 17
  preparation and 14
  self-awareness of 13
  self-doubt effects on 12-13
  self-efficacy and 1
  self-talk effects on 29
  state-like 10
  vicarious experiences for building 18, 24-25
self-confidence plan 15
self-correction 263-264
self-determination theory 153, 170
self-determined behavior 144
self-doubt 11-13, 23
self-efficacy. *See also* self-belief
  building of 24-25
  coach's effect on 18
  definition of 16
  emotional states' effect on 20-21
  mastery experiences effect on 18-20, 24-25
  past performance accomplishments effect on 18-20, 24-25
  physiological states' effect on 20-21, 24-25
  self-reflection and 216
  sources of 16-21, 24-25
  verbal persuasion effects on 16-18, 24-25
  vicarious experience effects on 18, 24-25
self-evaluation 152
self-fulfilling prophecy 9-10, 299
self-improvement 177
self-induced stress 89
self-reflection
  characteristics of 216-223
  consistency in 218
  after crisis moments 216
  critical 221-223, 249
  critical elements of 220
  definition of 216, 218

description of 215
feed forward 215-216
multiple angles and perspectives on 222
practical 221
self-awareness from 220
self-efficacy and 216
summary of 233
technical 220-221
three principles of 228-229
timing of 222-223
self-reflection models
after-action reviews 230-233
description of 223-224
six-stage cyclical model 224-228
self-regulation
of activation levels 91
definition of 6
description of 5-6
teaching of 35
self-regulation plan 13
self-reinforcement
anticipatory 132-134
strategies 131-132
self-talk
affirmations 36-38
awareness of 29
behavior and 30
buy-in 36
cognitive restructuring and 40-42
controlling of 38-42
definition of 16, 27
dysfunctional 39-40
examples of 27-28
grit mindset from 258
instructional 32-35
irrational thinking and 40-42
mindful approach versus 51
motivational 34-36
negative 39
performance and, relationship between 30-38, 43
positive 31
productive 3-4, 258
purposeful 38
self-awareness of 38
self-confidence affected by 29
significance of 28-29
systematic training of 43
timing of 31-36
training of 28-29
types of 31-36
self-talk logs 40-41
self-talk statements 37
senses, in imagery 73-74
setbacks 249, 254, 257, 270
Shiffrin, Mikaela 90
short-term goals 167, 172
Sinclair, Christine 183-184, 281, 312
situational cues 200
six-stage cyclical model 224-228
sleep 3, 100-102

SMART goals 168-169
Smith, Tommie 300-301
social cohesion 285-287
social loafing 284-285
social support 242-243, 283-284
somatic state anxiety 95
sport
failure rates in 157
mental toughness moments in 241
practicing the fundamentals of 182-183
specialization in 257
task orientation to 155
technical aspects of 2
sport psychology
description of 4, 47
imagery training in 80-85
mindful approach to 49-51
sport stacking 290
state anxiety 95, 97
state-like confidence 10
Stockton, John 290
storming stage 275-276
strategy 269-270, 321
strengths 13
stress
activation and 88-93
anxiety and 88-93
definition of 89
inevitability of 250
management of 88-98
meaning ascribed to 251
options in dealing with 244
perception effects on 93, 95, 124
self-induced 89
situations that cause 88
sources of 89-90
stress-related growth (SRG) 236-237, 249-251
subjective goals 166, 169
success
defining of 156, 241
Federer's principles for 263
orientation for 177
performance. See performance success
Summitt, Pat 176, 271
superstitions 204-206
supplementary motor area (SMA) 71
survival 237-238
systematic training 43

T
tactical training 2-3
talk, self. See self-talk
task cohesion 285-287
task-involved motivational climate 156-159
task orientation 155, 157-158
task-specific routines 207-208
taste 66, 74
teachable moments 241
TEA Check-In Guide 261-262
team. See also group
cohesion of 284-287

team *(continued)*
  conflicts in 276
  contributions of individual to 283-284
  development of 274-277
  diversity, equity, and inclusion in 291, 293, 306
  formal roles in 276, 280, 282
  forming stage of 274-276
  goal setting as 166
  group versus 274
  individual and, balancing of 281-283
  informal roles in 276
  leader of 280, 282-283
  mission statement for 288
  norming stage of 275-276
  performing stage of 275-276
  roles on 276-284
  social cohesion in 285-287
  social loafing in 284-285
  standard of excellence for 275
  storming stage of 275-276
  task cohesion in 285-287
team building 152, 285-287
team climate 17
team-first mentality 281
team members
  in forming stage 274
  roles of 276-284
team routines 211
Team USA women's hockey 260-261
teamwork 274
technical self-reflection 220-221
Terry's three principles of reflective work 228-229
Test of Attentional and Interpersonal Style (TAIS) 186-187
thoughts
  behaviors and 30*f*
  cognitive defusion 51-52
  cognitive restructuring of 40-42
  facts regarding 31
  focusing on 21-22
  productive 39-40, 42, 44
  self-awareness of 38-39
  stoppage of 39, 44, 51
  unproductive 39-40
total relaxation 106
track and field 301
training
  attributional 139-141
  autogenic 117-118
  imagery. *See* imagery training
  mental skills. *See* mental skills training
  self-talk 28-29
Training Wheels 286
transcranial magnetic stimulation (TMS) 70-71
transitions
  athletic identity and 309-311

athletic skill set redeployment after 318-319
  coping with 309
  crisis 311
  definition of 308
  examples of 307-308
  forced 316-318
  identity in 308-312
  non-normative 315
  normative 315
  predictable 315
  quasi normative 315
  role expansion in 312-316
  success in 309
  summary of 319-320
  vision and 312-316
  voluntary 316-318
trauma
  growth from 250
  inevitability of 250
  meaning ascribed to 250
  options in dealing with 244
True, Sarah 268
tunnel vision 91
Turcotte, Ron 1
Tyus, Wyomia 301-302

U
Union of European Football Associations (UEFA) Champions League 293-294, 296
United States Women's National Team (USWNT) 94-95, 193, 209, 239-240, 265, 273, 280-282, 302, 304, 314
unproductive thoughts 39-40

V
verbal persuasion 16-18, 24-25
vicarious experiences 18, 24-25
video recordings 19
Virtue, Tessa 129
vision 303, 312-316
visualization 67-68, 77
vividness 73-74
voluntary transitions 316-318

W
Wambach, Abby 306, 311-312
Wang, YiOu 161
warm-up 213
Wickenheiser, Hayley 259
Williams, Serena 1, 14-15, 168, 294
Williams, Venus 294
Wooden, John 134, 218, 298
WOOP 258
World Health Organization 290

Z
Zaharias, Mildred "Babe" Didrikson 87-88

ABOUT THE AUTHORS

Colleen M. Hacker, PhD, FNAP, is currently a Professor in the Department of Kinesiology at Pacific Lutheran University and is an internationally recognized speaker and consultant in Sport and Performance Psychology. Dr. Hacker is Fellow in the National Academies of Practice, is listed on the U.S. Olympic and Paralympic Committee Sport Psychology Registry, and is a Certified Mental Performance Consultant  (CMPC®). She has served on the Coaching Staff for six Olympic Games (both winter and summer) and more than a dozen World Championships, working with a wide range of Professional and Olympic athletes and teams. Dr. Hacker has delivered over 300 professional presentations and published more than 45 articles, book chapters, and a book. She has received numerous professional awards including the Distinguished Professional Practice Award from AASP, the American Psychological Association's Presidential Citation, and ESPNW named Dr. Hacker as one of 30 women in the country who "change the way sports are played." She has been inducted into seven different Hall of Fames either as an athlete or coach. Her strategies for peak performance are sought by corporations, business groups, professional and Olympic sport teams, and both print and television media appearing in the *New York Times*, *Washington Post*, CNN, and ESPN to name a few.

Mallory E. Mann, PhD, is an associate professor in the Department of Kinesiology at Pacific Lutheran University. Her educational background and training is situated between the cultural studies of sport and sport psychology. Dr. Mann's scholarship focuses on gender issues in sport as well as coaching effectiveness. She previously coached at both the NCAA Division I and Division III levels and, during her doctorate, Dr.  Mann served as a mental skills coach for individual athletes and a college sport team. Her applied work continues to focus in areas related to coach education and gender equity in sport.